The War of American Independence, 1775–1783

The War of American Independence, 1775–1783

Richard Middleton

PEARSON

Harlow, England • London • New York • Boston • San Francisco • Toronto • Sydney
Auckland • Singapore • Hong Kong • Tokyo • Seoul • Taipei • New Delhi
Cape Town • São Paulo • Mexico City • Madrid • Amsterdam • Munich • Paris • Milan

PEARSON EDUCATION LIMITED

Edinburgh Gate
Harlow CM20 2JE
United Kingdom
Tel: +44 (0)1279 623623
Fax: +44 (0)1279 431059
Website: www.pearson.com/uk

First edition published 2012

© Pearson Education Limited 2012

The right of Richard Middleton to be identified as author of this work has been asserted by him in accordance with the Copyright, Designs and Patents Act 1988.

Pearson Education is not responsible for the content of third-party internet sites.

ISBN: 978-0-582-22942-6

British Library Cataloguing in Publication Data
A CIP catalogue record for this book can be obtained from the British Library

Library of Congress Cataloging in Publication Data
A CIP catalog record for this book can be obtained from the Library of Congress

All rights reserved; no part of this publication may be reproduced, stored in a retrieval system, or transmitted in any form or by any means, electronic, mechanical, photocopying, recording, or otherwise without either the prior written permission of the Publishers or a license permitting restricted copying in the United Kingdom issued by the Copyright Licensing Agency Ltd, Saffron House, 6–10 Kirby Street, London EC1N 8TS. This book may not be lent, resold, hired out or otherwise disposed of by way of trade in any form of binding or cover other than that in which it is published, without the prior consent of the Publishers.

10 9 8 7 6 5 4 3 2 1
15 14 13 12 11

Set by 35 in 10/13.5pt Sabon
Printed and bound in Malaysia (CTP-VP)

Contents

	List of maps	vi
	Abbreviations	vii
	Preface	viii
	Maps	x
1	Britain and America come to blows, 1763–75	1
2	The fighting begins, 1775	15
3	Britain reasserts her authority, 1776	41
4	The unpredictable fortunes of war, 1777	69
5	France comes to America's help, 1778	103
6	Spain enters the conflict, 1779	140
7	Changing strategies, 1780	169
8	The North American frontier, 1775–82	211
9	No daylight at the tunnel's end, 1781	237
10	Resolution at Yorktown, 1781	270
11	End game, 1782	298
	Conclusions and consequences	321
	Appendix: Washington on the art of command	327
	Bibliography	328
	Index	338

List of maps

1 British and Native Indian Eastern North America, circa 1775 x
2 The European Theater xi
3 The Northern Theater xii
4 The Southern Theater xiv
5 The West Indies xv
6 The Siege of Yorktown, September to October 1781 xvi

Abbreviations

CAR	W.B. Willcox, ed., *The American Rebellion: Sir Henry Clinton's Narrative of his Campaigns, 1775–1783 with an Appendix of Original Documents* (New Haven, 1954)
Carter	Clarence E. Carter, *The Correspondence of General Thomas Gage, 1763–1775*, 2 vols. (Yale, 1931)
CJ	Journal of the House of Commons
DDAR	K.G. Davies, ed., *Documents of the American Revolution, 1770–1783: Colonial Office Series*, 21 vols. (Shannon, 1972–81)
Fortescue	Sir John Fortescue, ed., *The Correspondence of King George the Third from 1760–1783*, 6 vols. (London, 1927–28)
HMC	Historical Manuscripts Commission
NGP	Richard K. Showman et al., eds., *The Papers of Nathanael Greene*, 13 vols. (Chapel Hill, 1976–2005)
Ross	Charles Ross, ed., *Correspondence of Charles, First Marquis of Cornwallis*, 3 vols. (London, 1859)
Sandwich	G.R. Barnes and J.H. Owen, eds., *The Private Papers of John, Earl of Sandwich, First Lord of the Admiralty, 1771–1782* (Navy Records Society, 1933–38, LXIX, LXXI, LXXV and LXXVII)
Syrett	David Syrett, ed., *The Rodney Papers: Selections from the Correspondence of Admiral Lord Rodney*, 2 vols., 1742–1780 (Navy Records Society, Aldershot, 2005–7)
WGW	John C. Fitzpatrick, ed., *The Writings of George Washington from the Original Manuscript sources, 1745–1799*, 39 vols. (Washington, DC, 1931–44)
WP/RWS	W.W. Abbot et al., eds., *The Papers of George Washington, Revolutionary War Series*, 19 vols. (Charlottesville, 1985–)

Preface

War is still a widespread phenomenon, as events around the world testify. Hence its study remains valuable for shedding light on how wars start, the manner in which they are conducted, the reasons for their outcome, and the consequences arising therefrom. Even for the most powerful nations, war remains a dangerously unpredictable exercise.

The War of American Independence can be studied from many perspectives. To the British, the Americans were ungrateful rebels and traitors. The Patriots in contrast saw themselves as the defenders of liberty, asserting their rights against the tyrannical pretensions of an imperial oppressor. But perspective also depends on whether the viewer is looking from the center or the periphery, from the top or bottom of the social and political order, and whether as a combatant or civilian. Time is another factor. The British viewpoint about the War of Independence today is very different from that of Dr Johnson in 1774 when he asserted that Americans should be grateful for anything given them short of hanging.

The aim of this book, accordingly, is to explain why the War of Independence started, how it progressed, why it ended as it did, and what its consequences were. The emphasis is on the military, naval, and diplomatic activities of the principal combatants. Attention, therefore, is directed to strategy (or the lack of it) rather than tactics, except where such details are pivotal to the eventual outcome. For the same reason the spotlight is on the leaders rather than followers, since this is not a social history. The book focuses mainly on events in America, since a successful outcome there was the principal objective of Britain, France, and the Americans themselves, whether Loyalist or Patriot. Only Spain saw the conflict there as of secondary importance. Accordingly, events outside America are dealt with in less detail. India is excluded altogether, being so far from North America as to have no discernable impact there other than the diversion of some British and French resources in the later stages of the war.

The materials relating to this subject are vast, and time constraints have necessarily limited my investigations to the more important published collections, notably the Colonial Office Papers of Lord George Germain, the Admiralty Papers of Lord Sandwich, the Correspondence of George III, and the papers of George Washington and Nathanael Greene. I have been similarly selective in my use of secondary materials.

Because the struggle for independence was both a civil war and an international conflict, I use the term "Patriots" to describe the eventual victors, since until the Treaty of 1783 the Loyalists had as much right as the Patriots to be called "American." A dominant national identity in any case developed only during the nineteenth century. Finally, in quoting primary sources, I have modernized the punctuation and spelling to facilitate readability.

In producing this work I must acknowledge the contributions of other scholars to the subject, in particular that of Jonathan Dull, whose writings on the French Navy and diplomatic background have proved invaluable. Finally I should like to thank the editor of the series, Professor Hamish Scott and the editorial staff of Longman/Pearson Education for their great patience and advice in a project that has been too long in the making. For this and any errors or omissions, I alone am responsible.

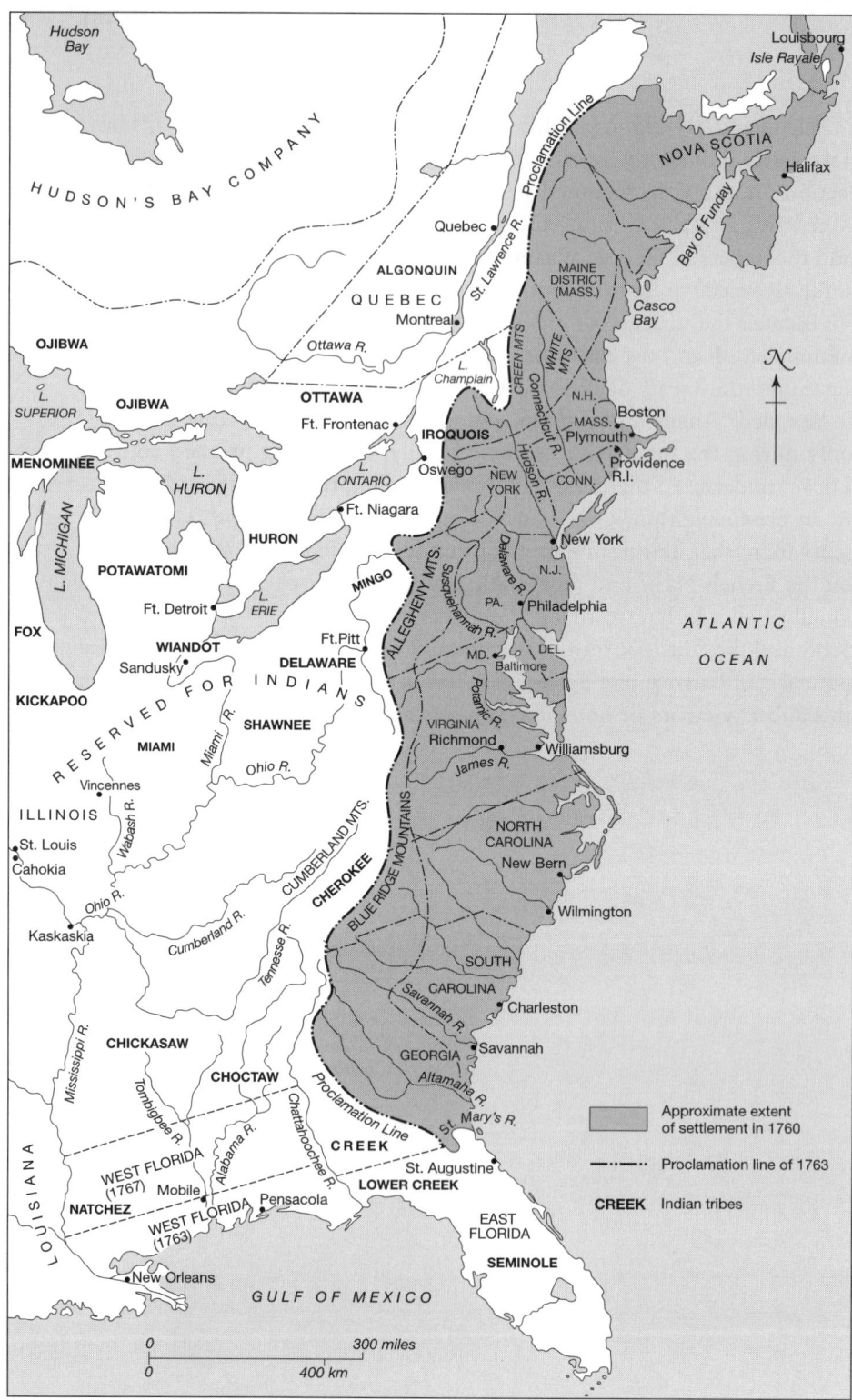

MAP 1 *British and Native Indian Eastern North America, circa 1775*

Adapted from Middlekauf, R. (1982) *The Glorious Cause: The American Revolution, 1763–1789*, Oxford University Press, page 33

MAP 2 *The European Theater*

Adapted from Mackesy, P. (1964) *The War for America, 1775–1783*, Originally published by Harvard University Press, 1964, reprinted by University of Nebraska Press, 1993, page 191

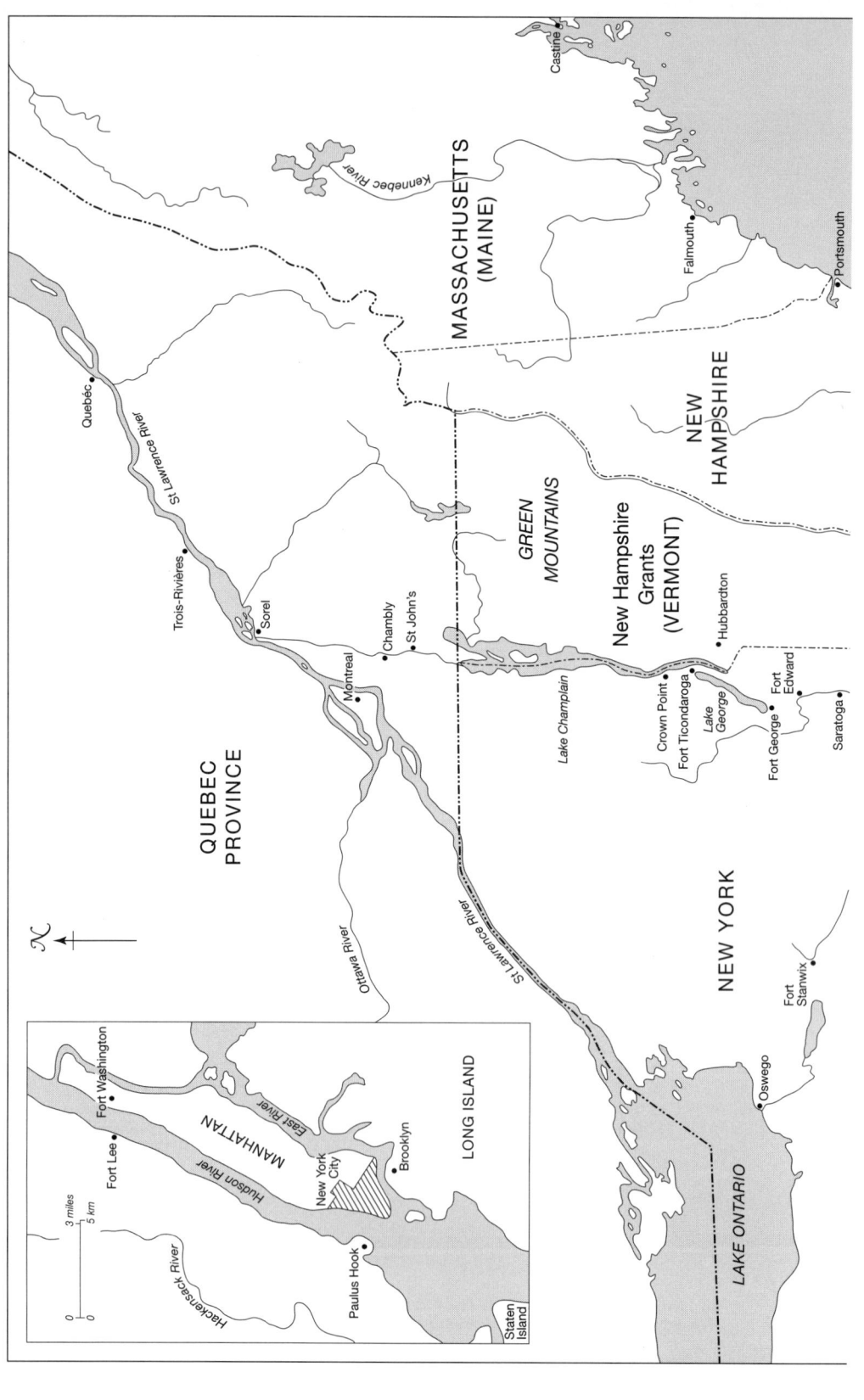

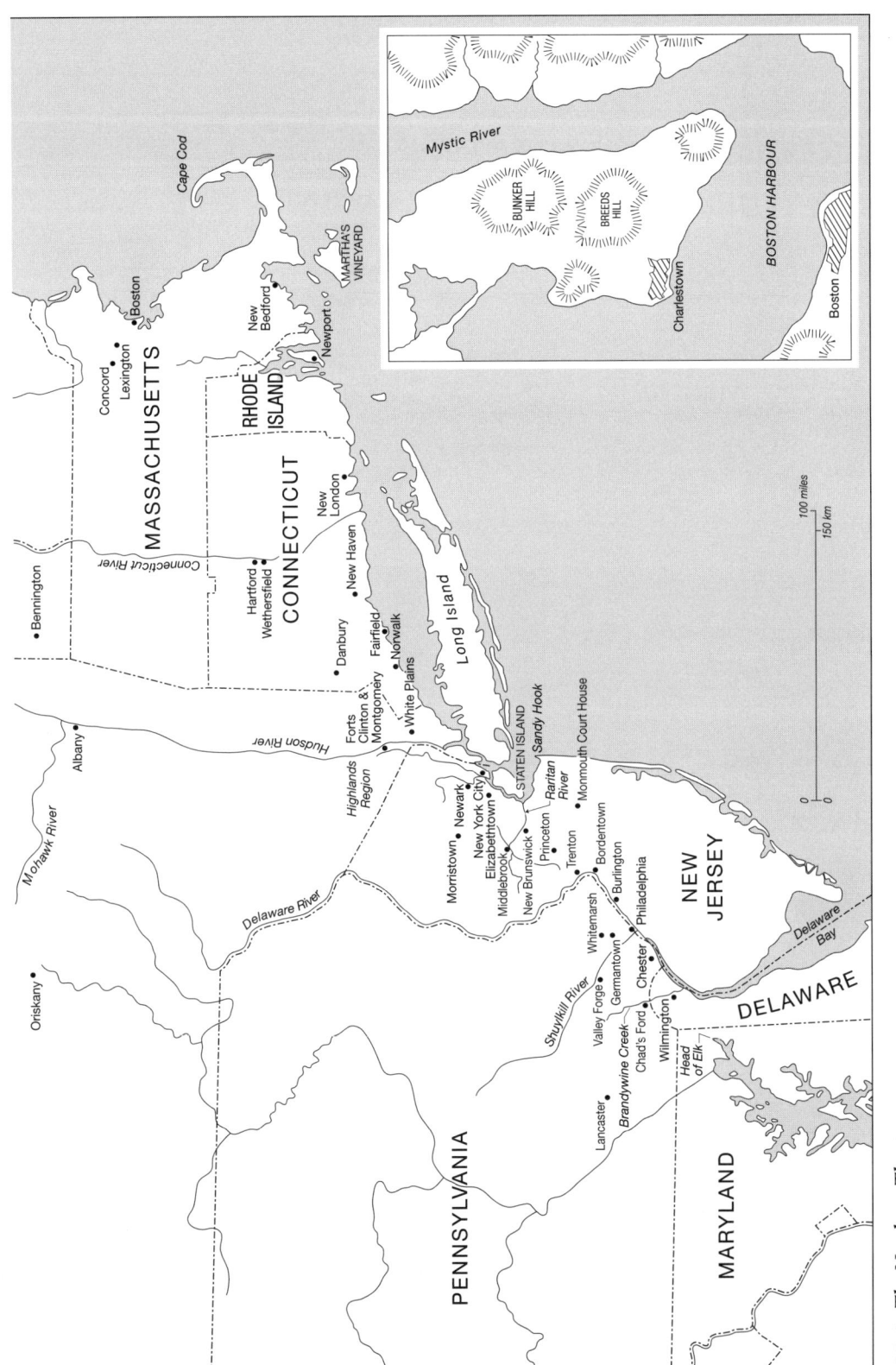

MAP 3 *The Northern Theater*
Adapted from Spring, M.H. (2010) *With Zeal and Bayonets Only: The British Army on Campaign in North America, 1775–1783*, University of Oklahoma, pages 2010, xix–xxi

MAP 4 *The Southern Theater*

Adapted from Nelson, D.P. (1985) *Anthony Wayne: Soldier of the Republic*, Indiana University Press, page 166

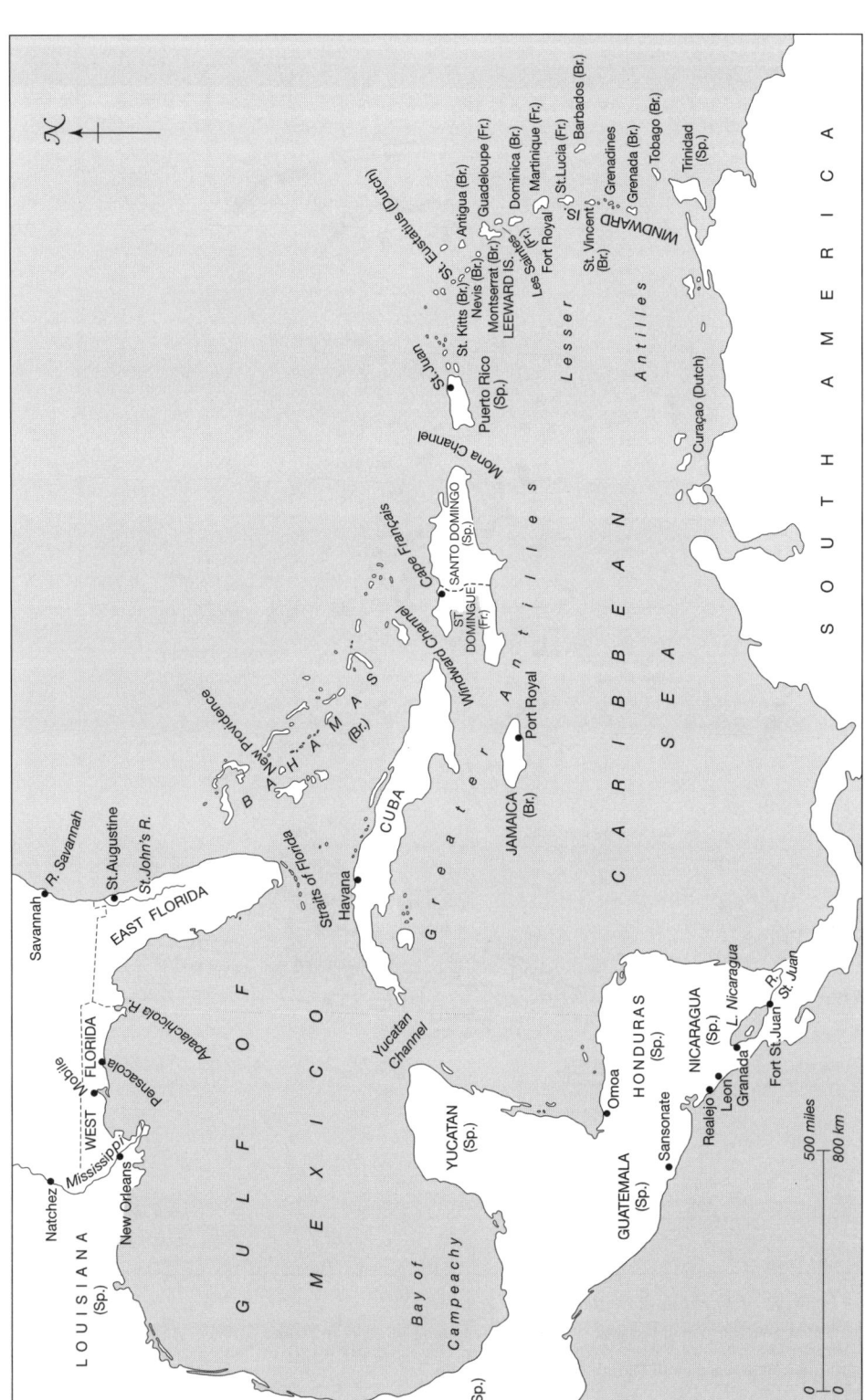

MAP 5 *The West Indies*
Adapted from Mackesy, P. (1964) *The War for America, 1775–1783*, Originally published by Harvard University Press, 1964, reprinted by University of Nebraska Press, 1993, page 226

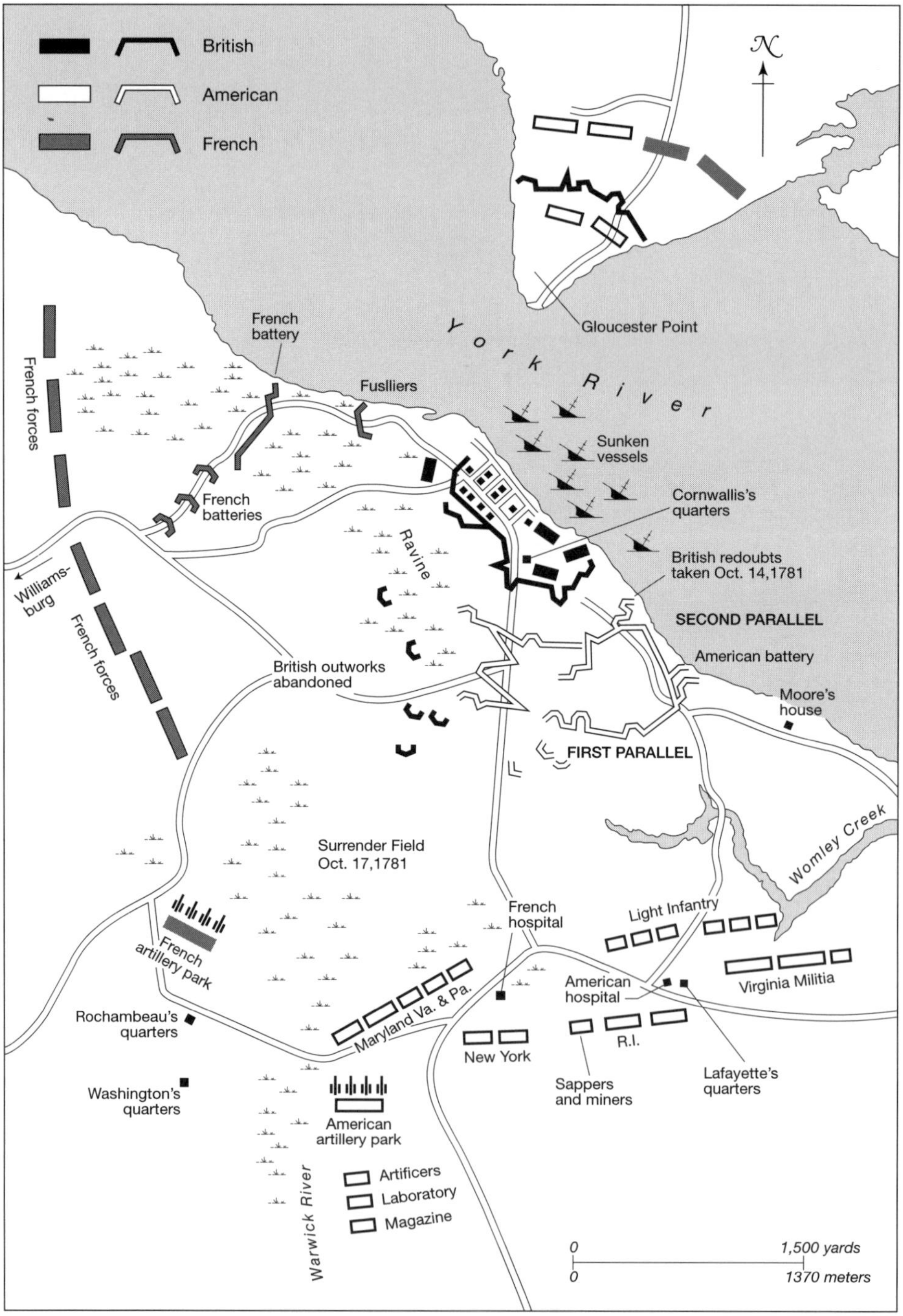

MAP 6 *The Siege of Yorktown, September to October 1781*

Adapted from the map of the siege of Yorktown, Sept. to Oct. 1781 in Ferling, J. (2007) *Almost a Miracle: The American Victory in the War of Independence*, Oxford University Press, page 514 (r/h side). By permission of Oxford University Press, Inc.

CHAPTER 1

Britain and America come to blows, 1763–75

John Bull and his empire

The signing of the peace of Paris in early 1763, which ended the Seven Years War, seemingly witnessed Britain at the zenith of its power. France and Spain had been checked in Europe while Britain's naval superiority allowed her to make important gains in North America, the Caribbean, Africa, and India. To many English-speaking commentators it seemed that Britain's empire was now comparable to that of Ancient Rome. The only downside was the widespread resentment in Europe at Britain's success, especially in France where Choiseul, the King's leading minister, was already strengthening the French navy in preparation for another war.[1]

However, none of this worried the victorious British. A glorious prospect seemingly awaited an empire based on trade and manufacturing. Orthodox mercantilism, still the accepted economic theory of the day, asserted that there was a fixed amount of wealth in the world. Hence the more one nation possessed, the less remained for others. The recent victories meant that Britain not only had supplies of raw materials from her colonies, but growing markets for her manufactures too. The Navigation Acts, which underpinned this system, also ensured that this trade was carried in British ships, creating a pool of seamen with which to man the Royal Navy.

Unfortunately there was just one downside to this happy prospect: the cost. The war had been carried on at great expense to the British exchequer, resulting in a doubling of the national debt to £128,000,000. This was considered highly undesirable. Until the capital was repaid, interest on the debt would have to be met by taxation, accounting for half the annual budget. The British taxpayer hence faced the anomaly that the peace of 1763 was going to be almost as costly as the war that preceded it.

The quest began therefore for new sources of revenue. One that had not been tried before was taxation of the colonies in North America. During the war, British officers and officials had noticed how prosperous the Colonists were. As one officer acerbically noted, "everybody has property and everybody knows it."[2] Among the white population there was almost no poverty since all enjoyed a decent income. Taxes on the other hand were low, since the provincial governments had no debts to service. The colonies had contributed to the war, but most of the burden had fallen on the British Treasury.

The ending of the conflict in 1763 accordingly led many Britons to conclude that the Colonists should now make a contribution to the cost of defending the empire. Much of the war had been fought to protect the frontiers of New England, New York, and Pennsylvania, resulting in the deployment of 30,000 British soldiers for the conquest of Canada and a frontier stretching to the Mississippi. These developments were hugely advantageous for the mainland colonies, offering them security from Indian and French attack as well as exciting prospects for expansion. Prior to 1755 each colony had provided its own internal security. However, such localism would no longer suffice, since troops were required in Canada where the French-speaking population was resentful of the British presence. Troops were also needed to contain the many additional Indian nations who were now in the British orbit. Finally, further forces were necessary to secure Florida and its residual Indian and Spanish population. British ministers calculated that an army of 10,000 men would be necessary to protect the gains made at the Peace of Paris.[3]

One person who accepted the need for a colonial financial contribution was George Grenville, who became first Lord of the Treasury in April 1763. Grenville had been overshadowed during the war by his brother-in-law, William Pitt, later Earl of Chatham, but was ambitious to make his mark by meeting the challenges of the peace. He saw two ways of getting America to pay a fairer contribution to the nation's expenses: firstly by improving the efficiency of the bureaucracy; and secondly by raising money through new taxes. The political classes in any case believed it was time to tighten British control over the colonies. The mercantilist system had clearly become lax in its enforcement, especially in New England, where royal authority was being seemingly undermined by undesirable democratic currents.

A start was accordingly made by ordering customs officers and other officials to return to America, since many of them were living in London, leaving their duties to be performed by ill-paid deputies. Greater powers were also given to the navy to suppress smuggling. After this Grenville introduced two new measures to raise taxes. The first of these, the 1764 Sugar or Revenue Act, imposed duties on the importation of molasses and other sugar products. This was followed in early 1765 with a Stamp Act, requiring all legal documents and printed materials, such as newspapers, to bear the cost of a stamp. However, both acts included additional regulations for making the collection of the revenue more effective. Customs officers were given powers to enter private premises to search for smuggled goods, while the Vice Admiralty courts were strengthened to ensure the more effective prosecution of offenders. Infractions of the Navigation Acts in America had previously been heard in the provincial common law courts, where sympathetic juries usually acquitted the defendants, whatever the evidence. The Vice Admiralty courts in contrast had only a judge to determine both the facts and verdict of a case without reference to a jury. This had long been the practice in Britain because ordinary subjects were not trusted to give impartial verdicts in revenue cases. Both measures accordingly caused little debate in Parliament.

The Grenville ministry was also responsible for one other measure in the restructuring of Britain's North American empire. This was the Proclamation of 1763 prohibiting further settlement west of the Allegheny Mountains. Most Indian nations had allied with France during the recent conflict and refused to accept the change in sovereignty. Under the leadership of the Ottawa Chief, Pontiac, they launched a series of surprise attacks on the British forts north of the Ohio and west of Allegheny Mountains, capturing every post except those of Niagara, Detroit, and Pittsburgh. To the British, Pontiac's War was yet another example of the Colonists' inability to defend themselves. Apart from abuses in the Indian trade, the uprising also underlined the desirability of more orderly settlement. On the fall of Canada in 1760, settlers had pushed westward against the wishes of the native peoples. Hence to calm Indian fears, a line was to be drawn along the crest of the mountains, forbidding settlement on the other side. Those wishing to acquire new lands should go to the maritime provinces of Canada or the recently acquired Spanish colony of Florida. Apart from quieting the Indians and reducing frontier costs, such settlement would have the additional advantage of buttressing the flanks of Britain's North American empire. It seemed a sensible measure, at least from London.[4]

The rights of British America

The actions of the British ministry came as a shock to the American Colonists, who like the inhabitants in Britain, had taken great pride in the triumph of the English-speaking peoples. They too could see a glorious future as partners in empire. The Reverend Samuel Cooper of Boston spoke for most Colonists when he exclaimed: "What scenes of happiness are we ready to figure to ourselves from the hope of enjoying, in this good land, all the blessings of an undisturbed and lasting peace." A glorious prospect beckoned through "our settlements extending themselves with security on every side, and changing a wilderness into a fruitful field."[5] Some even speculated that the center of the empire would eventually move from London across the Atlantic. However, the contentment was not just economic. The inhabitants felt pride in being part of a nation which since the Glorious Revolution of 1688–89 had protected their rights through constitutional government. This was in stark contrast to the absolute monarchies of Europe. Americans were proud to be Britons.

Now these assumptions were being undermined. The Colonists believed they had paid their fair share in money and manpower for the conquest of Canada. Furthermore, the expulsion of the French and defeat of their Indian allies meant that they no longer saw any reason for a large standing army. The Colonists had taken care of themselves before 1755 and could do so again. Accordingly, if Britain wanted to maintain a permanent military presence, it must be for more sinister reasons. The colonies, like Britain, had a long tradition of hostility to standing armies since the time of James II, believing them to be "absolutely inconsistent with civil liberty." Hence the continued deployment of troops must be "designed as a rod and a check."[6] Far from being partners, the Americans were to be slaves.

These suspicions about British intentions were supported by the administrative arrangements for enforcing the new taxes. The Colonists cherished their right to trial by jury and saw no reason for its curtailment in revenue cases, whatever the practice in Britain. It was a fundamental undermining of their liberty. Equally dangerous was the threat to their property posed by taxation, for without that, liberty was of little use. Finally the Proclamation of 1763 denied the right of the Colonists to cheap land. Though some New Englanders looked to Nova Scotia, the vast majority of those seeking land wanted to travel westward. Seemingly the Indian "savages" were being placated at the expense of the Colonists' birthright.

Initially the Colonists' reaction to these measures was muted. The frontier was still a minor consideration for most Colonists while the 1764 Sugar Act was presented by the ministers as a traditional mercantilist measure, regulating the trade of the empire by means of customs duties. The only provincial assembly to protest was New York. However, the Stamp Act was another matter. Here was an open attempt by Parliament to impose direct taxation on the daily lives of the Colonists. The first protests were made in May 1765 in the Virginia House of Burgesses where a fiery young lawyer, Patrick Henry, argued that the impositions were not only unconstitutional but against the rights of Englishmen. Anyone obeying them was a traitor. With such provocative language, colonial anger was not limited to words. Within weeks the people of Boston had taken to the streets, demolishing several properties, including the residence of the Lieutenant Governor, Thomas Hutchinson. Simultaneously, a call went forth for a joint protest by all the colonies. In response nine provinces sent delegates to New York, where they reaffirmed "the undoubted right of Englishmen, that no taxes should be imposed on them, but with their own consent." This led in turn to a general refusal to use the stamps on their arrival in November 1765, resulting in the closure of the law courts and ports. The powerlessness of royal government was apparent for all to see.

The reaction of the Colonists caught the British by surprise. The Stamp Act had caused little debate in Parliament, where Grenville had introduced it to an almost empty House of Commons. Only one speaker, Isaac Barré, had seriously questioned its equity and advisability. When ministers stressed the benign role of Britain in the founding of the colonies, he exploded: "They planted by your care? No your oppressions planted them in America," referring to the Puritan exodus to New England and departure of other migrant groups. His oratory, however, had been lost on the Commons where the bill was passed by 245 votes to 49.[7]

Fortunately for the Colonists, a change of ministry had occurred by the time that news of the Stamp Act protests reached London. The new government of the Marquis of Rockingham had strong links with the merchant classes, who bewailed the damage to their trade at a time of post-war recession. The new ministers accordingly opted for a repeal of the Stamp Act. However, all the parties in London agreed on the constitutionality of the Act, whatever the Colonists might say. Parliamentary sovereignty was the principle that underpinned the constitutional settlement of 1688–89 when King William III had saved England from the tyranny of James II. Consequently before Grenville's measure was repealed, a Declaratory Act was passed, reaffirming the sovereignty of Parliament over the colonies "in all cases whatsoever."

A tea party in Boston: Congress versus Parliament

Across the Atlantic, most Americans believed the repeal of the Stamp Act had restored the old benign relationship. They assumed that the Declaratory Act was mere face-saving. But as already noted, this was not the case. Consequently another clash was not long in coming. The ministry still needed revenue to pay the costs of defending and governing America while most Britons believed that a more positive assertion of Parliamentary sovereignty was required. One of those holding these views was Charles Townshend, the Chancellor of the Exchequer, who had taken office in 1766 following the collapse of the Rockingham ministry. He had noticed that most Americans were ready to accept the Sugar Act because it had the appearance of regulating trade rather than raising revenue. It was also an external rather than an internal tax, giving consumers the option to buy locally produced articles which did not carry the duty. Townsend accordingly proposed a new series of taxes on the importation of tea, glass, lead paints and paper. But he took advantage of the new act to tighten further the administrative machinery for enforcing the mercantilist system, by giving additional powers to the customs service and Vice Admiralty courts. Lastly he announced that the revenues so raised would be used to pay royal officials, notably the governors and judges, who had previously been dependent on the provincial assemblies for their salaries.

If Townshend believed he had neatly circumvented the difficulties of Grenville's previous measures, he was quickly disabused. Disguising the duties as a mercantilist measure cut no ice with the "Patriots," as opponents of the measures were beginning to be called. The act was clearly intended to raise revenue, not regulate trade, and was therefore as objectionable as the Stamp Act. The strengthening of the Vice Admiralty courts also raised anew the issue of trial by jury. Finally the payment of royal officials by the Crown appeared an attempt to sustain despotic government by removing any accountability to the people through their provincial assemblies.

Though the violence was less widespread this time, the opposition was in some respects more insidious. Once more the initiative was taken by Boston. Its leaders now proposed an inter-colonial boycott of British manufactures as a way of bringing economic pressure on the ministry. Action was accordingly taken in all the main American cities, though with mixed results. However, the enforcement of the boycott in Boston and the intimidation of the local officials led to the dispatch of troops for their protection. The cure proved worse than the symptoms, since the population now focused its anger on the soldiers, resulting in the "Boston Massacre" in March 1770, when five inhabitants were killed during a protest outside the Customs House.

In an effort to cool the situation, Hutchinson, now governor of Massachusetts, agreed to move the soldiers out of the town. He was supported in this conciliatory step by the ministry in London, where the King's new Treasury minister, Lord North, removed all the Townshend duties except that on tea to retain the principle of Parliament's right to tax. However, North's initiative was unavailing. The Patriots everywhere were now convinced of a long-term ministerial plot to deprive them of their liberty. The Massachusetts House of Representatives accordingly established a committee of correspondence to monitor the actions of the ministry and report any threat to the inhabitants' liberty. Even more ominously, the other provinces formed inter-colonial committees of correspondence for similarly watching the common threat posed by Britain. Sporadic incidents of violence also occurred, the most notorious being the seizure of a royal revenue cutter, the *Gaspée*, by the Rhode Island Patriots. During the incident several shots were fired and an officer wounded. The vessel was then burnt. All attempts to catch the perpetrators were of no avail.

In this climate it only required a spark to set off a wider conflagration, which inadvertently occurred when North attempted to provide financial support for the East India Company, one of Britain's foremost commercial establishments. To alleviate the company's distress, North passed a Parliamentary bill allowing the company to export tea directly to America, rather than via Britain as previously, where an additional customs duty was levied. The effect of the measure was to make the tea cheaper, even though Townshend's tax was still in force. To the Patriots, North's measure appeared a cunning plan to suborn the Colonists into drinking tea, thus acknowledging the right of Parliament to tax. This was something that the Boston Patriots, led by Samuel Adams, were determined to prevent. When Hutchinson refused to allow the East India company ships to return without unloading their cargo, several dozen Patriots disguised as Mohawk Indians boarded the vessels and cast the tea into the harbor.

The attack on the tea vessels in Boston was not necessarily the worst act of violence perpetrated by the Patriots since 1765. However, it was the last straw for the British government. Successive ministries had attempted to be conciliatory in the face of colonial protests. Now a measure that should have been beneficial to the average consumer had been used to justify another act of defiance. Clearly conciliation was not working. Although the violence had been directed at a private company rather than royal officials, it was an institution in which many of the British elite had a financial interest. The violence suggested that Massachusetts in particular was descending into anarchy through the actions of a small group of evil men, who were seeking to undermine the affection of the population for the King and mother country.[8] It was time to set an example before the colonies broke loose, with all the damaging consequences for the mercantilist system and wellbeing of the empire.

The Ministry accordingly introduced a series of measures to rectify this situation, making it clear to the colonies what their fate would be if they followed the example of Massachusetts.[9] First Boston was to be punished for the Tea Party by having its port closed until compensation had been paid to the East India Company. It was also to be occupied temporarily by several regiments of regular troops. However, the most important ministerial measure was the Government of Massachusetts Act which sought to remodel the political institutions of the province. Among the many obnoxious aspects of the existing charter in British eyes was the right of the lower assembly to name the council, which left governors politically isolated. Now the governor would have sole power to nominate the councilors. In addition, the powers of town meetings were to be greatly restricted. Adams had used such gatherings in Boston to mobilize opposition, especially when the provincial assembly was not sitting. In future the towns could hold meetings only once a year for the election of officials, unless they had the consent of the governor.

Two other measures affecting the colonies were passed by the North ministry at this time. The first was a bill allowing royal officials charged with any misdemeanor to be tried in another colony or even sent to Great Britain to ensure a fair hearing. The second was an act giving the province of Quebec a legislative council, the hope being that this would conciliate the inhabitants to the change in sovereignty. Its introduction now was purely coincidental. But the bill also extended the territory of the province on the other side of the Allegheny Mountains, thereby undermining the claims of the English-speaking provinces to that region. This upset many influential land owners and speculators.

All these measures had the widest political support in Parliament, even from the opposition Rockingham Whigs. As Lord Dartmouth, the Secretary of State for American affairs, observed: "The Constitutional authority of this Kingdom over its Colonies must be vindicated, and its laws obeyed throughout the whole Empire," for "if the people of America say no, they say in effect that they will no longer be a part of the British Empire."[10] The received wisdom at this stage was that a sharp slap would bring the recalcitrant colonies into line. General Gage, the newly appointed governor of Massachusetts, reflected this view when he assured George III: "They will be lions whilst we are lambs." But "if we take the resolute part they will undoubtedly prove very meek"[11] The only voice of caution was that of the former governor of West Florida, George Johnstone, who warned that the likely outcome would be "a general confederation to resist the power" of Britain.[12]

Johnstone was soon proved right. To the inhabitants of Massachusetts and the other colonies the acts were simply "intolerable." Closing the port of Boston was disproportionate to the offense, threatening the entire population with ruin. Even worse, the Massachusetts Government Bill overturned the political rights of the province's people, threatening them with an arbitrary government and certain slavery. The administration of justice was similarly objectionable, since it would allow corrupt officials to escape justice, providing a license for every kind of maladministration. Finally the Quebec Act seemed designed to placate the French Canadians as the prelude to employing them against the liberties of their English-speaking neighbors.

The Patriots in Boston responded by forming a "solemn League and Covenant" to ban the consumption of British goods.[13] But clearly wider action was desirable and the Patriot party in Massachusetts quickly appealed to the other colonies for a Congress to be held in September at Philadelphia. There was little delay in accepting this proposal. Although the regions of New England, the Mid Atlantic, Upper and Lower South had different religious, economic, and social structures, they could all see that what had been done to Massachusetts could be done to them should they assert their rights. Only Georgia failed to send a delegation, reflecting its lack of population and exposed frontier situation. The outcome in Philadelphia was a firm declaration by the Congress of the rights of the American people and a denial of Parliamentary sovereignty. In future the link with Britain would be through the Crown, though Parliament might still legislate on a courtesy basis for the regulation of trade and certain other matters of common interest.

To ensure acceptance of these terms, Congress proposed a boycott of British goods throughout the continent, enforced by means of a Continental Association. The hope was that such a boycott would have sufficient economic impact to bring the British ministry to terms. But Congress also adopted the resolves of Suffolk County in Massachusetts, authorizing its people to protect their liberties by the forming of their own de facto government.[14] The Massachusetts assembly, now termed a "congress," was to put the colony into a state of defense for which taxes were to be collected and the militia prepared.

In reality the Continental Congress was as misinformed as the ministry about what was politically acceptable to the other side. The British believed that any further concessions would be fatal to the empire. The belief persisted that the vast majority of the colonial population was loyal to the mother country and was being misled by a small mischievous minority. It was this thinking that led the ministry on 27 January 1775 to order General Thomas Gage, now Governor of Massachusetts, to make a demonstration of British military power by seizing the Patriot leaders in Massachusetts and imposing martial law. To help him execute these orders, the ministry simultaneously dispatched another 4,000 troops.[15] However contemptible the opposition, it was sensible to be prepared.

Gage, on leaving England, had initially been optimistic about enforcing the Intolerable Acts. However, since taking up his post he had witnessed the collapse of royal government throughout Massachusetts. Most of those accepting places on the new Council had been forced to flee or resign their posts, while the courts of justice had ceased to operate, because no juries could be empanelled. He now recognized that the government was not dealing with the "Boston rabble but the freeholders and Farmers of the Country."[16] Nor had the defiance been limited to Massachusetts. Since the meeting of Continental Congress in Philadelphia, Patriot officials were taking control everywhere, acting under its authority and that of their respective assemblies, now transformed into provincial congresses.

Perhaps most ominous for Gage was the treatment of those still loyal to the Crown. Following the establishment of the Continental Association, local committees had been formed to enforce the ban on British goods by inspecting premises and requiring that everyone take an oath in support. Those refusing to do so had their names publicized, making them targets for public hostility and acts of violence, the most popular being tarring and feathering. Such was the fate of the Connecticut "River God families" who had dominated the politics and economy of western Massachusetts. The Williams and Worthington families were slow to align themselves with the Patriot cause. They soon discovered the consequences of their defiance when a mob shut Israel Williams in a smokehouse for two days until he saw the error of his ways.[17] Not surprisingly most Loyalists quickly complied with what was required of them.

As for Gage, he was confined to Boston, apart from occasional patrols, while everywhere the provincial militia openly practiced its maneuvers in preparation for hostilities. This included the forming of elite companies of minutemen, pledged to take action at a moment's warning.[18] The situation was so ominous that Gage even suggested suspending the Coercive Acts. The only alternative was the dispatch of another 20,000 men, "since a small force rather encourages resistance than terrifies." But he still believed that "if a respectable force" was put into the field and the most obnoxious leaders detained, the government would emerge victorious.[19]

The first shot: Lexington and Concord

Gage's proposed suspending of the Coercive Acts was indignantly rejected in London, where the ministry prepared a further punitive measure restraining the trade of New England.[20] Nevertheless it prompted North to introduce a plan of conciliation, promising that if the colonies voted an adequate revenue for the provincial governments, Parliament would refrain from taxing them. As a further conciliatory gesture, he promised that the duties raised from the regulation of the trade would be used solely in America. But his colleagues simultaneously decided to dispatch three senior officers, Major Generals William Howe, Henry Clinton, and John Burgoyne, to stiffen Gage's resolve.[21] Gage had spent most of his military career in North America, following his arrival at the start of the French and Indian War, and had subsequently married into one of New York's leading families. It seemed that his long residence there had corrupted his ability to see what was required.

Unfortunately for North, his plan of conciliation proved still-born since it was overtaken by events in America. In mid-April Gage received Dartmouth's instructions to take decisive action. Accordingly on the night of 18 April 1775 he ordered a force of 800 Grenadiers and Light Infantry under Colonel Francis Smith to march to Concord where it was believed arms and ammunition had been stockpiled.[22] Several Massachusetts Patriot leaders were also thought to be in the area. The hope was that the detachment could reach its target without being observed. However, the preparations to cross the Charles River were quickly noticed and warnings sent ahead by Paul Revere, one of Boston's leading Patriots. The troops in any case were well short of their objective when they reached the hamlet of Lexington at 9.00 am, where they found 90 minutemen gathered on the green adjacent to the road. Smith immediately ordered them to disperse, not wishing to have a hostile force on his flank as he marched towards Concord. The provincials thereupon began to disband when shots rang out, prompting the British to return fire, killing several militiamen. There was much subsequent debate as to who was responsible for opening fire. In the wider context it is immaterial since both sides were determined to impose their views by force if necessary.[23]

The British then continued to Concord, only to find that the Patriot leaders had disappeared along with the supplies. But in carrying out their searches the soldiers set fire to several buildings which led to further firing. This time the militia was more numerous and ready to resist after the killings at Lexington. About noon, Smith ordered a retreat. However, he soon discovered that although the militia gave way before the regulars in close combat, they could inflict considerable damage as individuals, firing from the cover of hedges, walls, and buildings. By 3.00 pm Smith's contingent was on the verge of collapse and was saved only with the arrival of another 2,000 men equipped with cannon under Lord Percy. Smith had prudently requested this force on realizing that his intended strike at Concord had been discovered. With these reinforcements the British finally reached the Charles River where they were able to ferry themselves back to Boston. They had suffered 273 casualties, including 73 killed, three times as many as the New Englanders.[24]

The foray to Concord had proved unexpectedly expensive for the British. Percy admitted: "I never believed . . . that they would have attacked the King's troops, or have had the perseverance I found in them yesterday."[25] But even more expensive were the consequences. Far from collapsing, the New England militia poured in from every direction. The Massachusetts Congress had already made plans for an Army of Observation. Now it voted 30,000 men to be raised in conjunction with the other New England provinces. Within days the combined force had reached 20,000 men, allowing it to surround Boston. Everywhere the local Patriots were in arms, stockpiling ammunition and other stores ready for use. Nor was the trouble confined to New England, since all the provinces began expelling royal officials and preparing for hostilities.[26] By June, Gage estimated that the suppression of the rebellion would require a minimum of 15,000 men at Boston and another 10,000 in New York, with a third corps of 7,000 advancing from Canada.[27]

Continental Congress meanwhile had coincidentally reconvened in Philadelphia to consider the progress of its opposition to the Intolerable Acts. It now quickly took responsibility for the events at Boston and the conduct of the war. First it sanctioned on 14 June 1775 the raising of volunteer units from Pennsylvania, Maryland, and Virginia to reinforce the New Englanders.[28] Then it appointed George Washington as commander-in-chief. Washington at this point was attending Congress as a Virginian delegate, though he did so in the uniform of a Fairfax County militia colonel, reminding his colleagues of his experience during the French and Indian War, when he had first served as an aide to General Edward Braddock and later commanded a Virginian regiment.[29] His appointment in reality was prompted by the New England delegates to ensure support from Virginia and the other provinces. But it was an indication of the readiness of all the colonies to join what was now a war with Britain.

Congress's orders to Washington on 20 June 1775 were to take command of the forces at Boston and use "every method" in his power "to destroy or make prisoners of all persons" who were then "in arms against the good people of the United Colonies." Much would depend on his "prudent and discrete management," though he was to take the advice of his "council of war to order and dispose of the said Army as may be most advantageous."[30] It would be a difficult and onerous task, requiring luck, skill, and patience. Even Washington admitted that his "abilities and military experience" might "not be equal" to the task, since the auguries did not seem promising.[31]

Notes and references

1 Jonathan Dull, *A Diplomatic History of the American Revolution* (New Haven, 1985), 35–6. H.M. Scott, "The Importance of Bourbon Naval Reconstruction to the Strategy of Choiseul after the Seven Years War," *International History Review*, 1 (1970), 17–35.

2 Richard Middleton, *Colonial America: A History, 1565–1776* (Cambridge, Mass., 3rd edition, 2002), 220.

3 John Shy, *Toward Lexington: The Role of the British Army in the Coming of the Revolution* (Princeton, 1965), 45–79.

4 For the events surrounding Pontiac's War see Richard Middleton, *Pontiac's War: Its Causes, Course and Consequences* (New York, 2007).

5 Quoted in Bernhard Knollenburg, *Origin of the American Revolution, 1759–1766* (New York, 1960), 97.

6 Quoted in Knollenburg, *American Revolution*, 90.

7 Quoted in Edmund S. and Helen M. Morgan, *The Stamp Act Crisis: Prologue to Revolution* (Chapel Hill, 1962), 93.

8 Ira P. Gruber, "The American Revolution as a Conspiracy: The British View," *William and Mary Quarterly*, 26 (1969), 364–71.

9 Peter D.G. Thomas, *Lord North* (London, 1976), 76.

10 Dartmouth to Gage, 3 June 174, Carter/2, 165–66.

11 George III to North, 4 February 1774, Fortescue/3, 59.

12 *Dictionary of National Biography*.

13 Richard D. Brown, *Revolutionary Politics in Massachusetts: The Boston Committee of Correspondence and the Towns, 1772–1774* (Cambridge, Mass., 1970), 185–99.

14 David Hackett Fischer, *Paul Revere's Ride* (New York, 1994). The Suffolk resolves were the work of the Suffolk County Convention, which was in reality a reconstituted Boston town meeting to evade the provisions of the Massachusetts Government Act.

15 Dartmouth to Gage, 27 January 1775, Carter/2, 179–81.

16 Gage to Dartmouth, 2 September 1774, Carter/1, 369–72. Ibid., 12 September, 374. For a more detailed account of the collapse of Royal Authority in Massachusetts, see T. H. Breen, *American Insurgents, American Patriots: The Revolution of the People* (New York, 2010).

17 Gregory Nobles, *Divisions Throughout the Whole: Politics and Society in Hampshire County Massachusetts, 1760–1775* (1983), 167–177.

18 Robert Gross, *The Minutemen and their World* (New York, 1976), 59–60.

19 Gage to Dartmouth, 30 October 1774, Carter/1, 383.

20 Christopher Ward, *The War of the Revolution*, John R. Alden, ed., 2 vols. (New York, 1952), Vol. I, 22.

21 Dartmouth to Gage, 22 February 1775, Carter/2, 184–85.

22 Gage to Dartmouth, 22 April 1775, Carter/1, 396.

23 This was Gage's opinion in a subsequent letter to Dartmouth, 15 October 1775, Carter/1, 422.

24 John Ferling, *Almost a Miracle: The American Victory in the War of Independence* (New York, 2007), 30–33.

25 Quoted in Christopher Ward, *War of the Revolution* I, 50–51.

26 Gage to Dartmouth, 13 May 1775, Carter/1, 397–98. Ibid., 25 May 1775, 401.

27 Gage to North, 12 June 1775, Fortescue/3, 214–15.

28 Robert Middlekauf, *The Glorious Cause: The American Revolution, 1763–1789* (New York, 1982), 281.

29 Ferling, *Almost a Miracle*, 39–40. Edward G. Lengel, *General George Washington: A Military Life* (New York, 2005).

30 Instructions from Congress, 22 June 1775, WP/RWS/1, 21–22.

31 Address to Continental Congress, 16 June 1775 WP/RWS/1, 1.

CHAPTER 2

The fighting begins, 1775

Prospects and perspectives of the combatants

To most British and European observers, the Colonists' challenge appeared to offer little chance of success. Britain was at the height of its power following the Seven Years War and the defeat of France and Spain. It had a population of almost eight million, the largest merchant marine in the world, the most advanced industry, and a system of credit that was the envy of Europe. During the recent war the navy had mobilized almost 100 battleships of 60 to 100 guns and twice that number of frigates and smaller craft, the whole manned by 85,000 seamen.[1]

The military achievement had been almost as impressive, despite Britain's tradition of having only a small standing army. Towards the end of the Seven Years War the army had reached a strength of 120,000 men, organized in 95 foot and 20 cavalry regiments. In addition Britain had employed a substantial force of mercenaries in Germany in support of George II and George III as Electors of Hanover.[2] Finally there were the awesome resources of the British financial system to sustain this military and naval effort. The Bank of England and financiers of the City of London were able to raise millions of pounds at low rates of interest, which Parliament funded through long-term taxation.

The colonial resources in comparison appeared quite small. The continental colonies had barely 3,000,000 people, of whom 600,000 were slaves of African origin. Moreover a considerable proportion of the white population outside New England was strongly Loyalist. Another cause for caution was the lack of precedents for a successful rebellion by the subjects of a European monarch. The nearest example was that of Holland against Spain 200 years earlier, and that seemed of little relevance now.

Nevertheless the Patriots determined to persevere with their cause. If the recent history of Europe provided little inspiration, that of Ancient Greece and Rome gave them examples in which a few determined and honorable men had defied seemingly impossible odds. Moreover the Patriots were aware that the British army was far from invincible or sufficiently numerous to reconquer a territory stretching 1500 miles from Georgia to New Hampshire. Many remembered the disaster that happened to Braddock on the banks of the Monongahela River in 1755 when he had foolishly ignored colonial warnings about the inadequacy of regular tactics against the French and their Indian allies. Subsequent events during Pontiac's War had not changed these opinions.

The Patriots consequently believed that they could hold their own against the redcoats, whom they affected to despise as mercenaries who had sold their services to a corrupt ministry. The militias, in contrast, were freemen fighting for their farms and families. They would not be lacking in courage or skill when it came to battle, since nearly all of them were familiar with firearms in a frontier society, as had been demonstrated during the events at Lexington and Concord. The colonial cause was just, their men and women steadfast, and their population virtuous. There could be only one outcome: victory. However, independence was not yet on the agenda, since most Colonists desired a reconciliation that left them self-governing while still attached symbolically to the mother country.

The only cause for concern was the lack of unity, due to the colonies' different ethnic, religious, and economic background. Hence when John Adams attended the first Continental Congress in September 1774 he noted: "Philadelphia, with all its trade and wealth and regularity, is not Boston. The morals of our people are much better, their manners are more polite and agreeable; they are purer English," and were endowed with greater spirit, wiser laws, superior religion and better education.[3] But while Adams disparaged Pennsylvanians, John Rutledge of South Carolina was equally critical of the New Englanders for their "overruling Influence in Council . . . their low cunning, and those leveling principles which Men without character and without fortune in general possess."[4] For if the differences between New England and the Middle colonies were as Adams described, they were even more noticeable when compared with the southern colonies, whose economies depended on the production of cash crops like tobacco, rice, and indigo, for which a large slave workforce was necessary.

The 13 colonies in consequence had almost no tradition of intercolonial cooperation. The New England colonies had acted collectively during the seventeenth century, but no wider contacts had been made until the Albany Conference of 1754 when they met representatives from New York, Pennsylvania, and Maryland to discuss the defense of the frontier against French and Indian attack. It was during these discussions that Benjamin Franklin formulated a plan for colonial union. Nothing, however, resulted because the provincial assemblies feared that such a federal system would diminish their own importance. Eleven years later nine colonies met in New York for the Stamp Act Congress, presenting a brief appearance of unity. It was not until September 1774 that 12 of the 13 colonies formed a united front to Britain in the first Continental Congress. The discussions then revealed significant differences between the hard-line New Englanders, who wanted complete self-government for each colony and those from the middle colonies who wanted a more conciliatory approach, typified by Joseph Galloway's plan of union in which Congress would have become the partner of the British Parliament.[5]

Nevertheless, the need to cooperate was a more powerful force than the desire to disparage, for as Franklin observed, the Patriots would hang separately if they did not act together. Hence, further preparations were recognized as being necessary following the events at Lexington and Concord, even if reconciliation should prove the eventual outcome. Congress accordingly requested each province to provide men according to a quota based on population. Enlistments were initially for eight months, the assumption being that the crisis would be short-lived. But money would still be needed to implement these plans, and Congress began selling bills of credit and issuing currency.[6]

Meanwhile, across the Atlantic the British were reaching opposite conclusions to those of the Patriots. To the British it was inconceivable that the Americans should either want or have the ability to secede from the empire. Most of the inhabitants were of British stock, making the Patriot violence difficult to understand. The British constitution was the mildest in the world and offered the Colonists the greatest economic blessings. One had only to observe the phenomenal doubling of the population every 25 years and the growing prosperity of the mainland colonies. British rule had transformed a few isolated settlements into flourishing societies, all protected by the rule of law. It would be errant selfishness if the Americans seceded after Britain had done so much to defend them. As one official commented, "American Independence would be . . . the deepest and most disgraceful wound that Great Britain could possibly receive."[7]

It would mean the loss of "three millions of subjects to her prince, and to her merchants and manufacturers... an annual export and import trade of full four millions of money," which might eventually include "near five millions more from the West Indies." Britain would also lose "the sovereignty of a country which supplied her fleets [with] naval stores in abundance and a never failing nursery of hardy seamen." In short, the secession of the colonies would spell the end of Britain's greatness, including her ability to be "the arbiter of Europe."[8] The only beneficiaries would be France and Spain.

The second reason for taking a strong line with the colonies was the British belief that military success was certain. The colonies had barely a third of Britain's total population and no tradition of professional military or naval service. Until the late war the colonies had relied on their part-time militia for defense against the Indians. The volunteer corps raised between 1755 and 1763 had generally served as support units and had rarely performed with distinction when committed to battle. This was hardly surprising since they were usually raised in the spring and disbanded in the autumn. These were not the kind of units that could withstand a European professional army, trained over the years to maneuver in tight formation.[9] Accordingly those regulars who had served in America were generally contemptuous about colonial military ability. James Murray spoke for most when he asserted that the "American is an effeminate thing, very unfit for and very impatient of war."[10] Everyone agreed with George III that "when once those rebels have felt a smart blow, they will submit."[11] Hence extensive mobilization of the armed forces would not be necessary. The only augmentation to the army at the start of 1775 was the recruitment of another 4,383 men to strengthen 12 existing regiments.[12]

The British government's strategy at this point was based on the assumption that the old order would be restored, once the army had arrested the ringleaders of the conspiracy.[13] All that was required was a limited police action. The ministers had no concept of a people "numerous and armed," ready to fight for their rights and liberties. Resistance by the ordinary people was mere rebellion which could only end in their subjection, since they had neither the resources, nor intellect, nor leadership for a prolonged struggle in support of a legitimate cause. Only monarchs and aristocrats could make the grand decisions, as when Louis XV relinquished Canada as the price for the ending of the Seven Years War. The peasant farmers and bourgeoisie of Canada were not consulted. As for the mauling of Gage's men on the road from Concord, this was dismissed as the result of poor direction and bad luck.

The third reason for the ministerial hard line regarding America at this point was the seemingly peaceful situation in Europe. In 1770 Choiseul had been dismissed by Louis XV and replaced by a more pacific ministry, which abandoned the program of naval rearmament. Indeed in 1772 the French had even explored a rapprochement with Great Britain, prompted by the desire to counterbalance the central European powers, Austria, Prussia, and Russia. These three states had recently implemented the first partition of Poland while Austria and Russia were also threatening Turkey's Balkan provinces, both areas in which France had an interest. Britain in contrast had no such concern. Hence the talks came to nothing, since the North ministry believed that Britain had no need of allies, given her island situation and the distracted state of the Continent.[14] Any interference by Europe in Britain's colonial problems could be dismissed as improbable, meaning that she was free to crush the rebellion in whatever manner seemed most appropriate.

Accordingly on news of Lexington and Concord, there was still no reassessment of the ministerial policy. Dartmouth confidently told Gage that with the arrival of the five additional regiments, "we shall soon hear that you are no longer within the Town of Boston; [and] that the rebels who surrounded it have been dispersed, their works destroyed, and a communication opened with the country."[15] But to ensure colonial compliance, the navy was to enforce the New England Restraining Act more vigorously. Now the fleet was to "carry on such operations upon the seacoasts of the four governments in New England" as seemed "most effectual for suppressing, in conjunction with His Majesty's Land forces, the Rebellion." This included the seizing of all shipping, unless belonging to persons who could give "proof of their attachment to the constitution." Small squadrons would also operate around New York, Delaware Bay, the Chesapeake, and Charleston to prevent military stores from reaching Washington's forces at Boston.[16] Soon all would be set to rights.

Bunker Hill and the siege of Boston

What the ministry failed to appreciate was that the events at Lexington and Concord had caused a complete collapse of royal government throughout North America. The only place where a semblance of royal authority remained was in New York. Here an uneasy dual system operated. The Governor remained in office, supported by the warships and marines of the Royal Navy, while the assembly, acting as a Provincial Congress, wielded influence outside the city. But in other colonies the governors and other officers had no such support. Once news of hostilities arrived, flight to the nearest warship was the usual option, since the Crown's representatives lacked the means to rally the Loyalists. As Governor Martin of North Carolina commented from a frigate on the Cape Fear River, all attempts to contact supporters in the interior had been prevented by the Association committees. Those trying to reach him had "been intercepted . . . searched, detained, abused and stripped of any papers." Had Martin been provided with arms and ammunition six weeks earlier he might have done something effective. Now it was too dangerous to call on "the King's loyal subjects" in the face of "an increasing and spreading revolt that had actually enlisted half the country on its side by terror or persuasion."

Meanwhile the arrival in Boston of Howe, Clinton, and Burgoyne prompted Gage to make a new effort to assert British authority. As Burgoyne commented, it was preposterous that "ten thousand peasants" should "keep five thousand of the King's troops shut up" inside.[17] Gage's initial plan was to seize Dorchester Heights overlooking Boston from the south as the prelude to an attack on the rebel headquarters at Cambridge. However, on the morning of 17 June he discovered that the Patriots were entrenching themselves on Bunker Hill on the other side, bringing both the town and ships of the Royal Navy within cannon range. He resolved accordingly to make an immediate response before the rebels had time to complete their entrenchments. The attack was to be made by an elite force of 2000 regulars under Howe, who had led the Light Infantry and scaled the Heights of Abraham in 1759 prior to the battle for Quebec.

Unfortunately by the time these arrangements were ready it was two o'clock in the afternoon, giving the defenders ample warning of what was impending. Howe's plan was to advance in a broad line while the light infantry enveloped the Patriot entrenchments from the left. Only light resistance was anticipated from the New Englanders as the regulars advanced in close order on their first objective, Breeds Hill, expecting to carry the Patriot position with a single musket volley. The Colonists, however, were well entrenched and ably commanded by Artemis Ward, Israel Putnam, and Dr Joseph Warren. The British also found their advance obstructed by numerous picket fences. Three assaults proved necessary, the third with fixed bayonet, before the Patriots were finally driven from their positions. At the end of the day 226 redcoats were dead with another 800 wounded, of whom 300 were in hospital. Among the casualties were 92 officers, "a most dreadful account" in Howe's words.[18] The Patriot losses in contrast were 140 dead and 271 wounded.

These were casualties that the British could ill afford, as Gage readily acknowledged.[19] But even more importantly, the engagement had demonstrated "that the rebels are not the despicable Rabble too many have supposed them to be." They had shown extraordinary tenacity, the product of "a military spirit" allied to "an uncommon degree of Zeal and enthusiasm." Nor were they tactically naïve, for "wherever they find cover they make a good stand," which the countryside naturally afforded them. In consequence "the Conquest of this Country . . . can be effected only by time and perseverance, and strong armies attacking in various quarters".[20] It was a sobering analysis and a further warning to the British ministry that the suppression of the rebellion would not be a simple police action.

Two weeks later Washington arrived to take command. Unlike many New Englanders, he was not impressed by what he saw from his headquarters at Cambridge, near Boston. As one former regular commented, the problem was that "the privates are all generals but not soldiers."[21] In consequence Washington found that he had an "army of provincials under very little command, discipline, or order."[22] This led him to warn the men in his second set of General Orders that unless "exact discipline be observed and due subordination prevail," the glorious cause "must necessarily end in shameful disappointment and disgrace." But discipline could improve only if the men overcame their prejudices. Hence every man should remember that he was now a soldier "of the United Provinces of America." This required "all distinctions of colonies to be laid aside, so that one and the same spirit may animate the whole." A new continental identity was required.[23]

Washington was rightly punctilious about these matters since discipline alone could ensure success against the British. Until Bunker Hill it was assumed that the zeal of the average American would overcome the want of training.[24] The Patriots therefore had no need to practice marching in formation like European armies. But once the bravura of driving the British back to Boston had subsided, many soldiers found the hardships and tedium of camp life unbearable and asked to go home. Washington's invariable response to such requests was that those "who are engaged in the noble cause of Liberty, should never think of removing from their camp while the enemy is in sight."[25] Unfortunately his appeals too frequently fell on deaf ears, prompting many to desert.

Washington's other major problem on taking up his command was an insufficiency of numbers. He calculated that 22,000 men were needed to maintain the perimeter around Boston.[26] But as he told his fellow Virginian, Richard Henry Lee, the army mustered only 16,000 and was consequently "in an exceedingly dangerous situation." Washington was acutely aware that the British control of the rivers and coasts allowed them to strike wherever they wished. Washington in contrast had to remain stationary while "new modeling" his army in the presence of "the enemy from whom we every hour expect an attack."[27] However, by the third week of July he affected to be more confident. Discipline was improving, as were the Patriot defenses. He believed that if he could hold his position for the next few weeks he might win the war, for "if the enemy are not able to penetrate into the Country, they may as well . . . return home." Hence confining them to Boston "is the principal object we have in view, indeed the only" one.[28]

But much remained to be done. The army still had no uniforms and little money. Washington in lieu suggested the wearing of hunting shirts to give the men some identity and to boost morale.[29] This did not solve the problem of distinguishing ordinary soldiers from commissioned officers. Even Washington was stopped by sentries. He accordingly designed a series of hat cockades and colored sashes for the field officers, while non-commissioned officers were to wear an ordinary stripe on the right shoulder.[30] But most troubling was the lack of gunpowder, each regiment having just nine rounds per man. Hence when Washington occupied a hill close to Charleston Neck in late August, he was unable to exploit his advantage.[31] Fortunately the supply position improved with the appointment of Joseph Trumbull as Commissary General. Trumbull, a merchant by trade, was the son of the Governor of Connecticut and had already demonstrated his talents in securing supplies for that province's regiments.[32] Nevertheless Washington remained highly critical of the New Englanders. "Their officers generally speaking are the most indifferent kind of people." The men would probably "fight very well if properly officered," although they were "an exceeding dirty and nasty people."[33] He confessed to Richard Henry Lee: "My life has been nothing else . . . but one continued round of annoyance and fatigue" for which he would receive little thanks, especially as he refused to countenance any "irregularities" or "public abuses."[34] Being commander in chief was a uniquely thankless task.

One issue to surface in these early weeks was the treatment of prisoners. In a letter to Gage on 11 August 1775 Washington complained that his officers were being jailed "like common criminals without consideration for the Rights of Humanity" or rank. If such conditions continued, Washington would have to punish captured British officers similarly.[35] Gage responded that those in custody had been well treated, though "by the laws of the land" they should be hanged. Gage then raised the issue of the Loyalists, faithful subjects of the King, who were being forced to work like slaves to obtain food.[36] The treatment of prisoners was a difficult issue for both sides. To the British the Patriots were rebels who had forfeited the right to life. The Patriots on the other hand saw their countrymen as legitimate prisoners of war to be treated according to the law of nations. Fortunately for Washington, his threat to inflict the same punishment on captured British officers proved a powerful deterrent, despite Gage's bluster that his men would endure any punishment upholding "the rights of the state, the laws of the land, [and] the being of the Constitution."[37]

Congress widens the conflict: Canada

Although Washington hoped that the containment of the British in Boston would be sufficient to win the struggle, the Patriots recognized the desirability of securing the widest possible support to ensure the success of their cause. It was for this reason that approaches were now made to the Native American peoples. Most Patriots were averse to employing the Indians because of their perceived barbarity. However, they were acutely aware that the British might not be so squeamish. Emissaries were accordingly dispatched to the Iroquois Six Nations in August 1775, suggesting that they remain neutral in what was a white man's war. Similar approaches were made shortly afterwards to the Ohio and western nations at Fort Pitt. Most agreed to the idea. The Six Nations in particular expected to profit from the divisions among the white peoples, just as they had when the French held Canada.[38]

Congress also decided at the end of May 1775 to invite the Canadians to join them in the struggle to defend their "common liberty."[39] The appeal was disingenuous since the Patriots had little sympathy for their French-speaking Catholic neighbors. But it was recognized that the British were militarily weak in Quebec, having few soldiers to control a potentially hostile population. Indeed the Governor General Sir Guy Carleton had just 600 regulars after sending two regiments to Boston. His weakness was underlined by the capture in early May 1775 of Fort Ticonderoga on Lake Champlain by a force of irregulars from western New Hampshire under Ethan Allen and a small body of Massachusetts militia under Benedict Arnold.[40] The ease of the enterprise led both Allen and Arnold to urge an assault on Canada itself, since it would make control of the Indians easier. It would also close the door to a British invasion of New York by way of Lake Champlain. Congress accordingly agreed on 27 June to a preemptive strike against Montreal with a force of New England and New York troops under General Philip Schuyler. But Schuyler was to proceed only if the operation was "not too disagreeable to the Canadians."[41]

While planning new military ventures, the moderate party in Congress, led by John Dickinson, insisted on one last appeal to George III. This document, known as the Olive Branch Petition, asserted that the King should remember the colonial contribution during the previous war, which had helped raise Britain to "a power the most extraordinary the world has ever known." All that was required for the restoration of harmony was the repeal of the injurious statutes passed by Parliament since 1763.[42]

The British, however, were in no mood for conciliation. The Olive Branch Petition lay unread by either King or ministers. The prevailing sentiment in London, following news of Bunker Hill, was that force alone could bring the Americans to reason.[43] The ministry accordingly issued a proclamation on 23 August 1775 declaring all 13 colonies to be in a state of rebellion, which subjects everywhere were to help put down. The most that the ministry would consider was the appointment of commissioners "to grant general or particular pardons and indemnities . . . to such persons as they shall think fit." When a sufficient number had submitted, the officers of the Crown might "restore such province or colony . . . to the free exercise of trade and commerce, and to the same protection as if such province or colony had never revolted."[44]

However, before anything could be attempted, the ministry first had to expand the army and navy. At the start of 1775 the army's peacetime establishment numbered 30,000 men, of which 9,000 were in America and the West Indies, 4,300 in Gibraltar and Minorca, and the remaining 17,500 in Britain.[45] A further 7,000 men were on the separate Irish establishment. This was quite small compared to the establishments of the major European powers, but considered sufficient in peacetime, given Britain's island situation and powerful navy. Clearly this was now inadequate for the task of suppressing a major rebellion. As North informed George III on news of Bunker Hill, the conflict "is now grown to such a height, it must be treated as a foreign war and every expedient which would be used in the latter case" must now be adopted.[46] However, the expansion of the army in particular would be a matter of time. The country had a long tradition of hostility to standing armies since the time of Oliver Cromwell, which meant that recruitment would have to be by voluntary enlistment. Conscription was acceptable only if the country was threatened by invasion and then merely for a limited period and class of person.

The first method of expanding the army was by recruitment of the existing regiments, of which there were 78 in 1775. A second battalion could then be added to some regiments, doubling their size. Lastly, new regiments could be created, though the King was reluctant to do this because vested patronage interests made it difficult to disband them afterwards. Unfortunately for the ministry, the buoyant state of the economy in 1775 meant that recruits were scarce. As a result, by September 1775 the army still had only 32,700 men, leading Lord Barrington, Secretary at War, to declare that "no such number could be raised or procured" when told of the plan to field an army of 20,000 men in 1776.[47] To help out, the King agreed to the deployment of five Hanoverian regiments at Gibraltar and Minorca to release their British garrisons for service in North America.[48] Nevertheless, it was clear that no major military operations would be possible before the spring of 1776 and even this timetable would be at risk, if the French entered the conflict.

The slow expansion of the British army meant that for the next eight months the Patriots were free to pursue their military operations around Boston and in Canada. Since Schuyler was in poor health, much of the responsibility for the latter expedition fell on Richard Montgomery. Montgomery was the son of an Irish baronet who had held a captain's commission in the regular army during the French and Indian War. Afterwards he stayed in America to become a farmer and like Gage married into one of New York's leading Whig families. Montgomery left Albany on 25 August with 1700 New York and Connecticut militia, while Schuyler brought up the rear with another 300 men. Montgomery's first objective was St Johns on the Richelieu River, where Carleton, had gathered his regulars to block the route to the St Lawrence. However, the initial advance proved premature, since Schuyler and Montgomery had no artillery. The two commanders accordingly retreated to the Isle Aux Noix to await some ordnance from Ticonderoga.[49]

The plan to invade Canada by way of Lake George had been agreed before Washington took up his duties at Boston. He fully endorsed the scheme but thought its success would be more assured if a second strike was made against Quebec.[50] This led Washington to consider Benedict Arnold's idea for invading Canada by way of Maine. Arnold, like so many officers in the Revolutionary army, had no formal military training, though he had served with the provincial forces during the previous war. By profession he was a merchant from a prosperous Connecticut family. As relations with Britain deteriorated, he organized his own minuteman company and on news of Lexington and Concord took his unit to Boston.

It was here that his flair and organizational abilities caught Washington's eye. Arnold's orders, issued on 14 September 1775, were to advance on Quebec with a detachment from Washington's army via the Kennebec River. Like Montgomery he was to placate the Canadians at every opportunity and even abandon the enterprise if they proved hostile. He was to be equally conciliatory to the Indians, "convincing them that we come . . . not as robbers or to make war on them, but as friends and supporters of their liberties as well as ours." On reaching the St Lawrence, Arnold was to contact Schuyler and place himself under that general's command. The strictest discipline was to be observed at all times.[51]

Arnold took with him some Virginian and Pennsylvanian rifle companies which had been recruited shortly after Bunker Hill as part of Congress's drive to show support for the uprising around Boston. The rifle was unknown in New England, having been imported into the middle colonies by German settlers early in the eighteenth century.[52] The newcomers had delighted the local population with their prowess at shooting British sentries from long range, though Washington was less complimentary about the Pennsylvanian detachment, suggesting they "know no more of a rifle than my horse, being new imported Irish."[53] The rifle, as with most weapons, had advantages and disadvantages. It was far more accurate than the traditional musket, having twice the range. Unfortunately, it took twice as long to load. The weapon also had no attachment for a bayonet, making it less useful in close combat. However, the riflemen's knowledge of the backcountry made them eminently suitable for the kind of reconnaissance and skirmishing facing Arnold until he reached Quebec.[54] To instill some semblance of order, Washington appointed Daniel Morgan, a former Virginian wagon driver and frontiersman, to be their commander with responsibility for leading the advanced guard.

Washington also pondered his options regarding Boston. At the end of August he had taken post near Charleston "to bring on a general action" of the kind that had proved so propitious at Bunker Hill. The British, however, had merely responded with a cannonade from their ships. This passivity against an "enemy they affect to despise" puzzled Washington. Why did they not "come forth and put an end to the contest at once?" This emboldened him to consider making an attack himself. A successful assault on Boston would avoid the need for a long winter siege with all the attendant costs of sustaining the troops. It would also alleviate the danger of having no army when the present enlistments expired on the 1 January. Nevertheless, to Washington's disappointment, his field officers thought otherwise when he convened a council of war on 11 September 1775.[55]

One reason for their caution was the continuing lack of supplies. America could produce most things, including cannon. But saltpeter for making gunpowder was another matter. Fortunately it was possible to smuggle supplies into America from Europe, where many Dutch and French merchants were ready to trade at a price. Similar opportunities existed in the West Indies. The United Colonies of course had no navy at the start of the conflict, not least because the resources were lacking for building ships of war to match those of the Royal Navy. However, the ports of New England had a long tradition of fitting out privateers in previous wars with France and Spain and there were plenty of merchants now ready to arm their vessels to prey on British shipping. Most were of schooner construction, which allowed them to outrun the bigger warships of the enemy. The first such vessels put to sea shortly after Lexington and Concord and soon began making captures.

The success of these early cruisers led Congress to take a number of them into its pay. Among the first was the *Hannah*, which Washington deployed to prevent supplies getting into Boston as part of his plan to force the British to quit the town.[56] His expectations were partially fulfilled in November 1775 with the capture of the ordnance store ship the *Nancy*, which Washington described as an "instance of Divine favor," given his own shortage of munitions.[57] This encouraged Congress to authorize the construction of four frigates, the real start of the American navy. Unfortunately indiscipline on the new ships proved as great a problem as that among the land forces.[58] Nevertheless by early 1776 the Royal Navy's station commander, Admiral Shuldham, was acknowledging the speed with which the rebels prepared their vessels and their success in capturing British supply ships.[59]

Since the British continued to deny the rights of America, it was clear that some provision would have to be made to retain Washington's forces beyond 1 January 1776. Washington initially raised the matter in September 1775 with John Hancock, the President of Congress, who suggested that he first consult his officers.[60] The key issues were the number of men required, the length of their enlistment, and the means by which the army might be made more professional. When the officers met they unanimously agreed to an army of at least 20,300 men, comprising 26 regiments of 728 officers and men, each one organized into eight companies. The length of the service should be for a year, though with provision for an earlier discharge if hostilities ended. But no African American slaves were to be employed however great the shortage of recruits. Most of the council also vetoed the recruitment of free blacks.[61] These decisions were duly accepted by Congress with the additional proviso that Washington might call on the New England militia should insufficient men enlist for the service.[62]

One other decision by Congress for which Washington was duly grateful was that the army should not attempt to defend every town and village, since this would interfere with "the prosecution of those great plans which have been adopted for the common safety." Congress had accordingly resolved that "each Province should depend on its own internal strength" against minor "incursions". To do otherwise would "separate the Army into a number of small detachments, who would be harassed in fruitless marches and counter marches after an enemy whose conveyance by shipping" allowed them to "keep the whole coast in constant alarm."[63] This was something that had to be avoided.

Unfortunately affairs to the north were not going so propitiously as the Patriots hoped. The plan to invade Canada was risky so late in the season. Arnold's force had to traverse a 300-mile wilderness of forests, mountains, rivers, and lakes. During this odyssey 400 of his 1,100 men fell sick or deserted. At one point they were reduced to eating boiled moccasins, while muskets became crutches for those suffering from frostbite. The soldiers increasingly appeared like "amphibious animals as they were great parts of the time under water."[64] As Arnold approached the inhabited areas, some French farmers supplied food. However, few of them enlisted, despite Washington's proclamation inviting them to join the Patriots "in an indissoluble Union" to ensure "the Blessings of a free Government."[65] Being part of one English-speaking state was no more inviting than incorporation in another.

Arnold finally arrived on the southern side of the St Lawrence near Quebec on 5 November just as winter set in, his force now reduced to 600 men. Nevertheless he succeeded in crossing the river on 14 November, after first preparing a number of scaling ladders. But with no artillery there was little possibility of attacking Quebec with its high stone walls. Arnold accordingly set about isolating the city in order to starve its garrison into surrender. But even this proved too much for his emaciated men and after a few days he retreated to Point aux Trembles to await the arrival of Montgomery.[66]

To the south, Montgomery had experienced similar difficulties. Initially he found the reduction of St Johns insoluble until he captured the smaller post of Chambly in the rear. This not only cut the British supply line to Montreal, but also gave Montgomery a stock of artillery and powder, which allowed him to erect a battery overlooking St Johns. Finally on

2 November the garrison of 500 men surrendered, after a siege of 55 days. The loss of St Johns was a severe blow to the British since it left Montreal defenseless in the absence of Canadian help. Carleton quickly set off down the St Lawrence for Quebec with his remaining 150 men, narrowly escaping capture by Montgomery's patrols after his ship went aground near Sorrel. This forced him to complete his voyage in an open whaleboat, disguised as a Canadian peasant.[67]

Montgomery was now free to join Arnold, which he accomplished on 2 December 1775. The prospects were not inviting. Few Canadians had joined the "cause of liberty". Moreover, both Patriot forces were greatly diminished by desertions, following the expiry of the men's terms of enlistment, having now barely 1,000 men between them. Nevertheless the two commanders determined to continue the enterprise with an assault on the city during New Year's Eve. Since they had no artillery to breach the defenses, they resolved to use scaling ladders, the plan being for Arnold's forces to climb the north and eastern wall of the town while Montgomery traversed the southern side along the river. Aided by a snowstorm, Arnold's detachment managed to enter the lower town, led by the redoubtable Morgan. However, they were eventually repulsed, losing 100 dead and wounded and 400 prisoners. Arnold suffered a leg wound, while Morgan was among the captured. Montgomery was even less fortunate, being shot in the head as he searched for an entry into the town. Nevertheless Arnold hung on tenaciously in the hope of reinforcement.[68]

Congress meanwhile was widening its activities beyond the battlefield. In November 1775 it formed a secret committee for "corresponding with our friends in Great Britain, Ireland and other parts of the world." Among the former were the Rockingham Whigs, while in Ireland there was a growing body of Patriots who were disillusioned with the subordinate status of the Dublin parliament. But most important was the need to establish links with France. France was still the most populous and powerful nation in Europe, despite its defeats in the previous war. Its intervention could clearly change the course of the struggle.[69]

Informal contacts had already been made in London in the summer of 1775 between Arthur Lee, a Virginian planter, and Pierre Augustan Baron de Beaumarchais, the French dramatist and author of *The Barber of Seville*.[70] But although sympathetic, the French emissaries made it clear that France could do little until Congress had ended all ties with Britain. The Patriots in any case were unsure about a formal alliance, being fearful that the French might become their new colonial masters. At the very least Louis XVI might demand the return of Canada as the price of French help.

Hence Congress suggested an understanding about trade rather than a formal alliance.[71] It would suffice if France gave material assistance, since the Patriots could then fight their own battles.

This low-key response suited the French, as it would avoid an open breach with Britain until the Patriots had demonstrated the extent of their commitment to independence. On the first news of hostilities in July 1775 the French Foreign minister, the Comte de Vergennes, had dispatched Julien de Bonvouloir, a former army officer, to observe the situation and tell his listeners that France had no territorial ambitions regarding North America.[72] Other discreet contacts followed, notably by two merchants, Pierre Penet and Emanuel de Pliarne, who held their first meeting with the Secret Committee in early January 1776. Here they promised to establish "a branch of trade, sufficient to supply all the wants" of the Patriot forces.[73] Goods would be paid for by the sale of American produce.

These first contacts were sufficiently encouraging for Congress to dispatch its first envoy to France, Silas Deane.[74] The timing proved propitious for in May 1776 the French Council of State, led by Vergennes, determined to prepare for a more active role in the struggle. They resolved to resume Choiseul's former plan to reverse the terms of the Peace of Paris by helping the rebels dismember Britain's North American empire. First it agreed to make a grant of one million livres for the supply of arms to the Patriot forces. The shipment of these was to be organized by Beaumarchais through a bogus Portuguese corporation, Rodrique Hortalez and Company, to conceal any official French involvement. Secondly Louis XVI informed the council that he would urge his uncle, Charles III of Spain, to give similar covert financial assistance. But most importantly the council agreed to resume the buildup of the French navy to achieve parity with Britain. The responsibility for this was given to the recently appointed Minister of Marine, Antoine Sartine.[75] Under his direction, expenditure quickly increased to over 100 million livres, a fourfold increase on the last years of Louis XV.[76]

The political revolution: America declares her independence

The decision of France to give covert aid reflected important developments in America itself. In the aftermath of Lexington and Concord, all the provinces had established de facto governments pending a resolution of the disputes with Britain. As William Drayton noted of South Carolina, "a new government is erected. The [provincial] Congress is the legislature, the Council of Safety the executive power, the General Committee" a superior court, while "the district and parochial committees [act] as county courts."[77] Further steps had also been taken to deal with those still loyal to the Crown. Anyone who openly persisted in their loyalty now faced heavy fines and terms of imprisonment. As Washington commented to the governor of Connecticut in November 1775: "Why should persons who are preying upon the vitals of their country be suffered to stalk at large, whilst we know they will do us every mischief in their power."[78] The provincial congress took the hint by passing an act for seizing (though not yet confiscating) Loyalist property. Those detected giving aid to the British now faced up to three years' imprisonment.[79]

However, until early 1776 most Patriots still had no overt desire for independence or a republican form of government, though some members of Congress were beginning to believe that such outcome was likely. The majority of the political classes and even wider population remained fearful about what would happen if the colonies broke away from the mother country. Their fears were based on both ideological and practical considerations. Among the latter was the question whether the colonies could survive without the trade and protection of Great Britain, since France and Spain might see the disintegration of the empire as a chance to repossess their former colonies.

There were ideological considerations too. Educated Americans were familiar with the idea that government had begun as a contract with the people to avoid the disadvantages of living in a state of nature. Many feared that breaking the compact with Great Britain would lead to the destruction of civil society. Although John Locke and other Enlightenment philosophers argued that the state of nature was benign, there was no certainty that this would be the case. The seventeenth-century philosopher Thomas Hobbes had argued just as persuasively that a state of nature would lead to anarchy and rule by the strongest. Such prospect was a powerful deterrent, for few believed the common people were capable of governing themselves. Similar fears existed about Republicanism, which had disappeared as a form of government following the establishment of the Roman Empire 1,800 years before.[80]

However, events were starting to drive even the moderates towards independence and the creation of a republic. On 17 October 1775 the town of Falmouth (now Portland Maine) was bombarded by a British force, after the inhabitants refused to surrender their munitions and rebel leaders.[81] The raid was the result of instructions from England, following news of Lexington and Concord, that "every measure be pursued for suppressing by the most vigorous efforts by sea and land this unnatural rebellion."[82] Equally shocking to Patriot sensibilities was the proclamation of Lord Dunmore, the Governor of Virginia, in November 1775, offering freedom to any male slave whose master had joined the rebellion. Dunmore's announcement was in reality a cynical ploy to intimidate the planters. The appeal in any case proved counter-productive since it appeared that he was encouraging the slaves to kill their masters and seize their property.[83] Similarly, anger was generated by the news that the ministry was recruiting German and even Russian mercenaries. People also harbored suspicions about the intended use of the French Canadians and Indians. Seemingly the mother country was contemplating infanticide, the worst crime that any parent could commit.

It was in this gathering crisis that a pamphlet appeared titled *Common Sense*, which swept away the doubts and gloom that had perplexed the Patriot leaders at the start of 1776. The author, Thomas Paine, was a recent émigré from England. Paine argued that the British monarchy did not owe its authority to a compact with the people or enjoy divine blessing. It had been established by the Normans through conquest. History also showed that kings always brought misery to their peoples, not good governance. As to the dangers facing American society once it separated from Britain, these were greatly exaggerated. The common people were far too sensible to throw the country into turmoil. Reconciliation in any case was impossible after the events of 19 April 1775. Independence in contrast would bring many benefits. France might enter the war as an ally and all Europe would be keen to open its ports to American commerce. At home America had a glittering prospect embracing a whole continent. They should seize the opportunity by breaking with Britain.[84]

If the Patriot leadership had any doubts about the wisdom of this advice, they were removed by the course of the war at Boston. Since Bunker Hill, Gage's army had remained confined in the town, much to the dismay of Britons on both sides of the Atlantic. The problem was the location of Boston. As early as the summer of 1775 it had been recognized that the town was unsuitable for military operations, surrounded as it was by such hilly countryside. The army would be better redeployed in New York, where there was considerable Loyalist support.[85] But though tactically sound, such decision was surprising from a political and strategic viewpoint, since Boston was the center of the rebellion. However, no one faced up to the contradiction of simultaneously evacuating Boston while planning its recovery from New York or Rhode Island. The only certainty was that Gage was not to implement the scheme, since his inadequacies as a commander were now too obvious to ignore. Instead, he was to return to England, leaving Howe in charge.[86]

In the event, the British discovered that they would have to remain in Boston for the time being, since they lacked sufficient shipping to evacuate both the soldiers and Loyalist refugees. Howe was not unduly alarmed at the prospect. He believed that Washington's army lacked both the discipline and equipment to disturb him and would probably dissolve when the men's terms of enlistment expired in the New Year. His main concern was the availability of supplies to feed and warm the army and its dependents during the winter.[87]

Howe was correct in supposing that Washington was experiencing difficulty keeping his army together, since many soldiers were refusing to reenlist in the new military establishment which was to start on 1 January 1776. As the army melted away, Washington of necessity had to call on the New England Governments for their militia.[88] He also raised again the suggestion of recruiting free African Americans. Many people of color were anxious to enlist who might otherwise apply to the British.[89] Fortunately the number of enlistments increased as the date for the new establishment approached. Washington was also pleasantly surprised at the quality of the militia when they arrived.[90] Nevertheless, the failure to create a professional army, composed of men serving for at least three years, had produced the ludicrous situation now facing him. History had no parallel in which a commander had simultaneously "to disband one army and recruit another."[91] This made it even more surprising that Howe had not taken advantage of the army's weakness. Washington could only assume that the British commander had been ordered to await reinforcements from Europe.[92]

Howe's passivity led Washington to propose a Patriot attack on Boston in January to preempt the arrival of those reinforcements. However, his senior officers believed the army was too weak for such a challenging assignment, unless the New England provinces provided another 13 regiments of militia.[93] Despite this rebuff, Washington repeated his proposition in mid-February 1776. This time the officers agreed that the army should occupy Dorchester Hill, the hope being that it would provoke the British into making another ill-advised assault as at Bunker Hill, which might facilitate a Patriot counter-attack on the town.[94] One reason for their more positive attitude was that the army now had sufficient artillery for the prosecution of an effective siege. The previous November Washington had dispatched his senior artillery officer, Colonel Henry Knox, to bring some captured ordnance from Ticonderoga to Boston.[95] After heroic efforts

Knox managed to transport 44 cannon, 14 mortars, and a howitzer, reaching his destination in late January 1776.[96] The Patriots could now launch an offensive bombardment against the British positions.

Accordingly, on the night of 4 March Washington's forces occupied Dorchester heights, constructing temporary defenses out of wooden fascines, since the ground was too frozen for digging entrenchments. By next morning everything was in place.[97] The revelation that the Patriots were about deploy artillery was a devastating discovery for Howe. Boston was now within range of the Patriot guns, as were the ships of the Royal Navy, which could not respond, given the low trajectory of their cannon. Howe initially considered an assault but then reflected that it might lead to another Bunker Hill. An action would be doubly pointless, given his intention to evacuate Boston shortly.[98] He accordingly abandoned his plan, much to the disappointment of Washington who had 4,000 men at Roxbury ready for a counter-attack across Boston neck.[99]

Although Howe's preference was to go to New York, he found he had insufficient provisions to do so. He accordingly resolved to retreat to Halifax to reorganize his command and await the reinforcements and supplies being gathered in Europe.[100] In the meantime an unofficial truce operated, following an appeal by the Boston magistrates for the town to be spared further damage. The British agreed not to burn the public buildings, providing the Patriots ceased firing.[101] The troops and refugees then scrambled aboard the warships and such transports as were available. On 17 March the last soldiers departed from the harbor, leaving over 100 cannon and other military items, which Howe had not had time to destroy.[102] The town, so often the center of Patriot resistance, was free at last. For the Patriots it was cause for celebration and a boost to the growing demand for independence. To most Britons the evacuation was an "act of dishonor." As the Duke of Manchester acidly observed: "the army that was sent to reduce the province of Massachusetts Bay has been driven from the capital."[103] It was an ignominious end.

Any Patriot doubt about independence was also undermined by events off the battlefield. The British ministry had passed a Prohibitory Act in December 1775 imposing a total blockade on the ports of all 13 colonies. Congress now responded in early April 1776 by opening America's ports to the ships of all nations except those of Britain. At a stroke it had overturned the entire mercantilist system. Nor was this all, for six days later the first call was made by North Carolina for independence.[104] But before debating so momentous an issue, Congress decided that the provinces must first become sovereign states by the adoption of new constitutions "best conducive to the happiness and safety of their constituents in particular and America in general." Most adapted their old systems of government, replacing the royal governor with a nominee of the assembly, while the provincial council became a senate or upper house. The most revolutionary aspect of the new constitutions was the adoption in several states of a bill of rights. Unlike the English bill of 1689, the new articles emphasized the rights of the individual, rather than those of the legislature. But no rights were accorded to women, African Americans or Indians. Nor was the vote extended. Only the male propertied classes really benefited.[105]

Having encouraged the colonies to reform their constitutions, Congress then appointed a committee to consider the question of independence. The actual declaration was drafted by Thomas Jefferson one of the Virginian delegates. Under his guidance it began with a short prologue asserting the inalienable right of a people to "life, liberty and the pursuit of happiness." Since these had been denied by George III, the fundamental contract between the King and his people had been broken, leaving the inhabitants free to make new arrangements. The document was formally approved by Congress on 2 July and published two days later.[106]

Simultaneously, another committee prepared a "Plan of Confederation." This was urgently needed since the present Congress had no formal authority to conduct the war. Indeed many Patriots believed such agreement was essential before the break with Britain was made. However, the old inter-colonial jealousies remained strong, especially among the smaller states, which feared domination by Massachusetts, Pennsylvania, and Virginia. Others also feared the creation of a new central government. Article 2 of the document accordingly stated that the states were only entering into a "league of Friendship . . . for their common defense, the Security of their Liberties, and their mutual and general welfare." Each state therefore retained "its sovereignty, freedom and independence, and every power, jurisdiction and right which is not . . . expressly delegated to the United States, in Congress assembled." Among the delegated powers was the authority to make war, declare peace, negotiate treaties, maintain an army and navy, coin money, regulate Indian affairs, and establish a postal service. However, Congress had no power to levy taxes, though it could raise loans and print currency. Another weakness was its lack of judicial power. Without a system of courts, it could not enforce its decisions, which meant that each state could ignore the requests of Congress with impunity.[107]

Unable to tax, Congress had to rely on the old requisition system, as practiced by the British during the Seven Years War. Unfortunately this raised a further problem of how the contribution of each state was to be calculated, whether its quota was to be based on lands or population. The northern states wanted population, believing that slaves should be included as producers of wealth. The southern states for that reason insisted on the value of lands as the basis for any assessment. Hence no formal confederation had been agreed by the time of the Declaration of Independence. Not until 1777 was it agreed to base the quotas on the value of lands. Even then the articles were not officially accepted since a new dispute arose over the ownership of the western territories. Maryland had no lands beyond the Allegheny Mountains, raising fresh fears of domination by Virginia.[108] It accordingly refused to sign the articles until these lands had been donated for the benefit of the whole confederacy. The lack of agreement was unfortunate, since the forces that the British ministry had been assembling for the last six months were finally approaching, ready to compel the Patriots to resume their allegiance.

Notes and references

1. Richard Middleton, *The Bells of Victory: The Pitt-Newcastle Ministry and the Conduct of the Seven Years War, 1757–1762* (Cambridge, 1985), 150.
2. Middleton, *Bells of Victory*, 204.
3. L.H. Butterfield, ed., *The Adams Papers: Diary and Autobiography of John Adams* (Cambridge, Mass., 1962), vol. 2, 150.
4. Edward Rutledge to John Jay, 29 June 1776, Edward Cody Burnett, ed., *Letters of Members of the Continental Congress* (Washington, 1921), vol. 1, 517–18.
5. Robert Middlekauf, *The Glorious Cause: The American Revolution, 1763–1789* (New York, 1982), 245–52.
6. Ibid., 281.
7. Quoted in Piers Mackesy, *The War for America, 1775–1783* (Cambridge, Mass., 1964), 37.
8. *Clinton's Narrative*, CAR, 10.
9. Steve Brumwell, *Redcoats: The British Soldier and War in the Americas, 1755–1763* (Cambridge, 2002), 99–136.
10. Quoted in David Syrett, *The Royal Navy in American Waters, 1775–1783* (Aldershot, 1989), 33.
11. George III to Sandwich, 1 July 1775, Sandwich/1, 63.
12. Estimate for Augmenting his Majesty's forces, CJ/XXXV, 114.

13 Dartmouth to Gage, 27 January 1775, Carter/2, 178–83.
14 For the diplomatic background to Europe at this time, see H.M. Scott, *British Foreign Policy in the Age of the American Revolution* (Oxford, 1990), 160–206.
15 Dartmouth to Gage, 1 July 1775, Carter/2, 199–201.
16 Dartmouth to the Admiralty, 1 July 1775, DDAR/XI, 23.
17 Christopher Ward, *The War of the Revolution*, 2 vols. (New York, 1952), Vol. I, 73.
18 Howe to Lord Howe, 22 June 1775, HMC, Stopford-Sackville, II, 3–5. Howe to Germain, 22 June 1775, Fortescue/3, 220–24. For a Patriot account of the battle see Ward, *War of the Revolution: A Military History of the American Revolution*, I, 73–98. The skill of the British army in the use of the bayonet is discussed in Mackesy, *War for America*, 77–78.
19 Gage to Barrington, 26 June 1775, Carter/2, 686.
20 Gage to Dartmouth, 25 June 1775, Carter/1, 406–7.
21 Charles Royster, *A Revolutionary People at War: The Continental Army and American Character, 1775–1783* (New York, 1979), 122.
22 Washington to Samuel Washington, 20 July 1775, WP/RWS/1, 134–36.
23 General Orders, 4 July 1775, WP/RWS/1, 54.
24 Royster, *Revolutionary People*, 99.
25 General Orders, 18 July 1775, WP/RWS/1, 128.
26 Council of War, 9 July 1775, WP/RWS/1, 79–81.
27 Washington to Lee, 10 July 1775, WP/RWS/1, 99.
28 Washington to Samuel Washington, 20 July 1775, WP/RWS/1, 135–36.
29 Washington to Jonathan Trumbull, 4 August 1775, WP/RWS/1, 244.
30 General Orders, 23 July 1775, WP/RWS/1, 158–59. Ibid., 24 July 1775, 163.
31 Washington to Hancock, 4–5 August 1775, WP/RWS/1, 227. Washington to R.H. Lee, 29 August 1775, WP/RWS/1, 374.
32 Washington to Hancock, 10 July 1775, WP/RWS/1, 88.
33 Washington to Lund Washington, 20 August 1775, WP/RWS/1, 335–36.
34 Washington to R.H. Lee, 29 August 1775, WP/RWS/1, 375.
35 Washington to Gage, 11 August 1775, WP/RWS/1, 289–90.
36 Gage to Washington, 13 August 1775, WP/RWS/1, 301–2. Washington ignored the wider treatment of Loyalists by the Patriots, simply stating that the British Officers and Loyalists under his control had been correctly treated, 19 August 1775, WP/RWS/1, 326–27.

37 Washington to Gage, 13 August 1775, WP/RWS/1, 302.

38 Barbara Graymont, *The Iroquois in the American Revolution* (Syracuse, 1972), 71–80. For more information on Indian involvement, see Chapter 8.

39 Address of Continental Congress to the Inhabitants of Canada, 29 May 1775, Henry Steele Commager, *Documents of American History* (New York, 1963), vol. 1, 91–92.

40 Christopher Ward, *The War of the Revolution*, John R. Alden, ed., 2 vols. (New York, 1952), I, 64–69.

41 Hancock to Washington, 28 June 1775, WP/RWS/1, 42–43.

42 Petition of Continental Congress to the King, 18 July 1775, DDAR/XI, 40–42.

43 George III to North, 18 August 1775, Fortescue/3, 247–48.

44 Royal Proclamation for Suppressing Rebellion and Sedition, 23 August 1775, *English Historical Documents*, Vol. IX, *American Colonial Documents to 1776*, Merrill Jensen, ed. (London, 1955), 850–51.

45 Estimate of the Charges, CJ/XXXV, 35–36.

46 North to George III, 26 July 1775, Fortescue/3, 234.

47 Estimate for an Augmentation to His Majesty's forces, CJ/XXXV, 114. Barrington to Dartmouth, 31 July 1775, DDAR/XI, 59.

48 George III to North, 4 August 1775, Fortescue/3, 239. Memorandum by George III, 5 August 1775, Fortescue/3, 240.

49 Schuyler to Washington, 20 September 1775, WP/RWS/2, 17–21.

50 Washington to Schuyler, 20 August 1775, WP/RWS/1, 331–32.

51 Instructions to Colonel Arnold, 14 September 1775, WP/RWS/1, 457–59.

52 W.J. Wood, *Battles of the Revolutionary War, 1775–1781* (New York, 1995), xxvi–xxvii.

53 Washington to Samuel Washington, 30 September 1775, WP/RWS/2, 73.

54 Don Higginbotham, *Daniel Morgan: Revolutionary Rifleman* (Chapel Hill, 1961), 27–28.

55 Council of War, 11 September 1775, WP/RWS/1, 450–51.

56 Washington to Captain Broughton, 2 September 1775, WP/RWS/1, 98–400.

57 Washington to Reed, 30 November 1775, WP/RWS/2, 463–64.

58 Hancock to Washington, 14 June 1776, WP/RWS/4, 525–56.

59 Shuldham to Sandwich, 13 January 1776, Sandwich/1, 104.

60 Washington to Hancock, 21 September 1775, WP/RWS/2, 24–25. Hancock to Washington, 25 September 1775, WP/RWS/2, 48–50.

61 Council of War, 8 October 1775, WP/RWS/2, 123–24.

62 Thomas Lynch to Washington, 13 November 1775, WP/RWS/2, 365–67.

63 Washington to Brigadier Wooster, 2 September 1775, WP/RWS/1, 407.

64 Arnold to Washington, 13 October 1775, WP/RWS/2, 155–56.

65 Address to the Inhabitants of Canada, circa 14 September 1775, WP/RWS/1, 461–62.

66 Arnold to Washington, 8 November 1775, WP/RWS/2, 326. Ibid., 20 November 1775, 403–04.

67 Carleton to Dartmouth, 20 November 1775, DDAR/XI, 185–86; Schuyler to Washington, 28 November 1775, WP/RWS/2, 453–54. Ward, *War of Revolution*, I, 150–62.

68 Carleton to Howe, 12 January 1776, DDAR/XII, 41. Higginbotham, *Morgan*, 43–50. Arnold to Washington, 14 January 1776, WP/RWS/3, 81–83.

69 Middlekauf, *Glorious Cause*, 398.

70 Louis W. Potts, *Arthur Lee: A Virtuous Revolutionary* (Baton Rouge, 1981), 151–53.

71 Jonathan R. Dull, *A Diplomatic History of the American Revolution* (New Haven, 1985), 53–54.

72 Orville T. Murphy, *Charles Gravier, Comte de Vergennes: French Diplomacy in the Age of Revolution, 1719–1787* (Albany, 1988), 234.

73 Pliarne to Washington, 16 January 1776, WP/RWS/3, 69–70.

74 Samuel Flagg Bemis, *The Diplomacy of the American Revolution* (Bloomington, 1961), 34–35.

75 Murphy, *Vergennes*, 234–39. Jonathan Dull, *The French Navy and American Independence: A Study of Arms and Diplomacy, 1774–1787* (Princeton, 1975), 47–48.

76 Murphy, *Vergennes*, 245. Dull, *French Navy*, 49–56.

77 W.H. Drayton to W. Drayton, 4 July 1775, DDAR/XI, 36.

78 Washington to Trumbull, 15 November 1775, WP/RWS/2, 379.

79 Governor Trumbull to Washington, 1 January 1776, WP/RWS/3, 7–9.

80 Bernard Bailyn, *The Ideological Origins of the American Revolution* (Cambridge, Mass., 1967). Gordon S. Wood, *The Creation of the American Republic, 1776–1787* (Chapel Hill, 1969). Pauline Maier, *American Scripture: How America Declared its Independence from Britain* (New York, 1997).

81 Syrett, *Royal Navy in American Waters*, 7–8. Portsmouth Committee of Safety to Washington, 19 October 1775, WP/RWS/2, 206–7.

82 Dartmouth to the Admiralty, 1 July 1775, DDAR/XI, 23.
83 Middlekauf, *Glorious Cause*, 316.
84 T. Paine, *Common Sense* (Philadelphia, 1776).
85 Dartmouth to Howe, 5 September 1775, DDAR/XI, 90.
86 Dartmouth to Gage, 2 August 1775, Carter/2, 202–3
87 Howe to Dartmouth, 9 October 1775, DDAR/XI, 138–40.
88 Washington to Hancock, 28 November 1775, WP/RWS/2, 444–46.
89 Washington to Hancock, 31 December 1775, WP/RWS/2, 622–24.
90 Washington to Hancock, 18 December 1775, WP/RWS/2, 573–75.
91 Washington to Hancock, 4 January 1776, WP/RWS/2, 622–24.
92 Washington to Hancock, 9 February 1776, WP/RWS/3, 274.
93 Council of War, 16 January 1776, WP/RWS/3, 103.
94 Council of War, 16 February 1776, WP/RWS/3, 320–22. Plan for attacking Boston, 18–25 February 1776, ibid., 332–33.
95 Washington to Knox, 16 November 1775, WP/RWS/2, 384–85.
96 Inventory of Artillery, 17 December 1775, WP/RWS/2, 565–66.
97 Washington to Reed, 7 March 1776, WP/RWS/3, 369.
98 Howe to Germain, 21 March 1776, DDAR/XII, 81–84.
99 Washington to Hancock, 7–9 March 1776, WP/RWS/3, 420–25.
100 Howe to Germain, 21 March 1776, DDAR/XII, 83.
101 Washington to Reed, 9 March 1776, WP/RWS/3, 376.
102 Middlekauf, *Glorious Cause*, 308–11.
103 Quoted in William M. Wallace, *Appeal to Arms: A Military History of the American Revolution* (New York, 1951), 66.
104 Middlekauf, *Glorious Cause*, 315–16, 322.
105 R.B. Morris, ed., *Sources and Documents illustrating the American Revolution, 1764–1788* (New York, 1965), 148.
106 Maier, *American Scripture*, 97–153.
107 Ibid., 178–86.
108 Middlekauf, *Glorious Cause*, 603–5.

CHAPTER 3

Britain reasserts her authority, 1776

Patriots and Loyalists: The factors of identity

Historians on both sides of the Atlantic have usually portrayed the War of Independence as a struggle between two nations, downplaying that it was also a civil war between two sets of Americans: the Patriots and Loyalists. Older generations of historians have also tended to portray the conflict as a struggle between good and evil, between the honest freeholders of America and the corrupt dependents of the Crown. The decision to become a Patriot or Loyalist therefore was one of principle or self-interest. The inhabitants could either support the rights of the freeborn or the oppressive privileges of the Crown. In the stark terminology of the Whigs and Patriots, they must opt for either freedom or slavery.[1]

In reality, the factors determining the identities of the Loyalists and Patriots were more complex. Much depended on the religious affiliations and ethnicity of a region rather than abstract notions of individual rights or constitutional principle. In New England religion was a key factor. The New England colonies had been established in the seventeenth century as self-governing Puritan commonwealths and had only submitted reluctantly to the English Crown in the reign of James II. This "commonwealth" attitude persisted well into the eighteenth century, fanned by fears about the Anglican Church, which many New Englanders still believed was tantamount to Roman Catholicism. These factors made New England the most Patriotic of all the regions, its unanimity aided ironically by the homogeneity of the population whose ancestry was almost entirely English. Hence support for the Loyalist cause in New England was limited to royal officials and minority groups like the Anglicans and Quakers, who looked to the Crown for protection from the dominant majority.[2]

The middle states in contrast had much greater religious and ethnic diversity, affecting Patriot and Loyalist affiliations in rather different ways. In New York and New Jersey the principal groups were English Episcopalians, Scottish Presbyterians, Dutch Calvinists, and New England Congregationalists. The Episcopalians were naturally inclined to support the British cause, since the King was temporal head of that church. In contrast, the Scottish Presbyterians and New England Congregationalists were solidly Patriot, because of their historic opposition to the Crown in the seventeenth century and dislike of the Episcopalian Church as the Anglican Church was usually called.[3]

In Pennsylvania, a similar situation existed. The dominant ethnic and religious groups were the English and Welsh Quakers, the Presbyterian Scots Irish, and the German Lutheran and Calvinist churches. The Quakers were generally loyal, if only from a desire to protect their position from more recent arrivals, though their pacifism made them of limited value for the Crown once the war began. The Scots Irish on the other hand were solidly Patriot because of their experience in Ireland, where they had suffered both religious persecution from the Anglican Church and economic exploitation at the hands of landowners. The Germans in contrast were generally neutral, lacking familiarity with the political norms of the English-speaking peoples. This was especially true of the minority Dunkers and Mennonites, who like the Quakers believed in non-violence.[4]

A similar ethnic and religious mosaic existed in the southern colonies. The tidewater in Maryland, Virginia, and the two Carolinas was populated largely by people of English stock. They were also Anglican in their religious beliefs. This should have made them strongly Loyalist. However, the tidewater was dominated by the planter elite, who feared they had much to lose if the British enforced their measures. Property came before religion in their list of priorities. This was especially true after Dunmore's offer of freedom to Virginia's slaves if they joined the British. Independence accordingly seemed most likely to secure their wealth and power.[5]

The southern backcountry, however, had a quite different composition. Like Pennsylvania it had been heavily settled by Germans and Scots Irish. However, except in Virginia, the interior had become progressively alienated from the tidewater by the latter's refusal to grant representation in the provincial assemblies or establish effective local government. This had led in the 1760s to the formation of vigilante groups known as the Regulators, so called because they wanted a regulated and equitable system of local government. Feelings ran so high in the backcountry of North Carolina in

1771 that Governor Tryon had to suppress a full-scale rebellion with the help of the planter elite. Similar divisions afflicted South Carolina, though the disputes there were eventually settled without bloodshed. Nevertheless the Patriots in Charleston were so alarmed in 1775 about the affiliations of the backcountry that they dispatched two leading dissenting ministers, William Tennant and Oliver Hart, to secure support for their cause.[6]

John Adams subsequently estimated that one-third of the colonial population supported the Patriots, one-third were Loyalist and one-third neutral. In reality the Loyalists probably numbered about a fifth of the population while the Patriots were almost three times as numerous, depending on the region. The remaining 20 percent were either too remote or indifferent, being ready to accommodate whichever side was wining.

The greater numbers and better organization of the Patriots allowed them to seize control of all 13 colonies, using the machinery of government to crush their opponents. Here the delay of the British in mobilizing their forces and sending support proved fatal. While the regulars were confined to Boston, the Loyalists everywhere were either disarmed or forced into exile. Nevertheless, the knowledge that many Loyalists were biding their time encouraged royal officials to propose various measures for recapturing the initiative. Among the more vocal was William Campbell of South Carolina, who asserted that if Gage sent troops, the backcountry Regulators would rise up, allowing the speedy reduction of both the Carolinas and Georgia.[7]

Unfortunately the lack of manpower meant that Howe, Gage's successor, felt unable to help the Loyalists until November 1775 when he sent Governor Dunmore 300 regulars to test these claims. Few presented themselves when he landed at Norfolk later than month, except for some slaves responding to his offer of freedom. Undeterred, Dunmore sallied out with his regulars on hearing that the Patriots were assembling their forces at Great Bridge, a few miles from Norfolk. The attack on 9 December 1775 was badly planned and Dunmore's men were routed as they tried to cross a causeway. Dunmore then attempted to restore his authority on 1 January 1776 by bombarding Norfolk from a warship, which only confirmed to the Patriots that their enemy was intent on the destruction of their lives and property.[8] It was another example of the British inability to win the propaganda war. It was also a demonstration that the claims of Loyalist support were exaggerated.

A similar sequence of events happened in the Carolinas. The initial proposal was the sending of help to the Cape Fear region, where a number of Highlanders had settled following the disbandment of their regiments in 1763. According to Governor Martin, the Highlanders would be readily supported by the backcountry farmers, most of whom were former Regulators.[9] The ministry in London showed interest this time because it was clear by the autumn of 1775 that Loyalist help might be necessary in re-establishing royal authority. Howe was to dispatch Clinton with a battalion from Boston to assess the truth of Martin's assertions.[10] But as reports of Loyalist support in the south continued to arrive, the ministry decided to deploy part of the army then being assembled for the offensive in New York.[11] Accordingly a task force of five regiments was ordered to embark in December 1775 from Cork for Cape Fear, where it was hoped they would be joined by the Highlanders. Once royal authority had been restored, a proper militia was to be recruited from the loyal inhabitants to maintain order. Clinton and the naval commander, Sir Peter Parker, could then repeat the process, if they thought fit. However, if support for the Crown was not forthcoming, the expedition was to limit itself to establishing a "respectable post where the officers and servants of government may find protection." The flotilla should then return to New York to join Howe for the main offensive.[12]

Unfortunately several delays occurred due to the slowness of the Admiralty in assembling the necessary transports and the poorness of the weather. The Cork flotilla in consequence did not departed until 12 February 1776 and was then twice scattered by storms so that the troops did not arrive off Cape Fear until the start of May.[13] This was far too late to save the Loyalists of North Carolina. The Highlanders had assembled in late January 1776, under Colonel Donald McLeod, and marched towards Wilmington on the Cape Fear River, expecting to encounter a British army with a body of Regulators. Instead they met a superior force of North Carolina militia at Moore's Creek Bridge, 20 miles northwest of Wilmington. Here on 27 February 1776 McLeod attempted an ill-advised assault across a narrow planked bridge. His force in consequence was easily repulsed. Of the promised 5,000 Regulators there was no sign.[14]

News of the Highlanders' defeat convinced Clinton and Parker that Cape Fear was no longer a proper rallying point for the backcountry Loyalists. The two men decided to look for an alternative post "where the King's persecuted subjects and his officers might find an asylum" until order was restored.[15] Clinton favored the lower Chesapeake or adjacent Albemarle Sound. Parker, however, preferred the Charleston area, perhaps influenced by Governor Campbell. Two officers were accordingly dispatched to reconnoiter the latter objective, returning with the news that the rebel fortress on Sullivan's island, guarding the entrance to the harbor, was poorly defended. Clinton and Parker consequently resolved to make this their objective, believing that Sullivan's Island would not only provide the Loyalists with a refuge but might also lead to the fall of Charleston itself. At the very least it would provide a base from which to launch a subsequent attack.[16]

The flotilla arrived off Charleston harbor on 1 June 1776. However, the reports of Loyalist support proved even less well founded than those concerning North Carolina. Furthermore, the capture of Fort Moultrie on the southern tip of Sullivan's Island was more difficult than expected. The plan required Clinton's troops to land on an adjacent island before crossing at low tide to approach Fort Moultrie from the rear. Unfortunately Clinton neglected to establish the depth of the intervening channel, relying on the assertions of local pilots that the water would not be an obstacle. It proved too deep even at low tide when the troops assembled on 16 June. Since the expedition had few landing craft, the navy had to subdue the enemy fort on its own. This Parker attempted to do on 28 June, only to have three of his ships damaged by the defenders' guns, forcing him to abandon the attempt. The expedition then returned to New York with nothing accomplished.[17]

Loyalist resistance, in consequence, had been extinguished almost everywhere before the British mounted their main invasion, 15 months after the outbreak of fighting. The ineffectiveness of the Loyalists merely reinforced British prejudice that they were militarily of little value. It would be time enough to organize them once the regular army had subdued the rebels. Governor Tryon was a lone voice in arguing the need to give "employment and protection to the well affected part of His Majesty's subjects." Even in New York where the King's friends were relatively numerous, they were finding their situation "every day becoming more trying and distressing," because of harassment by "committees, congresses and minutemen in their persons and property." What was needed, Tryon argued, was "some great and distinguished person" to give voice and direction to the Loyalist effort.[18] His proposals went unheeded.

In one sense the British military were right not to depend on the Loyalists, given their passive ideology. Loyalists knew their place and awaited deliverance, since colonials did not initiate policy or take decisions. Their passivity was all the greater for being a minority. Minorities, especially those lacking self confidence, looked to others to rescue them. But while they waited, America was lost.

The two sides prepare

The failure of the Loyalists to make a greater impact was closely linked to the British underestimation of the rebellion and the need to expand its armed forces. As we have seen, no real mobilization was undertaken until news of Bunker Hill reached Britain in early August 1775, when it was recognized that Gage was correct about the need for a more substantial army to restore order.[19] Any doubts about this were removed by Howe in early January 1776 when he emphasized that a field army of 20,000 men was absolutely necessary, exclusive of any corps advancing from Canada, if offensive operations were to be undertaken. The rebel army was no longer "to be despised, having in it many European soldiers" and "young men of spirit in the country who are exceedingly diligent and attentive to their military profession."[20]

The creation of such a force would clearly be lengthy, given the cumbersome recruitment procedures and hostility to conscription. Between August and December 1775 a mere 17,750 men were recruited, raising the total strength of the army at home and abroad to just 50,000 men.[21] It was for this reason that the ministry began negotiations in September 1775 for the hire of 20,000 Russian infantry. However, Catherine the Great had no interest in squandering her army for a cause that could be of little advantage to her.[22] The ministers accordingly fell back on the expedient of hiring German troops, as in the previous war. Various German princes periodically hired out their forces as a source of revenue. The advantage for the hirer was that the troops were fully trained according to the discipline of the much admired Prussian army of Frederick the Great. Treaties were therefore signed in January 1776 for the hire of 18,000 soldiers from Brunswick and Hesse. The political consequences of hiring mercenaries were overlooked.

By early February 1776 the plans of the ministry were finally taking shape, as 12,000 Hessians, 3,500 Highlanders, and 1,000 elite Guards were to reinforce Howe for the offensive in New York.[23] A further eight British regiments, totaling 5,000 men, with a similar number from Brunswick (under Burgoyne), were to relieve Carleton at Quebec as the prelude to an invasion of the northern colonies via Lake Champlain.[24] Together Howe and Carleton would have 35,000 men in their respective field armies.

It had taken six months to assemble this force and much still remained to be done, not least its transportation across the Atlantic and sustenance once there. However, the British possessed considerable logistical experience of fighting a war across the Atlantic. During the French and Indian War they had mounted major sea-borne assaults against Louisburg and Quebec involving many thousands of men. The British had also undertaken various amphibious operations against the French coast.[25] Nevertheless, the shipping now required was greater than anything experienced before, comprising some 70,000 tons of transports, three times that of the previous war. There were other crucial differences too, as the British commanders were to discover. Although the expeditions of Jeffery Amherst and James Wolfe to Louisburg and Quebec in 1758 and 1759 had been self-sufficient, they still had access to nearby colonial resources. This would clearly not be the case this time. Until order was restored, 120,000 tons of shipping or 500 vessels would be required to carry and feed the two armies and fleet.[26]

The execution of these plans was primarily the responsibility of the Secretary of State for America, Lord George Germain, who had replaced the less martial Dartmouth in November 1775. Germain possessed military experience, having commanded the British troops in Germany during the previous war. However, he had never been to America and his understanding of the continent, as for all the ministers, was limited. Moreover Germain was a potential liability at home because his earlier career had ended in disgrace following a court-martial for failing to obey orders during the battle of Minden in 1759. Opponents in the House of Commons were certain to exploit his implied cowardice if affairs took a turn for the worse.[27] But for the moment his speaking abilities were an asset in Parliament, though his cold haughty demeanor did not endear him to most colleagues.[28]

In contrast to Pitt in the previous war, Germain gave Howe and Carleton considerable latitude in the execution of their orders. Germain saw his task as one of organizing the means, leaving the commanders to decide how best to use them. As he told Carleton at the beginning of 1776: "These operations must be left to your judgment and discretion, as it would be highly improper, at such a distance to give any positive orders." Everything was left to the "knowledge and military experience" of the commanders.[29] However, the outlines of the campaign had already been sketched by Howe in previous letters to Dartmouth. The main army under his command was to occupy New York before "opening a communication" with Carleton advancing from Canada. Once the two armies had made contact they could either act together or "take separate routes into the province of Massachusetts Bay as circumstances may arise." The center of the rebellion should then be quashed.[30]

Since the Royal Navy would have an important role supporting the army in the early stages of the campaign, the ministry decided to appoint

Howe's older brother, Richard Lord Howe, to command the naval forces in America. This was welcome news for Howe since he had great confidence in his brother's "experience" of "conjunct war." Richard Howe had commanded the naval forces during the coastal expeditions to France in 1758 with much applause from his military colleagues. His orders were to prevent all sea-borne commerce as defined by the Prohibitory Act while simultaneously cooperating with the army "in the most vigorous execution of such measures" as were necessary for ending the revolt. This included attacking American ports, destroying rebel property, and giving help to the Loyalists.[31]

Finally the Howe brothers were to act as peace commissioners. This part of their remit originated with North as part of his 1775 conciliation plan. The other ministers were less enthusiastic about the idea but agreed, providing it did not interfere with the prosecution of the war. The purpose of the commission was "to induce such a submission" as was consistent "with the just ... dependence" of the colonies. In pursuance of this objective the commissioners could "issue proclamations ... promising a free pardon ... to any person or persons" who within a certain time "returned to their allegiance," always excepting those who were not worthy of the King's mercy. To increase the chances of a submission, the Commissioners could suspend the Prohibitory Act and reopen ports or coasts, though only after all illegal congresses had been dissolved and armed bodies disbanded. Then if a province agreed to contribute satisfactorily to a common defense fund and the expenses of civil government, Parliament would cease levying any taxes other than those for the regulation of trade.[32]

North's colleagues were right to be skeptical about the peace commission since submission was the last thing on Washington's mind following the British evacuation of Boston. Even before that event, he had recognized that New York would be the likely scene of future operations, given its strategic location between New England and the other colonies to the south. He had been sufficiently concerned in early January 1776 to send Charles Lee, a former regular officer, to secure the city with help from neighboring Connecticut.[33] Once the British intention to evacuate Boston was clear, Washington had dispatched a further six regiments in case Howe sailed there rather than Halifax.[34] Then in early April he headed for New York himself, recognizing that Boston was finally safe.

Washington reached New York on 13 April 1776. Although Lee had begun digging entrenchments, much remained to be done. Even by the middle of May, Washington still had barely 10,000 men to defend a city that appeared almost indefensible, surrounded as it was by navigable rivers and inlets. In addition the troops under his command were hardly the professionals he had expected following the decision to create a new army for 1776. He would therefore have to fight defensively, being acutely aware that the Patriot cause depended on his ability to keep the Continental army in being. Defeat now would mean not only the loss of New York City and the control of the Hudson River, but the separation of New England from the rest of the confederacy.[35]

Washington was not helped at this point by the diversion of resources to Canada. Despite the repulse of Montgomery and Arnold, Congress determined to persevere in its attempt to wrest that country from the British. Since Washington had no troops to spare, Congress created in January 1776 three additional regiments to reinforce the army there.[36] However, at the end of March Congress decided Canada was still so important that Washington was to send four of his own battalions, followed by another six corps four weeks later.[37]

The weakening of Washington's army would have been acceptable had there been a reasonable prospect of success. Unfortunately the northern army was still insufficient to capture Quebec and the situation further deteriorated with the arrival of the first British relief ships. This forced the Patriots to abandon their cannon in a precipitate retreat to the Sorrel River to avoid being cut off.[38] Nevertheless the arrival of the additional troops in early June 1776 determined John Sullivan, the new commander, to attack the British post at Trois Rivieres to encourage Canadian support.[39] He made his decision unaware that Carleton had been massively reinforced by Burgoyne. Sullivan's offensive in consequence turned into yet another retreat, this time down Lake Champlain to Crown Point.[40] Sullivan's ability to resist was not helped by a serious outbreak of smallpox in his army. In addition morale was poor, according to Schuyler, because of "an illiberal and destructive jealousy ... between the troops" raised in Connecticut and New York.[41] The invasion of Canada had proved a costly failure, which the cause of independence could ill afford, given the threat to New York.

Washington by this time had set up his main camp in June 1776 on Long Island, where he formed a defensive line along Brooklyn Heights. From here he could cooperate with the troops in Manhattan, while keeping the road to New England open at Kingsbridge. This was a huge area to defend with an army that still only numbered 14,000 men fit for duty. Some posts were 15 miles apart. Washington could only hope that the various militias would come to his aid once the enemy appeared.[42] However, the auguries were not promising. The New York Provincial Congress bluntly affirmed that it could do little, given the widespread hostility of the inhabitants and the exposed situation of its coastline.[43]

Otherwise Washington's defensive stance suited his army since it was still too poorly trained to withstand a regular army in open combat. Eighteenth-century warfare required troops to be able to march in a column or line, wheeling to the right or left as required. They also needed to be able to load their weapons in a synchronized fashion to ensure maximum effect.[44] Such coordination could be achieved only after prolonged exercise, which was not possible for men on short-term enlistments. But there were other attributes necessary for a well disciplined army. The men required proper uniforms rather than simple hunting shirts. They also needed muskets equipped with bayonets, not fowling pieces. Finally they must be disciplined to execute any order, however unpleasant. The errant attitude to discipline was demonstrated by some Connecticut militia cavalry who refused to do guard duty or dig trenches, claiming that they could be employed only when on horseback. Despite his want of troops, Washington instantly dismissed them to avoid setting a precedent.[45]

Finally the cohesion of Washington's army, like that of Schuyler, was threatened by regional jealousies among the different units. As Washington pointed out in his general orders of 1 August 1776, the army must avoid these disputes since they could only "injure the noble cause in which we are engaged." The men should remember that "the honor and success of the army" depended "upon harmony and good agreement." Since "the provinces" were fighting a "common enemy . . . all distinctions" must be "sunk in the name of an American."[46]

The lack of discipline meant that a war of movement was not practical for the moment. The troops therefore continued improving the defenses, though Washington advised his officers not to neglect exercising their men in the art of maneuver. The shovel could not entirely replace the musket. But morale remained surprisingly high, bolstered by the news on 9 July that Congress had declared the American states to be independent.[47] It was also helped by the news of the repulse of Clinton and Parker at Charleston, which demonstrated what a small number of new raised troops could do against the might of the British army and navy.[48] This was just as well since the British were now ready to commence their operations around New York.

The British invasion of New York

Since the evacuation of Boston, Howe had been preparing his forces at Halifax for a campaign based on New York. His plan, he told Germain on 7 June 1776, was to start with "a landing upon Long Island." Should "the enemy offer battle on the open field," Howe would "not decline it," since he had every prospect of success, given the calibre of his troops. Once the reinforcements arrived, he could then divide his forces to complete the subjugation of the rebels. His only concern was that he would have to take orders from Carleton, the senior officer, once the two armies met on the Hudson.[49]

In the event, Howe abandoned his plan for an immediate landing on Long Island after learning about its hilly interior and the reported strength of Washington's army.[50] Instead he occupied Staten Island at the end of June, where he set about entrenching his force while awaiting the ministry's reinforcements from Germany, England, and Ireland. The delay also allowed him to reconnoitre the countryside. Howe had been advised that the Patriots had obstructed the North River, as the lower part of the Hudson was known. However, on 12 July the navy managed to get two vessels past the batteries at Fort Washington half-way up Manhattan. This opened the possibility of approaching the city from the rear, thus facilitating the interception of Washington's supplies.[51]

Unfortunately for Howe, his reinforcements had still to appear. Clinton and Parker returned from Charleston only on 1 August while the 1,100 Guards and first division of the Hessian troops, totaling 7,000 men, finally arrived on 12 August. This still left the second Hessian division of 5,000 men to appear. But Howe's timetable was governed by another factor. Until the middle of August the regiments lacked their camp equipment, which Howe considered essential for field operations. As a result, six weeks passed before he was ready to advance with his 25,000 troops.[52]

Nevertheless, Howe's slow proceedings have perplexed historians. Washington's forces were not strong, comprising only 23,000 men as late as 19 August, of whom almost half were militia.[53] This failure to exploit his weakness has led to suggestions that the Howe brothers were sympathetic to the Patriot cause.[54] They had undoubtedly been touched by the colonial response to the death of their eldest brother, Lord Augustus Howe at Ticonderoga in 1758, which led the Massachusetts Assembly to vote money towards the erection of a statue in Westminster Abbey. Their empathy helps explain Richard Howe's readiness to undertake informal negotiations with Benjamin Franklin during the winter of 1774 as part of North's attempts at conciliation. Certainly both Howe brothers seem to have been free of the prejudice typical of most Britons regarding the Colonists, recognizing that this was a civil war, not a peasant revolt. It was for this reason that Richard Howe insisted on a peace commission that was worded in the "mildest though firmest" language, to induce the colonies "to lay down their arms and return to their duty".[55]

However, the Howe brothers would not have sabotaged their field operations, since both were professional soldiers. The Patriots were still rebels and traitors who had to be subdued. Shortly before his appointment, Lord Howe told Parliament that "if he was commanded, it was his duty to obey and he could not refuse to serve."[56] The most that can be said is that the Howe brothers may have slowed their operations on occasion in the belief that the Patriot cause was about to collapse. As one officer commented, it was right "to treat our enemies as if they might one day become our friends."[57]

While awaiting the final elements of their armada, the Howe brothers issued their first proclamation as peace commissioners, promising a pardon to all who were willing to take the oath of loyalty to George III and acknowledge Parliament's sovereignty. Those helping in the restoration of lawful government would be rewarded. The proclamation had the dual purpose of encouraging the Loyalists while giving the rebels reason to pause. It was also a timely counter to the Declaration of Independence which had been announced ten days earlier.[58] The Commissioners sent a copy to Washington, but he refused to receive it because it was not addressed to him as "General of the American army."[59] Technically Washington was a rebel in British eyes, whereas he insisted on the status of a belligerent as befitted the commander of an independent state. In any case this clumsy gesture was in vain, since the Patriots had made their choice. As Franklin informed the two commissioners in a private letter, independence was the only option, given Britain's "wanton barbarity and cruelty" against "defenseless Towns." The British had not only "incited massacres by rebellious slaves and Indians," but had also brought "foreign Mercenaries to deluge our Settlements with Blood." Unsurprisingly, these "atrocious injuries" had extinguished "every remaining Spark of Affection for the Parent Country."[60]

Howe finally began his operations by crossing to Long Island on 22 August with 15,000 men. His plan was to gain Brooklyn Heights as the prelude to an attack on Manhattan. After that he proposed forcing the Hudson River to facilitate a meeting with the northern army, providing he could get sufficient transports past the Patriot batteries. His advance took him to Guana Heights where Washington had belatedly placed his army to gain maximum advantage from the rising ground. He hoped that the British would make another frontal attack as at Bunker Hill. Unfortunately Washington neglected to secure his left flank adequately at

Jamaica Pass.[61] This allowed Howe early on 27 August 1776 to approach with the right wing of his army from the east, threatening the Patriot lines around Brooklyn and retreat across the East River. The center and left wing of Howe's army then launched a frontal assault, forcing the rest of Washington's troops under Generals Stirling and Sullivan back towards the River. Fortunately for Washington, Howe failed to follow up his advantage by storming the entrenchments around Brooklyn itself. As he told Germain on 3 September, he had restrained his forces, even though on the verge of success, "as it was apparent the lines must have been ours at a very cheap rate by regular approaches" without risking "the loss that might have been sustained in the assault."[62] It was to be one of many missed opportunities that a bolder commander might have exploited. The Patriot losses were some 800 dead, wounded, and captured, among the latter being Stirling and Sullivan.[63]

Fortune then smiled on Washington a second time when contrary winds prevented the Royal Navy from entering the East River. With foresight the Howe brothers should have had vessels in place before the battle. Although hulks had been sunk across the main channel, smaller warships might have navigated the shallower waters on the Long Island side of the river. This would then have ensured Washington's entrapment.[64] It was yet another missed opportunity for destroying the Patriot army, of which Washington took full advantage by ferrying his men back across the East River on the night of 29 August 1776 to momentary safety in New York. The British discovered his departure only at dawn next day.[65]

Nevertheless, the situation of the Continental army was grim, as desertion and sickness increased, always the signs of low morale. At the beginning of September Washington had barely 9,000 men exclusive of militia, whose reliability was seriously in doubt.[66] These were pitifully inadequate forces to attempt the defense of Manhattan. But to give up the city without a struggle would be a severe blow to Patriot morale. Its surrender would also provide the British with a naval base and center for winter quarters. On the other hand, to stay and fight would place the Continental army in a certain trap, given that Manhattan was surrounded by water.[67] Washington wanted to burn the city before abandoning it, but the decision was a political one for Congress. After much heart-searching the members merely agreed that New York should not be burnt, leaving Washington to hold or abandon it.[68]

Before making a final decision, Washington sought the advice of his senior commanders. He pointed out the danger of being surrounded on Manhattan. The question was how to deal with the threat. Everyone accepted that the army must act defensively, fighting "a war of posts," on the principle "that we should on all occasions avoid a general action ... unless compelled by necessity." Nevertheless the majority of the council still wanted to hold the city, tempting Howe into another Bunker Hill style assault. The British had yet to navigate the Harlem River at the northern end of Manhattan, which left Kingsbridge open as an escape route in case of a defeat.[69]

However, the decision was quickly reversed when the council realized that the British were intending to surround Manhattan before storming the city. On 11 September several vessels appeared at the confluence of the North and Harlem Rivers, while another group entered Hell Gate, the tricky channel leading to the Harlem River at its eastern end.[70] Washington accordingly reconvened his Council on 12 September when it was agreed to evacuate the city, removing the bulk of the army to Harlem Heights. A second division simultaneously occupied Kingsbridge to protect the army's escape route in case the British landed above Manhattan to outflank the new positions.[71]

Howe meanwhile was considering his options in the belief that the rebellion might shortly collapse. This optimism undoubtedly explained Lord Howe's readiness to send a message to Congress suggesting talks, indicating that the commissioners had far wider powers than the mere granting of pardons. The result was a meeting on 11 September 1776 between Howe and Edward Rutledge, John Adams, and Benjamin Franklin. The conference on Staten Island began with a dinner. But despite the pleasantries, the discussions quickly stalled. Howe made it clear that he could not enter into a treaty with Congress. The envoys responded that they could negotiate only as the delegates of free and independent states, whatever the military situation. They then pointed out to Howe the benefits to Britain from such a relationship. But this was something Howe had not been authorized to consider.[72] The gap between the two sides was as great as ever.

Sir William accordingly began preparations for another amphibious assault, this time on Manhattan. First he dispatched three ships up the North River as a diversion before landing his main force at Kips Bay on the East River. The troops experienced only fleeting resistance on 15 September, even though the Patriot forces along the shore were protected by entrenchments. The first cannonade by the ships was enough to panic the men into flight. Fortunately the site was close to the new position on Harlem Heights where Washington was able to reform the men's ranks. Nevertheless, the remaining forces still in the city were in grave danger of being cut off.[73]

However, by the time that Howe was ready to march across Manhattan to the North River, the garrison had joined Washington, though at the expense of their baggage and artillery. Howe seemingly hesitated to execute this maneuver because he was still awaiting the second Hessian division, having barely 12,000 men in his main field army. His forces had been stretched by the need to support the Loyalist seizure of Fort George in New York City.[74] His caution was perhaps justified when some British light infantry were nearly cut off, after reconnoitering Washington's positions at Harlem. It was a welcome boost to the morale of the Patriot army following the evacuation of New York and the events at Kips Bay.[75]

Nevertheless, the situation of the Patriots was increasingly dire, as Washington explained to Hancock. He was referring not only to its current plight but to its future existence, since in three months it would be on "the eve of another dissolution," similar to that of December 1775. Better terms of service must be offered if the army was to be recruited, since appeals to patriotism were futile when everyone else was moved only by self-interest. People would not reenlist "when men find that their townsmen and companions are receiving 20, 30 and more dollars for a few months service" in the militia. In Washington's view "nothing but a good bounty can obtain them" for "the continuance of the war." Accordingly everyone should receive at least 30 dollars on signing, a new suit of clothes every year, and 100 to 150 acres of land at the end of their service. With such encouragement an army might be raised capable of defeating the enemy.[76]

But to effect this, Congress must overcome its "jealousy of a standing army" since "the evils to be apprehended from one are remote." The fact was that a militia could never be an adequate substitute for a professional army. "Men just dragged from the tender scenes of domestic life, unaccustomed to the din of arms, totally unacquainted with every kind of military skill . . . when opposed to troops regularly trained, disciplined, and appointed . . . makes them timid and ready to fly from their own shadows." To bring such men "to a proper degree of subordination is not the work of a day, a month or even a year." The reality was that the militia "do not think themselves subject to" the rules of war. The effect of their insubordination was to undermine the morale of those who were. But the creation of an effective military force meant that the rules of war must also be strengthened regarding discipline. "For the most atrocious offences a man receives no more than 39 lashes and these perhaps (through the collusion of the officer who is to see it inflicted) are given in such a manner as to become rather a matter of sport than punishment." The consequences were that soldiers often deserted 30 to 40 at a time and everywhere plundered the inhabitants, burning down their houses to conceal their crimes.[77] This was in stark contrast to the conduct of the British who so far had operated with respect for the civilian population and their property.[78]

By the time that Washington finished his letter to Hancock, Congress had already recognized the need for a more professional force. On 16 September 1776 it voted to create an army of 88 battalions, totaling 66,000 men, to be raised according to the population of each state. The men were to serve for the duration of the war, receiving a bounty of 20 dollars on enlisting and 100 acres on being discharged.[79] However, until these resolves were implemented, Washington would again have to rely on the militia to sustain him over the New Year.[80]

Meanwhile Howe was busy securing his position in New York City before making another move against Washington. He already accepted that a further campaign would be necessary. The second division of the Hessians had still to arrive and it appeared that he could have no "dependence upon General Carleton's approach." From Howe's perspective the Patriots were still a formidable force when entrenched on favorable ground, despite their recent setbacks. The best way to overcome these obstacles without unacceptable casualties was by turning the enemy's flank. But this posed "innumerable difficulties," not least a lack of landing craft and men to handle them. To remedy this deficiency Howe proposed the deployment of "eight or ten line of battleships with supernumerary seamen for manning boats." But men were also needed to fill the regimental ranks, since Loyalists were reluctant to enlist because of the severity of regular discipline.[81]

Organizing the defenses of New York City meant that Howe was not ready to advance against Washington before the end of September, when his caution once again came into play. The Patriot army had 14,759 fit for duty with another 3,427 on independent commands.[82] But rather than attack Washington frontally on Harlem Heights, Howe resolved to outflank him by landing on the eastern side of Westchester County between Throgs Neck and New Rochelle. This would allow him to approach the Patriots from the rear, thus reducing the likelihood of casualties.

The army accordingly took to its boats on 12 October, landing eventually six days later at Pell's Point. The delay in disembarking gave Washington sufficient time to move the bulk of his army to White Plains, leaving General Nathanael Greene at Fort Washington on the west side of Manhattan with 3,000 men to dispute the passage of the Hudson.[83] White Plains offered excellent defensive positions from which to confront Howe. Consequently when Howe arrived on 25 October, he found Washington's forces drawn up in good order. Nevertheless he decided to force a battle by attacking the Patriot right wing on Chatterton's Hill. The position was successfully carried on 28 October, but Howe again failed to press home his advantage. This allowed Washington to withdraw to yet another defensive line at North Castle, where he awaited a further British assault.[84]

To his surprise none was forthcoming. Instead word was received that Howe was withdrawing towards Kingsbridge and the North River. This suggested that he was planning either to invade New Jersey or to attack Fort Washington.[85] Faced with these uncertainties, Washington's Council determined on 6 November to split the army into three divisions. Charles Lee with the largest force was to remain at White Plains while Washington crossed the North River with another 4,000 men to strengthen the defense of Fort Lee on the New Jersey side of the river. A further 3,000 would garrison the Highland forts, commanding access to the upper reaches of the Hudson River.[86] The council surprisingly failed to order the simultaneous evacuation of Fort Washington, now isolated on Manhattan. Washington personally wanted to abandon the fort since its guns and those of Fort Lee on the other bank had not prevented the Royal Navy from sailing up the Hudson.[87] However, the decision to hold the fort had been taken "by a full council of General Officers," in response to a "resolution of Congress . . . that the Channel of the River" be retained.[88] Washington accordingly could do no more than advise Greene: "As you are upon the spot, [I] leave it to you to give such orders as to evacuating Mount Washington as you judge best."[89]

Greene replied reassuringly that the garrison was in no immediate danger, since it could be ferried expeditiously across the Hudson to Fort Lee. The commander, Colonel Robert Magaw, also believed he could hold his position until the end of December.[90] It proved an unwise assessment, since Magaw had to defend not only Fort Washington but a perimeter stretching between the Hudson and Harlem Rivers with vastly inferior numbers. Furthermore, most of the defenses consisted of shallow entrenchments. This was an opportunity that even Howe could grasp, especially as the second division of the Hessians had finally arrived after a passage of 21 weeks. On 16 November he struck with his main army, capturing almost the entire garrison of 3,000 after a brief engagement. Among the booty was a huge quantity of ordnance and other stores which the Continental army could ill afford to lose.[91] Some junior British officers thought an example should have been made on this occasion. The rules of European warfare entitled the victors to put the vanquished to the sword if they refused an initial summons to surrender. This severity "would have struck such a panic as would have prevented the Congress from ever being able to raise another Army."[92]

One note of cheer for Washington at this time was the news that Carleton had abandoned his advance from Canada.[93] Despite Burgoyne's arrival in early June, he and Carleton failed to catch the retreating Patriots before they reached Lake Champlain, where Arnold had assembled a flotilla with which to dispute the passage of the lake. As a result Carleton had to construct his own armament to win back naval superiority. Eventually a fleet of sufficient size was built.[94] But although Arnold's flotilla was finally destroyed on 13 October, the campaigning season was effectively at an end.[95] Carleton did occupy Crown Point, but the Patriots still held Ticonderoga. With the weather steadily deteriorating, he resolved to return to St Johns rather than risk a siege.[96]

Nevertheless, there was to be no respite for Washington's own forces, for the capture of Fort Washington induced Howe to attempt a further advance into New Jersey. On 20 November Major General Charles Earl Cornwallis, one of Howe's senior officers, crossed the Hudson with 4,000 regulars to trap the Patriot forces in Fort Lee. Fortunately Greene was able to withdraw in time to join Washington near Hackensack so that there was no repetition of the events at Fort Washington.[97] But any hopes of confronting Cornwallis disappeared when 2,000 Maryland and New Jersey militia disbanded at the expiry of their terms of service. The New Jersey units were especially anxious to return to their families now that the British were approaching. Washington was also hampered by the refusal of Lee at White Plains to come to his aid, even though it was clear that the British were directing their attention towards Philadelphia rather than the communication with New England.[98] Indeed, Lee was openly challenging Washington's authority, arguing that generals on a "detached" command "cannot have too great a latitude."[99]

In this situation Washington could only retreat again, after making several fruitless appeals to the militia. His plan was to reach the River Delaware before the British, so that he could use it as a shield to protect Philadelphia while rebuilding his army. His route first took him to Newark and then Brunswick, both places being evacuated just as the British advance guard entered from the other side.[100] Fortunately for Washington, Howe then ordered Cornwallis to halt at Brunswick, since his "design" went "no further than . . . [the] possession of East New Jersey." Several days passed before Howe realized the "advantage that might be gained by pushing on to the Delaware and the possibility of getting to Philadelphia." He accordingly joined Cornwallis on 6 December with a substantial reinforcement to continue the chase in person.[101]

Once again Howe paid the price for his dilatory style of warfare, since his halting of Cornwallis had allowed Washington to ferry both his forces and stores to relative safety in Pennsylvania. Hence on Howe's arrival on 8 December at Trenton, he found that Washington had not only crossed the river but taken all the boats with him.[102] Howe would have to construct new vessels to continue the pursuit, which was hardly practical given the prevailing weather and lack of tools.

After a few days Howe decided to send his men into winter quarters in a line of posts between the Hudson and the Delaware. The weather had turned cold, making it probable that Washington's army would follow the example of the New Jersey militia and disband. Going into winter quarters was normal practice for European professional armies, when conditions made the movement of large numbers and men and supplies impractical. Howe admitted to Germain that his chain of posts was "rather too extensive," but he had had been "induced to occupy Burlington to cover the county of Monmouth," in which there were many loyal inhabitants. Furthermore the likely "submission of the country to the southward" and "the strength of the corps placed in the advanced posts" led Howe to conclude that they would "be in perfect security."[103]

The seeming collapse of the Patriots led Lord Howe to issue another proclamation offering a pardon to all those who resumed their allegiance in the next 60 days. The offer was inclusive despite "the atrocious delinquency of some of the leaders and instigators of the war."[104] The success this time was palpable. Within three weeks almost all New Jersey had taken the oaths while "several persons of property" had similarly indicated their readiness to submit in Pennsylvania, even though the army had not yet entered that province.[105] The same conciliatory spirit also prompted him to issue new instructions for the enforcement of the Prohibitory Act. In future the blockading warships were to seize only those vessels engaged in contraband or the export and import of goods. Subsistence activities like fishing should be allowed. In addition the officers were to cultivate an "amicable correspondence" with the inhabitants since Howe believed this was the best way of detaching "them from the prejudices they have imbibed."[106]

The establishment of the posts in New Jersey was not quite the end of Howe's campaign. He now felt sufficiently strong to send Clinton with 7,000 men to occupy Rhode Island. The navy desired a base there because the rivers around New York tended to freeze in winter, making the navy's ships vulnerable to attack. The Newport anchorage on the other hand was well protected and ice-free. It also offered a convenient location from which to blockade the southern New England coast. Finally, possession of Rhode

Island would provide a springboard for the reconquest of Massachusetts. Clinton achieved his mission on 8 December with little bloodshed, trapping several Continental frigates under Commodore Hopkins at Providence.[107] It was another indication that the rebellion was about to collapse.

Trenton and Princeton: The Patriot cause retrieved

Howe was seemingly correct in his opinion that Washington's army was about to dissolve. It now numbered barely 3,000, and the enlistments of half of these would shortly end. Washington still expected Lee to join him, but his authority was so precarious that he could only plead with his subordinate to comply.[108] He told a relative that unless the army was speedily enlarged "the game will be pretty well up."[109] He was equally frank with the Governor of Connecticut, telling him that when the enlistments expired, he would be left with a few sickly southern regiments to protect Philadelphia. It was clear that Howe was only waiting for a sufficient depth of ice to cross the Delaware into Pennsylvania.[110] In anticipation Washington sent his correspondence and other incriminating papers deep into the interior of Virginia, since there was little to stop the British from marching to Philadelphia and beyond.[111] Others thought similarly, including John Dickinson, author of the Olive Branch Petition. He had retired to his farm in Delaware to await a negotiated peace, simultaneously advising his brother, a senior militia officer, to dispose of any Continental currency.[112]

One person who did not despair was Paine, who produced another eloquent pamphlet, appropriately titled *The Crisis*, in which he wrote the immortal words: "These are the times that try men's souls." He reminded his readers that "the summer soldier and the sunshine Patriot" might desert but those who did their duty would receive "the love and thanks of [every] man and woman." The Patriots should remember that "Tyranny, like hell, is not easily conquered." The consolation was that "the harder the conflict, the more glorious the triumph."[113] Winston Churchill's speech promising "blood, toil, tears and sweat" to the British people in 1940 was a similar response to a desperate emergency.

Among those still determined to do their duty was Washington himself. The problem was how and where to act, since every day increased the danger that the army would melt away, leaving Philadelphia and a large swathe of the country under British rule. It was at this moment that Joseph Reed, Washington's Adjutant General, reported that some New Jersey militia was planning to attack the British posts between Bordentown and Burlington.

Perhaps Washington could "make a diversion or something more at or about Trenton?" Reed continued: "If we could possess ourselves again of New Jersey or any considerable part of it, the effects would be greater than if we had never left it." Reports all indicated that the British had gone into winter quarters and were not about to attack the Patriots.[114]

This was the spur that Washington needed. Accordingly, on Christmas night he ferried over a substantial portion of his remaining troops to attack three Hessian regiments at Trenton, using the same boats with which he had retreated. The Hessian commander, Johan Rall, had participated in the capture of Fort Washington and was utterly contemptuous of his opponents. He had accordingly taken few precautions while his men enjoyed the Christmas festivities. The Patriots consequently arrived undetected at Trenton at 8.00 on the morning of 26 December with 2,400 men supported by artillery. Within an hour 1,000 Hessians had been captured with little resistance. The success would have been even greater but for the failure of two other detachments to cross the river because of ice, thus allowing the remaining Hessians to escape. Nevertheless Washington was well pleased as he prudently retreated back that same evening across the Delaware with his captives.[115] Two days later a grateful Congress voted him dictatorial powers for six months, including authority to raise troops, appoint officers below brigadier, and take from the inhabitants whatever he wanted "for the use of the army."[116]

The success at Trenton and the additional authority from Congress naturally encouraged Washington to consider another strike. Several factors now appeared to favor this. The first was the discovery that the British had abandoned all their posts in southern New Jersey.[117] The second was that the army had now been reinforced by Lee's division, though without its commander, who had foolishly allowed himself to be captured after taking quarters outside his camp. Other units were also arriving, including a substantial number of Pennsylvania militia. Washington accordingly felt strong enough to return to Trenton on New Year's Eve with the aim of pushing the British back to Brunswick, thus liberating most of New Jersey.[118] But before crossing the river he first used his new powers to offer ten dollars to those whose enlistments were about to expire if they would extend their service by one month. Almost all did.[119]

In one crucial respect Washington had misread British intentions. Howe had withdrawn the Delaware River garrisons to concentrate his forces for a counter-attack under Cornwallis, with the objective of trapping Washington. By 1 January Cornwallis was ready to proceed with some 7,000 picked men and a large train of artillery. By 4 pm on 2 January 1777 he had seemingly accomplished his objective, since Washington's army was still on the outskirts of Trenton, separated from its boats upstream. Some senior officers suggested an immediate attack, fearing that Washington might re-cross the river during the night. Cornwallis, however, disliked an action so close to nightfall, especially as his advance guard had failed to dislodge the Patriots from the protective cover of Assunpink Creek. He commented: "We have got the old fox safe now. We'll go over and bag him in the morning."[120]

But instead of attempting to re-cross the Delaware, Washington unexpectedly made a night march along a back road to Princeton. Shortly after daybreak he surprised the British rearguard of three regiments under Colonel Mawhood, capturing 200 prisoners.[121] It was yet another boost to morale. Washington momentarily contemplated continuing to Brunswick. But as he explained to Congress, "the harassed state of our own Troops (many of them having had no rest for two nights and a day) and the danger of losing the advantage we had gained by aiming at too much, induced me, by the advice of my Officers, to relinquish the attempt."[122] He accordingly set off for Morristown, where he had already established a fortified encampment. Cornwallis did not follow, being too concerned about the safety of Brunswick. Washington was consequently able to complete his withdrawal without further difficulty.

Morristown was an admirable site, protected as it was by a range of hills, swamps, and rivers. It was also well placed for watching the motions of the British, should they advance on Philadelphia or move northwards towards New England. Perhaps most importantly, it would allow the army to recuperate. It numbered perhaps 3,500 men, as units continued to go home on the expiry of their enlistments. Those that remained were tired and needed rest: it was time for winter quarters.

These factors were not immediately apparent to the British, who still feared for their remaining posts in New Jersey. Howe accordingly gave orders for the various garrisons to withdraw towards New York. By 6 January 1777 the British were confined to the towns of Amboy and Brunswick with nothing else to show for their efforts since the capture of Fort Lee. "The unfortunate and untimely defeat at Trenton," Howe informed Germain, "has thrown us farther back than was at first apprehended, from the great encouragement it has given the rebels." A large body of New England militia had even threatened the British post at Kingsbridge, insolently calling on the defenders to surrender.[123]

But apart from the loss of territory, the British had squandered something more important, the confidence of the New Jersey Loyalists. They had been subject to surveillance and intimidation for 18 months, during which time the Patriots had established their authority at every level. Nevertheless they had welcomed the return of the British in November 1776, expecting the old order to be restored. The British retreat after Trenton left them facing a cruel dilemma, following a proclamation from Washington. They could either reaffirm their loyalty to the United States or withdraw to the British lines in 30 days.[124] In the latter case they could take only a few personal effects and as enemies of the American states would be liable to the confiscation of their property. But even those who reaffirmed their citizenship were still open to persecution by Patriot mobs and local magistrates. Very few would make the mistake of welcoming the British again, as Howe found when he reentered New Jersey briefly in June 1777. The British had failed to realize that there was no substitute for permanent possession if they wished to retain the hearts and minds of the population.

There was one other consequence following the British retreat to New York. The advance into New Jersey had allowed them for the first time to secure provisions from the local population. That option was now closed. Hereafter the army would once again have to depend for most of its food and forage on a supply chain stretching 3,000 miles across the Atlantic, imposing a huge burden on the resources of the nation. It was to be one of several factors that undermined Britain's chances of regaining her colonies.[125]

Trenton and Princeton, in contrast, restored Washington's reputation, not least in France where his maneuvers were critically acclaimed. It was clear that the Patriot cause was far from finished. Indeed the British attempt to recover the colonies had achieved little in either political or military terms. The rebel army was still in existence while all 13 provinces remained under Patriot control.

Notes and references

1 See for example Edmund S. Morgan, *The Birth of the Republic, 1763–1789* (Chicago, 1956).

2 William H. Nelson, *The American Tory* (Oxford, 1961).

3 Philip Ranlet, *The New York Loyalists* (Knoxville, 1986).

4 James H. Hutson, *Pennsylvania Politics, 1746–1770: The Movement for Royal Government and its Consequences* (Princeton, 1972).

5 Thad W. Tate, "The Coming of the Revolution in Virginia: Britain's Challenge to Virginia's Ruling Class, 1763–1776," *William and Mary Quarterly*, XIX, 1962, 323–43.

6 Rachel N. Klein, *Unification of a Slave State; The Rise of the Planter Class in the South Carolina Backcountry, 1760–1808* (Chapel Hill, 1999), 82–83.

7 Campbell to Dartmouth, 19 September 1775, DDAR/XI, 116–18.

8 Dunmore to Dartmouth, 6 December 1775–18 February 1776, DDAR/XII, 57–68.

9 Paul H. Smith, *Loyalists and Redcoats: A Study in British Revolutionary Policy* (Chapel Hill, 1964), 19.

10 Dartmouth to Martin, 15 September 1775, DDAR/XI, 106–7.

11 North to George III, 15 October 1775, Fortescue/3, 265–68.

12 Dartmouth to Howe, 22 October 1775, DDAR/XI, 158–161. Germain to Clinton, 9 December 1775, DDAR/XI, 208–10.

13 David Syrett, *The Royal Navy in American Waters, 1775–1783* (Aldershot, 1989), 35–36.

14 Narrative of proceedings of Loyalists in North Carolina, 25 April 1776, DDAR/XII, 112–13.

15 *Clinton's Narrative,* CAR, 27. Smith, *Loyalists,* 25.

16 Clinton to Germain, 8 July 1776, CAR, 373–76.

17 Parker to Admiralty Secretary, 9 July 1776, CAR, 376–78.

18 Tryon to Dartmouth, 3 January 1776, DDAR/XII, 31–32.

19 Dartmouth to Gage, 2 August 1775, DDAR/XI, 62–63.

20 Howe to Dartmouth, 16 January 1776, DDAR/XII, 44–47. It is not clear what Howe's evidence was for his claim that Europeans were serving with the Patriots' army at this time.

21 Estimates for 1776, CJ/XXXV, 414–15. Ibid., Estimate of the Augmentations, 471.

22 Dartmouth to Howe, 5 September 1775, DDAR/XI, 100. George III to North, 3 November 1775, Fortescue/3, 275–76.

23 Germain to Howe, 5 January 1776, DDAR/XII, 33–36. Ibid., 28 March 1776, 93–96.

24 Germain to Carleton, 17 February 1776, DDAR/XII, 56–57.

25 Richard Middleton, "The Coastal Expeditions to France, 1757–1758", *Journal of the Society for Army Historical Research*, LXXI, 1993, 74–92. See also David Syrett, *Shipping and Military Power in the Seven Years War: The Sails of Victory* (Exeter, 2008).

26 Piers Mackesy, *The War for America, 1775–1783* (Cambridge, Mass., 1964), 64–65. For a detailed analysis, see David Syrett, *Shipping and the American War, 1775–1783* (London, 1970).

27 Piers Mackesy, *The Coward of Minden: The Affair of Lord George Sackville* (London, 1979).

28 Gerald S. Brown, *The American Secretary: The Colonial Policy of Lord George Germain, 1775–1778* (Ann Arbor, 1963), 24, 38–41.

29 Mackesy, *War for America*, 60.

30 Howe to Dartmouth, 9 October 1775, DDAR/XI, 138–40. Howe to Dartmouth, 26 November 1775, DDAR/XI, 191–92.

31 Ira D. Gruber, *The Howe Brothers and the American Revolution* (New York, 1972), 79. For Howe's previous experience in the conduct of amphibious operations, see Middleton, *British Coastal Expeditions*, 74–92.

32 Instructions to the Commissioners for restoring Peace in America, 6 May 1776, DDAR/XII, 120–25.

33 Instructions to Charles Lee, 8 January 1776, WP/RWS/3, 53–54.

34 Orders to Colonel Mifflin, 24 March 1776, WP/RWS/3, 527–28. Washington to Stirling, 27 March 1776, WP/RWS/3, 553–54.

35 Middlekauf, *Glorious Cause*, 333.

36 Hancock to Washington, 20 January 1776, WP/RWS/3, 154–55.

37 Hancock to Washington, 25 March 1776, WP/RWS/3, 532–33. Ibid., 23 April 1776, WP/RWS/4, 114–15.

38 Thomas to Washington, 8 May 1776, WP/RWS/4, 231–32. Carleton to Germain, 14 May 1776, DDAR/XII, 137–38.

39 Sullivan to Washington, 5 June 1776, WP/RWS/4, 440–43.

40 Sullivan to Washington, 12 June 1776, WP/RWS/4, 465–67. Carleton to Germain, 20 June 1776, DDAR/XII, 152–53. Sullivan to Washington, 24 June 1776, WP/RWS/5, 92–93. Ibid., 2 July 1776, WP/RWS/5, 186–87.

41 Schuyler to Washington, 12 July 1776, WP/RWS/5, 286–88, 92–93.

42 Washington to Hancock, 8 August 1776, WP/RWS/5, 625–28.

43 New York Convention to Washington, 9 August 1776, WP/RWS/5, 652–54.

44 H.C.B. Rogers, *The British Army of the Eighteenth Century* (London, 1977), 66–81.

45 Washington to Hancock, 17 July 1776, WP/RWS/5, 356.

46 General Orders, 1 August 1776, WP/RWS/5, 534.

47 General Orders, 9 July 1776, , WP/RWS/5, 245–47.

48 General Orders, 21 July 1776. WP/RWS/5, 411–12.

49 Howe to Germain, 7 June 1776, DDAR/XII, 145–47.

50 Howe to Germain, 7 July 1776, DDAR/XII, 157–59.

51 Howe to Shuldham, 7 July 76, Sandwich/1, 143. Shuldham to Howe, 11 July 1776, Sandwich/1, 144–45. Howe to Germain, 6 August 1776, DDAR/XII, 177–79.

52 Mackesy, *War for America*, 86.

53 Washington to Lund Washington, 19 August 1776, WP/RWS/6, 82–83.

54 Gruber, *Howe Brothers*, 351–65. One early historian of this view was the Loyalist, Charles Stedman, *The History of the Origin, Progress, and Termination of the American* War (London, 1794), 198–99.

55 Howe to Germain, 26 March 1776, HMC, Stopford-Sackville, II, 25–26.

56 Quoted in David Syrett, *Admiral Lord Howe: A Biography* (Annapolis, MD, 2006), 42.

57 Mackesy, *War for America*, 24.

58 Syrett, *Howe*, 51.

59 Washington to Hancock, 14 July 1776, WP/RWS/5, 304–7. Peace Commissioners to Germain, 11 August 1776, DDAR/XII, 182–83.

60 Quoted in Syrett, *Howe*, 52.

61 Edward G. Lengel, *General George Washington: A Military Life* (New York, 2005), 141–45

62 Howe to Germain, 3 September 1776, DDAR/XII, 216–18.

63 Washington to Hancock, 31 August 1776, WP/RWS/6, 117–18.

64 Quoted in Conway, *American Independence*, 217.

65 Howe to Germain, 3 September 1776, DDAR/XII, 216–18.

66 Washington to Abraham Yates, 30 August 1776, WP/RWS/6, 170–71.

67 Washington to Hancock, 2 September 1776, WP/RWS/6, 199–200.

68 Hancock to Washington, 3 September 1776, WP/RWS/6, 207.

69 Washington to Hancock, 8 September 1776, WP/RWS/6, 248–52.

70 Washington to Hancock, 11 September 1776, WP/RWS/6, 280–81.

71 Council of War, 12 September 1776, WP/RWS/6, 288–89.

72 Viscount Howe to Germain, 20 September 1776, DDAR/XII, 225–27.

73 Washington to Hancock, 16 September 1776, WP/RWS/6, 315.

74 Proceedings of the Army at New York, September 1776, Sandwich/1, 156–59.

75 Washington to Hancock, 18 September 1776, WP/RWS/6, 331.

76 Washington to Hancock, 25 September 1776, WP/RWS/6, 394–400.

77 Ibid., 398–400.

78 General Orders, 19 September 1776, WP/RWS/6, 340–41.

79 Hancock to Washington, 24 September 1776, WP/RWS/6, 388–90.

80 Washington to Hancock, 4 October 1776, WP/RWS/6, 463–66.

81 Howe to Germain, 25 September 1776, DDAR/XII, 232.

82 Washington to Lund Washington, 30 September 1776, WP/RWS/6, 441.

83 Council of War, 16 October 1776, WP/RWS/6, 564–65.

84 Harrison to Hancock, 29 October 1776, WP/RWS/7, 49. Washington to Hancock, 6 November 1776, WP/RWS/7, 96. Howe to Germain, 30 November 1776, DDAR/XII, 258–64.

85 Washington to Greene, 7 November 1776, WP/RWS/7, 107.

86 Council of War, 6 November 1776, WP/RWS/7, 92. Washington to Hancock, 6 November 1776, WP/RWS/7, 96. See also Washington to Lee, 10 November 1776, WP/RWS/7, 113–15.

87 Washington to Hancock, 9 October 1776, WP/RWS/6, 507.

88 Washington to Augustine Washington, 19 November 1776, WP/RWS/7, 103–4.

89 Washington to Greene, 8 November 1776, WP/RWS/7, 115–16.

90 Greene to Washington, 9 November 1776, WP/RWS/7, 119–20.

91 Howe to Germain, 30 November 1776, DDAR/XII, 261–63.

92 Quoted in Wallace, *Appeal to Arms*, 122.

93 Arnold to Washington, 6 November 1776, WP/RWS/7, 93.

94 Carleton to Germain, 28 September 1776, DDAR/XII, 232–34.

95 Carleton to Germain, 14 October 1776, DDAR/XII, 237. Captain Charles Douglas to Philip Stephens, 21 October 1776, DDAR/XII, 237.

96 Mackesy, *War for America*, 96.

97 Washington to Hancock, 21 November 1776, WP/RWS/7, 182–83.

98 Washington to Lee, 21 November 1776, WP/RWS/7, 193–94.

99 Lee to Washington, 30 November 1776, WP/RWS/7, 235. The issue of Lee's insubordination is discussed by John W. Shy, "Charles Lee: The Soldier as Radical", in George Nathan Billias, ed., *George Washington's Generals and Opponents: Their Exploits and Leadership* (New York, 1994), 22–48.

100 Washington to Hancock, 30 November 1776, WP/RWS/7, 232–33. Ibid., 1 December 1776, 243–44.

101 Howe to Germain, 20 December 1776, DDAR/XII, 266–68.

102 Washington to Brigadier Maxwell, 8 December 1776, WP/RWS/7, 278–79.

103 Howe to Germain, 20 December 1776, DDAR/XII, 266–68.

104 Peace Commissioners, 30 November 1776, DDAR/XII, 257.

105 Peace Commissioners, 22 December 1776, DDAR/XII, 274–75. Gruber, *Howe Brothers*, 146–47.

106 Viscount Howe to Parker, 22 December 1776, DDAR/XII, 271–72.

107 *Clinton's Narrative*, CAR, 57–58.

108 Washington to Lee, 10 December 1776, WP/RWS/7, 288–89.

109 Washington to Samuel Washington, 18 December 1776, WP/RWS/7, 369–71.

110 Washington to Trumbull, 21 December 1776, WP/RWS/7, 406–8.

111 Washington to Lund Washington, 17 December 1776, WP/RWS/7, 291.

112 Pennsylvania Council of Safety to Washington, 17 December 1776, WP/RWS/7, 363–64.

113 Quoted in Christopher Ward, *The War of the Revolution*, John R., Alden, ed. (New York, 1952), I, 287.

114 Reed to Washington, 22 December 1776, WP/RWS/7, 414–16.

115 Washington to Hancock, 27 December 1776, WP/RWS/7, 454–56. For a full account see David Hackett Fischer, *Washington's Crossing* (New York, 2004).

116 Hancock to Washington, 27 December 1776, WP/RWS/7, 461–62.

117 Cadwalader to Washington, 27 December 1776, WP/RWS/7, 451–52.

118 Washington to Heath, 28 December 1776, WP/RWS/7, 468.

119 Washington to Morris, 31 December 1776, WP/RWS/7, 497.

120 Franklin and Mary Wickwire, *Cornwallis and the War of Independence* (London, 1971), 95. Cornwallis was keen on fox hunting, ibid., 30.

121 Howe to Germain, 5 January 1777, New York, DDAR/XIV, 27–28.

122 Washington to Hancock, 5 January 1776, WP/RWS/7, 519–23.

123 Howe to Germain, 20 January 1777, DDAR/XIV, 33.

124 Proclamation Concerning Persons Swearing British Allegiance, 25 January 1777, WP/RWS/8, 154–55.

125 Arthur Bowler, *Logistics and the Failure of the British Army in America, 1775–1783* (Princeton, 1975), 47–48. Syrett, *Shipping*, 123–24.

CHAPTER 4

The unpredictable fortunes of war, 1777

The British plan a new offensive

The setback in New Jersey was largely ignored in London when the ministry met to consider the situation. They continued to assume that the colonies would return to their allegiance once their evil leaders had been removed. However, they realized that the campaign of 1776 had not been entirely successful. A further effort therefore would be needed to complete the collapse of Congress and restore royal authority. As in 1776, Germain believed the generals should decide how these objectives were to be achieved.

Howe's initial proposal was that Clinton should first take Providence with 10,000 men before advancing on Boston. A second army of 10,000 men under Howe would simultaneously move up the Hudson River to isolate New England, while 8,000 troops kept Washington in check in east New Jersey. Once New England had been subdued, Howe would then attack Philadelphia, after which an advance might be possible into Virginia, leaving the two Carolinas and Georgia to be reduced the following winter. This was an ambitious program, though fully consistent with Howe's desire "to finish the war in one year by an extensive and vigorous exertion of His Majesty's arms." The scheme, however, would require an additional 15,000 men. If recruiting methods in Britain were insufficient to meet these demands, Howe suggested further approaches to Russia and the German principalities for the hiring of troops.[1]

Howe composed these thoughts before Washington's flight across the Delaware. The speed of the British advance and the readiness of the population to return to their allegiance led him to alter his views. In a second dispatch on 20 December 1776, he told Germain that an advance across the Delaware would prove most decisive in bringing the rebellion to an end. Philadelphia was the rebel capital, which Washington was bound to protect, thus forcing him to fight a pitched battle. The capture of the city also promised to increase support for the crown. The decision, however, had serious implications for the other parts of Howe's previous plan. Howe would need a minimum of 10,000 men for this operation, leaving just 9,000 for other services, unless his request for an additional 15,000 men was granted. The simultaneous invasion of New England, therefore, would have to wait, since 2,000 men would be needed to garrison Rhode Island and another 4,000 at New York. This left just 3,000 men to "act defensively upon the lower part of Hudson's River . . . to facilitate in some degree the approach of the army from Canada." Quite what the Canadian army would do on its arrival at Albany Howe did not say, except that its "subsequent operations . . . will depend on the state of things at the time."[2]

As Howe suspected, his plea for 15,000 men was not well received in London when his first letter arrived in early January 1777. The total strength of the army for the coming year was not expected to exceed 60,000 men when the estimates were presented to Parliament.[3] The best that Germain could promise was another 6,000 German troops, plus 1,800 recruits for the British regiments. If further manpower was required Howe should raise more provincials. In any case Germain believed that Howe would still have a field army of 35,000 troops, more than enough for the tasks outlined in his letter of 30 November 1776, especially in view of the "greatly weakened and depressed" state of the enemy.[4]

While dealing with Howe's arrangements, Germain was simultaneously completing the details regarding the army in Canada. As the most senior officer in North America, Carleton was the obvious choice for the command. However, Germain disliked Carleton personally, having already made one attempt to limit his military responsibilities.[5] Any inducement to restore that authority was removed by Germain's conviction that Carleton had caused the disappointing end to the 1776 campaign because of his failure to reach Albany. He was encouraged in these views by Burgoyne. Impatient of delay and clearly believing he could do better, Burgoyne had returned to England late in 1776 to seek the command for himself. He probably knew that Germain detested Carleton and that Howe was jealous of Carleton's seniority which would make him overall commander should there be a junction of the two armies. It was accordingly easy for Burgoyne to fan the flames about Carleton's undue caution, thus providing Germain with an excuse to relieve him of his responsibilities.[6] During the forthcoming campaign Carleton was to devote himself to his duties as governor, leaving the conduct of military operations to Burgoyne.[7]

Burgoyne was not without ability. His troops called him "gentleman Johnny," because of his impeccable manners and even-handed discipline. He had also shown both organizational and tactical ability in the Seven Years War while serving in Portugal.[8] Burgoyne now submitted a paper dated 18 February 1777, containing his ideas for the deployment of the forces in Canada. First the main army of 11,000 men should sail across Lake Champlain to Ticonderoga, while a diversionary force of Indians and Loyalists under Colonel St Leger advanced down the Mohawk Valley to Fort Stanwix. Once at Ticonderoga, the main army would then have two options. If the "only object of the Canadian army was to effect a junction with Howe" it should take "immediate possession of Lake George ... as the most expeditious and most commodious route to Albany." From here it could either open a communication with New York or remain on the Hudson River, while Howe acted "with his whole force to the southward."

But if a simple union at Albany was not intended, Burgoyne's second option was for the Northern army to march eastwards from Ticonderoga to join Clinton in southern New England. "Should the junction between the Canada army and Rhode Island armies be effected upon the Connecticut [River], it is not too sanguine an expectation that all the New England provinces will be reduced."[9] However, if the ministry disliked both proposals, Burgoyne could sail from Quebec to New York for a joint operation with Howe. Nevertheless, he doubted that "any expedition from the sea can be so formidable to the enemy, or so effectual to close the war, as an invasion from Canada by [way of] Ticonderoga."[10]

In making his proposals Burgoyne may have been inspired by the example of Wolfe, who had enjoyed a similar independent command in 1759 at Quebec. However, Burgoyne's scheme was different in one key respect. Wolfe could call on the Royal Navy to evacuate his force should a siege prove too difficult. Burgoyne would have no such luxury in the forests and lakes of upper New York. He would be on his own, unless either Howe or the Loyalists came to his aid in unprecedented numbers. Even when he reached the Hudson there was no certainty that the Royal Navy could support him. The Patriots had several forts through the Highlands with a boom across the Hudson to prevent access and no attempt had yet been made to assess the strength of these obstacles. Nevertheless the dangers of his isolation and navigational difficulties on the Hudson were overlooked. Amherst, the conqueror of Canada in 1760, who might have sounded a cautionary note, was out of favor with George III.[11] The scene was thus set for what was to prove a major blow to the British hopes of restoring their empire in North America.

Five days after receiving Burgoyne's "Thoughts," Howe's second dispatch of 20 December arrived with his plan for concentrating on Philadelphia rather than the Hudson River. This should have warned Germain that the campaign was losing cohesion. But instead of ordering Howe to focus on his first scheme for advancing up the Hudson, he merely commented in his reply of 3 March 1777 that "the King entirely approves of your proposed deviation from the plan which you formerly suggested." Germain's single criticism of Howe's new proposals was the lack of any provision for a "warm diversion upon the coasts of the Massachusetts Bay and New Hampshire" to divert resources from the Continental army.[12]

Since Howe ruled out the possibility of any offensive from Rhode Island, Burgoyne's second proposal for a thrust towards the Connecticut River was disregarded. Germain instead accepted his first suggestion for an advance by 8,000 regulars, 2,000 Canadians, and 1,000 Indians by way of Ticonderoga to Albany, which he believed would help sever New England from the middle colonies. Burgoyne's orders, accordingly, were "to pass Lake Champlain and from thence by the most vigorous exertion of the force under his command to proceed with all expedition to Albany" where he was to "put himself under the command of Sir William Howe." St Leger was similarly "to proceed... down the Mohawk River" for a union at Albany. But until their arrival there, both commanders were to "act as exigencies may require," adopting the best measures "for making an impression on the rebels and in bringing them to obedience." But "they must never lose view of their intended junctions with Sir William Howe as their principal objects."[13]

Germain's emphasis to Burgoyne and Carleton about the need for a junction at Albany is extraordinary, given his failure to mention this essential point in his orders to Howe of 3 March 1777. He did subsequently send Howe a copy of Carleton's instructions regarding Burgoyne's deployment but ignored the subject thereafter in several succeeding letters. Not until 18 May did he raise the topic again after receiving a subsequent letter from Howe dated 2 April further spelling out his plans. Then he merely acknowledged Howe's decision to go to Philadelphia, adding the caveat that "whatever you meditate it will be executed in time for you to cooperate with the army ordered to proceed from Canada"[14] Germain seemingly anticipated that Howe would defeat Washington and capture Philadelphia before the end of June, allowing him to return to New York for an advance up the Hudson. Apart from Germain's obvious lack of geographical knowledge, his failure to lay down a clear sequence for the coordination of the two armies more than anything explains the debacle that followed.[15]

Meanwhile Washington was preparing for another defensive campaign, since without help from Europe, he was powerless to stop the British from continuing their attempts to re-establish their authority. However, in one respect a defensive war suited Washington. Except for the British enclaves in New York, Rhode Island, and New Jersey, the Patriots controlled all 13 states and enjoyed *de facto* if not *de jure* independence. The longer this situation continued, the greater their legitimacy among the population. Hence they merely had to wait in positions of their choosing for the British to attack, which they must do if their cause was to succeed. In the interim, if Washington could deny the British forage for their horses, food for their troops, and recruits for their dwindling ranks, he might yet force them from the continent without the need for a battle, given their long supply line across the Atlantic.[16] The result, as one British officer ruefully noted, was a constant struggle for forage, which "kept the army the whole winter in perpetual harassment" and had cost "more men than the last campaign."[17]

Otherwise Washington's energies were devoted to creating the new Continental army which Congress had authorized in September 1776. The problem was that Congress lacked the money to make good its promises, not being able to support its credit through taxation. Everything therefore depended on the states. By way of encouragement, Washington pointed out that if the latter completed their enlistments he would not have to call on their militia so often, which must surely be a blessing for their farmers and artisans.[18] Nevertheless progress was slow, with the new recruits barely matching losses through desertion. A further complication was the need to inoculate the newly raised troops against smallpox, a process that required quarantining for several weeks.[19] By the middle of March 1777 Washington had just 3,500 men at Morristown, of which 1,000 were militia whose enlistments were about to expire.[20] Indeed for two months he faced the possibility of having no army at all. Despite this, Howe remained inactive, blaming deep snow and poor roads for his failure to venture into New Jersey.[21] Apart from foraging excursions, the only operation undertaken by Howe before June was an amphibious raid on the town of Danbury in Connecticut to seize some Continental supplies.[22] Washington could only ascribe this inactivity to a lack of wagons and horses. Whatever the cause, Howe's passivity was certainly fortunate for the Patriot cause.[23]

Nevertheless, the situation was deeply disappointing to Washington since he was convinced that with a properly paid and disciplined army he could drive the British out of New Jersey and perhaps New York too.[24]

The chances to prepare such an army remained slim, given the readiness of the states to recruit their own militias rather than the ranks of the Continental army. As Washington told the governor of Massachusetts, this amounted to a policy of weakening "the hands of the continent under the mistaken idea of strengthening your own." The governor should reflect that with only "a small Continental army in the field," it would be impossible "to watch the motions of the enemy and oppose them where they may in reality direct their operations."[25]

In these circumstances, Washington had to request once again the services of the militia, since by the middle of May 1777 he still had a mere 8,188 men at Morristown, organized into five divisions or ten brigades. The caliber of the troops also left much to be desired.[26] However, their equipment was beginning to improve, following the arrival of two French ships in March 1777 with 23,000 muskets and bayonets, the first substantial shipments by Hortalez and Company. A third vessel, the *Amphitrite*, appeared soon afterwards loaded with brass field guns, muskets, flints, and clothing.[27] The day of the fowling piece as a weapon of war for the Patriots was finally over.

The *Amphitrite* also brought a number of French officers. Most had come on the recommendation of Silas Deane in Paris, who had little knowledge about the newcomers' military credentials or their lack of English. He also overlooked the fact that the issue of commissions to such persons caused resentment among the existing officers. The tension was most acute in the artillery. But Washington could do little other than ask Congress to act circumspectly, limiting appointments to below that of lieutenant, unless the applicants could speak English.[28]

Howe goes to Philadelphia

Howe initially intended to go to Philadelphia by marching through New Jersey while a subsidiary force sailed up the Delaware.[29] However, after hearing that he would not be substantially reinforced, he resolved to withdraw his garrisons from New Jersey and sail with his entire army to Philadelphia via the Delaware River. This would obviate the need for a line of posts to protect his communication with New York. It would also mean that he would not have to cross the Delaware, which had caused such difficulty the previous December. As before, he did not consider the effect of abandoning the remaining posts in New Jersey at Newark and Elizabethtown, even though he now had over 2,500 Loyalists serving in provincial units.

Howe informed Germain of his decision to go by sea on 2 April 1777. Curiously he made no reference about its consequences for the army advancing from Canada.[30] However, in a letter to Carleton three days later, he made it clear that he knew about Burgoyne's scheme but could do little to help, since Howe had insufficient men "to detach a corps in the beginning of the campaign to act up the Hudson's River, consistent with the operations already determined on." Cooperation at such a distance would in any case be difficult, since Howe would "probably be in Pennsylvania when that corps is ready to advance." Burgoyne must therefore rely entirely on his own resources and judgment as to what was "most conducive to the advancement of His Majesty's service." The best that Howe could do was "to have a corps upon the lower part of Hudson's River sufficient to open the communication for shipping through the Highlands ... which corps may afterwards act in favor of the northern army." But Howe did not doubt that once in possession of Albany, Burgoyne would find "the friends of government in that part of the country so numerous and so ready to give every aid and assistance" that it should "prove no difficult task to reduce the more rebellious parts of the province."[31]

Having absolved himself of any obligation to help Burgoyne, Howe completed his own campaign preparations, following a final delivery of camp equipage and recruits for the regiments. By early June everything was ready. Nevertheless, Howe delayed the evacuation of New Jersey. One reason was his need to secure more forage in case the victualling fleet from Ireland was delayed.[32] But he also wanted to fight a decisive battle "where the enemy's principal strength still remains."[33] He still believed that the destruction of Washington's army was the surest means of ending the rebellion. Washington by this time had occupied a new camp at Middlebrook, eight miles west of Brunswick. From here he could observe any advance by Howe on Philadelphia or the Hudson River for a junction with Burgoyne. His new position, like that at Morristown, constituted "a strong piece of ground" and was well protected by hills and rivers.[34]

On 13 June 1777 Howe accordingly set off down the road to Philadelphia, hoping to lure Washington from his fastness at Middlebrook. Washington, however, refused to engage. He would only fight on his own terms, even if that meant giving up Philadelphia, for as he told Arnold on 17 June, "while we have a respectable force in the field, every acquisition of territory they may make will be precarious and perhaps burthensome."[35] He said the same to Reed, pointing out that Howe's possession of territory increased the chances of a strategic error. People were wrong to think that fighting was the only way to conduct a war. The essential thing was to keep the "one great end in view," namely the preservation of the army. In the meantime his network of spies and reconnaissance by Morgan's riflemen kept him well informed of the British maneuvers. Washington was also pleased at the support given by the New Jersey militia, whose readiness to participate was so different from the previous year. This must have given Howe "a greater shock... than any event which had happened in the course of this dispute."[36]

The failure to engage Washington finally led Howe at the end of June to return to "the principal objects of the campaign." But while awaiting transportation at Amboy, he heard that Washington was advancing towards him. Howe immediately assembled an elite force of troops on 26 June, hoping to outflank the Patriot army before it could regain its entrenchments at Middlebrook. The stratagem once again proved unsuccessful, though one of Washington's divisions lost a few cannon before regaining the heights.[37] Howe then ferried his army over to Staten Island on 30 June where the main embarkation was to take place. Aides noted that he seemed "a good deal disappointed" at not being able to catch his foe.[38]

Shortly after this, Clinton returned from leave in England carrying Germain's letter of 18 May, "trusting" that Howe would be ready to cooperate with the army from Canada on the completion of his own operations.[39] Clearly this would not now be possible if Howe went to Philadelphia, given the lateness of the season. Nevertheless, he determined to persevere with his existing scheme, offering by way of justification that Burgoyne would not make the rendezvous in time, since he was likely to "find full Employment for his Army against that of the Rebels opposed to him." Howe then launched into a tirade about the difficulties facing him. The war was "now upon a different scale with respect to the increased powers and strength of the enemy than it was last campaign." Their officers were "much better and the addition of several from the French service and a very respectable train of artillery" had made them a formidable adversary. Only substantial reinforcements could achieve "the reduction of the northern provinces." Indeed "three armies should be employed to make" that conquest "effectual."[40] He was already making excuses in case of any setback.

Any doubts Howe had about proceeding to Philadelphia were removed a few days later with the news that Burgoyne had successfully advanced down Lake Champlain to Ticonderoga. This convinced him that the northern army could handle the situation, even if Washington marched northwards against Burgoyne. The "strength of General Burgoyne's army is such as to leave me no room to dread the event."[41] It would therefore be safe for him to set out for Philadelphia. Germain was about to reap the fruits of allowing his generals so much latitude instead of giving them precise instructions.

Nevertheless, for Washington, Howe's intentions were utterly baffling as 18,000 troops began embarking on 150 transports for an unknown destination. They might be going up the Hudson River to meet Burgoyne. Alternatively the embarkation could be a ruse to draw Washington away from Philadelphia. Equally it might be the prelude to an attack on New England. Another possible objective was Charleston. Hence, Washington determined to remain in New Jersey until Howe committed himself. At Middlebrook he could go northwards to meet Burgoyne, eastwards to help New England; or southwards to defend Philadelphia while keeping an eye on New York.[42] It was a good example both of Washington's strategic insight and tactical acumen.

As we have seen, Howe expected to sail to Philadelphia via the Delaware River rather than the Chesapeake, since it was closer to New York in case it was necessary to reinforce the troops on the Hudson. However, on arriving at the mouth of the Delaware Howe became worried that Washington might have fortified the likely landing sites at Wilmington and Newcastle. He was also discouraged by the narrowness of the channel and the presence of floating batteries and other obstacles. Accordingly, he decided to approach Philadelphia via the Chesapeake as the best route for his amphibious force. The journey in consequence took the flotilla another four weeks to reach its preliminary objective, the Elk River at the top of Chesapeake Bay.[43] This meant that Howe was only starting his campaign in the last week of August.

There was a further penalty for taking this route. After six weeks at sea during the hottest period of the year, his men required time to recuperate. Even more distressed were the army's horses. On setting out Howe had ordered just three weeks' forage. Not surprisingly most of the horses were dead or unusable, depriving Howe not only of his cavalry but his supply train as well. In these circumstances he had to seek whatever he could from the local population. Until now supplies had been obtainable by cash or a promissory note redeemable at the office of the Commissary or Quarter Master General. However, this time force proved necessary, given "the prevailing disposition of the inhabitants." Many had "taken up arms and by far the greater number deserted their dwellings, driving off at the same time their stock of cattle and horses" to prevent them falling into British hands.[44] Not that the practices of the Patriot army were much better, as Washington reminded his men in yet another appeal to stop looting. "We complain of the cruelty and barbarity of our enemy," but their own depredations were equally vile. "Why had they taken up arms if it was not to protect the property of their countrymen?"[45]

Howe's delay at the Head of Elk meant that Washington had sufficient time to reach Wilmington on the east bank of the Brandywine River, where he began entrenching his army. John Adams noted that the Continental troops had an irregular step on passing through Philadelphia, not having "quite the appearance of soldiers."[46] Adams had no experience of military life other than watching redcoats drilling on Boston Common. But his observations accurately reflected the fact that Washington's army still lacked the discipline and self-confidence of a truly professional army. Despite this, Washington determined to attempt another Bunker Hill style engagement, sensing that Congress expected a more aggressive style of generalship.[47]

Washington's determination to contest the British advance meant that Howe had another opportunity of doing what he had failed to achieve since arriving in America. The resources of the two combatants heavily favored the British, who numbered 16,500 men to just 11,000 on the Patriot side. Washington's position, however, offered a number of advantages. The Brandywine was a considerable stream which could be crossed only at certain places. At Chad's ford Washington's army was astride the road to Philadelphia, allowing it to fall back towards the city should that be necessary. However, a static defense meant that the initiative would lie with Howe, increasing the danger of his being outflanked, as at Brooklyn Heights. Washington was aware of the danger, spending every day surveying the roads. He also had a corps of light troops "constantly near the enemy ... to give them every annoyance."[48] Nevertheless Washington once more failed to assess the situation with regard to the fords upstream.[49]

Howe quickly seized his chance. While the Hessian forces under General Knyphausen threatened Washington's front, Howe and Cornwallis crossed the river a few miles above at Jeffries Ford, which lay unguarded except for a few militia. The size of the British thrust was then misreported, allowing Howe to approach Washington's position before the full gravity of the situation was revealed.[50] The right wing of the army under Sullivan in consequence had to turn 90 degrees to face this unexpected threat. At this point the battle became general as Knyphausen attacked Washington's center from the other side of the Brandywine while Howe and Cornwallis closed on the Patriot right. The superior discipline and numbers of the British and Germans were not to be denied.[51] Nevertheless the victory was not decisive since the Patriots still managed to retreat, helped by a courageous stand by Greene's division. Among those wounded was the young Marquis De Lafayette, who had recently come to America to fight for the cause of liberty.[52] Howe now paid another penalty for approaching Philadelphia by sea, namely the loss of his cavalry, which prevented a more vigorous pursuit. However, he blamed nightfall for any loss of momentum, telling Germain that "the enemy's army escaped a total overthrow" for want of "an hour's more daylight."[53] The Patriots then staged a further rally a few miles back, after which Washington made for Chester before crossing to comparative safety over the Schuylkill River.[54] Once again a complete victory had eluded Sir William Howe.

For the next two weeks Howe and Washington played a game of cat and mouse as Washington sought to protect Philadelphia without hazarding a battle unless on ground of his choosing. Congress again invested him with special powers so "that the army may be more effectually supplied with provisions and other necessaries."[55] In the meantime he did everything possible to harass Howe's flanks and rear. But the danger of dividing his forces was soon demonstrated when Anthony Wayne's Pennsylvania brigade was surprised by a detachment under Lord Grey, who gave a classic demonstration of the bayonet's use in close-quarter fighting. To ensure silence, the British commander ordered his troops to rely solely on their bayonets. This allowed total surprise, resulting in the killing or capture of 200 Americans on the night of 20 September without a shot being fired in what came to be called the "Paoli Tavern Massacre."[56] Howe next moved up the Schuylkill River, seemingly threatening Washington's supplies at Reading. It proved a ruse, for during the night Howe doubled back, crossing the Schuylkill unopposed. This placed him between Washington and Philadelphia, which Cornwallis entered on 26 September 1777.[57]

Although a considerable number of inhabitants welcomed the British, few came forward to receive the latest pardon or enlist in the provincial units. Moreover the British began to realize that the capture of Philadelphia was not equivalent to seizing London or Paris, since it was merely the capital of a province. Congress itself had removed to the sparser comfort of Lancaster eight days earlier where it continued to function as before. It was another illustration of the inability of the British to grasp the nature of the conflict in which they were engaged. Moreover the occupation of Philadelphia was far from secure, since the Patriots still held Fort Mifflin and Fort Mercer below the city, thus preventing the delivery of supplies via the Delaware River. Washington quickly exploited the situation by strengthening the garrisons while the militia harried the British lines of communication.[58] Howe in consequence had to deploy a considerable force to reduce the Delaware forts while maintaining a respectable garrison in the city. As a result he had barely 9,000 men in his main camp at Germantown, which he carelessly failed to entrench.[59]

These developments led Washington to believe that Howe had presented him with another opportunity for a battle on favorable terms. He was encouraged in his optimism by the news that Burgoyne's invasion of New York had stalled.[60] Washington's plan was to march during the night of 3 October in four columns so that his troops converged on the British line at daylight. Initially all went well, since the Patriot approach was aided by fog. Unfortunately this made it difficult to know where each unit was located, which led to two brigades firing on each other. More time was lost attempting to reduce a British strongpoint at Chew House. This allowed Howe to launch a counter-attack which forced the Patriots back, though still in order. Washington, like many commanders following a setback, blamed first the conditions and then his men for giving way, rather than admitting that his plan had been too complex.[61] But as Wayne pointed out, the action revealed that the British could be beaten in close combat. Next time the result would be different.[62]

For Howe it had been a lucky escape and he now took the precaution of fortifying the city with his troops inside. However, the army and fleet still had to open the navigation of the Delaware River, for as Howe's commissary Daniel Weir commented, "The whole country around us is possessed by the enemy." It was difficult even to secure fresh provisions for the hospitals, since it was impossible to "go an hundred yards beyond our lines without a large escort."[63] An assault on Forts Mifflin and Mercer on 23 October was beaten back with the loss of 400 men and a 64-gun battleship. Not until the middle of November was the task completed.[64] Then having made one further attempt to engage Washington to the northwest of Philadelphia, Howe ordered his army into winter quarters, "being unwilling to expose the troops longer to the weather in this inclement season".[65]

For Washington, the events at Germantown had been another blow to his hopes of defeating the British. It seemed that victory had again been snatched from him due to fog and poor discipline. However, he could take comfort from the rumors of a success in the north against Burgoyne. The year might still end brightly for the Patriot cause.

Burgoyne meets his match: Saratoga

Initially Burgoyne's plan to invade New York via Lake Champlain had gone relatively well, following his return to Canada in May 1777. Awaiting him at Quebec was a force of 3,700 British regulars, 3,000 Brunswick Germans under Baron von Riedesel, 650 Canadians and Tories, and 400 Indians from the seven St Lawrence nations.[66] This was substantially fewer than what he had requested, but he made no complaint, such was his confidence. Before starting, Burgoyne issued a proclamation that the inhabitants should befriend his troops or face the wrath of the Indians, unaware that such a threat was likely to be counter-productive. He also issued a fatuous appeal to the Indians not to harm civilians. As one observer suggested, this was equivalent to releasing lions from the King's menagerie on the understanding that they would not harm the other animals.[67]

Nevertheless his preliminary preparations were remarkably smooth, being ably assisted by Carleton, despite the latter's grievance at being deprived of the command. After attending to St Leger's requirements, Burgoyne was able to set off down Lake Champlain on 20 June to face his first test, the fortress of Ticonderoga, where the Patriot Northern Army under General St Clair was based.[68] On paper St Clair had 5,000 men but in reality his numbers did not exceed 3,000, because of desertion and the expiry of enlistments. The fort itself was in a poor state and had a long outer defense line. There was another problem too. Ticonderoga was overlooked by three hills: Mount Defiance, Mount Hope, and Mount Independence. Only the latter two had been fortified, because of the lack of manpower, though Mount Defiance was considered too steep for placing artillery. It proved a mistake since Burgoyne's engineers quickly established a battery on 5 July, which allowed him to command both the fort and the approaches by lake. St Clair immediately recognized that his position was untenable. On 6 July he ordered a retreat to Skenesborough, at the southern end of Lake Champlain.[69]

This was an encouraging preliminary success for Burgoyne, the only setback being Carleton's refusal to garrison Ticonderoga, because this contravened Germain's order to restrict his responsibilities to the province of Canada.[70] Burgoyne in consequence had to leave 900 of his own men behind, a serious weakening of his force. Nevertheless for the moment the Patriots were in flight and the British in hot pursuit. Burgoyne's advanced guard under General Simon Fraser eventually caught St Claire's rearguard at the foot of Lake Champlain near the infant settlement of Hubbardton. The result was a vicious wood fight on 7 July 1777 in which Fraser eventually had the upper hand, though only after he was joined by Riedesel from the other side of the lake.[71] Nevertheless the majority of St Claire's force escaped along Wood Creek to Fort Edward astride the Hudson River. Here they were joined by Schuyler with his reserve of just 700 men.

The lack of troops was partly because Washington was still uncertain about Howe's intentions, fearing a British advance up the Hudson River against the Highland forts.[72] But Schuyler was also weakened by the lack of militia from New England, where he was suspected of being a British sympathizer. He decided accordingly to abandon both Fort Edward and Fort George to concentrate his forces at a more defensible site, first near Saratoga and then at Stillwater. Simultaneously he appealed to Washington for more help.[73]

Washington responded this time with several initiatives. First he asked Hancock to place Arnold in charge of the New Englanders serving with Schuyler, being an officer from the region "in whom the militia will repose great confidence."[74] Next he appealed to the militias of western Massachusetts and New Hampshire, pointing out that they faced an enemy "who not content with hiring mercenaries to lay waste your country, have now brought Savages with the avowed and express intent of adding murder to the desolation."[75] To make their contribution more effective he simultaneously asked Benjamin Lincoln to mobilize the militia on the western border of New Hampshire from where they could threaten Burgoyne's flank. Finally he agreed to the dispatch of a brigade from the Highlands to join Schuyler.[76]

Burgoyne meanwhile was pondering his next step. Prudence suggested he return to Ticonderoga and haul his boats over to Lake George, since there was a well established road from Fort George, at the other end of that lake, to Fort Edward on the Hudson River. However, Burgoyne was reluctant to do this, since it would appear like a retreat. On the other hand the difficulties already encountered in the pursuit of the Patriots could not be ignored. He decided accordingly to continue on his present course along Wood Creek, while making every effort "at Ticonderoga to get gunboats, bateaxu and provision vessels into Lake George." This could then become the main supply route for the army to Fort Edward where "a junction of the whole" could be effected.[77]

The advance down Wood Creek proved difficult, since St Clair had destroyed all the bridges and felled trees across the path. The result was not only the loss of three weeks but the arrival of the army on 6 August at Fort Edward in an exhausted state, having expended much of its supplies and lost most of its draft animals. Moreover, the Patriots had driven off all the inhabitants and their cattle, though Burgoyne interpreted this as "an act of desperation and folly" rather than a sensible act of military necessity. One benefit from his advance via Wood Creek was that the Patriots had abandoned Fort George and burnt their vessels, thus opening the way for the rest of his artillery and supplies by that route. This was just as well since Burgoyne had received intelligence that the enemy was gathering at Saratoga to give battle.[78]

A few days later Burgoyne received a copy of Howe's letter to Germain of 16 July 1777 confirming that he was going to Philadelphia, though with the promise that he would leave additional troops at New York in case Washington advanced up the Hudson River against him.[79] This information, however, did not seemingly trouble Burgoyne since he made no reference to it in his reply on 6 August 1777. He merely informed Howe that he was still bringing up his artillery, provisions, and bateaux from Lake George for use on the Hudson. He was therefore unlikely to reach Albany before 22 August.[80]

Burgoyne accordingly resumed his advance on Albany a few days later, encouraged by news that St Leger had reached Fort Stanwix. But he quickly realized that even the short distance to Saratoga was placing an intolerable strain on his supply chain, given his lack of horses and need to protect every convoy. This led him to consider an alternative way of providing for his army by sending a detachment to the Connecticut River where he believed there were copious supplies of cattle and carriage. If true, it would allow him to dispense with the ever-lengthening supply chain with Lake George.[81]

Burgoyne's second reason for this foray was to secure horses for Riedesel's dragoons, who had arrived in Canada without their mounts. The dragoons were to be accompanied by some Tories and Indians, the whole amounting to about 800 men under Colonel Friedrich Baum. Burgoyne undoubtedly liked the idea since it dovetailed with his earlier enthusiasm for an advance into Connecticut. He was also confident that there were many Loyalists in the area. Baum's orders were accordingly "to try the affections of the people ... to mount Riedesel's dragoons, to complete Peter's corps [of Loyalists] and to obtain large supplies of cattle, horses and carriages." Baum, who spoke no English, was also to take prisoner anyone acting "under the directions of Congress, whether Civil or military."[82] In the meantime Burgoyne began building a raft bridge across the Hudson River to counter any move by Schuyler's army at Stillwater.[83]

The expedition left on 11 August and quickly ran into trouble. Unknown to Burgoyne, a young woman, Jane McCrea, had recently been brutally scalped by the Indians near Fort Edward, news of which had aroused the New England settlements east of the Hudson River.[84] Baum's entire force was quickly surrounded on 15 August near Bennington by the New Hampshire militia under Brigadier John Stark. The situation was made worse by Baum's inability to tell friend from foe, which led him to welcome Stark's militia as friends. Once the shooting started, the Indians fled, as did the Tories, leaving the dragoons in a desperate fight until their ammunition ran out. A reinforcement of 600 Brunswick troops fared little better. In the event Burgoyne lost 900 men that he could ill afford. He also lost most of his remaining Indians, who were angered by his refusal to let them fight in their own way after the killing of Jane McCrea. For most warriors war had little appeal without the chance to revenge past wrongs, seize plunder, and take captives for adoption or ransom.[85]

Burgoyne now faced a critical decision. His army was still relatively intact and had enough supplies, carriages, and bateaux to return to Lake George. There were good reasons for so doing, as he admitted to Germain on 20 August. St Leger had not yet taken Fort Stanwix and there were few signs that the Loyalists would join him, while the enemy could clearly raise 4,000 militia from the upper Connecticut River settlements. He also knew that Howe had gone to Philadelphia and that Washington was sending substantial reinforcements to the Northern front. No attempt had yet been made by Clinton to open the route to Albany. All the indications were that Burgoyne's army was in danger of being cut off. He acknowledged "had I a latitude in my orders I should think it my duty to wait in this position . . . where my communication with Lake George would be perfectly secure," until something "happened to assist my movement forward." However, Burgoyne did not believe he had such latitude, since his instructions were "positive to 'force a junction with Sir William Howe.'"[86] Quite why he chose to interpret his orders in this manner is unclear. He had a reputation for being a gambler. It may be that he was also a prisoner of his own bombast. He had proclaimed what he would do to the rebels if they failed to lay down their arms. Halting now would be interpreted as cowardice, undermining his standing in the army.

He accordingly determined to press on for Albany, after he had completed 25 days' provisions and received some additional companies and recruits en route from Lake Champlain. He was aware that once he crossed "the Hudson River and proceed towards Albany all safety of communication ceases" with Lake George. However, he did not consider the crossing as a point of no return, since he told Germain that he would still have "the chance of fighting my way back to Ticonderoga," providing he did not tarry too long. But "should I succeed in forcing my way to Albany and find that country in a state to subsist my army, I shall think no more of retreat but at the worst fortify there and await Sir William Howe's operations."[87]

Burgoyne could have marched to his objective down the eastern side of the Hudson River. However, Albany was on the west bank where the river was wider and its banks more likely to be fortified. Crossing the river at Saratoga would be easier, though he would have to build a new bridge of boats, since his previous raft structure had been swept away. The bridge would then have to be dismantled, since the boats were needed to transport the army's provisions as they marched down the river. As a result Burgoyne was not ready to start his advance until 13 September.

Up to this time Burgoyne's forces had seen little of the Patriot army, which had been weakened by the need to send reinforcements for the relief of Fort Stanwix.[88] Schuyler had in consequence retreated for a second time to the mouth of the Mohawk River. But his days as commander were numbered. The New Englanders had long distrusted Schuyler and his credentials were further tarnished by the loss of Ticonderoga, which many attributed to treachery.[89] News of that debacle now provoked Congress into removing both Schuyler and St Clair in favor of Horatio Gates and Arnold, who both enjoyed the confidence of the New England states.[90]

Gates was another former British army officer who had stayed in America at the end of the previous war and thrown in his lot with the Patriots. Though of an un-soldierly appearance, he had proved an able administrator as Washington's adjutant general. His appointment proved fortunate in that Washington had already reinforced his command with several regiments from the Highland forts. Among the new arrivals was Morgan with 300 Virginia riflemen to provide a "counterpoise to the Indians," being able to "fight them in their own way."[91] By early September Gates had over 7,000 men under his command compared to Burgoyne's 4,500. He now felt strong enough to move back to Stillwater, where Arnold was fortifying some ground overlooking the Hudson River known as Bemis Heights.[92]

News of these movements prompted Burgoyne to resume his advance, sensing that the Patriots were ready to offer him the chance of a decisive battle. His plan on 19 September 1777 was a flanking movement to take some high ground to the left of Gates's army as the prelude to a general assault. Unfortunately Fraser took so long to execute the maneuver that the center and left wing of Burgoyne's army were unable to deploy effectively. Then to the British surprise, Arnold and Morgan sallied forth with the left wing of the Patriot army to engage Fraser among the trees near an isolated homestead called Freeman's farm. Although the British ultimately held the center ground, they did so only at the cost of some 530 men, suffering particularly from Morgan's sharpshooters posted in the trees. Among the casualties was Fraser. Equally disconcerting was the fact that the Patriot entrenchments on Bemis heights were not even tested. The only sour note for the Patriots was an outbreak of acrimony after Arnold accused Gates of not recognizing the contribution of his men. Gates responded by relieving Arnold of his command.[93]

Incredibly, Burgoyne still did not appreciate fully the dangers of his situation. As he explained to Clinton on 27 September, he believed he could maintain his position at Saratoga until mid-October, providing a communication was opened with New York. This was essential because he now realized that he was unlikely to secure sufficient provisions at Albany to subsist him during the winter. Hence if Clinton was uncertain about the navigation of the Hudson, Burgoyne would have to retreat before ice closed the rivers and lakes. Clinton accordingly must tell him categorically "whether he should proceed to Albany or to make good his retreat to Canada."[94]

While awaiting a reply, Burgoyne began fortifying his position to protect his boats with the provisions. However, the longer he waited, the worse his position became. By the end of September Gates had over 11,000 men, all enthused by the battle at Freeman's farm. Large numbers of New England militia were also across the river, threatening the British line of retreat. Nor was this all, for another corps of New England militia had almost recaptured Fort Ticonderoga, simultaneously destroying the shipping at the nearby landing place.[95] As a result the British no longer controlled Lake George and were effectively trapped, unless they could break through the lines on Bemis Heights or were relieved by Clinton in New York.

Burgoyne finally recognized the gravity of his situation only in early October when he decided to make another attempt to breach the Patriot lines. First he sent out a large part of his army on 7 October for a reconnaissance in force. However, they had not gone far when Morgan and Arnold, the latter acting in defiance of Gates, attacked the British column from the front, flank, and rear, forcing Burgoyne to retreat to Saratoga. His discomfiture was indicated by the abandonment of the sick and the loss of six cannon. Another was the destruction of his boats and baggage by the militia firing from the opposite bank. Such provisions as were saved amounted to a mere four or five days' supply.[96]

Back in New York Clinton pondered how to answer Burgoyne's messages. One thing was certain: he could not give Burgoyne directions, "not having received any instructions" from Howe "relative to the northern army." Burgoyne surely did not suppose that Clinton could get "to Albany with the small force" which he then had at New York. All he could do was attack the Highland forts, in line with Burgoyne's suggestion that "even the menace of an attack would be of use."[97]

But there was to be no escape for the British, trapped by the Hudson River, even though Clinton succeeded on 6 October in capturing the two principal Highland posts, Fort Montgomery and Fort Constitution, which had been denuded of troops to strengthen the field armies.[98] This allowed Clinton to dispatch General Vaughan with 3,000 men further up the Hudson River to Kingston, which he reached on 15 October. But he was still 45 miles from Albany and all accounts of Burgoyne's situation suggested that it was "impracticable to give him any further assistance." Another reason for turning back was the pilots' assertion that the river was not navigable for warships beyond Kingston. Vaughan also noted the increasing number of rebels on both sides of the river as it narrowed towards Albany, making further progress both difficult and dangerous.[99]

Burgoyne considered his options at a council of war on 12 October. He suggested that the army could wait on events; attack the Patriot positions; retreat in an orderly fashion towards the Hudson River above Fort Edward; or run away in the night, leaving the artillery and baggage, in the hope of finding an undefended ford.[100] Most of these suggestions were dismissed as impractical though a tentative agreement was reached in favor of a nighttime withdrawal. However, scouts reported next morning that the enemy controlled all the fords and had also blocked the road from Fort Edward to Lake George.[101] Hence at a second council of war on 13 October Burgoyne introduced the subject of capitulation, asking whether "an army of 3,500 fighting men and well provided with artillery were justifiable upon the principles of national dignity and military honor in capitulating." All those present agreed that it was.[102]

Accordingly later that day Burgoyne swallowed his pride and asked for terms. Gates was more than ready to comply, fearful that Clinton might yet mount a rescue. The result was a convention rather than a traditional surrender. The British and Germans were to enjoy the honors of war, with the right to return to Europe or be exchanged with Patriots of equal rank, thus allowing them to fight once more. Accordingly on 16 October 5,800 officers and men marched out to lay down their arms. Among the haul were 27 pieces of field artillery and several thousand muskets, no small booty for the Patriot forces.[103]

Burgoyne's hope that his men could return to the fray were soon dashed, since Congress refused to accept the Convention. When the details were submitted, the members rightly felt that the terms were too lenient and insisted that Burgoyne's men become prisoners of war. The one consolation for the British was that the lateness of the season precluded any invasion of Canada. The commanding officer at Ticonderoga, on learning of Burgoyne's surrender, quickly abandoned the fortress to concentrate the remaining troops and armed vessels at St Johns. The control of Lake Champlain for a time at least ensured that Canada was safe.[104]

Even so, the consequences could not but be damaging. Burgoyne had personified the British belief that a few regiments were sufficient to return the population to its allegiance. This was clearly shown to be false. The damage was all the greater because Howe's capture of Philadelphia had not proved the blow it might have been at the start of the rebellion. Moreover, as the battle of Germantown demonstrated, Washington's army was still a threat, especially as the Delaware had yet to be opened. It was for this reason that Howe ordered Clinton to vacate the Highland forts and send him five battalions by way of reinforcement. Control of the Hudson had been a key part of the British plan to recover New England. Now the keys had been thoughtlessly discarded because Howe had overextended himself at Philadelphia.[105] The opportunity was not to arise again, since the Patriots not only rebuilt their existing posts but began a massive new structure at nearby West Point.

In Britain, Saratoga had less impact than might have been expected. The setback, if anything, stiffened the resolve of the nation not to be beaten by such contemptible opponents, even though France and Spain might seek to profit from Britain's difficulties. The King still spoke for the great majority when he affirmed that "to treat" on the basis of "Independence can never be possible."[106] Nevertheless, fear of French and Spanish intervention was enough to persuade the Rockingham Whigs to accept independence in principle.[107] The ministry would in consequence face a more divided Parliament.

Naturally answers were demanded in Britain as to who was responsible for this debacle. Among those quick to absolve themselves were the generals. Burgoyne insisted that his instructions required him to advance on Albany whatever the circumstances. Had he stopped at Fort Edward "his conduct would have been held indefensible by every class . . . in government, the army and the public." The subsequent outcome therefore was no more than "an honorable misfortune," given the lenient terms of the convention. He did make one concession, that he had been deluded about the military ability of the Patriots. The Continentals in particular had acquitted themselves in the "fundamental points of military institution, sobriety, subordination, regularity and courage."[108]

Howe equally refused to accept responsibility for Saratoga because of his failure to advance up the Hudson. He had "positively mentioned" in his "letter to Sir Guy Carleton . . . that no direct assistance could be given by the southern army." Burgoyne therefore could have no complaint.[109] But in the subsequent Parliamentary inquiry both Howe and Burgoyne preferred to blame Germain rather than each other. Howe argued that Germain had not given him sufficient instructions regarding the northern army and had sent inadequate reinforcements. Burgoyne, in contrast, asserted that Germain had interfered too much, a charge in which he was supported by Carleton.[110]

In reality all three men were responsible for the outcome of the campaign. Germain failed to ensure that the two armies were part of a coordinated strategy with clear attainable objectives. His acceptance of Burgoyne's plan. knowing that Howe intended to go in the opposite direction, is difficult to understand. One explanation is that like most Britons, he believed the regular army could not be beaten whatever the odds. The generals, therefore, could make their own decisions. This allowed Howe to pursue his campaign without regard to the wider objectives of the war. Nevertheless, Howe's indifference to Burgoyne's progress was especially willful, given his responsibility for the northern army once it reached Albany. Finally Burgoyne adopted unrealistic goals and then compounded his errors by distorting his orders. The instruction to advance to Albany did not mean that he had to destroy his army and make his men prisoners of war.[111] Generals are usually given latitude to ensure the preservation of their command.

One immediate casualty was William Howe, who asked to be relieved of his command on news of Burgoyne's debacle. He was prompted ostensibly by the ministry's refusal to accept his recommendations for promotion.[112] But Howe undoubtedly realized that much of the opprobrium for Saratoga would be laid at his door. His departure in any case was not inappropriate. For two years he had conducted an overly cautious campaign when a vigorous pursuit of Washington might have brought about a collapse of the Patriot cause. If his actions had been guided by a desire to be conciliatory, the policy had not worked. Howe seemingly lacked the killer instinct, perhaps because he wanted confidence. On forwarding his 1776 campaign proposals, Lord Howe observed that his brother believed the scheme "to be of greater compass than he feels himself equal to direct." Essentially Howe was a good corps officer rather than a commander-in-chief. This made him ill-equipped for the political and strategic aspects of the struggle.[113]

Another near casualty was Washington. In the aftermath of Saratoga various Congressmen and senior officers believed that Gates was the man to command the army. After two and a half years Washington still had no victory.[114] The discontent was fanned by Thomas Conway, a former colonel in the French army's Irish brigade, whom Washington had declined to promote in October 1777 because of his lack of seniority and overrated abilities. Conway then used his influence in Congress to secure a place on the Board of War, giving him further scope for mischief.[115] However, Gates gave no overt encouragement to the malcontents, and the issue subsided.[116] But the Conway episode revealed that the Patriots were no different from their British counterparts when it came to rank and field command. After one fracas, John Adams observed that the officers high and low "quarrel like cats and dogs . . . scrambling for rank and pay like apes for nuts." It was a most unedifying spectacle for a nation that proclaimed Republican virtue and simplicity.[117]

The maritime dimension, 1775–1777

While the British army labored to reconquer the Continental colonies, the Royal Navy had also been engaged in a complementary campaign to end the rebellion.

On the outbreak of hostilities in 1775 the British fleet was expected to perform two tasks. The first was supporting the army's operations along the coast, giving aid to the officers of the Crown and other Loyalists. The second was the stopping of Patriot commerce to make the Colonists submit through economic pressure. Some officials, notably Barrington, believed that a blockade of the American coast might achieve the ministry's objectives without the need for a full-scale military reconquest.[118] Orders were accordingly sent to the fleet in early July to seize all New England shipping unless the owners were of proven loyalty.[119] As the rebellion spread, so did the need for a wider blockade, resulting in December 1775 in the Prohibitory Act, which placed a ban on all colonial trade, making ships and cargoes liable to confiscation.

The first responsibility for supporting the army was performed relatively well in the period 1775 to 1777. However, the same could not be said for the blockade and interdiction of colonial commerce. This was partly due to the large number of Patriot privateers, which began operating shortly after Lexington and Concord. But the main reason was the Royal Navy's lack of ships even when the blockade was limited to New England. The Admiralty calculated in early July 1775 that some 50 frigates and cruisers would be necessary for the execution of these orders.[120] However, the ministry was as slow to mobilize the navy as it was to expand the army. As a result, by October 1775 the North American squadron still had only 12 frigates and 20 sloops or other small craft.[121] This was quite insufficient, especially when so many warships were required to support Gage in Boston. The inadequacy of the navy's presence was especially noticeable in the south where Governor Martin reported in August 1775 that there was only one sloop of eight guns to intercept the rebel commerce. Warlike stores were consequently flooding into the colony to the great detriment of the royal cause. Nevertheless all appeals to Boston for assistance had remained unanswered.[122] Rebel shipping was accordingly free to come and go not only to Europe, but also to the Spanish, Dutch, and French islands in the West Indies.

The Admiralty in response proposed to have 70-plus warships in American waters during 1776. This would allow a dozen vessels to be periodically refitted or employed as convoys, leaving 60 for enforcing the blockade.[123] But once the army began its operations at New York, fewer than ten cruisers were left for the suppression of commerce between Halifax and Long Island.[124] The Delaware and Chesapeake were even more scantily patrolled. As one of Admiral Howe's captains commented, the need to attend the army meant that the rebels in the south were free to export their tobacco and grain with which to pay for their supplies of gunpowder and other items.[125] Even by November 1776 only two warships were patrolling the entrance to the Delaware, with another two off Savannah and three at St Augustine. Most alarmingly the Chesapeake was empty after the sole sloop there had been ordered back to New York.[126] The Patriots consequently were never critically short of saltpeter in the first two years of the war, which was the one item that they could not produce for themselves. Without this the rebellion might have collapsed.

Another consequence of the navy's lack of ships was its inability to protect British supply vessels. The most notorious failing in this respect was the capture of the *Nancy* ordnance ship in November 1775. This vessel not only had no escort, but lacked even a detachment of marines and thus fell an easy prey to the New England schooner *Lee*.[127] This and other such mishaps led the Ordnance Board in August 1776 to request that its cargoes in future be carried either on the Royal Navy's 44-gun frigates or on specially constructed vessels of appropriate armament and design.[128] Unfortunately the request took no account of the Admiralty's priorities. As Sandwich explained to Germain, the 44-gun vessels were needed on other services. In any case such deployment would be "perverting" them "from their proper use." As to building special vessels, this too was impossible given the workload of the royal dockyards. If the Ordnance wanted to protect their cargoes, they should follow the example of the Treasury, which was hiring armed merchantmen to transport the army's victuals to North America.[129] Given such attitude, the Ordnance similarly had to make its own arrangements by buying some "old India men" for transporting its weapons and munitions.[130]

The Ordnance was not the only department to experience a lack of cooperation from the Admiralty. In May 1776 two transports carrying four companies of Highlanders were captured in Boston harbor. The station commander, Admiral Shuldham, had left insufficient warships to warn approaching vessels that the town had been vacated.[131] The incident prompted Germain to ask Sandwich why a more effective blockade had not been established in America.[132] Sandwich replied that it was Lord Howe's responsibility to prevent such incidents. Eventually Sandwich agreed to the dispatch of another 12 frigates, telling Howe that he must prevent the rebel cruisers from doing "so much mischief" in the future. But he acknowledged to Howe that while his squadron was "attending the operations of the army, other services must in some degree give way to the principal object."[133] Assuredly this would change once the army had established itself and taken control of the coastal areas.

One reason for Sandwich's lack of sympathy with Germain and the Ordnance Board was that from the summer of 1776 the Patriots had begun equipping privateers for operations in Europe. The first such vessel was the *Rover* of Salem, which captured several merchantmen off the Portuguese coast in late August of that year. Soon others appeared off Britain itself.[134] They were able to do so because the navy had just two 32-gun frigates, eight sloops and nine cutters left for the protection of British and Irish waters.[135] The lack of cruisers was partly due to the demands of the American service but also because the majority of the ministry refused to accept the need for full mobilization, believing that the rebellion would quickly collapse.

Another reason for the privateers' success was France's benign attitude, which allowed them to dispose of their prizes in its ports and get fresh supplies without re-crossing the Atlantic. The North ministry made diplomatic protests demanding an end to these infringements of French neutrality. However, there were limits as to what could be done, since the British ministers were anxious not to push France into an open alliance with the rebels. The privateers consequently continued to sail as they pleased, forcing the Admiralty to adopt an expensive convoy system to protect their most valuable East and West Indian commerce. This in turn meant fewer frigates and sloops for policing ordinary commerce on either side of the Atlantic. During 1776 Lloyds insurance brokers registered the loss of no fewer than 229 merchant vessels, most in the unprotected coastal trades.[136]

The ending of military operations in America in December 1776 allowed Howe to focus once more on enforcing the blockade, following the receipt of Germain's letter. During the next three months he had two squadrons operating off the American coast, one of 14 frigates under Commodore Peter Parker, based on Rhode Island, the other of 16 frigates commanded by Commodore Hotham, centered on the Chesapeake.[137] However, the Rhode Island squadron was constantly diverted to finding forage and fuel for the garrison at Newport, while Hotham was hampered by the need to send five of his vessels to Antigua for refitting. In the following three months Hotham made just 25 interceptions while hundreds of other rebel cargoes sailed without restriction.[138] Nor did the blockade affect the Patriot naval effort since few privateers were among the captures. The reason, as Howe acknowledged, was that the privateers were too fast and too familiar with the navigation for the heavier ships of the Royal Navy.[139]

This was embarrassingly demonstrated in May 1777 when Commodore Manley escaped from Boston in the 32-gun *Hancock*, one of Congress's new frigates, to rendezvous with several other privateers from Marblehead. In this emergency the navy had few ships to call on, as Howe informed the Admiralty when it complained about Manley's escape. None of the 29 ships of war then at New York could be spared because of the need "to co-operate in the expected movements of the army." Manley's cruise culminated in the capture of the 28-gun Royal Navy frigate, the *Fox*, off the Newfoundland banks.[140] The Admiralty was especially mortified by this incident, blaming Howe for unnecessarily dispersing his smaller ships. Clearly he must pay more attention to seeking out the enemy's large cruisers.[141] But one thing he should understand. No more ships could be sent from England. The seas around Britain "were so full of privateers and the demand for convoys and cruisers so great that we know not how to supply them."[142]

Howe did not take this criticism lightly. He pointed out that it was difficult to know what the Patriots were doing in their numerous ports and rivers. He then reminded the Board: "I have always conceived the first object of my instructions to be for co-operating with the army in the services the General is to undertake." Unfortunately, "the progress of the army" had not been sufficient to release "the ships of war from constant attendance." The rebels still controlled the countryside "many leagues above the entrance of the rivers leading thereto," making the army dependent on the navy for its supplies. New York, Rhode Island, and the Delaware were all "examples of this necessity." Hence, "until the army is competent to ensure such communication, the deficiency must be furnished from the fleet." Otherwise Howe had done his best with the remaining ships. Although he had a large fleet, it was still insufficient, given the excessive wear on the ships and crews and the need for regular refits and rest. But if the Board knew better how to station his fleet, it should tell him.[143]

The *Fox* was shortly recaptured when two British frigates, the 32-gun *Flora* under Captain Brisbane and the 44-gun *Rainbow* under Sir George Collier fortuitously met Manley off Newfoundland. While Brisbane retook the *Fox*, Collier pursued Manley in his flagship, the *Hancock*, forcing his surrender.[144] But this success did little to halt the movement of rebel shipping, though Collier at Halifax did his best in the summer of 1777. After destroying a rebel base at Machias, he cruised off Maine and New Hampshire, "going sometimes into the enemy's harbors," both to keep "the militia and troops in continual alarm" and to prevent them "from joining the rebel army collecting against General Burgoyne."[145] But even Collier admitted the counterproductive effects of these raids, which had created such "inveteracy and rancor" among the local population as would take a "generation" to repair.[146] It was for this reason that Howe wanted his captains to be as conciliatory as possible.

Nevertheless, Collier's activities were precisely the kind of maritime war that Germain wanted to pursue. He believed such policy would inhibit New Englanders from enlisting in the Continental army, while ensuring the destruction of their privateer bases. The enforcing of the blockade would then be easier, thus reducing the need for more ships from England.[147] However, both Howe brothers objected that such activities would interfere "materially with the more important operations of the campaign."[148] By the end of August 1777 half of the navy's 80 warships in America were still supporting the army.[149]

There was one other factor behind the Admiralty's failure to institute an effective blockade. This was Sandwich's concern about the intentions of France.[150] From the summer of 1776 he was increasingly anxious about the need to build up the home fleet by equipping the larger ships of the line. Insufficient attention therefore was given to the commissioning of frigates and sloops. A paper presented to Sandwich on 25 August 1777 revealed that there were still only 10 frigates in the British Isles, though a further 11 would be in service by the end of the year. Another 20 new vessels might be launched in the next 18 months, but this would barely compensate for those needing repair. In the meantime 17 ships of the line were attempting the dual role of escorting the trade and intercepting commerce raiders, tasks for which they were not suited.[151]

The lack of frigates and cruisers stemmed from North's earlier determination to cut government spending on becoming First Lord of the Treasury in 1770. Most new frigates and sloops were built in merchant yards. However by 1775 just £17,574 was voted by the Commons for such construction.[152] This freeze in the merchant building was reversed only at the end of 1776 when the Commons voted £169,261 for the service of 1777, in addition to £254,547 for the royal yards.[153]

With such ill-timed parsimony, it is not surprising that enemy privateers sailed freely around the British Isles, as Admiral Palliser, Sandwich's closest colleague on the Admiralty, readily admitted in September 1777: "It is truly mortifying we have nothing proper to send after them," he commented to Sandwich. The only solution was a further large increase in new construction since the demands on the navy could only get heavier. "The Americans are increasing theirs at an amazing rate, besides their innumerable small privateers."[154] The French were similarly exerting themselves in the building of both frigates and battleships. But despite this the naval estimate for 1778 was only marginally larger than that for 1777. Sandwich and North seemingly still thought that the rebellion would collapse before France was ready to enter the war. In the meantime British merchant losses continued to grow, reaching 331 vessels by the end of 1777.[155]

But whatever the problems around the British Isles, Sandwich believed that any failings across the Atlantic were not his fault. With 90 warships Howe had more than enough vessels to stop the rebel commerce, crush their privateers, and prevent supplies reaching Washington's army. The reason why none of these objectives had been achieved was the excessive use of the fleet in support of the army. Admittedly, the length of the coast made it impossible to blockade rebel shipping entirely. Nevertheless, the fleet should have distressed the Patriots "infinitely more than has hitherto been done." The opportunity to make them "tired of the war" had been missed.[156]

With the capture of the Delaware forts and the end of military operations, Howe once again was able to focus on the blockade of the American coast. From the end of November 1777 he had two substantial detachments based on Rhode Island and Halifax to patrol the coasts of New England. Two more squadrons were to perform the same duties between New York and the Delaware, while a third patrolled the Chesapeake. Unfortunately this left just five frigates between Cape Fear and St Augustine to prevent the export of rice, indigo, and tobacco from the Carolinas and Georgia.[157] But even in the most heavily policed areas the rebel commerce continued to flourish, aided by the complexities and extensiveness of the coastline. As an instrument of economic attrition, the navy had been a failure. Moreover, its ability to influence the ending of the rebellion could only be further reduced if France entered the war, as she was clearly tempted to do.

In the first three years of the conflict Britain's military and naval effort to regain the colonies had been hugely ineffective. When the map of America was unfurled at the end of 1777, Britain's presence was confined to three small enclaves at Newport, New York, and Philadelphia. Otherwise all 13 states remained firmly in Patriot control. It was not much to show for such an effort against campaigning a supposedly weak opponent. The North ministry had squandered a unique opportunity to impose its will. It would not have another such chance.

Notes and references

1. Howe to Germain, 30 November 1776, DDAR/XII, 264–66.
2. Howe to Germain, 20 December 1776, DDAR/XII, 268–69.
3. Estimates for the Year 1777, CJ/XXXVI, 22–23.
4. Germain to Howe, 14 January 1777, DDAR/XIV, 31–33
5. Germain to Carleton, 22 August 1776, DDAR/XII, 187–88.
6. Even George III was aware of Germain's dislike of Carleton, George III to North, 13 December 1776, Fortescue/3, 406. See also Gerald Saxon Brown, *The American Secretary: The Colonial Policy of Lord George Germain, 1775–1778* (Ann Arbor, 1963), 88–93.
7. Germain to Carleton, 26 March 1777, DDAR/XIV, 53–54.
8. Richard J. Hargreaves, *General John Burgoyne* (Newark, 1983), 64–71.
9. "Thoughts for Conducting the War from the Side of Canada," 28 February 1777, DDAR/XIV, 41–46.
10. Ibid., 46.
11. J.C. Long, *Lord Jeffery Amherst: A Soldier of the King* (New York, 1933), 200–41.
12. Germain to Howe, 3 March 1777, DDAR/XIV, 47–49.
13. Germain to Carleton, 26 March 1777, DDAR/XIV, 53–56.

14 Germain to Howe, 18 May 1777, DDAR/XIV, 84–85. Brown, *American Secretary*, 113.

15 A story subsequently arose that Germain had written a letter for Howe regarding Burgoyne's plans but had forgotten to sign and post it, Brown, *American Secretary*, 108–12.

16 Washington to Sullivan, 3 February 1777, WP/RWS/8, 237. Washington to Hancock, 4 February 1777, WP/RWS/8, 249–50.

17 Quoted in Arthur Bowler, *Logistics and the Failure of the British Army in America, 1775–1783* (Princeton, 1975), 69.

18 Circular to the New England States, 24 January 1777, WP/RWS/8, 134–35.

19 Washington to Hancock, 4 February 1777, WP/RWS/8, 249–52.

20 Return of American Forces in New Jersey, 15 March 1777, WP/RWS/8, 576.

21 Howe to Germain, 2 April 1777, DDAR/XIV, 65.

22 Howe to Germain, 24 April 1777, DDAR/XIV, 72–73.

23 Washington to Hancock, 26 January 1777, WP/RWS/8, 160–62. Washington to John Washington, 24 February 1777, WP/RWS/8, 439–40.

24 Washington to Augustine Washington, 12 April 1777, WP/RWS/9, 144.

25 Washington to James Warren, 23 May 1777, WP/RWS/9, 512–13.

26 Washington to Hancock, 12 May 1777, WP/RWS/9, 394–95. Ibid., 21 May 1777, 491–93.

27 Hancock to Washington, 26 March 1777, WP/RWS/8, 637. Heath to Washington, 23 April 1777, WP/RWS/9, 244–45.

28 Washington to Hancock, 9 May 1777, WP/RWS/9, 371. Ibid., 6 June 1777, 618–19.

29 Howe to Germain, 20 January 1777, DDAR/XIV, 33.

30 Howe to Germain, 2 April 1777, DDAR/XIV, 64–65.

31 Howe to Carleton, 5 April 1777, DDAR/XIV, 66.

32 Bowler, *Logistics*, 68–69.

33 Howe to Germain, 3 June 1777, DDAR/XIV, 102–3.

34 Washington to Augustine Washington, 1 June 1777, WP/RWS/9, 586–87. Ibid., 29 June 1777, WP/RWS/10, 149–50.

35 Washington to Sullivan, 14 June 1777, WP/RWS/10, 41. Washington to Arnold, 17 June 1777, WP/RWS/10, 59.

36 Washington to Reed, 23 June 1777, WP/RWS/10, 113–14.

37 Washington to Hancock, 28 June 1777, WP/RWS/10, 137.

38 Howe to Germain, 5 July 1777, DDAR/XIV, 127–9. Ira D. Gruber, *The Howe Brothers and the American Revolution* (New York, 1972), 229.

39 Germain to Howe, 18 May 1777, DDAR/XIV, 84.

40 Howe to Germain, 7 July 1777, DDAR/XIV, 129–30.

41 Howe to Germain, 16 July 1777, DDAR/XIV, 145.

42 Washington to Putnam, 1 July 1777, WP/RWS/10, 165–66. Washington to Hancock, 2 July 1777, WP/RWS/10, 168–69. Washington to Heath, 4 July 1777, WP/RWS/10, 189.

43 David Syrett, *Admiral Lord Howe: A Biography* (Annapolis, MD, 2006), 68–69. He actually landed six miles below the Head of Elk, Washington to Hancock, 27 August 1777, WP/RWS/11, 78.

44 Howe to Germain, 30 August 1777, DDAR/XIV, 181. Piers Mackesy, *The War for America, 1775–1783* (Cambridge, Mass., 1964), 125.

45 General Orders, 4 September 1777, WP/RWS/11, 142–43.

46 Robert Middlekauf, *The Glorious Cause: The American Revolution, 1763–1789* (New York, 1982), 385.

47 John Ferling, *Almost a Miracle: The American Victory in the War of Independence* (New York, 2007), 146.

48 Washington to Hancock, 30 August 1777, WP/RWS/11, 93. Ibid., 9 September 1777, WP/RWS/11, 175.

49 W.J. Wood, *Battles of the Revolutionary War, 1775–1781*(New York, 1995), 96.

50 Sullivan to Washington, 11 September 1777, WP/RWS/11, 197–98. Ibid., 2 pm, 198.

51 Howe to Germain, 10 October 1777, DDAR/XIV, 203–9. Knyphausen to Germain, 21 October 1777, DDAR/XIV, 238–41.

52 Initially Washington was unsure how to deal with Lafayette, looking on him as one of the "numberless applications for employment by foreigners." Washington to Benjamin Harrison, 19 August 1777, WP/RWS/11, 4–5. For the first few months Lafayette had to accept a position on Washington's staff with the honorary title of Major General.

53 Howe to Germain, 10 October 1777, DDAR/XIV, 202–4.

54 Washington to Hancock, 11 September 1777, WP/RWS/11, 200–1.

55 Hancock to Washington, 17 September 1777, WP/RWS/11, 254.

56 Wayne to Washington, 21 September 1777, WP/RWS/11, 286–87.

57 Council of War, 23 September 1777, WP/RWS/11, 294–96. Howe to Germain, 10 October 1777, DDAR/XIV, 205–6.

58 Washington to Colonel Arendt, 23 September 1777, WP/RWS/11, 298.
59 Howe to Germain, 10 October 1777, DDAR/XIV, 206–7.
60 Council of War, 28 September 1777, WP/RWS/11, 338–39. General Orders, 28 September 1777, WP/RWS/11, 337.
61 Washington to Hancock, 5 October 1777, WP/RWS/11, 393. Howe to Germain, 10 October 1777, DDAR/XIV, 207.
62 Wayne to Washington, 4 October 1777, WP/RWS/11, 389–90.
63 Quoted in Bowler, *Logistics*, 71.
64 Lord Howe to Stephens, 25 October 1777, DDAR/XIV, 243–46. Ibid., 23 November 1777, DDAR/XIV, 257–61.
65 Howe to Germain, 13 December 1777, DDAR/XIV, 272–73.
66 Burgoyne to Germain, 15 May 1777, DDAR/XIV, 78–79.
67 Christopher Ward, *The War of the Revolution: A Military History of the American Revolution*, John R, Alden, ed. (New York, 1952), I, 405.
68 Burgoyne to Germain, 22 June 1777, DDAR/XIV, 119–21.
69 Burgoyne to Germain, 11 July 1777, DDAR/XIV, 133–40. St Clair to Washington, 17 July 1777, WP/RWS/10, 308–11.
70 Carleton to Germain, 16 August 1777, DDAR/XIV, 160–61.
71 Burgoyne to Germain, 11 July 1777, DDAR/XIV, 137–38. St Clair to Washington, 17 July 1777, WP/RWS/10, 308–11.
72 Washington to Schuyler, 16 June 1777, WP/RWS/10, 53. Ibid., 20 June 1777, WP/RWS/10, 90–1.
73 Schuyler to Washington, 10 July 1777, WP/RWS/10, 244–45. Ibid., 14 July 1777, WP/RWS/10, 279–80. Ibid., 4 August 1777, WP/RWS/10, 506.
74 Washington to Hancock, 10 July 1777, WP/RWS/10, 240–41.
75 Washington to the Brigadiers of Militia, 18 July 1777, WP/RWS/10, 317–18.
76 Washington to Schuyler, 24 July 1777, WP/RWS/10, 396–98.
77 Burgoyne to Germain, 11 July 1777, DDAR/XIV, 139.
78 Burgoyne to Germain, 30 July 1777, DDAR/XIV, 153–55.
79 Howe to Germain, 16 July 1777, DDAR/XIV, 145. Gruber, *Howe Brothers*, 234.
80 Burgoyne to Howe, 6 August 1777, DDAR/XIV, 156.
81 Burgoyne to Germain, 20 August 1777, DDAR/XIV, 163.
82 Quoted in Wood, *Revolutionary Battles*, 144–45.

83 Burgoyne to Germain, 20 August 1777, DDAR/XIV, 164.
84 Arnold to Washington, 27 July 1777, WP/RWS/10, 433–34.
85 Burgoyne to Germain, 20 August 1777, DDAR/XIV, 162–65.
86 Burgoyne to Germain, 20 August 1777 (Private), DDAR/XIV, 166–67.
87 Burgoyne to Germain, 20 August 1777 (Private), DDAR/XIV, 167.
88 Schuyler to Washington, 13 August 1777, WP/RWS/10, 606–7.
89 Trumbull to Washington, 25 July 1777, WP/RWS/10, 420–22.
90 New England Congressional delegates to Washington, 2 August 1777, WP/RWS/10, 10.
91 Washington to Governor George Clinton, 16 August 1777, WP/RWS/10, 635–37.
92 Ward, *War of the Revolution*, II, 498.
93 Don Higginbotham, *Daniel Morgan: Revolutionary Rifleman* (Chapel Hill, 1961), 70–71.
94 Burgoyne to Clinton, 27 September 1777, DDAR/XIV, 190–91
95 Brigadier Powell to Carleton, 18 September 1777, DDAR/XIV, 185–86. Ibid., 23 September 1777, 187–89.
96 Burgoyne to Germain, 20 October 1777, DDAR/XIV, 233.
97 Copy of Notes by Clinton on a discussion with Captain Campbell, 5 October 1777, DDAR/XIV, 191–92.
98 Clinton to Howe, 9 October 1777, DDAR/XIV, 197–99. G. Clinton to Washington, 20 October 1777, WP/RWS/11, 560–62.
99 William B. Willcox, *Portrait of a General: Sir Henry Clinton in the War of Independence* (New York, 1964), 183–88. *Clinton's Narrative*, CAR, 80.
100 Minutes of a Council of War, 12 October 1777, DDAR/XIV, 212–15.
101 Burgoyne to Germain, 20 October 1777, DDAR/XIV, 234.
102 Minutes of a Council of War, 13 October 1777, DDAR/XIV, 214.
103 Middlekauf, *Glorious Cause*, 384.
104 Powell to Germain, 8 November 1777, DDAR/XIV, 253–54.
105 Howe to Germain, 21 October 1777, DDAR/XIV, 238.
106 George III to North, 13 January 1778, Fortescue/4, 14–15.
107 Frank Gorman, *The Rise of Party in England: The Rockingham Whigs, 1760–82* (London, 1975) 371–74, 386–88.
108 Burgoyne to Germain (private), 20 October 1777, DDAR/XIV, 236–37.

109 Howe to Germain, 22 October 1777, DDAR/XIV, 241–43.

110 Mackesy, *War for America*, 142.

111 This was a point made by Germain to George III, 15 December 1777, Fortescue/3, 514.

112 Howe to Germain, 22 October 1777, DDAR/XIV, 243.

113 Lord Howe to Germain, 25 September 1775, HMC, Stopford-Sackville Mss, II, 9. William Howe's lack of confidence is also argued by Gruber, *Howe Brothers*, 57.

114 James Craik to Washington, 6 January 1778, WP/RWS/13, 160–61.

115 Washington to R.H. Lee, 16 October 1777, WP/RWS/11, 529. Conway to Washington, 29 December 77, WP/RWS/13, 40–41.

116 Ferling, *Almost a Miracle*, 282–84.

117 Quoted in Higginbotham, *Morgan*, 99.

118 Mackesy, *War for America*, 38–39.

119 Dartmouth to Admiralty, 1 July 1775, DDAR/XI, 23–24.

120 Memorandum by Admiral Palliser, July 1775, Sandwich/1, 64–66.

121 Disposition of His Majesty's ships and vessels in North America, 9 October 1775, DDAR/XI, 141–42.

122 Martin to Dartmouth, 28 August 1775, DDAR/XI, 88–92.

123 Memorandum from Admiral Palliser, December 1775, Sandwich/1, 76–77.

124 Mackesy, *War for America*, 100.

125 Gruber, *Howe Brothers*, 141.

126 Disposition of His Majesty's Ships in North America, 5 November 1776, DDAR/XII, 244–46.

127 David Syrett, *The Royal Navy in American Waters, 1775–1783* (Aldershot, 1989), 6.

128 Townshend to Germain, 21 August 1776, DDAR/XII, 185–86.

129 Admiralty to Germain, 28 August 1776, DDAR/XII, 208–9.

130 Sandwich to Howe, 17 October 1776, Sandwich/1, 159–62.

131 Washington to Hancock, 16 June 1776, WP/RWS/5, 4. David Syrett, *Shipping and Military Power in the Seven Years War: The Sails of Victory* (Exeter, 2008), 183.

132 Germain to Admiralty, 16 August 1776, DDAR/XII, 184–85.

133 Sandwich to Howe, 17 October 1776, Sandwich/1, 160–64.

134 David Syrett, *The Royal Navy in European Waters during the American Revolutionary War* (Columbia, SC, 1998), 6.

135 State of the Fleet, 20 June 1776, Fortescue/3, 378–80.

136 Alfred T. Mahan, *The Major Operations of the Navies in the War of American Independence* (Boston, 1913), 61.

137 Howe to Commodore Peter Parker, 22 December 1776, DDAR/XII, 269–74.

138 Viscount Howe to Stephens, 31 March 1777, DDAR/XIV, 56–61.

139 Howe to Admiralty, 5 June 1777, DDAR/XIV, 103–6.

140 Syrett, *Royal Navy in American Waters*, 71–72.

141 Palliser to Sandwich, 22 July 1777, Sandwich/1, 233–35.

142 Sandwich to Howe, 3 August 1777, Sandwich/1, 293–96.

143 Howe to Stephens, 10 December 1777, DDAR/XIV, 268–70.

144 Captain Brisbane to Howe, 11 July 1777, Sandwich/1, 299–300. Report by Sir George Collier, 13 July 1777, DDAR/XIV, 142–45.

145 Collier to Germain, 16 August 1777, DDAR/XIV, 160–61. Ibid., 11 October 1777, Halifax, DDAR/XIV, 210–12.

146 Collier to Sandwich, 9 October 1777, Sandwich/1, 302–3.

147 Germain to Howe, 3 March 1777, DDAR/XIV, 48.

148 Howe to Germain, 3 June 1777, DDAR/XIV, 102–3.

149 Disposition of HM's ships and vessels in North America, 28 August 1777, DDAR/XIV, 175–80.

150 Sandwich to North, 21 July 1776, Sandwich/1, 213–14.

151 Memorandum from Palliser, 25 August 1777, Sandwich/1, 242–44.

152 Estimate for Building and Rebuilding, 20 December 1774, CJ/XXXV, 56–57.

153 Estimate of Vessels Building, 15 November 1776, CJ/XXXVI, 37–39.

154 Palliser to Sandwich, 29 September 1777, Sandwich/1, 249.

155 Mahan, *Major Operations*, 61.

156 Paper on the War in America, 8 December 1777, Sandwich/1, 327–34.

157 Disposition of HM's Ships and Vessels in North America, 9 March 1778, DDAR/XV, 63–66. Howe to Stephens, 16 March 1778, DDAR/XV, 702.

CHAPTER 5

France comes to America's help, 1778

The French connection, 1775–1778

The French governments of Louis XV and Louis XVI had followed the growing tensions between Britain and her American colonies since the time of the Stamp Act, believing they might provide the means for reversing the 1763 Treaty of Paris. In French eyes Britain had become too powerful for the balance of power and the good of Europe. The separation of the continental colonies from Britain would help correct this imbalance because much of her wealth and power came from those territories. Such separation would be doubly advantageous if that trade and wealth could be diverted to France. France would once again be the leading power in Europe and the arbiter of its destinies, a position that she had enjoyed until the humiliating peace of 1763.[1]

Nevertheless, the French had to tread warily on the outbreak of hostilities in April 1775, as her foreign minister Vergennes well knew. France's finances were still weak while her army and navy had yet to recover fully from the defeats of the recent war. Although Choiseul had greatly increased French naval spending in the 1760s, this had not been sustained after his dismissal in 1770. There were also some reservations about supporting a rebellion against the lawful authority of a reigning monarch. The French in any case did not wish to reawaken European fears by attacking George III as Elector of Hanover. For the past hundred years French aggrandizement had led other European powers to unite against her. This had resulted in four costly wars, none of which had brought much benefit to France. But another advantage of diplomatic restraint was that it might encourage those same European powers to be more benevolent to France. Austria, Prussia, and Russia had all been alienated by the recent arrogance of Britain, especially with regard to maritime affairs. By courting these nations the isolation and defeat of Britain would be more certain.[2]

The French from the start made it clear to the Patriots that formal assistance could be given only if they ended all ties with Britain. The French feared that their old nemesis, William Pitt, Earl of Chatham, might return to office and seek to reconcile the Colonists by inviting them to help attack France's Caribbean possessions. This was not as fanciful as it seemed. Memories of the brutal French and Indian wars were still vivid in English-speaking North America, especially among New Englanders. The two peoples also had little in common in terms of their institutions and values, France being a Catholic absolutist monarchy, the colonies a collection of small protestant states.[3] It was for this reason that Vergennes had sent Bonvouloir to emphasize that France had no territorial ambitions in North America. She would not seek the return of Canada.

Initially the French stance suited the Patriots. They were still wary of any formal alliance, fearing that France might attempt to become their new colonial master. Others remained hopeful of a reconciliation with the mother country. However, by September 1776 the military situation had sufficiently deteriorated for Congress to seek a formal treaty of commerce and amity. The presentation of its proposals was entrusted to Franklin who was to join Lee and Deane in a tripartite commission. But for the moment formal recognition was too much for the French. Such action was certain to bring a declaration of war for which France was not yet ready, since Sartine still had work to do before the various squadrons were ready to confront the Royal Navy. The Patriots in any case had to prove themselves militarily, since the mission's arrival that December coincided with news of Washington's retreat through New Jersey.[4] The French therefore continued to restrict their help to munitions and loans for essential supplies. The furthest that the ministers would go before news of Saratoga was the provision of frigates for escorting the supply ships into the Atlantic.[5]

Official neutrality did not stop French army officers from offering their services, as in the case of Lafayette. The French, as we have seen, also allowed Patriot privateers to use their ports, despite protests from Britain. Vergennes attempted to assure the British ambassador in Paris that his country was doing everything possible to prevent these violations of its neutrality, pointing to the treatment of Captain Conyingham, a notorious privateer, who had been thrown into prison in May 1777 after bringing some prizes into Dunkirk.[6] But as Franklin told the Congress, the French ministry "privately profess real friendship, wishes success to our cause, winks at the supplies we obtain here as much as it can without giving open grounds of complaint to England." Vergennes' twin objectives were thus achieved of providing the American states with "essential aids," while allowing France to continue "preparing for war."[7]

Those preparations were largely naval, since France's peacetime standing army of 170,000 men was more than adequate for any service, especially given the peaceful state of Europe. By the end of 1777 Sartine's preparations were sufficiently advanced for Vergennes to consider hostilities, now that Washington's dogged resistance and Burgoyne's surrender had proved the military worth of the United States. Nevertheless, the path to a formal understanding was not easy. The Patriots still clung to the notion that the French would give assistance without expecting anything in return other than access to America's trade.[8] The French in contrast remained wary of exposing themselves to British anger. Ideally they wanted Spanish support before making an open declaration. The two crowns had been closely linked since 1701 when the Bourbons became the ruling family in both countries. Those ties had been strengthened in 1761 by the Family Compact between Louis XV and his cousin Charles III, which committed both powers to aid the other in the event of a war with Britain. However, the Spanish still wanted time to complete their military and naval preparations, since they also had a boundary dispute with Portugal to resolve in South America.[9]

The French therefore for the moment would have to proceed alone. One reason for not delaying further was the appearance in early January 1778 of a British envoy in Paris with instructions to talk to Franklin, Deane, and Lee about a possible reconciliation.[10] The timing was not entirely auspicious for Vergennes, since a crisis had suddenly arisen in Europe over Hapsburg plans to exchange its territory in the Low Countries for Bavaria. The scheme would greatly increase Austrian power in southern Germany and was immediately seen by Prussia as a threat to itself. This was precisely the kind of dynastic issue which had led France into numerous territorial conflicts in the past to the detriment of her maritime interests. However, in line with his new policy of moderation in European affairs, Vergennes resolved not to become involved, even though France was technically allied to Austria in a defensive treaty. Such stance would instead allow France to devote her resources to the struggle with Britain.[11]

This was a momentous change in France's traditional foreign policy regarding Europe and indicates the importance that Vergennes now placed on the maritime rivalry with Britain. The Franco-American agreement of 6 February 1778 affirmed that the purpose "of the present defensive alliance" was to maintain "the liberty, sovereignty and independence . . . of the said United States." Each side accordingly agreed to do their utmost "to attain the proposed end," by coordinating their military and naval resources against Britain. However, the war was not to be entirely defensive. The French renounced all claim to North America, leaving the reduction of Canada to the American Patriots, "which in case of success shall be confederated with or dependent upon the United States." America in return acknowledged the French right to seize Britain's Caribbean islands. Both parties also agreed not to make peace without the "formal consent of the other." Finally a separate secret article recognized the need to facilitate the entry of Spain into the alliance, the tacit assumption being that Florida would be the price for her admission.[12]

The new treaty was remarkably generous to the United States. It effectively committed France to a war with Britain, with few guarantees of anything in return, other than the notional advantages stemming from the destruction of Britain's North American Empire. Admittedly the French were not obliged to intervene directly in the land war. The expectation was that France would continue to supply munitions and money so that the Patriots could fight their own war. The French were still wary of stirring up hostility should they send troops to the continent, a sentiment that was likely to be reinforced by the ingrained aversion to standing armies.[13] However, the French would dispatch a fleet to North America to destroy Howe's squadron. The British army would then be cut off from its supplies and forced to surrender. Travelling with the French squadron would be Conrad Alexander Giraud, the new French minister to the United States.[14]

Britain's strategic options

News of the Franco-American alliance had yet to be announced when the British ministers considered their plans for 1778. Nevertheless, they had plenty to think about. At the end of December they received a letter from William Howe warning that "a successful termination to the war" would not be possible without a large reinforcement. Burgoyne's defeat had not only animated the Patriot cause, but allowed Gates to reinforce Washington's army. Hence if additional troops were not forthcoming, the army would be restricted to its three principal posts at New York, Rhode Island, and Philadelphia. Of course the evacuation of one of these would allow a "corps to act offensively." But it would have an adverse effect on the Loyalists and be "strongly against His Majesty's interests."[15]

A large reinforcement for the moment was impossible. The regular army currently numbered little more than 60,000 men, though plans were in progress for increasing its strength. Eleven new corps, totaling 15,000 men, had been agreed, following offers from "many noblemen and gentlemen of extensive influence and some great cities" such as London, Manchester, and Bristol. However, few if any of these new corps would be available for Howe's army in North America.[16] If France entered the war, Britain's defenses would have to be strengthened, not only at home but overseas in the West Indies and elsewhere. The ministry was considering a bill to conscript "all able bodied, idle and disorderly persons" without "some lawful trade or employment." But the history of such measures was not encouraging, since magistrates tended to impress only the socially undesirable. Universal conscription was still incompatible with the liberties of the nation, whatever the emergency.[17]

Despite these difficulties, the King and his ministers all agreed that there would be no recognition of America, since they believed this would reduce Britain to the status of a second-rate power. Nevertheless, some change in the conduct of the American war was inevitable. Even George III acknowledged this when he told North that the army might have to act defensively in the next campaign, holding rather than expanding its bases in Canada, Nova Scotia, Florida, Rhode Island, and New York.[18] He was inclined to this view after being told by Amherst that a land war was not feasible following the loss of Burgoyne's army, since it would require an additional 40,000 to rectify the situation. As the former conqueror of Canada, Amherst knew what he was talking about. A "sea war" therefore was the "only wise plan." If the navy prevented "the arrival of military stores, clothing and the other articles necessary from Europe" it "must distress them and make them come into what Britain may decently consent to."[19]

However, as Sandwich had earlier pointed out, even a maritime war in America was not without objection. The experience of the previous three years demonstrated that much more was required if the navy was to implement both an effective blockade and support for amphibious landings. The army must first secure such ports "as the King's ships can resort to at all times and seasons" to "give them shelter and refreshments for their men." They must also have "proper facilities for careening and refitting," otherwise the squadrons would become unseaworthy, as had happened with Lord Howe's vessels. Only Halifax currently offered such facilities. The most suitable locations appeared to be Newport on Rhode Island, New York, Philadelphia, and Port Royal in South Carolina. The downside was that such facilities would be very expensive and would also tie down so many troops as to restrict further land operations. The ministry should also remember that no "force will be sufficient entirely to execute the purpose of blocking up all the rebel's port and putting a total stop to their privateering." "Along so extensive a coast, full of harbors and inlets, many ships will in spite of all our efforts get in and out by taking advantage of their knowledge of the coast, of dark and long nights, and events of wind and weather favorable to their purposes."[20] Amherst's suggestion for a purely maritime war did not appear to be the answer.

A decision was also needed on a replacement for Sir William Howe. The ministers' initial choice was Amherst, because of his previous success during the French and Indian War, but he quickly declined because of his views about the impracticality of a military reconquest.[21] The ministry therefore turned to Clinton, the next most senior officer in America. Clinton had been in America since June 1775, having previously served in Europe during the Seven Years War. However, according to one contemporary, he was "vain" and "open to flattery," which made him easily "misled by aides de camp and favorites." He was also indifferent "to all business not military," suggesting a lack of political acumen.[22] Moreover his experience in Germany was not the best preparation for the kind of warfare now being waged. Nevertheless he had shown tactical skill in his seizure of the Highland forts and might prove the man to defeat Washington in battle.

The orders to Clinton, dated 8 March 1778, began with a reaffirmation by Germain of the ministry's view that most Colonists wished "to enjoy their rights under the British constitution." Therefore this was not the time "to slacken any preparations which have been judged necessary for carrying on the war." Nevertheless it was clear that the "war must be prosecuted on a different plan from that upon which it has hitherto been carried on." Accordingly, if Clinton was not able "to bring Mr. Washington to a general and decisive action early in the campaign," he was to relinquish the idea of carrying on offensive operations by land." Instead he was to cooperate with the navy, as Amherst suggested, in making raids against the American coast, especially New England, "with the aim of destroying every ship and vessel, wharfs, stores and materials for ship building, so as to incapacitate them from raising a marine or continuing their depredations upon the trade of this Kingdom." If necessary he could evacuate Philadelphia to facilitate these operations.[23]

However, ministry's ambitions did not end here since Germain also wanted Clinton to launch a winter expedition against South Carolina and Georgia once operations had ended in the north. Those colonies had played little role in the rebellion, suggesting that Loyalist sentiment might be strong. Two thousand men therefore ought to be sufficient to capture Georgia, while

5,000 should be sufficient for taking Charleston. Germain affirmed that the King put great store on the southern provinces, since their recapture would restore to Britain a very valuable branch of commerce, while depriving the rebels "of their foreign credit" and the principal means of paying for their supplies. Lastly Germain reminded Clinton of the need "to raise and embody the well affected inhabitants." Germain had been impressed by the support given to Washington by the state militias. If the same assistance could be elicited for the Crown, the rebellion might quickly collapse.[24]

Five days after issuing these orders, the French ambassador informed the British ministers about the Franco-American alliance. This raised some truly ominous problems. In previous conflicts France had been forced to divide its resources between a land and sea war because of the need to confront her European enemies. Now the reverse was true. France had no overt enemies while Britain faced a generally hostile Europe. The French in consequence could give their undivided attention to the maritime war. They could either send men and ships to North America or alternatively attack Britain's possessions in the West Indies. Everywhere British trade and shipping would be in danger, including the convoys to sustain the war in America. Even the coastal operations of the army there would be at risk. Other targets included the British presence in India and her interests in the Mediterranean. Most audaciously, France might threaten an invasion across the English Channel, since nothing was so well calculated to paralyze the country. This had been demonstrated in 1756 when the fleet of Admiral Byng was prevented from sailing for the Mediterranean to relieve Minorca because of such fears. Nor was this the end of France's options, since she could always make trouble in Ireland.[25] She could also threaten Hanover, which Britain was bound to assist. France's one weakness was her finances which made it difficult for her to sustain a long war, despite having over twice Britain's population. But this would be more than compensated should Spain join the conflict with her still-considerable army and navy, and flow of treasure from her colonies. But whatever the French did, the war hereafter would be as much a maritime struggle as a military one. American Independence consequently was as likely to be won in the English Channel or Caribbean as on the battlefields of New York and New Jersey.

It was this daunting scenario that led Lord North to believe that Britain was "totally unequal" to a war simultaneously with the colonies and the "House of Bourbon." "Peace with America and a change in the Ministry are the only steps which can save this country" he informed George III on 25 March 1778.[26] This could best be done by negotiating with the opposition and by inviting Chatham into the Cabinet, since he had credit with the Colonists and talents as a war minister which North did not possess. But whoever was appointed "must be the director and dictator of the leading measures of government."[27] George III, however, refused. To replace loyal servants with members of the opposition would be dishonorable and he had no faith in Chatham, given previous attempts to "accept the services of that perfidious man."[28] He was ready to receive some individuals who agreed to "come to the assistance of my present efficient Ministers; but whilst any ten men in the kingdom will stand by me I will not give myself up into bondage," meaning the imposition on him of a ministry led by the opposition. If the nation felt otherwise, then "they shall have another King."[29] After a few days North agreed to remain until the end of the Parliamentary session.[30] The one change for the moment was the decision to invite Amherst to attend the Cabinet meetings as military advisor.[31]

Whatever the composition of the ministry, further radical rethinking was clearly necessary regarding the conduct of the war. Momentarily the King suggested opening negotiations with Franklin, commenting how "desirable it would be to end the war with that country," since this would allow Britain "to avenge the faithless and insolent conduct of France." Above all Britain could then attack the French in the West Indies, crippling their finances, since the sugar islands produced most of their customs revenue. However, Canada, Nova Scotia, and Florida must be retained, since these would be the means "to keep... the abandoned colonies" in awe.[32]

George III's views as usual reflected what his ministers were thinking. Their position was summed up by Amherst in a note for Sandwich: "The contest in America being [now] a secondary consideration, our principal object must be distressing France and defending and securing our own possessions against their hostile attempts."[33] The orders to Clinton were accordingly modified. Instead of the expedition to Georgia and the Carolinas, Clinton was to dispatch 5,000 men to St Lucia in the Leeward Islands. St Lucia reputedly had the finest harbor in the West Indies, providing a base from which to attack France's most profitable sugar islands, Martinique and Guadeloupe. But reinforcements would also be required in Florida to guard against a possible Spanish attack on St Augustine and Pensacola. Philadelphia therefore would have to be evacuated. Moreover, if Clinton still felt that he had insufficient troops to hold New York, he was to retire to Rhode Island or Halifax.[34]

The pending entry of France into the war also had important consequences for the Royal Navy in America the Royal Navy, since the defense of the mother country was now its first priority, as Sandwich constantly insisted. Lord Howe was accordingly to send back 20 cruisers for deployment around the British Isles. In addition he was to detach another 13 vessels for the expedition to St Lucia, leaving just 37 warships in North America itself.[35] Clearly the plans for an amphibious war there had been seriously weakened, while an effective blockade was virtually impossible. The only consolation was that Spain had yet to declare hostile intentions.

Finally the ministry recognized that an offer of peace to the Colonists was desirable, both to undermine the alliance with France while allowing Britain to concentrate on the maritime war. A commission under Lord Carlisle was accordingly to negotiate on the following terms: Britain would refrain from taxing the colonies internally, leaving Parliament responsible for regulating the empire's trade. Effectively the Colonists would return to the relationship which they had enjoyed in 1763, as they had previously demanded. Most of the other complaints listed in the Declaration of Independence were also conceded: the preservation of the colonial charters; the ending of treason trials in England; and the granting of tenure to the judges. And while the "sovereignty of the mother country" was to be formally retained, the commissioners could incorporate something akin to Congress in the final settlement.[36] In effect the British were offering partial dominion status. What the ministry overlooked was that such terms were hardly likely to appeal when the army was simultaneously retreating from Philadelphia and even New York. Nevertheless Germain for one remained confident for several months that "a treaty will take place and that we shall be at liberty to act with our whole force against France."[37] It was wishful thinking of the most naïve kind.

Naval preliminaries in Europe

Although war had yet to be declared between Britain and France, it was clearly about to happen, since the French recognition of American independence constituted a denial of Britain's mercantilist system and the integrity of her empire. However, any unilateral opening of hostilities might prejudice Britain's standing among the other European powers. Ideally France must be made to appear the aggressor.

Ironically the French ministry similarly wanted to avoid responsibility for starting hostilities. Since the summer of 1776 Sartine had been preparing two large squadrons, one at Brest on the Atlantic coast under Admiral d'Orvilliers, and the other at Toulon in the Mediterranean under Admiral d'Estaing. The French plan was for the Toulon squadron of 11 battleships and 6 frigates, with 4,000 troops on board, to sail immediately for America. The hope was that d'Estaing could pass through the Straits of Gibraltar before hostilities began, since it was essential that he disable Howe's fleet before undertaking any joint operation with Washington.[38] Hence French naval commanders everywhere were to act circumspectly until d'Estaing reached America. The main fleet at Brest, accordingly, put to sea on a training exercise with instructions to avoid hostilities unless provoked. But troops would simultaneously be assembled along the northern coast of France as though threatening an invasion. This would then compel the British, as in 1756, to keep a large fleet in the Channel, thus preventing the dispatch of any help to Howe across the Atlantic.[39]

The plans of Vergennes and his colleagues were unknown when news of the Franco-American alliance was received in London. The initial fear of the British ministers was that the Brest and Toulon fleets might combine to assist an invasion across the Channel. But the ministers also recognized that one of the French squadrons might cross the Atlantic to help the Patriots or attack the British West Indian islands. The result was considerable uncertainty and division in the ministerial ranks. Sandwich wanted to make the defense of the Channel the navy's priority to protect the homeland from invasion.[40] Germain on the other hand pleaded for strengthening the fleet in North America, since the destruction of Howe's squadron would leave the army dangerously vulnerable. He suggested that if Sandwich did not want to send more ships to America, he should deploy a squadron at Gibraltar to prevent d'Estaing leaving the Mediterranean.[41]

The Cabinet initially agreed to Germain's idea for a Mediterranean presence. However, Sandwich continued to insist that the Admiralty had insufficient ships to do this and two weeks later his view prevailed.[42] He also continued his opposition to the sending of more vessels across the Atlantic. The most that he would agree was the preparation of a squadron under Admiral Byron of 13 battleships for service there, once d'Estaing's destination was known. As Sandwich pointed out to North, even without Spanish assistance, the Brest and Toulon squadrons numbered nearly 40 battleships.[43] The danger was too great to release Byron. Not until 5 June 1778 was it clear that d'Estaing had passed the Straits of Gibraltar for North America, thus allowing Byron to depart with his 13 ships of the line. His orders were to track d'Estaing and bring him to battle.[44]

Historians have traditionally blamed Sandwich for this inability to maintain squadrons simultaneously in the Channel, Mediterranean, West Indies, and North America, suggesting that he had allowed the fleet to decay after the previous war. However, since becoming First Lord in 1770 he had instituted a program of building and repair so that the navy could match the achievements of Lord Anson's Admiralty in the previous war. This included a three-year supply of timber to ensure that ships did not fall to pieces after being built with unseasoned wood. He also resumed building in merchant yards which had ceased after the Seven Years War.[45] However, as we have seen, he had not been exempt from Treasury demands for economy. At the end of 1772 North requested a reduction in the number of battleships on guard duty as part of his program to cut the national debt. North believed it was safe to do so because of the tranquil state of Europe and recent friendly overtures from France.[46] Sandwich had responded by cutting the building program instead, both in the royal and merchant yards.[47] As a result no 74-gun ships, the workhorse of the battle fleet, were ordered between 1775 and 1777, new building being limited to six 64-gun vessels.[48] The same frugality affected the construction of new frigates.

As the difficulties in America mounted, Sandwich urged on several occasions that the navy be put on a proper wartime establishment, especially in the early summer of 1776 when his agents reported increased activity in French naval yards.[49] This time North had to concede the need for greater mobilization. From October 1776 the number of ships in commission was steadily increased, as was the use of press gangs to man them.[50] Construction in the royal and merchant yards was also enhanced from a peacetime average of £280,000 in the late 1760s to £423,000 for 1777.[51] But still more was required. As Sandwich told North in August 1777: "I lay it down as a maxim that England ought for her own security to have a superior force in readiness at home to anything that France and Spain united have in readiness on their side." In other words, Britain must be able to match a two power two-power standard set by her rivals. North again responded positively by agreeing to an increase in total expenditure of over £5,000,000, compared to £2,100,000 in 1774.[52] As a result 41 ships of the line were ready for home service by March 1778 with another 15 "getting forward." Eight more were preparing to receive men while a further nine were already in America and the West Indies.[53] Although many crews still had to be completed, Lord Hawke, the victor of Quiberon Bay in 1759, affirmed that no better fleet had been seen in the Kingdom. George III was equally commendatory after a visit to the royal dockyards.[54]

Unfortunately, the French and Spanish had been increasing their naval forces even faster. As a result of Sartine's endeavors, the French currently had 33 ships of the line and 48 frigates in European waters, while Spain had 32 of the line and 8 frigates. This meant that the Bourbon powers would have 65 battleships for service in Europe, compared to the Royal Navy's current strength of 41.[55] In earlier wars between 1689–1713 and 1744–48, Britain had enjoyed Dutch naval support, while in the recent Seven Years War she had been able to crush the French navy before Spain came to its assistance. This time the Royal Navy was entering a war without Holland as an ally, facing her two closest rivals with their fleets greatly enhanced since the previous conflict.

The blame for this situation must primarily rest with North because of his earlier demands for economy. But Sandwich too must share some of the responsibility for adopting Anson's fleet in 1759 as his benchmark instead of one based on the current navies of France and Spain. The result was a deficiency of ships which the Admiralty was never able to rectify until after the war due to the time required for building such vessels.

The departure of Byron allowed North's Cabinet to focus on the defense of Britain. The Channel fleet, or Western squadron as it was often called, was the strategic lynchpin in Britain's security. Not only could it prevent Britain from being invaded across the Channel, it was also the prime means of protecting the inward and outward bound shipping for the West Indies, Canada, the Mediterranean and the East Indies. This important responsibility now rested with Admiral Augustus Keppel. Keppel had risen to flag command in the previous war when he commanded the naval squadron during the capture of the French west coast island of Belle-Ile and had served as second in command the following year at the siege of Havana. In his career he had shown himself to be a competent rather than inspired commander. His appointment was surprising in that he was associated with the Whig opposition. However, his seniority and aristocratic connections meant that he could not be ignored for this important assignment. Not for the first time, political considerations rather than ability were Sandwich's prime consideration in making a senior appointment.

Having decided on a commander, the next issue to decide was where to station Keppel's squadron. There were two options. One was a close blockade of Brest to prevent the French putting to sea. The second was to allow their squadrons to emerge in the hope of catching them before they disappeared into the Atlantic. A close blockade of Brest had been attempted by Anson in 1759 which had directly contributed to Hawke's victory in Quiberon Bay, thus ending the threat of invasion during that war.[56] However, maintaining vessels on such an exposed station was arduous for both the ships and crews, requiring frequent rotation to keep them serviceable. Clearly the navy currently had insufficient ships to do this. Sandwich therefore decided on the second tactic of periodic cruises in the hope of catching the French fleet in open water, when the greater experience of the British vessels should prove decisive. The drawback was the difficulty of finding the French once they got to sea.

The initial orders to Keppel were to escort a convoy with troops and supplies for Gibraltar and Minorca past Ushant. After this he was to cruise off Brest to prevent a junction of the French and Spanish squadrons, while simultaneously protecting British convoys as they entered and left the Channel. However, Keppel was not to precipitate hostilities against individual French warships and he was to greet Spanish vessels in a friendly manner, unless they indicated hostile intentions. But should the French or Spanish appear in overwhelming force, he was to retire to St Helens to await reinforcement.[57]

Keppel finally set sail on 12 June with 20 battleships, but quickly returned when he learnt that the French at Brest not only had more capital ships but a superiority in frigates too.[58] Nevertheless, he was ready to return by early July with a considerably increased fleet of 29 ships of the line, accompanied this time by four frigates with coppered hulls, a new method of protecting ships' bottoms from barnacles, which greatly improved their speed.[59] His orders were as before, to cruise off Brest though he could extend his station to the Scilly Isles and Cape Lizard for the better protection of the trade. This time he was to attack and capture all French shipping, whether vessels of war or merchantmen, since war was now inevitable following the detention of two French frigates sent to spy on Keppel's squadron.[60]

Meanwhile the Brest fleet under Admiral d'Orvilliers had also put to sea on 10 July with 32 ships of the line. D'Orvilliers' orders were to cruise in the western approaches for a month. However, he was not to seek a confrontation as war had not yet been formally declared. He was also to avoid being driven up the Channel.[61] Nevertheless, the two fleets were not long in sighting one another, though d'Orvilliers endeavored to avoid battle to give his crews more time to prepare. He accordingly kept to the windward of Keppel for several days.[62] However on 27 July the wind turned in Keppel's favor, allowing him to catch the French rear. D'Orvilliers then tacked about to confront the British, though his plan was still to fight a defensive action. French naval doctrine since the early eighteenth century emphasized the need to avoid close engagement with the more experienced crews and robust vessels of the British. This could best be done by firing on the rigging of their opponents so that they were unable to use their heavier armament and superior discipline at close quarters. But the French had other reasons for adopting such tactics. Strategically they saw naval power as a means of supporting their colonies and trade.[63] The defense of metropolitan France did not depend ultimately on the fleet but on the size of its army. The exact opposite, of course, was the case for Britain where the Royal Navy was the main line of defense. Hence for the British the destruction of an enemy fleet always took precedence over the protection of the trade or conduct of amphibious operations.

As the two fleets passed in opposite directions, the French aimed their cannon at the British rigging while keeping under full sail. This maneuver cost the French more casualties, losing 730 seamen to 400 British, but the damage to Keppel's rigging prevented him from pursuit. This allowed d'Orvilliers to retreat under cover of night, leaving Keppel the apparent victor. But it was a hollow victory, since Keppel had to return to port to repair his shattered masts.[64] The real beneficiary, therefore, was d'Orvilliers, since he had disrupted Keppel's operations while preserving his own fleet. Nevertheless the engagement revealed that the French were still unable to command the Channel, despite the disabling of Keppel's fleet. There would be no invasion this year nor would the lines of communication be disrupted with North America. On the other hand the Royal Navy had failed to inflict a decisive blow on the French while unsupported by Spain. The consequences of this would become clear in 12 months' time.

The Battle of Ushant had one other consequence, namely an outbreak of dissention among the senior officers of the Royal Navy, involving Keppel and the commander of his rear division, Vice-Admiral Palliser. The dispute was colored by political considerations because of Keppel's links with the Rockingham Whigs. Palliser in contrast was a member of the Admiralty Board and protégé of Sandwich. Nevertheless, relations between the two commanders had been correct before the battle. However, on returning to Portsmouth Palliser discovered that he was being anonymously blamed for the failure to fight a decisive battle, because he had not supported the van and center of the fleet. Palliser quickly demanded that Keppel refute these insinuations. When Keppel refused, Palliser published his own version of the battle and then took the unusual step of demanding that Keppel face a court martial for misconduct and neglect of duty. Keppel had little difficulty in refuting these charges, leading the court to conclude that the accusations against him were "malicious and unfounded."[65] Palliser in consequence had to demand a court martial to clear his own name. He too was acquitted though with a less ringing endorsement, being reprimanded for not keeping Keppel informed about the state of his squadron during the battle.[66]

The net result of these proceedings was to divide the fleet along both political and personal lines, with consequent damage to its morale and effectiveness. Even two years later Sir George Rodney commented how "The Unhappy difference between Mr Keppel and Sir Hugh Palliser" had "almost ruined the Navy," regarding its discipline and the readiness of officers to execute orders.[67] The episode exposed the danger of making appointments on political grounds rather than merit, as the Treasury Secretary, John Robinson, had warned Sandwich the previous year. "Every command [needs] to be filled with men of the greatest experience in service and ability." To do otherwise only increased the danger of operational failure and subsequent recrimination. One way of alleviating the latter was for Sandwich to insist that the most senior appointments to the fleet be taken by the whole Cabinet. This would then avoid charges of favoritism, something that Sandwich was clearly guilty of.[68]

While the senior officers squabbled, the more mundane tasks of the fleet continued to suffer for want of sufficient vessels. Well before Ushant, Sandwich acknowledged that "our deficiency of frigates is an irretrievable misfortune, as our trade must be exceedingly exposed for want of convoys and cruisers."[69] This was graphically demonstrated in the spring of 1778 when the American privateer, John Paul Jones, launched a series of raids round the British Isles, during which he captured a Royal Navy sloop off Belfast Lough.[70] Although such raids were minor pin pricks, they had a psychological impact out of all proportion to the damage caused. The British homeland was being violated. It was symptomatic of the Royal Navy's inadequate resources and its inability to command the seas and determine the outcome of the war in America and elsewhere.

Valley Forge and the fashioning of a new army

While a maritime war was enveloping Western Europe, the armies in North America were preparing to take the field again after four months in winter quarters.

Howe's men had spent the winter in relative comfort. Since the British usually paid for their subsistence, many farmers around Philadelphia were willing to cross the lines to meet their needs, especially after Howe opened a market for them in the city.[71] Washington's army in contrast had few such benefits at Valley Forge, 20 miles to the west. Washington had chosen this location because of its defensible position. Unfortunately the site offered little shelter or access to supplies without money, as Washington informed Henry Laurens, the new President of Congress, shortly after his arrival. The troops were supposed to "have two days provision" in case of "any sudden call" for the intercepting of enemy foraging parties. Such supplies had rarely been available, thus obstructing them in that vital task. In addition there was no soap for washing or vinegar for fumigating lodgings. Clothing too was in short supply, "few men having more than one shirt . . . and some none at all." A want of shoes was another hardship. Finally the shortage of blankets forced many men "to sit up all night by fires, instead of taking comfortable rest in a natural and common way." As a result 3,000 men were "unfit for duty because they are barefoot and otherwise naked."

All these deficiencies, Washington observed sarcastically, were the result of Congress's facile assumption that "an inferior army" could confine a stronger "one in all respects [better] appointed." Hence unless Congress acted promptly the prospects for the forthcoming campaign would be severely constrained. He told Laurens: "We have not more than three months in which to prepare a great deal of business. If we let these slip or waste, we shall be laboring under the same difficulties all next campaign." The army was like a clock. If one part malfunctioned the rest would not work either.[72]

The worst failing of Congress was its inability to make good its promises regarding food and clothing. Feeding the army was the responsibility of Trumbull, the Commissary General. His task had proved relatively easy during the investment of Boston, since the credit of Congress was good, while the army, largely composed of New England militia, was among friends willing to supply its needs. Thereafter the problems rapidly got worse, not least because the army was operating in several divisions, which made it difficult for Trumbull to keep in contact.[73] He was also frustrated by a lack of authority following the decision of Congress to enforce a closer inspection to prevent embezzlement. By July 1777 Trumbull was threatening to resign. In desperation Washington warned Hancock that "without something is done in aid of Mr. Trumbull immediately, the army must be disbanded."[74] This prompted Congress to dispatch its War Committee to assess the problems, providing Washington with an opportunity to emphasize what was needed to ensure a successful campaign.[75] Despite this Congress still failed to act.

As a result, by early February 1778 the Continental army faced starvation with little prospect of relief, since the states of New Jersey, Pennsylvania, Maryland, and Delaware appeared exhausted. The normal diet of the men was meat, bread, butter, salt, and rum. But for several days they had no meat or bread, forcing them to subsist on biscuits made of flour and water.[76] Some officers urged Washington to forage in the European manner. However, he believed that living off the land would undermine the principles of the Revolution and preferred to appeal once more to the nearby states for help.[77] But some forcible requisitioning was unavoidable and Washington could only instruct his officers to sequester foodstuffs on as an equitable basis as possible, offering receipts for eventual payment.[78]

Unfortunately these receipts were worthless since Congress could only pay for goods with its rapidly depreciating currency. The farmers retaliated by hiding their livestock in the woods and swamps. Others, especially in Bucks County, used byways to reach Howe's market. The army did its best to prevent this trade, much of which was carried on by women.[79] But their interception did nothing to increase the affordability of supplies for the Continental army, as the officers in one brigade had earlier reported when trying to purchase liquor for treating wounds and boosting morale. On seven occasions the price had risen by 50 percent since their previous offer. Unless action was taken to protect them from such inflation, they would have to quit the service.[80]

Congress's only response to these problems was the formation of another committee in January 1778 to ensure closer control of the army. Washington dutifully wrote a long summary of what was necessary to make it fit for purpose. Among the required changes was proper provision for the officers; effective recruitment of the regiments; an Inspector General to ensure a standard drill; an office of Provost martial to supervise discipline; an efficient Quarter Master and Commissary department; and a revision to the articles of war to allow more graduated punishments from 100 lashes to death by hanging.[81]

In reality Congress itself needed reform, as Washington confided to selected correspondents. A critical weakness was its inability to make decisions, not least because the states failed to send delegates of "the first abilities among us." But things would go more smoothly if Congress put aside its prejudice that "standing armies are dangerous to a state." Such fears might have legitimacy in societies where the soldiers had few ties with ordinary citizens, being solely "mercenaries and hirelings." But this was not the case in America, where the troops had "all the ties and interests of citizens," including property. It was essential that Congress and the Army were considered "as one people, embarked in one cause." To do otherwise was to damage morale and lead to the very thing that Congress was trying to avert, the suppression of liberty.[82]

Despite Washington's remonstrance, few changes were forthcoming. Even his request for the appointment of Nathanael Greene as Quarter Master

General took three months to process.[83] Not surprisingly, the army continued to decline, as Washington confided to one senior officer towards the end of March 1778. "By death and desertion we have lost a good many men since we came to this ground and have encountered every species of hardship that cold, wet and hunger and want of clothes were capable of producing." In the circumstances it was remarkable "that we have been able to keep the soldiers from mutiny or dispersion."[84] The same discontent was true of the officers. By 1778 over 200 had retired from the service. Many others had been retained only with the greatest difficulty.[85]

Nevertheless, the months at Valley Forge were not entirely wasted. The winter of 1777 was the first occasion when the army did not dissolve on the expiry of one-year enlistments. This allowed more time to prepare for the field. Washington always believed that discipline and order were the keys to success. The militias could suppress the Tories and keep the population obedient, but they were not equipped for capturing fortified conurbations like New York, Newport, and Philadelphia. Only a properly organized field army could do this.

Washington was grateful therefore to be offered late in February 1778 the services of an officer formerly in the army of Frederick the Great, Baron von Steuben. One of the main problems with Washington's army was the lack of regularity in its training methods. This was especially true of its parade ground maneuvers which were essential for moving large bodies of men on the battle field.[86] As Steuben subsequently noted: "With regard to military discipline, I may safely say no such thing existed." Each officer "had a system of his own, the one according to the English, another according to the Prussian or French style."[87] Steuben now offered to teach Washington's men the standard Prussia drill, as used by the best army in Europe. He would also serve without rank or pay while he demonstrated his talents.

Washington quickly agreed, proposing a system of assistant inspectors to help implement it.[88] Steuben first drilled Washington's own guard to show the trainee inspectors how a body of men should uniformly load muskets and use their bayonets. He then arranged for his methods to be written down as a manual for distribution to the whole army.[89] Steuben emphasized from the start that the officers must drill their men rather than leaving it to the sergeants. But even Steuben realized that he would have to modify his teaching methods. Writing to a friend, he commented how in Prussia, Austria, and France "you say to your soldier, do this, and he doeth it." In America Steuben was obliged to say, "this is the reason why you ought to do that" before a soldier complied.[90] Of course Washington had been explaining the rudiments of military life since he first arrived at Boston in June 1775, realizing that the average recruit required a longer induction to soldiering than those in the armies of Europe.

The introduction of the system was not without some hostility. Complaints were made that Steuben was exceeding his powers, "being too much prejudiced against the American Officers from an ignorance of their abilities."[91] The feeling that too many foreigners were being promoted at the expense of local talent was never far away. It was for this reason that Washington limited Steuben to his duties as Inspector General rather than allowing him to act as a field officer.[92] However, he remained firm that there must be no deviations from the new system, since "any alterations would again plunge the army into that contrariness and confusions from which it is endeavoring to emerge."[93] Nevertheless the hostility to foreign officers meant that the plan for an inspectorate was only confirmed by Congress in April 1779.[94]

Having survived the winter, the main task now was to recruit the ranks. At Washington's request, this had been taken out of the hands of his officers and made the responsibility of the states. The notional strength of the army was supposed to be 66,000 men, but by the end of March 1778 they had still not determined how to meet their quotas.[95] Most inclined to adopt a system of voluntary enlistment. The problem, as one correspondent observed, was that "men will not encounter every hardship and danger merely for the sake of being starved and naked and treated with contempt and neglect." The only alternative was drafting from the militia. But this too had drawbacks, since most states allowed the better off to pay for substitutes, which often produced recruits of inferior quality.[96] By early May the army still had only 11,000 men at Valley Forge, with another 1,400 at Wilmington and 1,800 on the Hudson River.[97] Fortunately for Washington, Howe felt unable to attack because of the lack of "green forage" for his draft animals[98] Nevertheless, another defensive campaign was likely, until France came to America's aid.

Clinton: Retreat and retrenchment

The training and recruitment of Washington's army was still far from complete when news arrived on 30 April that the French had signed a treaty of mutual defense.[99] At a stroke the whole strategic position changed, since it was clear Britain would have to reduce her effort in America, unless she could miraculously increase her armed forces. Washington was sufficiently elated to ask his Council about the advisability of an early attack on Philadelphia or New York to quicken that withdrawal. But despite the more positive outlook, his officers still believed that it would be best to remain on the defensive until a more favorable opportunity presented itself.[100] This response seems to have annoyed Washington, since he subsequently asked his officers for their opinions in writing rather than in open council, arguing "I can digest everything at my leisure and act with more secrecy," in contrast to decisions determined by "a majority of votes and known to numbers" of people.[101]

The opportunity for action was not long in arriving, for in mid-May word came that the British were preparing to evacuate Philadelphia. Washington immediately ordered Lafayette with the advanced guard to observe their movements. But the ploy almost ended in disaster, when Clinton anticipated the Patriot move by setting a trap. Only the slow advance of one of his divisions allowed Lafayette to retire to Valley Forge unscathed.[102] In the circumstances the caution of Washington's council had been justified.

Clinton meanwhile was attempting to balance Germain's orders to evacuate Philadelphia while simultaneously sending 8,000 men to Florida and the West Indies. It was soon apparent that it was not possible to do both at once, since the navy had insufficient ships to convey the rest of the army to New York, let alone transport the expedition to St Lucia.[103] Accordingly he decided to implement his orders in stages by first withdrawing to New York before dispatching the expedition to the West Indies. Even so, not everyone would be able to travel by water because of insufficient shipping. Clinton's eventual plan was for the 3,000 Loyalists to travel by sea, while the core of his army, some 10,000 men, marched through New Jersey by way of Allentown and Brunswick.[104]

For the Loyalists, the evacuation of Philadelphia was a bitter blow, made no more palatable by the advice of the Howe brothers that they make peace with the rebels. Their "deplorable situation" was typified by Joseph Galloway who, "deprived of a fortune of £70,000," was "now left to wander like Cain upon the earth, without home and without property."[105] Most Loyalists still wishing to leave opted for New York, abandoning their possessions to save their lives. But before they left they had the indignity of watching an elaborate masked ball, celebrating General Howe's departure in the manner of a conquering hero.[106]

The Loyalists were not the only persons upset by the pending evacuation of Philadelphia. The Carlisle peace commission arrived on 8 June ignorant of what was about to happen. They immediately condemned the abandonment of Philadelphia as "a fatal, ill concerted and ill advised retreat, highly dishonorable to His Majesty's arms and most prejudicial to the interest of his dominions."[107] In many states the deadline was approaching when the population had to take a final oath of loyalty or suffer banishment and the confiscation of their estates. "Many of the principal inhabitants" in consequence took the advice of the Howe brothers, "seeing that they were to be deprived of the protection of the King's forces."[108] The commissioners were not surprised, therefore, when Congress rejected their peace proposals. "The Treaty of Alliance with France, the evacuation of Philadelphia, the leaving open the whole coast of America to foreign supplies, the free entrance for prizes," and the "prospect of further assistance from Europe" had so elated the rebels that no other answer could be expected.[109]

Clinton finally set off from Philadelphia on 18 June 1778. Although he tried to keep his forces together, his march was encumbered by a 12-mile baggage train, carrying everything from the officers' personal possessions to iron forges. Initially Clinton protected the train by marching along two parallel roads. But after reaching Allentown he had to choose either the road to the coast at Sandy Hook or that to the Hudson River near Staten Island. He opted for Sandy Hook. He accordingly placed the German troops under Knyphausen at the front, leaving Cornwallis with 6,000 men, the cream of the British infantry, to protect the rear, the plan being to launch a counter-attack if Washington got too close.[110]

Getting close to the British was precisely what Washington intended after he left Valley Forge on 19 June, taking a more northerly route across the Delaware. Less baggage allowed him in a few days to catch the British near Monmouth Court House, where Clinton had stopped to refresh his men after marching through the intense heat of a summer day. Most of Washington's officers still advised caution about disputing the British retreat. However, Washington's own instincts were to attack, given the improved discipline of the Continental army and Clinton's difficulties in protecting his baggage train. In the end a compromise was agreed. Lafayette would command an enhanced detachment to harass the flanks and rear of the enemy, while the main army with Washington followed close behind, ready to give support.[111]

Among those advising caution was Charles Lee, who had recently rejoined the army following an exchange of officers. Captivity had not lessened his disenchantment with Washington or his desire to succeed him. He now demanded the command of Lafayette's corps, even though he had initially declined the assignment as being merely the "proper business of a young volunteer general" Since Lee was the army's second most senior officer, Washington necessarily had to agree.[112]

On 28 June 1778 Lee began implementing his orders to harass the British rear. His advance, however, required a difficult march over three ravines. Clinton immediately saw this as an opportunity to draw the Patriot army into a battle on favorable ground. Lee, on seeing the advancing ranks of the British, promptly ordered a withdrawal. However he failed to communicate his intention to Wayne on his left. As a result many units became entwined, resulting in considerable confusion until the men regained the crest of the first ravine, where Washington organized a makeshift defense.[113] Clinton then attempted to turn the Patriots' flanks but without success. By this time both armies were too exhausted to continue the engagement. Clinton was accordingly able to resume his retreat to Sandy Hook, which he reached on 1 July 1778.[114] Five days later his entire force had been ferried over to New York.

Washington never forgave Lee for ruining what he believed had been a golden opportunity to attack Clinton. He implicitly accused him of wantonly disobeying orders by retreating prematurely, and he repeated his charge when Lee demanded a court martial to clear his name.[115] Washington was not normally vindictive. He may have acted thus because of Lee's earlier defiance during the retreat through New Jersey in December 1776. Lee eventually got his court martial but was found guilty on three minor technicalities and suspended from command for 12 months. In reality his career was finished once Congress had confirmed the court's decision.[116] Historians have been divided over his guilt, though Clinton believed Lee had been justified in retreating with the elite of the British army advancing towards him.[117]

Clinton's arrival in New York proved fortunate, for a few days later d'Estaing appeared off Sandy Hook, with his 12 ships of the line and instructions to concert operations with Washington.[118] Howe had just six battleships at New York until Byron arrived. All that Howe could do was to form a defensive line inside the harbor and hope that d'Estaing found the sand bars obstructing the main channel too difficult to navigate.[119]

This duly happened. Although Washington had recruited pilots to help the French warships, d'Estaing did not relish having to force his way into the harbor past Howe. After 11 days of fruitless probing for an alternative channel, d'Estaing decided to sail to Rhode Island, where Sullivan with a force of Continentals and New England militia was watching the British garrison in Newport.[120] Washington readily accepted the new objective, sending two divisions under Lafayette and Greene to reinforce Sullivan, while he positioned the rest of the army at White Plains to threaten New York.[121] Clinton was sufficiently disturbed by these movements to consider momentarily evacuating the city in favor of Halifax.[122]

The allied prospects of securing Rhode Island were seemingly good, since the British garrison comprised little more than 4,000 soldiers, seamen, and marines. The initial plan was for d'Estaing to secure the three channels separating Newport from the mainland so that Sullivan could cross over from his camp at Tiverton. The joint forces could then lay siege to the enemy garrison.[123] But from the start relations between d'Estaing, a cultured aristocrat, and Sullivan, the son of Irish indentured servants, were poor. These social differences reinforced French prejudice that the local inhabitants were not competent in the arts of war. Surely the sons of mere laborers could never be generals.[124]

But before the allies could implement their plan, Howe appeared after being reinforced by several ships from Byron's squadron. The passage of the latter had not been smooth since leaving England in early June. Half-way across the Atlantic Byron's ships had been dispersed and damaged by a hurricane.[125] After assessing the strength of the new arrivals, d'Estaing immediately put to sea, having a slight advantage in the size of his ships. However, the two fleets were also dispersed by a storm before they could engage. D'Estaing temporarily returned to Rhode Island, leaving Howe to make for New York.[126] But after inspecting his ships, d'Estaing decided that his fleet was too badly damaged to continue the siege. He accordingly set off for Boston for repairs, despite angry protests from Sullivan, during which the Patriot commander made some very unflattering comments about d'Estaing's officers.[127]

The withdrawal of the French fleet on 22 August 1778 meant that Sullivan also had to abandon the siege of Newport, though he persisted for a few days until news arrived that a British task force was on the way under Howe and Clinton. This prompted the garrison to launch a counterattack on 30 August on the retreating Patriots, but without success.[128] Since his "prey had flown" Clinton then proposed an amphibious attack on d'Estaing in Boston harbor before the Frenchman could refit his vessels, but Howe rightly dismissed the idea as impractical. He preferred to fight a purely naval battle with d'Estaing without the complication of an accompanying army.[129] Nevertheless Washington was sufficiently worried to move part of his army to Danbury on the Connecticut River in case such an attempt was made.[130]

The first test of Franco-American cooperation had not proved fruitful and it required all the diplomatic skills of Washington and Lafayette to smooth the acrimony.[131] Sullivan's tirade was certainly undiplomatic. However, had d'Estaing stayed inside Narragansett Bay on Howe's first appearance, he might have anticipated the situation at Yorktown in 1781 when a union of the French and American forces forced the surrender of Cornwallis's army.[132] Equally, if Howe had entered Narragansett Bay on his second appearance instead of going to Boston, he might have trapped Sullivan's army at Newport and anticipated Clinton's capture of Lincoln's army at Charleston.[133] Counter-factual history, however, is no substitute for what happened. The most that can be said is that the events at Rhode Island represented a missed opportunity for two relatively balanced forces.

The rescue of the garrison at Rhode Island was Admiral Howe's last act in North America, having received permission to return to England. D'Estaing too wanted to leave New England for warmer waters, once his repairs were completed. However, these would take some weeks. Clinton accordingly took advantage of d'Estaing's disablement to implement Germain's call for coastal raiding. The first town to suffer in early September was New Bedford, followed by Martha's Vineyard, during which a number of privateers, prize vessels, stores and buildings were destroyed. Clinton justified these depredations as a way of convincing "these poor deluded people" of the fate awaiting them should they continue to resist.[134] Few Britons questioned the wisdom of such policy, though the Peace Commissioners pondered whether such devastation was "consonant with the dignity and humanity of a great nation." Doubts were also expressed about its practicality along such an extensive coastline. The only outcome was likely to be the permanent alienation of the population.[135]

There was little that Washington could do to counter these attacks other than recommend the construction of better defenses. But as he pointed out to Laurens, British possession of these "towns while we have an army in the field will avail them little," since they could only be held with a strong garrison.[136] There were other ways of hurting the enemy. A few weeks earlier Washington had asked his officers to reconsider plans for an invasion of Canada. They responded that such a project still offered considerable benefits, including control of the northern Indians, an advantageous trade, and the opening of the western territories to settlement. Although the British controlled Lakes Champlain and Ontario, alternative routes existed that would allow an invading force to link up with the Canadians.[137]

It quickly became apparent that the resources for such a venture were not available. Many soldiers who had enlisted in 1776 were due to complete their term of service and few replacements were in prospect. The Virginia state legislature was acting as though the war was already over, even though its Continental regiments wanted 2,731 men to complete their ranks. The legislators preferred sending men to Kentucky in the hope of extending the State's territory rather than securing what they already possessed.[138]

With no further military operations in the offing, Washington ordered his officers to consider the question of winter quarters.[139] But first warm clothing must be found if the men were to be retained in service. The troops were still "desperately" short of blankets, stockings and shoes, which meant that a great part of the army would not be able to march in an emergency.[140] Inflation was also eroding the ability of the officers and men to make their lives more comfortable, souring "the temper of the army exceedingly." Unless "some measures can be devised and speedily executed to restore the credit of our currency, restrain extortion and punish forestallers," Congress might well have to quit the war."[141]

Certainly there appeared little chance of an offensive against Canada, even though the need for it had resurfaced, following Indian attacks on the settlements of Cherry Valley and Wyoming.[142] Only the entry of Spain into the conflict, the defeat of the Royal Navy, or a British withdrawal from New York and Rhode Island could make such an enterprise feasible. At present the most that could be contemplated was an attack on Detroit or Niagara.[143] Despite the entry of France into the war, the initiative still seemed to remain with the British.

Britain ventures into Georgia

The arrival of Byron's squadron at New York and the disablement of d'Estaing meant that Clinton could finally carry out his orders to send an expeditionary force to St Lucia in the West Indies.[144] Help was certainly needed there, given the dispersed situation of Britain's possessions, scattered as they were from the Leeward and Windward Islands in the east to Jamaica in the west. The islands were also vulnerable because of their small white population and huge African slave force. Many planters believed submission to the French was preferable to confronting a slave rebellion.[145]

Unfortunately for Clinton, the delay in sending the expedition had allowed the French on Martinique to seize the neighboring island of Dominica. Hence any British success at St Lucia would merely be exchanging one sugar island for another of a similar size and would not constitute a fatal blow to French power in the area. Nevertheless the St Lucia task force, under General Grant and Commodore Hotham, finally left New York on 3 November 1778, reaching Carlisle Bay in Barbados on 10 December.[146] Here they were joined by the main British squadron under Admiral Samuel

Barrington. The flotilla then turned northwards, arriving off St Lucia three days later, to the surprise of the French. The troops quickly took possession of the island's main points, but their progress was threatened on 9 December 1778 by the return of d'Estaing to the West Indies with his flotilla of 12 battleships. Barrington in contrast had just seven such vessels, though the odds would be reversed once Byron arrived.[147] Unfortunately "foul weather Jack," as he was known to his men, had experienced another storm while waiting for d'Estaing to sail from Boston. This had forced him to undertake fresh repairs at New York.[148]

In this crisis Barrington acted as Howe had done earlier at New York. He placed his fleet inside the principal anchorage under the protection of the army's guns. D'Estaing then landed his amphibious force of 4,000 men to attack the British rear, in cooperation with the Island's militia. His troops however failed to break through the British lines, despite three assaults. D'Estaing was sufficiently discouraged by this setback to order a withdrawal on 29 December 1778 to Martinique.[149] The British West Indian islands, with the exception of Dominica, had for the moment survived.

Simultaneously to preparing the St Lucia expedition, Clinton also considered his instructions for reinforcing Florida. However, Germain had now readopted his previous idea of a campaign in Georgia and South Carolina. The continued neutrality of Spain meant that Florida was relatively safe. Germain accordingly suggested to Clinton on 5 August 1778 that he should make an attempt on Georgia, if South Carolina appeared too formidable.[150] After initial skepticism, Clinton consented. The task force would not have to be large, and would not weaken his forces in the north where Washington remained a threat. Such operation would also help reassure the Loyalists that Britain was not abandoning its attempts to regain America.

Clinton received his revised instructions at the end of October 1778 and immediately arranged for the dispatch of 3,000 men under Colonel Archibald Campbell. Campbell's orders were to "take possession of Savannah in Georgia and afterwards to pursue such measures as may be found most effectual for the recovery of that province." Campbell's force comprised one British regiment, the 71st Highlanders, two Hessian regiments and four battalions of New York and New Jersey provincials.[151] For the first time the Loyalists comprised a significant element in a British military operation.

The decision to send so many provincials reflected recent success in recruiting 7,000 men to the royal colors.[152] Earlier Germain had suggested that Clinton draw "over from the rebels the Europeans in their service," meaning recent immigrants from Ireland and Germany.[153] Clinton responded by targeting the Irish, many of whom he believed had not assimilated into the wider population. The result was the Volunteers of Ireland under the command of Lord Francis Rawdon, himself an Irish noble. Most of the 380 recruits were deserters from Washington's army, many being lured by the prospect of a free pardon for crimes (other than murder) committed in Ireland. Enlistment in the Volunteers would allow them to return home once the war had ended. By October 1778 Clinton reported that the Volunteers were proving a fine body of men and had even won the commendation of Cornwallis. Indeed Clinton wanted to make the unit into a regular regiment, since Rawdon's officers all had royal commissions.[154]

Campbell's task force set sail on 27 November 1778, arriving off Savannah late on 23 December. Georgia was a small state and its defenses were weak, the main reliance being 700 Continentals under General Robert Howe.[155] Such force was not likely to halt Campbell's progress, especially when he was informed by a slave about a secret path through a swamp on the right of Howe's position. After a brief exchange on 29 December 1778, the Patriots fled, leaving 400 of their number dead, wounded or captive.[156] Savannah was again the capital of a loyal colony. Campbell proudly observed that he was "the first officer . . . to take a stripe and a star from the rebel flag," a reference to the national flag which Congress had adopted in June 1777. A number of the respectable inhabitants now formed a loyal corps of rifle dragoons to patrol the country while Campbell advanced up the Savannah River to Ebenezer. Here he could watch the Patriot army in South Carolina commanded by Benjamin Lincoln.[157] Charleston, the fourth-largest American city, was within striking distance.

It was at this point that General Augustine Prevost arrived from East Florida with another 2,000 men, following orders from Clinton to send reinforcements.[158] Prevost was keen to maintain the military momentum and readily agreed to Campbell's proposal to advance with 1,000 men to Augusta while Prevost destroyed Lincoln's army at Purrysberg, 15 miles to the north. But although a number of Loyalists welcomed Prevost, he soon found the swamps and rivers along the coast difficult to traverse. More importantly the Patriot forces had been considerably reinforced in late December with units from North Carolina and Virginia. For the moment Prevost found it advisable to limit himself to a watching brief at Ebenezer.[159]

Campbell's advance up the Savannah River in contrast had been seemingly rather more successful. Little opposition was encountered on the way to Augusta, where a majority of the inhabitants welcomed him on 30 January. The oath of loyalty was then administered to some 1,400 people and 20 companies of militia formed to defend the population against the rebel attacks from South Carolina.[160] Patrols simultaneously scoured the countryside to encourage other Loyalists to enlist. Attempts were also made to contact the Creek Indians, whose support John Stuart, the southern superintendent, had repeatedly promised.[161]

The lull was deceptive, since the Patriot militia under Andrew Pickens had not been idle, especially when news was received that 600 North Carolina Loyalists were marching to join Campbell at Augusta. Although the Loyalists under Colonel James Boyd were numerically superior to Pickens, they allowed themselves to be surprised on 11 February 1779 at Kettle Creek, 50 miles north of Augusta, and routed with the loss of Boyd and 40 of his followers. Five others were then taken to Charleston for hanging. Campbell subsequently rescued 300 of Boyd's men but their condition was pitiful.[162] It was yet another example of the British inability to liaise with their supporters.

The defeat of Boyd and the approach of a further 1,200 North Carolina militia meant that Pickens and General Andrew Williamson now had some 4,000 men in the vicinity of Augusta, threatening Campbell's communications and very existence. Any hesitation about retreating was removed by the desertion of the Loyalists. As Campbell informed Clinton on 4 March 1779: "The Militia of Georgia ... on seeing the rebels increased on the opposite banks of the River found many excuses for going home to their plantations" despite every "argument to convince them that if they did not join the army in defense of the frontiers, the rebels would constantly make incursions and plunder them of their property."[163] He accordingly withdrew on 14 February 1779 towards Hudson's Ferry, 50 miles above Savannah, leaving the inhabitants in Augusta "to the Fury of the Rebel Army." On this occasion Williamson proved a humane conqueror. No plundering was allowed, though ten leading Tories were taken into custody to ensure the good behavior of the rest.[164]

Campbell shortly returned to England, though not before issuing a proclamation on 4 March 1779 that civil government had been restored. He had been instructed by the Peace Commissioners before the start of his mission to establish a civil administration, should he receive a welcome from the population. They recognized that the longer the rebels remained in power the more people became familiar "with the habits of their new situation," thus making it "daily more difficult" to win them over.[165] Germain readily agreed with these arguments, informing Campbell that former royal officials in the southern colonies had been ordered to return to their posts. The re-establishment of civil government, including an assembly, would show the population that the days of military government were coming to an end.[166]

Despite Campbell's proclamation, civil government had clearly not been restored, since the King's writ ran no more than a few miles outside Savannah. Moreover, Georgia still had no assembly, giving it the appearance of being under military rule. But even if one were called, as Governor Tonyn of Florida noted, the likelihood was that it would produce "men of the most turbulent tempers and leveling principles and of no support to the government." The only hope was that all would be different once "the malignant spirit of rebellion had subsided and men of moderation and temper had been elected."[167]

Prevost remained on the defensive for a few weeks, hoping that the restoration of constitutional government might reinvigorate the British cause. However, towards the end of April 1779 he learnt that Lincoln had gone to Augusta with his Continentals, leaving General William Moultrie with 2,000 militia at Purysburg. Prevost immediately advanced to take advantage of the situation and he was soon rewarded. The Patriot defenses collapsed so quickly that Prevost shortly found himself on the Ashley River opposite Charleston itself.[168] Morale in the city was so low that Governor John Rutledge even offered to declare South Carolina neutral for the rest of the war, leaving the question "whether the state shall belong to Great Britain or remain one of the United States" to a subsequent peace treaty.[169] It was a remarkable indication of the Patriots' weakness, though the negotiations were partly a ploy to give Lincoln time to come to the city's rescue. Prevost in any case replied that his instructions made no provision for a neutrality. The garrison must surrender unconditionally.[170]

News of these events quickly brought Lincoln back with his Continentals. This placed Prevost in a quandary, since he lacked sufficient artillery and other materials for a siege. Loyalist support was also lacking, not least because of rebel barbarity in enforcing the laws against them. Prevost determined consequently to retire towards Savannah, leaving 900 men under Colonel John Maitland on Port Royal Island as a forward base. He could then return to Charleston, once he had been reinforced and received the necessary naval support.[171]

Clinton was privately critical of Prevost for risking his army by so precipitate an advance.[172] James Wright, the governor of Georgia, agreed. Prevost's invasion of South Carolina had made it impossible to call elections or restore order in his province.[173] Clearly the British still lacked the key to regaining and retaining the political support of the population. But the incident was also a warning to the Patriots about their weak situation which had reduced them to beg for assistance from d'Estaing in the West Indies.[174]

Notes and references

1 Jonathan R. Dull, *A Diplomatic History of the American Revolution* (New Haven, 1985), 57–59. Orville T. Murphy, *Charles Gravier, Comte de Vergennes: French Diplomacy in the Age of Revolution, 1719–1787* (Albany, 1982), 213.

2 Murphy, *Vergennes*, 215–16. Jonathan Dull, *The French Navy and American Independence: A Study of Arms and Diplomacy, 1774–1787* (Princeton, 1975), 20–21.

3 Dull, *French Navy*, 27. William C. Stinchcombe, *The American Revolution and the French Alliance* (Syracuse, NY, 1969), 2.

4 Dull, *Diplomatic History*, 53–56. Murphy, *Vergennes*, 242–43.

5 John Ferling, *Almost a Miracle: The American Victory in the War of Independence* (New York, 2007), 199.

6 Dull, *Diplomatic History*, 80–81.

7 Quoted in David Syrett, *The Royal Navy in American Waters, 1775–1783* (Aldershot, 1989), 65.

8 Robert Middlekauf, *The Glorious Cause: The American Revolution, 1763–1789* (New York, 1982), 403–4.

9 Dull, *Diplomatic History*, 70. Samuel Flagg Bemis, *The Diplomacy of the American Revolution* (Bloomington, 1961), 55–56.

10 Andrew Stockley, *Britain and France at the Birth of America: The European Powers and the Peace Negotiations of 1782–1783* (Exeter, 2001), 11–12.

11 Murphy, *Vergennes*, 258–59, 291–309.

12 Dull, *Diplomatic History*, 165–69.

13 Lee Kennett, *The French Forces in America, 1780–1783* (Westport, Conn., 1977), 6.

14 Dull, *French Navy*, 109–12.

15 Howe to Germain, 30 November 1777, DDAR/XIV, 264–65.

16 Germain to Clinton, 8 March 1778, DDAR/XV, 58. Augmentation of the Army, 22 January 1778, CJ/XXXVI, 597.

17 Statutes at Large, 18 Geo III, Chapter 10. The bill received the royal assent on 28 May 1778, CJ/XXXVI, 997. For attempts to raise troops previously by these means, see Richard Middleton, *The Bells of Victory: The Pitt-Newcastle Ministry and the Conduct of the Seven Years War, 1757–1762* (Cambridge, 1985), 25–26.

18 George III to North, 4 December 1777, Fortescue/3, 500–1.

19 George III to North, 13 January 1778, Fortescue/4, 14–15. Cabinet Minute, 17 January 1778, Fortescue/4, 20–21.

20 Sandwich to North, 8 December 1777, Sandwich/1, 327–32.

21 George III to North, 15 January 1778, Fortescue/4, 14. J.C. Long, *Lord Jeffery Amherst: A Soldier of the King* (New York, 1933), 237–41.

22 Piers Mackesy, *The War for America, 1775–1783* (Cambridge, Mass., 1964), 213.

23 Germain to Clinton, 8 March 1778, DDAR/XV, 57–62.

24 Ibid., 57–61.

25 North to George III, 30 December 1777, Fortescue/3, 530–31.

26 North to George III, 25 March 1778 Fortescue/4, No. 2247.

27 North to George III, 21 March 1778, Fortescue/4, 70–72.

28 George III to North, 16 March 1778, Fortescue/4, 59–60.

29 George III to North, 17 March 1778, Fortescue/4, 65.

30 North to George III, 30 March 1778. Fortescue/4, 88.

31 George III to North, 16 March 1778, Fortescue/4, 62.

32 George III to North, 26 March 1778, Fortescue/4, 80. Stephen Conway, *The British Isles and the War of American Independence* (Oxford, 2003), 63.

33 Amherst's Idea about the change of War in America, [March 1778], Sandwich/1, 365.

34 Secret Instructions for Sir Henry Clinton, 21 March 1778, DDAR/XV, 74–76.

35 Sandwich's Advice about the Change of the War in America, March 1778, Sandwich/1, 359–60. Cabinet Minute, 14 March 1778, Sandwich/1, 361. State of the Force in North America, 15 March 1778, Sandwich/1, 362.

36 Instructions to the Commissioners for Quieting the Disorders in North America, 12 April 1778, DDAR/XV, 81–93.

37 Germain to Clinton, 5 August 1778, DDAR/XV, 177–78.

38 D'Estaing to Washington, 8 July 1778, WP/RWS/16, 38–39.

39 Dull, *French Navy*, 110.
40 Lord Sandwich's Opinion, 4 April 1778, Sandwich/2, 22–23.
41 Germain to North, 27 April 1778, Fortescue/4, 121.
42 Lord Sandwich's Opinion, 6 April 1778, Sandwich/2, 23.
43 Sandwich to North, 7 May 1778, Sandwich/2, 49–50.
44 Summary of Instructions to Admiral Byron, 1778, Sandwich/2, 374–76.
45 N.A.M. Rodger, *The Insatiable Earl: A Life of John Montagu, 4th Earl of Sandwich* (London, 1993), 137–40, 197. Estimates for Building and Rebuilding, 1769, 1770, CJ/XXXII, 53, 634.
46 North to Sandwich, 5 September 1772, Sandwich/1, 19–23. H.M. Scott, *British Foreign Policy in the Age of the American Revolution* (Oxford, 1990), 166–67, 181–90.
47 Sandwich to North, 10 September 1772, Sandwich/1, 23–6.
48 Daniel A. Baugh, "Why did Britain lose command of the sea during the war for America," in Jeremy Black and Philip Woodfine, eds., *The British Navy and the Use of Naval Power in the Eighteenth Century* (Leicester, 1988), 153–55.
49 Cabinet Minute, 20 June 1776, Sandwich/4, 212–13. Sandwich to George III, 23 October 1776, Fortescue/3, 396–97. Nicholas Tracy, *Navies, Deterrence and American Independence: Britain and Sea Power in the 1760s and 1770s* (Vancouver, 1988), 126–34.
50 Rodger, *Sandwich*, 235. Scott, *British Foreign Policy*, 235.
51 Estimate for Building and Repairs for the Service of 1769, CJ/XXXII, 53. Ibid., 1777, CJ/XXXVI, 37–39.
52 Sandwich to North, 3 August 1777, Sandwich/1, 235–38. N.A.M. Rodger, *Command of the Ocean: A Naval History of Britain, 1649–1815* (New York, 2004), 644.
53 State of the Present Naval Force, 15 March 1778, Fortescue/4, 54.
54 George III to Sandwich, 14 April 78, Sandwich/2, 24. Memorandum of a visit to Portsmouth, 2 May 1778, Fortescue/4, 126–30.
55 Sandwich to North, 6 March 1778, Sandwich/1, 349–52. Dull, *French Navy*, 360.
56 R. Middleton, "British Naval Strategy, 1755–1762: The Western Squadron", *Mariner's Mirror*, LXXV (1989), 349–67.
57 Summary of Orders to Admiral Keppel, 25 April to 5 June 1778, Sandwich/2, 369–74.
58 Keppel to Sandwich, 21 June 78, Sandwich/2, 98.

59 Keppel to Sandwich, 6 July 1778, Sandwich/2, 109.

60 Summary of Orders to Admiral Keppel, 1778, Sandwich/2, 372–3. David Syrett, *The Royal Navy in European Waters during the American Revolutionary War* (Columbia, SC, 1998), 38.

61 Dull, *French Navy*, 119–120.

62 Keppel to Shuldham, 24 July 1778, Sandwich/2, 127. Keppel to Sandwich, 29 July 1778, Sandwich/2, 128.

63 Rodger, *Command of the Ocean*, 272–73.

64 Keppel to Sandwich, 29 July 1778, Sandwich/2, 128–29. Palliser to Sandwich, 31 July 1778, Ibid, 129–32.

65 Jackson to Sandwich, 10 February 1779, Fortescue/4, 269–70.

66 Syrett, *Royal Navy in European Waters*, 55–57. Rodger, *Sandwich*, 249.

67 Rodney to Sandwich, 16 February 1780, Sandwich/3, 201.

68 Robinson to Sandwich, 18 August 1777, Sandwich/1, 238–40.

69 State of the force at Home, March 1778, Sandwich/2, 21.

70 Ferling, *Almost a Miracle*, 372–73.

71 Arthur Bowler, *Logistics and the Failure of the British Army in America, 1775–1783* (Princeton, 1975), 72.

72 Washington to Laurens, 23 December 1777, printed in Saul K. Padover, *The Washington Papers: Basic Selections from the Public and Private Writings of George Washington* (New York, 1955), 155–57.

73 Washington to Trumbull, 18 February 1777, WP/RWS/8, 366. Ibid., 12 May 1777, WP/RWS/9, 407. Trumbull to Washington, 9 July 1777, WP/RWS/10, 236.

74 Trumbull to Washington, 19 July 1777, WP/RWS/10, 342–43. Washington to Hancock, 9 July 1777, WP/RWS/10, 234–35.

75 Washington to Congressional Committee, 19 July 1777, WP/RWS/10, 332–36.

76 Washington to Robert Hooper et al., 15 February 1778, WP/RWS/13, 549. Middlekauff, *Glorious Cause*, 413

77 Circular to the Governors of New Jersey etc, 19 February 1778, WP/RWS/13, 589.

78 Washington to Wayne, 9 February 1778, WP/RWS/13, 492–93.

79 Washington to Brigadier Lacey, 23 January 1778, WP/RWS/13, 323. Ibid., 351, Lacey to Washington, 26 January 1778.

80 Officers of General Wayne's brigade to Washington, 15 August 1777, WP/RWS/10, 631–32.

81 Washington to the Continental Committee of Congress, 29 January 1778, WP/RWS/13, 376–404.
82 Washington to John Banister, 21 April 1778, WP/RWS/14, 573–79.
83 General Orders, 24 March 1778, WP/RWS/14, 285–86.
84 Washington to Cadwalader, 20 March 1778, WP/RWS/14, 234–35.
85 Washington to Laurens, 28 March 1778, WP/RWS/14, 292–94.
86 Washington to McDougall, 23 May 1777, WP/RWS/9, 506–7.
87 Quoted in Christopher Ward, *The War of the Revolution* (New York, 1952), II, 551.
88 Washington to Smallwood, 1 May 1778, WP/RWS/15, 7–8.
89 Washington to Laurens, 30 April 1778, WP/RWS/14, 681–82. Ibid., 22 July 1778, WP/RWS/16, 129.
90 Middlekauf, *Glorious Cause*, 419.
91 Varnum to Washington, 5 May 1778, WP/RWS/15, 54–55.
92 Washington to Laurens, 24 July 1778, WP/RWS/16, 150–52.
93 General Orders, 4 May 78. WP/RWS/15, 27–28.
94 General Orders, 27 April 1779, WGW/14, 445–46.
95 Washington to General Armstrong, 27 March 78, WP/RWS/14, 326–28.
96 B. Dandridge to Washington, 12 April 1778, WP/RWS/14, 484–86.
97 Council of War, 8 May 1778, WP/RWS/15, 79–81.
98 Howe to Germain, 19 April 1778, DDAR/XV, 103.
99 Washington to Smallwood, 30 April 1778, WP/RWS/14, 684–85.
100 Council of War, 8 and 9 May 1778, WP/RWS/15, 79–86.
101 Washington to St Clair, 4 October 1779, WGW/16, 402–3.
102 Washington to Lafayette, 18 May 1778, WP/RWS/15, 151–52. Washington to Laurens, 24 May 78, Ibid., 210–11.
103 Clinton to Germain, 23 May 1778, DDAR/XV, 126.
104 Clinton to Germain, 5 June 1778, DDAR/XV, 132–33.
105 Quoted in Ward, *War of Revolution*, 568.
106 Ira D. Gruber, *The Howe Brothers and the American Revolution* (New York, 1972), 298–99.
107 Commissioners for Quieting Disorders to Germain, 15 June 1778, DDAR/XV, 142.
108 Commissioners for Quieting Disorders to Germain, 15 June 1778, DDAR/XV, 140–42.

109 Commissioners for Quieting Disorders to Germain, 5 July 1778, DDAR/XV, 159.

110 Clinton to Germain, 5 July 1778, DDAR/XV, 159–63.

111 Council of War, 24 June 1778, WP/RWS/15, 520–21. Washington to Lafayette, 25 June 1778, ibid., 539.

112 Lee to Washington, 15 June 1778, WP/RWS/15, 403. Lee to Washington, 25 June 78, WP/RWS/15, 541–42. Washington to Lafayette, 26 June 1778, WP/RWS/15, 555.

113 Washington to Laurens, 1 July 1778, WP/RWS/16, 2–6.

114 Clinton to Germain, 5 July 1778, DDAR/XV, 159–62.

115 Lee to Washington, 30 June 1778, WP/RWS/15, 594. Washington to Lee, 30 June 1778, WP/RWS/15, 595.

116 Washington to Laurens, 16 August 1778, WP/RWS/16, 318–19. General Orders, 22 December 1778, WP/RWS/18, 486–88.

117 *Clinton's Narrative*, CAR, 95. General Lee's Defense at his Court Martial, 9 August 1778, CAR, 388–90.

118 D'Estaing to Washington, 8 July 1778, WP/RWS/16, 38–39.

119 Admiral Howe to Stephens, 6 July 1778, DDAR/XV, 163–64. Syrett, *Royal Navy in American Waters*, 97–99.

120 Washington to Sullivan, 17 July 1778, WP/RWS/16, 92–93. Alexander Hamilton to Washington, 20 July 1778, WP/RWS/16, 109.

121 Washington to d'Estaing, 22 July 1778, WP/RWS/16, 125. Council of War, 25 July 1778, WP/RWS/16, 160–64. Washington to Lafayette, 27 July 1778, WP/RWS/16, 185–86.

122 Clinton to Germain, 27 July 1778, DDAR/XV, 173–74.

123 Sullivan to d'Estaing, 24 July 1778, WP/RWS/16, 178–79. Colonel Laurens to Washington, 4 August 1778, WP/RWS/16, 243–50.

124 Middlekauf, *Glorious Cause*, 430–31.

125 Syrett, *Royal Navy in American Waters*, 101.

126 M. Le Comte de Lapeyrouse Bonfils, *Histoire de la Marine Française*, 3 vols. (Paris, 1845), III, 47–50.

127 Sullivan to Washington, 23 August 1778, WP/RWS/16, 358. Lafayette to Washington, 25 August 1778, WP/RWS/16, 369–74.

128 Greene to Washington, 28–31 August 1778, WP/RWS/16, 396–98. Piggott to Clinton, 31 August 1778, DDAR/XV, 188–92.

129 William B. Willcox, *Portrait of a General: Sir Henry Clinton in the War of Independence* (New York, 1964), 252–53. David Syrett, *Admiral Lord Howe: A Biography* (Annapolis, MD, 2006), 86–87.

130 Washington to Gates, 10 September 1778, WP/RWS/16, 553–54.
131 Washington to Greene, 1 September 1778, WP/RWS/16, 458–59. Washington to Lafayette, 1 September, WP/RWS/16, 460–61.
132 Syrett, *Royal Navy in America Waters*, 104–5.
133 Willcox, *Portrait of a General*, 250. Syrett, *Royal Navy in American Waters*, 109–10.
134 Quoted in Willcox, *Portrait of a General*, 251 [Clinton to Unknown, 21 September 1778].
135 Commissioners for Quieting Disorders to Germain, 21 September 1778, DDAR/XV, 203.
136 Washington to Laurens, 3 October 1778, WP/RWS/17, 237–38.
137 Board of Officers to Washington, 10 September 1778, WP/RWS/17, 550–51.
138 Colonel James Wood to Washington, 12 November 1778, WP/RWS/18, 127–28.
139 Washington to General Officers, 14 October 1778, WP/RWS/17, 373. Council of War, 16 October 1778, WP/RWS/17, 399–400.
140 Washington to Measam, 2 October 1778, WP/RWS/17, 230. Washington to Measam, 28 October 1778, WP/RWS/17, 617–18.
141 Washington to Morris, 4 October 1778, WP/RWS/17, 253.
142 See Chapter 8, section on "The devastation of Iroquoia."
143 Washington to Laurens, 11 November 1778, WP/RWS/18, 94–106.
144 Clinton to Germain, 15 September 1778, DDAR/XV, 201.
145 Mackesy, *War for America*, 225–28.
146 Ibid., 230–31.
147 Charles Stuart to Sandwich, 8 January 1779, Sandwich/2, 344–46.
148 Syrett, *Navy in American Waters*, 114–15.
149 Stuart to Sandwich, 8 January to 3 February 1779, Sandwich/2, 343–62.
150 Germain to Clinton, 5 August 1778, DDAR/XV, 177–78.
151 Clinton to Germain, 25 October 1778, DDAR/XV, 232.
152 Ferling, *Almost a Miracle*, 416.
153 Germain to Clinton, 8 March 1778, DDAR/XV, 60.
154 Clinton to Germain, 23 October 1778, DDAR/XV, 227–29.
155 Lincoln to Washington, 19 December 1778, WP/RWS/18, 466–67.
156 Campbell to Germain, 16 January 1779, DDA/XVII, 33–38. Lincoln to Washington, 5 January 1779, WP/RWS/18, 576–77.

157 Campbell to Germain, 16 January 1779, DDAR/XVII, 39–42.

158 Clinton to Germain, 25 October 1778, DDAR/XV, 232.

159 Prevost to Clinton, 14 February 1779, DDAR/XVII, 65–67.

160 Campbell to Clinton, 4 March 1779, DDAR/XVII, 72–73.

161 For the Native American involvement, see Chapter 8, section on "The southern mosaic."

162 Paul H. Smith, *Loyalists and Redcoats: A Study in British Revolutionary Policy* (Chapel Hill, 1964), 102–3. Edwardn J. Cashin, *The King's Ranger: Thomas Brown and the American Revolution on the Southern Frontier* (Athens, Ga., 1989), 89–92.

163 Campbell to Clinton, 4 March 1779, DDAR/XVII, 72–73. Smith, *Loyalists*, 102.

164 Cashin, *King's Ranger*, 91.

165 Commissioners for Quieting Disorders to Germain, 16 November 1778, DDAR/XV, 253–59.

166 Germain to Campbell, 16 January 1779, DDAR/XV, 31–33.

167 Tonyn to Germain, 3 July 1779, DDAR/XVII, 155–58.

168 Prevost to Clinton, 21 May 1779, DDAR/XVII, 127–29. Ibid., 10 June 1779, 141–43.

169 Quoted in Robert D. Bass, *Swamp Fox: The Life and Campaigns of General Francis Marion* (Orangeburg, 1959), 24.

170 Prevost to Germain, 10 June 1779, DDAR/XVII, 141–43.

171 Prevost to Germain, 4 August 1779, DDAR/XVII, 175–76.

172 *Clinton's Narrative*, CAR, 134.

173 Wright to Germain, 31 July 1779, DDAR/XVII, 171.

174 Henri Doniol, *Histoire de la participation de la France à l'éstablishment des États-Unis d'Amérique: Correspondence diplomatique et documents*, 5 vols. (Paris, 1886–1892), 4, 161–62. For the outcome of South Carolina's appeal to d'Estaing, see below, Chapter 6.

CHAPTER 6

Spain enters the conflict, 1779

Spain and the American war

Spain, like France, had followed with interest Britain's growing troubles in North America. Initially, Charles III agreed with his nephew, Louis XVI, that detaching the colonies would be a useful weakening of Britain's power. He accordingly matched Louis XVI's grant of one million livres for the purchase of arms and ammunition.[1] However, the creation of 13 independent republics in the summer of 1776 posed a dilemma for the Spanish monarchy. Although Britain might be weakened, the independence of these states could set a precedent for Spain's own colonies in central and South America.[2]

Another reason for caution was that Spain, like France, was still recovering from the previous war. In addition her confidence had not been improved in 1775 by an embarrassing end to her expedition to punish the corsairs of Algiers for their constant harassment of merchant shipping along the north coast of Africa. Resentment also lingered that France had not supported Spain against British claims to the Falkland Islands in 1771.[3] Nevertheless Spain had a number of long standing issues to settle with Britain, not least the recovery of Minorca and Gibraltar. The loss of the latter in 1704 was a cause for national shame, situated as it was on the Spanish mainland. Jamaica and Florida were also considered legitimate targets, having once been Spanish colonies. Consequently, Vergennes' invitation to enter the war in 1778 was of considerable interest to the government in Madrid, since it offered Spain an opportunity to regain her lost territories.[4]

The Spanish, however, were divided on their best course of action. The foreign minister, Count Floridablanca, wanted an immediate alliance with France. Charles III on the other hand hoped to profit from the situation by threats rather than actual force. Certainly no military action could be contemplated until the annual treasure fleets from Mexico and Peru had arrived, bringing their precious cargo of silver to finance the completion of Spain's warlike preparations.[5] Hence the need for caution initially prevailed. In the autumn of 1778, the Spanish accordingly made an offer of mediation to Britain and France, though in tones that clearly favored the latter. Essentially Spain would support whoever accommodated her in the recovery of Gibraltar and Minorca. Had Britain agreed to surrender those territories, Spain would have remained neutral, leaving France to fight alone. The British ministry, however, rejected the proposal, not least because of public contempt for Spain as a military and naval power. The Spanish ministry was accordingly left with the choice of either declaring war or accepting a humiliating snub. Any inducement regarding the latter was outweighed by the flagrant disrespect shown to Spanish shipping by the Royal Navy.[6]

Although the British affected to despise Spain, its threat to intervene was a serious matter. The army in metropolitan Spain was admittedly below its nominal strength of 70,000 men and had little prospect of rectifying the deficit, despite a system of conscription, which, as in Britain, was highly unpopular.[7] On the other hand Spain had the third-largest navy among the European powers, comprising some 57 ships of the line. When the squadrons at Ferrol and Cadiz were added to those of France at Brest and Toulon, the result would be a decided superiority over the Royal Navy.[8] Sandwich's own calculations at the end of 1778 were that France and Spain could deploy 80 battleships in European waters compared to 55 for Britain. This made invasion a possibility. At the very least the Bourbon powers would be able to dominate the Mediterranean, thus allowing Spain to attack Minorca and Gibraltar. Spain would also be able to threaten Britain's most valuable Caribbean possession, the island of Jamaica, as well as East and West Florida.[9] Finally the entry of Spain would put yet more pressure on Britain's extended lines of communication and her ability to conduct the war in America.

The threat from Spain became a reality on 12 April 1779 when the courts of Madrid and Paris signed an alliance committing them to a war with Britain "to avenge their respective injuries." Among the latter was the ending of "that tyrannical empire which England ... claims to maintain upon the ocean." The Treaty of Aranjuez specified that the two nations would fight until Spain had recovered Gibraltar, Minorca, and the two Floridas, and expelled the illegal logwood cutters along the coast of Honduras. In return Spain would help France secure a share of the Newfoundland fishery, a stronger presence in India, and permanent possession of Dominica in the West Indies and Senegal in West Africa, both of which had been ceded to Britain at the end of the previous war.[10] However, the convention did not commit Spain to supporting American Independence, though she was indirectly tied to that objective by the requirement not to make a separate peace.[11]

The two governments decided that an immediate invasion of Britain would be the best means of securing their objectives. The Spanish argued that their resources were insufficient to sustain a long war, even after the arrival of the annual treasure fleets from the silver mines of Mexico and Peru. A successful invasion of Britain, in contrast, could give the two governments everything they wanted.[12] The plan seemed the more plausible following the battle of Ushant, which revealed that the Royal Navy was far from invincible. However, the treaty was concealed for several weeks so that Spain could complete her naval preparations at Ferrol and Cadiz. The delay would also permit her forces in Cuba and elsewhere in America to secure themselves from British attack and prepare for more offensive operations. Not until 16 June 1779 was the agreement acknowledged in London and war declared.

The delay in announcing the alliance meant that there would not be time to coordinate operations elsewhere. The two powers accordingly agreed to pursue separate objectives once the invasion had been attempted. For Spain this meant the reduction of Gibraltar and capture of West Florida. The French in contrast would focus on the West Indies, following news that Britain had captured St Lucia. Twelve ships of the line with several thousand troops had already been assembled in March 1779 under Admiral La Motte Picquet for dispatch to Martinique, though contrary winds delayed their sailing until early May.[13] These commitments meant that there would be no military or naval help for the American Patriots in 1779. They would have to make do with French weapons and money, at least until France had regained the initiative in the Caribbean.[14] In any case a British defeat in the West Indies should be as helpful to the Patriots as the dispatch of French forces to North America, since the loss of Britain's sugar islands would undermine her ability to finance the war.

Britain faces invasion

News of the Spanish-Franco accord started a new discussion in Britain about the war's objectives and its sustainability. North raised the question of cost, arguing "that the advantages to be gained by this contest could never repay the expense." But George III resolutely refused to listen. North's reasoning was "only weighing such events in the scale of a tradesman behind his counter." Some things were more important than the loss of money. Should America succeed in its bid for independence, the West Indies must succumb, given their dependence for supplies from North America. Ireland would then "follow the same plan and be a separate state" so that Britain "would soon be a poor island indeed."[15]

Likelihood of war with both Bourbon powers had already led North to request once more that he be relieved of an office which he was no longer capable of executing. He told George III: "In critical times it is necessary that there should be one directing minister, who should plan the whole operations of government, and control all the other departments of administration so far as to make them cooperate zealously and actively with his designs, even though the contrary of their own." He was of course thinking of Pitt's example during the Seven Years War. The King must understand that North himself was "not capable of being such a minister."[16] Nevertheless George III was adamant. He was prepared to dispense with Germain, recognizing that the American Secretary was dogged by "his former misfortunes."[17] But he would not hear of North's retiring, even though Sandwich pointed out that it was essential to have a first minister who was capable and willing to coordinate the decisions of the Cabinet.[18]

In an attempt to keep the ministry together, George III called a Cabinet meeting on 21 June 1779 to address his ministers. This was something that he rarely did, though there was nothing unconstitutional in his action, whatever the assertions of later Whig historians.[19] He compared the present crisis with that of 1588 when Queen Elizabeth I had been assailed by the Spanish Armada. The ministers must remain firm. He still believed that one more campaign could end the rebellion, or at least leave Britain in possession of Canada, Nova Scotia, and Florida.[20] In these views George III undoubtedly spoke for the majority of the nation.

The plan of the Bourbon allies was for a fleet of 55 battleships to seize control of the Channel after first defeating or dispersing the Royal Navy. They would then convoy 20,000 troops under the Comte de Vaux from St Malo and Le Havre to the Isle of Wight. A further reinforcement of 10,000 would follow, allowing the troops to besiege Portsmouth. The loss of this base was expected to cause the collapse of British resistance, since there were few troops in England, the main defense being a poorly organized militia.[21] At the very least it would lead to the collapse of British credit and ability to finance the war. But to increase the general alarm, the French plan included the dispatch from Lorient of a cruiser squadron under Jones, to create a diversion around the coasts of Britain.

The plausibility of the scheme was privately acknowledged by George III, given what a few ragged Highlanders under the Young Pretender, Bonnie

Prince Charlie, had achieved in 1745. The British army was hardly better prepared for such an emergency this time.[22] Its strength was not expected to exceed 91,400 men, an increase of just 14,440 on the previous year. Of these, 30,346 horse and foot were for service in Britain and the other 47,000 for deployment overseas.[23] Plans were in train for the passing of another Recruiting Act, allowing the conscription of unemployed indigent men. However, the results of the previous year had not been encouraging, only 1,463 men having been secured.[24]

These were clearly inadequate resources should the enemy succeed in landing. Nevertheless, the French and Spanish were not as strong as initially appeared, especially at sea. Their crews were less well trained, especially those in the Spanish fleet. In addition they had had little experience of fighting combined operations involving crews speaking different languages and using different signaling systems. Some British officers believed that 30 battleships were as many as any commander could direct at sea.[25] There were other factors too. The allies, unlike the British, had no suitable bases in which to take cover in the Channel, where westerly gales posed the danger of ships being blown onto a lee shore. In such circumstances their fleets might be driven up the Channel away from their objective like the Armada in 1588. Even in good weather they still had to escort the troop transports while fending off their enemy.

The British fleet had some other advantages too. It was beginning to benefit from the first fruits of the industrial revolution. Most important was the introduction of copper sheathing to keep the hulls free of barnacles and mollusks, which made ships faster and less liable to decay, thus reducing the time spent in port. By August 1779 Sandwich was able to assert that "the coppering of battleships is now become almost general."[26] The French in contrast had only just begun to follow suit. Another improvement was the introduction in 1779 of a new type of French ammunition, called langridge, which d'Orvilliers had used against the sails and rigging of Keppel's fleet. Until now the British had relied on grapeshot for this purpose. Langridge in contrast comprised a canister packed with jagged metal which exploded on hitting the target, causing much more severe damage.[27] This did not mean that the Royal Navy was abandoning its traditional tactic of battering opponents into submission, since the new ammunition was merely intended to immobilize an enemy prior to close bombardment. Indeed, to increase the effectiveness of its traditional tactics, the navy now introduced a third weapon, the carronade. This gun had a shorter barrel than the normal 32-pounder cannon. However, it could still fire the same weight of shot at close range while its reduced weight meant that it could be mounted on the upper decks, thus increasing a vessel's firepower without upsetting its balance.[28]

It is no coincidence that these improvements coincided with the appointment in July 1778 of Sir Charles Middleton as Comptroller of the Navy Board, the department responsible for the building and equipping of the fleet. Middleton, later Lord Barham, was the former captain of a 50-gun ship. He quickly established a reputation for efficiency. One of his colleagues at the Navy Board commented shortly after his arrival: "The load of business he gets through at the Board, at the Treasury, at the Admiralty and his own house is astonishing, and what I am confident no other man will be able to execute."[29] Within two years almost all the capital ships had been coppered and most of the frigates as well. He also ensured that canister shot was widely available. However, the introduction of the carronade proved more difficult. Middleton wanted these weapons mounted on the 44- and 50-gun ships so that they could be deployed in a line of battle against larger enemy vessels. He had an uphill struggle convincing the Ordnance Board and ships' officers as to their utility.[30]

Nevertheless, under Sandwich and Middleton, the Royal Navy by 1779 was close to its maximum strength in the previous war, the yardstick by which everything was measured. Eighty ships of the line were in commission, of which half were for the Channel. Another ten were building or being refitted, and expected to join the fleet during the year.[31] Equally significant was the resumption of merchant building, not only of frigates and sloops, but 74- and 64-gun battleships as well.[32] However, many of those ships in commission still wanted men, even though the number of seamen by April 1779 stood at almost 73,000 with another 15,277 in the marines, making a grand total of 88,210. This was fractionally more than the highest figure in the previous war.[33] But as usual the figures did not include the sick, so that by June 1779 the ships at Portsmouth were still 15 percent short of their complement. Their quality also left much to be desired.[34]

The Admiralty had been using the traditional press gang system since the autumn of 1776 to complete the manning of the fleet. However, the shortage this time was so serious that it adopted the extreme measure of pressing even those who were protected by act of Parliament. But before taking so grave a step, Sandwich sought the advice of Lord Thurlow, the Lord Chancellor, the Crown's most senior law officer. Fortunately for Sandwich, Thurlow was clear: "The law should not stand in the way" during "a crisis more alarming than this country ever saw before," though a bill of indemnity would be required to make the action retrospectively legal.[35] Inevitably collateral disruption occurred, not least to the convoys waiting with provisions for the armies in North America.[36] It was a classic case of short-term expediency and long-term damage.

One other difficulty facing Sandwich was that of finding a suitable commander, since Keppel refused to serve, following his court martialing on the unsubstantiated charges of a subordinate officer and friend of Sandwich. His allies in the navy simultaneously requested George III to remove Palliser from all his employments. They too refused to serve until this had been done.[37] In this situation Sandwich had to select the elderly Sir Charles Hardy, who had held various commands during the previous war and had not been involved in the Palliser–Keppel controversy.[38] To assist him, Sandwich appointed Richard Kempenfelt as his "post" captain or chief of staff. Kempenfelt was one of the most respected officers in the navy, who had missed high command because of the archaic system of promotion. He was also one of the most innovative, recognizing that the navy urgently needed a more efficient signaling system. He had recently been devising one similar to that of the French which Middleton urged should be introduced at the earliest convenient moment.[39]

Hardy's orders at the end of May 1779 were to blockade the French fleet at Brest, unless it had already departed, in which case he was to patrol the Channel approaches west of Lizard Point, since the security of Britain and Ireland were to "be the principal objects" of his cruise.[40] But as in 1778 Hardy could return to port if the Bourbon fleets appeared too strong. Opinion was divided whether he should seek battle immediately or wait until the enemy attempted to escort their invasion flotilla across the Channel when they would be at their most vulnerable.[41] For the moment he was to keep his options open.

Hardy finally got to sea on 16 June 1779 with a fleet of some 30 battleships. However, it was not long before he was back in the Channel, though from the force of the wind rather than the strength of the enemy. While sheltering in Torbay, he requested the delivery of fresh water supplies. This led him to suggest readopting the system of the previous war when the western squadron was supplied at sea with food, beer, and water by transports from Plymouth. To this Sandwich readily agreed, since he was anxious to keep Hardy on his station.[42] Once ships came into port they often undertook inessential repairs, while crews deserted so that days turned into weeks, leaving the western approaches open to the enemy. At Torbay Hardy had a much better chance of regaining his station once the weather improved, which he effected in the second week of August.[43]

By now the French and Spanish were far behind their invasion timetable. Originally the two courts wanted to complete their Channel operations by the end of August so that the Spanish could return to the siege of Gibraltar, which they had begun to blockade in early July.[44] However, the Spanish navy had found this schedule too onerous, though the French had done their best to be ready by the end of May for a union of the two fleets at Ferrol in northern Spain. The Spanish dockyards and machinery of government were simply not capable of operating at such speed. Bad weather also played its part.[45] The allied armada in consequence reached the Channel only in early August, by which time the French battleships had barely a month's supply of provision left. The joint fleets also mustered only 50 battleships rather than the 66 originally planned. Nevertheless their timing proved propitious, because Hardy had taken a new station west of the Scilly Isles, leaving the Channel open for the combined fleet. D'Orvilliers and Admiral Cordoba accordingly entered Plymouth Sound with some 45 ships of the line on 17 August within sight of the Royal Navy's second most important dockyard, capturing a British battleship in the process. Seemingly the way was now open for the French army under the Comte de Vaux at St Malo and Le Havre to board their transports and begin the invasion.[46]

In the absence of Hardy, the defense of Britain therefore apparently rested on the forces assembled by Amherst as commander-in-chief. These amounted to a field army of 20,000 regulars, and the uncertain services of some 39,000 militia.[47] But the main dilemma facing Amherst was whether to scatter his army along the coast to repulse the enemy on the beaches or keep his men together so that he could strike them more effectively once they had landed. Common sense dictated the latter. He accordingly concentrated his infantry in two camps in Kent and Essex to cover London. Except for the naval bases at Portsmouth and Plymouth, the Channel coast was effectively defenseless, apart from the militia and dragoon patrols.[48]

The sight of the enemy fleet in Plymouth Sound understandably led to a panic. The commissioner of the naval dockyard momentarily considered setting fire to it, thinking that a landing was imminent. The local army commander, General Lindsay, similarly took fright, believing that the town and yard were indefensible. He begged Amherst to replace him.[49] Fortunately the ministry itself did not give way to panic. Sandwich pointed out to the commissioner that the enemy was unlikely to attempt the harbor until they had secured the surrounding coast. All the reports indicated that the countryside was flocking to the defense of the town, including 600 Cornish miners. The commissioner therefore should focus on getting as many ships as possible ready for sea.[50]

Twenty-four hours later the combined fleet had disappeared. The reason was that Cordoba and d'Orvilliers had turned back to search for Hardy, whom they needed to defeat before starting the invasion itself. The two fleets finally sighted each other on 31 August, though Hardy had already signaled his 38 capital ships two days earlier to make "a closer order of sailing in preparation for a battle." His plan was to lure the enemy fleet into the Channel, being confident of any engagement in those waters.[51] D'Orvilliers took the bait and attempted to follow. However, the Spanish proved unable to keep up with their French colleagues, which prevented them from forming a line of battle or catching Hardy.[52] In reality both allied fleets were ready to quit. Their supplies were running low and the French crews were suffering from widespread sickness.[53] The decision was accordingly made to return to Brest, where they arrived on 11 September. The intention was to rest the crews and resupply the ships before making another attempt. However, the two commanders rapidly concluded that it was too late to continue the enterprise. Cordoba accordingly was to return to Cadiz to strengthen the blockade of Gibraltar while the French refitted in Brest ready for operations elsewhere. The Channel invasion threat for the moment was over.[54]

The episode was not without cost to Britain, since the Royal Navy's preoccupation with the invasion meant that the waters round the British Isles were open to enemy privateers. As already mentioned, the French determined to add to Britain's woes by equipping a squadron under Jones to sail round Scotland into the North Sea, with instructions to do as much damage as possible along the way.[55] Jones set off from L'Orient in mid-August. After securing several prizes, he arrived off Leith, the port of Edinburgh, threatening fire and destruction. Only a storm prevented him from seizing the defenseless town. Then on 23 September he intercepted a British Baltic convoy off Flamborough Head in the North Sea, capturing one of the Royal Navy's copper-bottomed frigates, the *Serapis*, in an epic struggle which led to the sinking of Jones's own vessel. He finally ended his cruise by taking the *Serapis* and his other prizes into the Dutch port of Texel.[56] The threat of invasion might have receded, but as North commented to Sandwich, unless Jones was stopped, "much shame and blame" "would accrue to the ministry."[57]

The inability of the Royal Navy to meet the various demands on it forced Sandwich to present a defense of his administration of the navy in a paper for the Cabinet. He pointed out that the fleet currently comprised 88 ships of the line, of which 42 were with Sir Charles Hardy, another 23 were in the West Indies, 8 in the East Indies, 5 in America and 13 at home re-fitting or acting as guard ships. This effectively equaled the 97 battleships assembled by Anson during the last invasion threat in 1759, since many of the present ships were superior in size and number of guns.[58] Sandwich then addressed the question: "Why with a force as great if not greater than ever before, we have an enemy superior to us?" The reason was clear if comparison was made with previous wars: "England till this time was never engaged in a sea war with the House of Bourbon thoroughly united, their naval force unbroken, and having no other war or object to draw off their attention and resources." This time "we unfortunately have an additional war upon our hands [in America] which essentially drains our finances and employs a very considerable part of our Navy and army." However, Sandwich acknowledged that in the first three years of the conflict the Admiralty had not observed the two-power standard, implicitly criticizing the Treasury for its cuts to the naval budget: "Had we been early enough in our preparations, and had not suffered them [France and Spain] to go on arming and building without keeping pace with them, their superiority would certainly not have been so decided."[59]

Twentieth-century governments might have addressed the loss of naval superiority by building new dockyards and slipways. However, this was alien to eighteenth-century thinking. The accepted mode of proceeding was to maximize the output of current facilities rather than the creation of new ones. Hence Sandwich warned: "we have no other source to draw from and no possibility of augmenting our strength." Accidents meant that "our numbers may be delayed or diminished but cannot be increased."[60] The ministry must work with what it had.

One person who refused to accept such pessimism was Middleton. He pointed out that most of the ships now had coppered hulls which allowed them to refit more quickly and stay on station longer. He also reminded Sandwich of the increased firepower of the navy from carronades and Howitzers. But even Middleton could not hide the lack of frigates. A doubling of their number was urgently needed.[61] This led Middleton to question Sandwich's assertion that the nation had reached the limit of its resources. He should understand that "what was done in the last war is no guide for this." In any case more could be achieved by careful planning and dispatch. It was inexcusable that ships were completed before arrangements had been made for their stores and equipment. Finally he reminded Sandwich, as had Robinson previously, that "selecting out the most deserving in all ranks will prove a stronger bulwark to your administration than a phalanx of peers and MPs."[62] The promotion of political appointees led invariably to controversy, as the Keppel–Palliser controversy demonstrated.

Sandwich did not accept all of Middleton's arguments. Nevertheless, the estimates for 1780 provided for a 20 percent increase in naval construction, the majority of it in merchant yards. The downside was that the new vessels would require time to deliver.[63] Meanwhile the hemorrhaging of the merchant marine continued. By the end of 1779, Lloyds Insurers had registered the loss of another 487 merchant vessels. This was not only a loss for the individual owners, but a diminution in customs revenues, a crucial part of the nation's sinews of war.[64] Fortunately there had been no major disruption to the North American supply convoys or those to and from the East and West Indies. Even so, there was no room for complacency on the part of Sandwich and the Admiralty.

Stalemate in America

The intention of Spain to go to war was not known when the British Ministry sat down to decide its American campaign plans for 1779. Despite the lack of success in 1778, the ministry continued to believe that reunion with Britain was what most Colonists desired. Only "the tyranny of their leaders prevented them from avowing" their loyalty.[65] The ministers were encouraged in these views by refugees like Galloway, who argued that the middle colonies especially were tired of the rebellion. Once Washington had been defeated, "the King's authority could be reestablished under men of weight and authority, supported by the loyal militia."[66]

The British ministry consequently made few changes to its strategic objectives in North America, despite the possibility of conflict with Spain, though there was some discussion about methods. Amherst again asserted that the best way of "obtaining success appears to be by small corps of troops with ships of war making attacks on every part of the American coast" to convince the rebels of the folly of their enterprise.[67] Most of the ministers, however, were against a purely maritime war, for which the ships were not currently available. Germain still hoped for a major land campaign in New York. He was supported by General James Robertson, who was about to return to America as Governor of New York. Robertson suggested that a field army of 12,000 men plus 2,000 provincials should be retained to defeat Washington and seize the rebel posts in the Highlands. Civilian government could then be established in lower New York, as Campbell had been instructed to do in Georgia, to show the other provinces what they might expect on the re-establishment of lawful government.[68]

Germain was sufficiently impressed to relate Robertson's ideas to North in preparation for a meeting of the Cabinet. In his formal orders to Clinton on 23 January 1779, Germain accordingly reaffirmed that the ministry's "great end" was "the re-establishment of legal government in the revolted colonies." The precise means of doing this were left to Clinton. Naturally "it is most earnestly wished that you may be able to bring Mr. Washington to a general and decisive action at the opening of the campaign." But if that could not be effected he should have sufficient troops to force Washington "to seek safety in the Highlands of New York, or the Jerseys." This would then leave the rest of "the inhabitants" in the province free to return "to the allegiance of His Majesty." Elections for an assembly could follow which in turn would remove the "ill founded apprehensions of being ruled by military laws."[69]

Although the ministry had rejected Amherst's idea of a purely maritime war, it did recommend the deployment of two corps of 4,000 men against the coasts of New England and the Chesapeake. "By entering the rivers or inlets" of the rebels, the two detachments were to "seize or destroy their shipping and stores and deprive them of every means of fitting out privateers" or "of carrying on commerce." However, Clinton should ensure that the corps sent to Virginia was also strong enough to attack Maryland "so as to give protection to the loyal inhabitants of Jersey or the lower counties on the Delaware," should they be disposed "to deliver themselves from the tyranny and oppression of their rebel committees." Lastly the rebels should be further tested "on the side of Canada by a succession of parties of Indians," "supported by detachments of troops," with the aim of "alarming and harassing the frontiers."[70]

To achieve these objectives, Clinton was to receive two Scottish battalions of 1,000 men each, plus 4,200 recruits for the existing British and German corps, amounting to 6,600 men. Recent returns indicated that these additions should bring Clinton's field army to over 28,000 regulars, more than sufficient for dealing with Washington. But any further reinforcement was not to be considered, for as Germain had previously told the peace commissioners, America was no longer "the only object of attention," since the "whole power of France" had to be contended with and very likely that of Spain in due course. If Clinton wanted more men, he should look to the Loyalists.[71] They needed encouragement. It was for this reason that Germain now proposed to give Loyalist officers the same status as their provincial counterparts in the previous war, "that is to say when they are on service with the British officers they shall take rank as juniors of the rank to which they belong." They would also receive half pay on being discharged. The common soldier was to be rewarded too. Every man enlisting in a properly organized unit would receive a bounty of £2.2s.6d and be entitled to 100 acres at the end of the emergency. Hopefully the Loyalists would now play a more prominent part in the struggle to subdue the rebels.[72]

Few challenged these assumptions about the depth of Loyalist feeling and their readiness to serve. Lord Grey, the former corps commander in America, was a lone voice when he warned the House of Commons that most Colonists were hostile to Britain and that the Loyalists would always be a timid minority, making it difficult to end the rebellion even with overwhelming military superiority. His testimony appeared so damning that North feared it would result in a vote of censure.[73] But few were sufficiently knowledgeable to assess the validity of such opinions. The war in America would continue much as in 1778, even if Spain entered the war.

The British belief that the rebels were close to collapse was not entirely fanciful, as Washington admitted to George Mason, a leading Virginian, late in March 1779. At no time since the commencement of hostilities had the Patriot cause been "in such eminent danger." The people in general "seem to think the contest is at an end" and that "to make money and get places" were "the only remaining things to do." This was helping the British "to pull down the goodly fabric we have hitherto been raising at the expense of so much time, blood and treasure." Such indifference was very discouraging after the enemy had so recently been "on the point of evacuating America." This led him to conclude that "nothing ... can save us but a total reformation in our own conduct or some decisive turn of affairs in Europe." Shamefully, the latter was more likely.[74]

At the heart of the Patriots' difficulties was the depreciation of the currency, which undermined every attempt at procuring men and supplies. By April 1779 Washington jokingly commented that it required a wagon load of Continental paper to purchase a similar quantity of provision.[75] Fortunately the army had experienced a better winter than in 1777 at Valley Forge. The countryside around Middlebrook was more accessible and the men healthier than at any time since the formation of the army.[76] But conditions were still harsh, and problems remained, especially with the supply of clothing. The lack of warm clothing was one reason for a threatened mutiny in the Connecticut brigade. But however justified the men's discontent, Washington insisted on swift action. He told Putnam their commander. "In cases of this kind," the senior officer must "use every means for discovering the authors of the mischief," after which "instant punishment should be inflicted." The rest could then be reclaimed through clemency.[77]

The prospects for the forthcoming campaign, accordingly, were not bright when Washington met Gerard, the French envoy. Clearly the key to any successful outcome was French naval superiority in America, since that would allow an attempt on either New York or Rhode Island. However, if the British proved too strong in the north, d'Estaing perhaps could assist Lincoln against Prevost in Georgia. Another attempt might then be considered on New York, providing Byron did not follow d'Estaing from the West Indies. Once the British had been expelled from the mainland, the Patriots could then cooperate with the French "elsewhere," meaning the West Indies.[78] But whatever plan was adopted, Washington warned Laurens, the Patriots must first recruit their forces since there would be no quick ending to the war, as so many seemed to think.[79]

Across the Hudson River Clinton was similarly considering his prospects as he awaited instructions from London. He informed Germain on 4 April that although it was time to start planning, so much depended "upon circumstances that I cannot yet inform your Lordship to what point I shall direct the small force which I can spare from this post." One option was to build on the recent success in Georgia, perhaps by making "an attempt against Charleston." However, this would not be advisable during the summer and while the movements of the French fleet were unknown. But Clinton would commit 6,000 men to such a project the following October, provided the French and Spanish did not intervene.[80]

Clinton finally received Germain's orders in early May outlining the ministry's thoughts on the forthcoming campaign and the size of his reinforcement. Clinton was not pleased at the contents. The small number of new troops meant that it would be very difficult striking a decisive blow against Washington, especially if he "persists in his present post" above New York.[81] He was, moreover, appalled at Germain's plans for the provincials. In the first place the scheme had "given great discontent to the officers of the regular regiments," who were angry that provincials were being advanced to stations to which they had no claim. Secondly Clinton was likely to experience constant difficulty from having to devolve "the command of important detachments . . . upon heads entirely unequal to the task." Finally the recruitment of the provincials was too haphazard to warrant the granting of permanent commissions. Loyalist units invariably took the field incomplete. "The whole provincial line" in consequence was "over-officered; and the professional merit of some, with the [political] connections of others, render it scarcely possible to remedy the fault."[82]

Until the promised reinforcements arrived, Clinton decided to implement Germain's proposal for a raid on Virginia. It was widely believed that Washington relied on the export of tobacco from that province for the purchase of military stores. Virginia was also supporting the rebel army in

South Carolina under Lincoln.[83] Another reason for Clinton's choice was that he had a congenial naval colleague. Commodore Sir George Collier was relatively unique among the officers of the navy in his eagerness to work with the army. He was temporally in command until a more senior flag officer arrived from England. Collier had previously suggested an attack on Falmouth, a major privateer base and source of fuel for Boston.[84] He readily agreed therefore to Clinton's proposed attack on Virginia, even though he had few battleships and wanted men for his remaining vessels.[85] The troops were to be commanded by General Edward Mathew.

The flotilla, comprising 1,800 British, German, and Loyalist troops departed from New York on the 5 May 1779, arriving off the Capes of Virginia four days later. A landing was quickly made on the Elizabeth River. Here the British found numerous warehouses full of tobacco, munitions, seasoned oak, and other naval stores, as well as the keels of several 24- and 36-gun warships. Equally gratifying was the widespread show of support for the Crown. Collier accordingly suggested the establishment of a base at Portsmouth on the Elizabeth River. "By securing this the whole trade of the Chesapeake is at an end, and consequently the sinews of the rebellion destroyed." It would also provide the navy with a convenient base for refitting the smaller ships of war.[86] However, Mathew doubted that he had sufficient forces for such a commitment and felt that his orders required him to be back in time for Clinton's operations on the Hudson.[87]

The two commanders accordingly returned to New York to support Clinton's "big blow" against Washington, which had so far eluded him and his predecessors. Clinton's plan was to move up the Hudson River to attack the Patriot forts of Stony Point and Verplancks Point, which protected King's Ferry, a few miles below the Highlands. Their seizure, he believed, might tempt Washington into a battle to protect the communication between New England and the middle states.[88]

Clinton's offensive began promisingly with the capture on 30 May 1779 of the two forts, being ably assisted by Collier who directed the naval bombardment. However, Washington refused to leave his mountain fortress at Peekskill, where he had 8,000 men with another 3,000 at West Point. Clinton accordingly returned to New York, leaving a "considerable corps" as bait in the two posts. He believed that by keeping most of his army on transports at Staten Island, he could relieve Stony Point within 24 hours, should Washington move against its garrison.[89]

In the meantime he complied with Germain's wish for maritime operations by dispatching Collier and Tryon on a fresh series of attacks along the New England coast. The first landing on 5 July was directed at

New Haven, followed by visits to Fairfield on July 8, and Norwalk on 11 July. At New Haven all opposition ceased when Tryon threatened to burn the town. Only the public stores and some shipping were in consequence destroyed. But at Fairfield the inhabitants were not so lucky. Due to persistent small arms fire, "the greatest part of the village" was set alight in retaliation for "the fire of the rebels from their houses." Despite this the British still met considerable resistance at Norwalk, where the local militia had been reinforced by 250 Continental troops. Here many salt pans were destroyed along with the magazines, stores, and vessels in the harbor. A similar fate was inflicted on the "greatest part of the dwelling houses."[90]

The destruction of so much private property led once again to questioning about such operations. Tryon himself was unrepentant, despite the accidental burning of two churches at Fairfield, apprehending "no mischief to the public from the irritation of a few in the rebellion."[91] But Washington was closer to the truth when he commented that such operations amounted to little more than the burning of defenseless towns. "How conduct of this kind is to effect the conquest of America the wisdom of a North, Germain or Sandwich best can tell: it is too deep and refined for the comprehension of common understandings." What he did know was that such operations further alienated New England from Britain, thus undermining the chances of any reconciliation.[92]

Clinton expected Washington to march to the aid of the New England towns. Instead he sent Wayne down the west bank of the Hudson to surprise the garrison at Stony Point. Wayne's force comprised an elite corps of light infantry which Washington had recently established. The troops were to storm the parapets at midnight on 15 July 1779 without firing a shot, placing "their whole dependence on the bayonet," a tactic whose effectiveness Wayne had experienced at Paoli in 1777. The result was a resounding success, since the British saw the approaching Patriots only when it was too late to use their cannon. Soon the garrison was calling for quarter, losing 130 dead and wounded, and over 500 captured. The Patriots' losses in contrast were just 15 killed and 83 wounded. The action was over long before Clinton could get his transports in motion. It was a considerable boost for the morale of the Patriot army.[93]

Washington did not attempt to retain Stony Point, preferring to withdraw Wayne's corps to the security of the Highlands. Clinton then reoccupied the post, while Washington strengthened West Point in anticipation of another British attack. Digging trenches was all that Washington could do at this point. As he told Lincoln in Charleston, he had no troops for other operations, since the states were amused by dreams of peace. The army consequently had received few recruits and these had been obtained only by an enormous bounty for a mere nine months' service.[94] Congress responded by urging the states to offer the officers half pay for life and extra money for the ordinary soldiers if they served for the entire war. Provision should also be made for the widows of those killed in action.[95] But these were resolutions only. The states still had to implement them and most were slow to do so.

Fortunately for Washington, the loss of Stony Point had once again paralyzed Clinton's ability to take the initiative. Not that he accepted any blame for the setback, telling Germain that with proper reinforcement he would not have had to play cat and mouse to bring Washington to battle. But Clinton's defensive mentality was the product of other factors too. Governor Frederick Haldimand in Canada wanted 2,000 men to strengthen the defenses there.[96] Clinton also feared that d'Estaing might appear from the West Indies, where the French had a considerable superiority in capital ships.[97] The situation was all the more dangerous in that the ministry was sending only a modest reinforcement of four battleships to North America because of demands elsewhere.[98] This meant that every British port from Halifax to Savannah was under threat, not to mention the supply convoys from England.

Then on 3 August news arrived that Castine at the mouth of the Penobscot River in Maine was under attack. Castine had been established as a refuge for northern Loyalists.[99] However, the post was very isolated, prompting Massachusetts to launch an assault. The forces assembled were a testimony to Massachusetts' commitment to its own part of the war. The naval commander, Dudley Saltonstall, had a force of 17 warships and 19 transports, carrying 2,500 militia under General Solomon Lovell. But despite their overwhelming advantage, the two commanders made hard work of the siege after arriving on 25 July 1779. Nevertheless they were close to success on 11 August when Collier's squadron of six ships, led by the 64-gun *Raisonable*, was seen approaching Penobscot Bay.[100]

Saltonstall momentarily considered giving battle but his confidence quickly evaporated, given his crew's lack of experience and size of their ships. Some of the American vessels attempted to run for the open sea, but most retreated into the Penobscot River, where they were burnt. The entire flotilla of 37 vessels was either taken or destroyed, leaving the crews and troops to undertake the long trek home through the forests of Maine.[101] A delighted George III commented: "Sir George [has] performed more by his spirited and able exertions with his small force than has been effected in any former year of the rebellion when the force was so greatly superior."[102] It demonstrated what could be done by a resourceful commander. However, the rigidity of the ranking system meant that Collier was too junior to be appointed permanently to the North American station.[103] He also lacked the right political connections. The position instead was given to Marriott Arbuthnot, a former commissioner of the Halifax dockyard and friend of Sandwich. He was now almost 70 years of age with an undistinguished career. He was also of a rather volatile temperament, just the sort of man to fall foul of Clinton.[104] It was another example of Sandwich's mistaken reliance on patronage rather than merit in the making of appointments.

Clinton's operations meanwhile were stalled because he was still awaiting the reinforcements from England with Arbuthnot and the return of Grant's corps from St Lucia. The former had unfortunately been delayed by bad weather and Arbuthnot's decision to aid the island of Jersey following an incursion by the French.[105] The latter had been detained in the West Indies, where the balance of naval power had changed following the arrival of La Motte Piquet with reinforcements from France. This superiority had allowed d'Estaing to capture the islands of St Vincent on 18 June and Grenada on 4 July 1779. Byron in response had attempted to engage d'Estaing off Grenada the day after its capture, despite having only 21 battleships to d'Estaing's 25. However his fleet had suffered serious damage during the action to its rigging and sails, thus necessitating a return to Antigua, leaving the remaining British islands vulnerable to attack. Clinton in consequence could expect little military or naval help from the West Indies, even during the hurricane season.[106]

Clinton was so disillusioned by this turn of events that he requested permission to resign in favor of Cornwallis. He told Germain that the delays to the reinforcements had rendered his plan of operations useless. Originally the capture of Stony Point and Verplanks was to have been the prelude to an advance up the Hudson to bring Washington to battle. This was now impractical due to the lateness of the season and Washington's judicious dispositions, which together ruled out any further "offensive operations in this country."[107] Nor did Clinton's spirits revive when Arbuthnot finally arrived in early September 1779, since he brought a mere 3,500 troops, half the number promised by Germain. The situation of the navy was no better. Arbuthnot had just 36 vessels for all his tasks, less than half the number with Howe in 1777. Moreover, with only five capital ships, he would be powerless to oppose d'Estaing should the French fleet appear.[108]

As Clinton's hopes declined so those of Washington improved, following news of d'Estaing's success at St Vincent and Grenada and the entry of Spain into the war.[109] Although the French had not promised any help for the Patriots in 1779, Washington was naturally hopeful that d'Estaing would sail northwards during the hurricane season to assist in the reduction of New York or Rhode Island. The mood of optimism was increased by the success of Major Henry Lee in taking 150 prisoners at the British post of Paulus Hook, opposite Manhattan. The incident was only marred by contention in the Patriot ranks because Lee was a cavalry officer while the majority of his command were infantrymen. The curse of petty jealousy was never far below the surface.[110]

Then in mid-September news arrived that d'Estaing had indeed come to North America and was before Savannah with 24 battleships, 14 frigates and several thousand troops. Washington quickly issued orders to prepare for an attack on New York.[111] He also wrote to d'Estaing outlining his hopes for such an operation, once Savannah had been captured, reassuring the French commander that he could have 30,000 men ready in three weeks. He did not say that half of them would be militia.[112] Washington of course was misinformed about French intentions, which had not been communicated either to him or Congress. D'Estaing's orders were to return to Europe with most of his fleet once he had completed his operations in the West Indies. However, the appeals for help from South Carolina, following Prevost's invasion, had proved too powerful to ignore. D'Estaing accordingly set off for a short visit to Georgia on his way back to France.[113]

The arrival of d'Estaing in North American waters was sufficiently alarming for Arbuthnot and Clinton to convince them that it would be prudent to abandon Rhode Island. In Arbuthnot's view the post "had never been of the smallest use to the navy," while Clinton acknowledged that it constituted a serious drain on the army. It was also a hostage to fortune, as had been demonstrated the previous year when Howe had relieved the post with difficulty. It was time to concentrate British resources at Halifax and New York where Arbuthnot began sinking vessels to prevent d'Estaing from entering the harbor. Clinton simultaneously evacuated Verplanks and Stony Point, now that he had no prospect of forcing a passage up the Hudson. Both operations were completed at the end of October.[114] These developments were gleefully noted by Washington in a letter to one of his Virginian correspondents. "The enemy have wasted another campaign . . . without doing a single thing [towards] advancing the end in view." Their inactivity had allowed the Patriots to crush Britain's

Indian allies, the Iroquois Six Nations, without any interference from Clinton at New York. The British actions were difficult to reconcile with any military principle or even common sense.[115]

However, Washington's hopes of a joint operation with d'Estaing were soon dashed. Initially affairs seemed promising, since the French arrival at Savannah caught Prevost by surprise, after d'Estaing had slipped away from the West Indies without being noticed by Byron.[116] Prevost was fortunate in being able to recall Maitland from Port Royal Island. Even so, d'Estaing and Lincoln had a superiority of three to one in troops. They began entrenching on the night of 23 September and opened their bombardment on 3 October. But after several days, d'Estaing, conscious of his orders to return to France, insisted on abandoning a regular siege in favor of a coup de main. The new plan was to storm the defenses in a surprise attack on the morning of 9 October.[117] Fortunately for the British, a deserter had informed them of the scheme, resulting in the repulse of their opponents with heavy loss.[118] D'Estaing, who was wounded in the action, was so discouraged by the outcome that he determined to sail back to France immediately, leaving Lincoln to withdraw towards Charleston.[119]

A second Franco-American operation had ended with no outcome, though it showed what a union of the French and American forces might achieve. For the British it was a further alert that their position in North America was far from secure. Nevertheless, for Washington it was a disappointing end to the campaign, leaving his army with the prospect of another dreary winter at Morristown and West Point.[120] Clearly everyone must now realize that there would be no quick ending to the war, unless the states made an effective contribution to the common cause.

Britain, Spain, and Gibraltar

Although Britain had survived the Bourbon invasion attempt of August 1779, the situation facing its ministry was still critical. The entry of Spain into the war had considerably increased the demands on the Britain's resources elsewhere. Gibraltar was blockaded by the Spanish fleet based at Cadiz and Minorca was also threatened, while Jamaica and the other islands in the West Indies were vulnerable to attack from Cuba and elsewhere, following Byron's setback at Grenada. If the sugar islands were lost, Britain might have to sue for peace on the most abject terms, just as the Bourbon powers had been compelled to do at the end of the Seven Years War in 1762.[121] More ships were urgently needed there once the hurricane season was over.

However, the most immediate issue at this point was the relief of Gibraltar, which was considered essential for the protection of British trade in the Mediterranean, providing as it did a convenient anchorage just east of the Straits. It had a substantial garrison of five British and three Hanoverian regiments, totaling 5,380 men. The Spanish had commenced hostilities on 5 July 1779. The aim of the Spanish at this point was to starve the fortress into surrender, since its high cliffs, massive stone walls and elevated batteries made it impregnable to a conventional assault. The Spanish accordingly fortified the isthmus leading to Gibraltar while a squadron of ships of varying sizes kept a close watch to prevent supplies arriving by sea.[122]

The problem was how to save Gibraltar and Britain's other overseas possessions without putting the homeland at risk or compromising Clinton's situation in North America. Despite Cordoba's returned to Cadiz, Hardy's squadron would still be inferior to d'Orvilliers's fleet, if detachments were made for the relief of Gibraltar and the West Indies. This was something that Sandwich refused to contemplate until winter made major fleet deployments in the western approaches and other areas around the British Isles inadvisable. He told the Cabinet: "I hold it as a fundamental point that nothing is to be taken from Sir Charles Hardy's fleet till his cruise is ended, which it is supposed will last at least two months from his time of sailing."[123] Only after the threat of invasion had ceased would he consider making detachments to the Mediterranean and West Indies.

As a result some weeks passed before consideration could be given to the relief of Gibraltar, Minorca, and the West Indies. The plan finally discussed on 4 November 1779 was a complex one. First the Channel fleet was to escort the transports with 3,000 troops for Jamaica and the Lesser Antilles into the Atlantic. Then it was to turn southwards with the rest of the convoy for the relief of Gibraltar and Port Mahon. When this was accomplished five ships of the line would set off for the Leeward Islands, leaving the rest of the fleet to return to England with the empty storeships.[124]

This was a crucial mission for which an officer of resource was required. None of the flag officers recently deployed with the Channel squadron were deemed to have the right credentials. Sandwich accordingly turned to Sir George Rodney, who had distinguished himself during the previous war in the capture of Havana. He was thus familiar with the area to which he was going. His appointment had another advantage in that he had not been involved in the Keppel Palliser controversy. However, he had a reputation for peculation and was intensely disliked by most colleagues.[125]

The plan was for him to command the fleet until it reached Gibraltar, after which he would proceed with the five battleships for the West Indies to join the 15 already there under Sir Peter Parker, who had temporarily replaced Byron.[126] Admiral Robert Digby with the rest of the Channel fleet would then return to Portsmouth.

Rodney set sail on 25 December 1779. First he escorted the West Indian troop convoy into the relative safety of the Atlantic before turning south towards Gibraltar. Not long afterwards on 8 January he sighted a Spanish convoy of 15 merchantmen, escorted by a ship of the line and several smaller vessels, which were quickly captured.[127] But this was only the prelude to a greater prize for on 16 January near Cape St Vincent another group of ships were sighted. It proved to be a fleet of 11 battleships under Admiral Langara, which had been stationed to intercept British vessels heading for Cadiz. The French had warned their allies of Rodney's impending arrival. However, the Spanish believed that the united fleets of Langara and Cordoba could handle the situation, doubting that the British would send the Channel fleet so far away.[128] Unfortunately for the Spanish, Cordoba was then driven back into port by a storm, leaving Langara to face Rodney alone. Rodney immediately gave the order for a general chase, which enabled his copper-bottomed battleships to overhaul Langara, despite the danger of being driven onto a lee shore.[129] To increase the chances of success, Rodney instructed his captains to engage the first available Spanish vessel instead of attempting to form a line of battle. This saved time and reduced the danger of the British ships being raked by enemy fire as they sought their correct position. Five of Langara's battleships struck their colors while another two sank before their prize crews could save them. In terms of enemy losses, it was a major success.[130] The only downside was the continued bickering among the officers of the fleet, which Rodney attributed to "the unhappy differences between Mr Keppel and Sir Hugh Palliser."[131] In reality his cavalier style of command was largely to blame.

Rodney reached Gibraltar on 15 January 1780. Here the precious supplies of food, fuel, and ammunition were unloaded for the garrison while an escort set off with the vessels destined for the relief of Port Mahon in Minorca. This part of the operation was also successful, since the Spanish had still to invade the island and had no major naval units in the area. The convoy returned unchallenged on 13 February, leaving Rodney to set off for the West Indies.

The capture of the Spanish convoy and victory over Langara was not the only success during this operation, for shortly afterwards the ships with Digby returning from Gibraltar fell in with a French convoy heading for Mauritius and the French stations in India. Several rich prizes were taken along with a French ship of the line.[132] The haul might have been even bigger since the Indiamen on leaving Brest had been accompanied by a larger convoy for the West Indies. Here was another consequence of the Royal Navy's not having sufficient ships to simultaneously relieve Gibraltar and maintain a close watch on Brest. Nevertheless, it was a promising start to the New Year, for which Rodney was given the freedom of the City of London and a vote of thanks from the two houses of Parliament.[133]

The success of Rodney and Digby brought one additional benefit in that they restored confidence in the City of London, thus helping North finance the war. Early in March 1780 he succeeded in raising 12 million pounds at 4 percent interest, five million more than the previous year. Government borrowing was now close to the maximum raised during the Seven Years War.[134] George III commented: "I can never suppose this country so far lost to all ideas of self importance as to be willing to grant American Independence." To do so would condemn the country to "a very low class among the European states."[135] The revived confidence of the ministry was reflected in Sandwich's ambitious new building program.[136] The army too was to be strengthened with another 16 infantry regiments, making a prospective total of 112,000 men.[137] The power of Great Britain was not yet exhausted.

Notes and references

1 Samuel Flagg Bemis, *The Diplomacy of the American Revolution* (Bloomington, 1957), 23–28.

2 W.N. Hargreaves-Mawdsley, *Eighteenth Century Spain, 1700–1788: A Political, Diplomatic and Institutional* History (London, 1979), 129–30. John Lynch, *Bourbon Spain, 1700–1808* (Oxford, 1989), 319–20.

3 Lynch, *Bourbon Spain*, 311.

4 Orville T. Murphy, *Charles Gravier, Comte de Vergennes: French Diplomacy in the Age of Revolution, 1719–1787* (Albany, 1988), 261–63.

5 Jonathan Dull, *The French Navy and American Independence: A Study of Arms and Diplomacy, 1774–1787* (Princeton, 1975), 102.

6 Jonathan R. Dull, *A Diplomatic History of the American Revolution* (New Haven, 1985), 107–8. Hargreaves-Mawdsley, *Spain*, 131.

7 John Lynch, *Bourbon Spain*, 308–10.

8 Ibid., 315–6. Dull, *French Navy*, 83.
9 Sandwich to North, 15 October 1778, Sandwich/2, 179–80.
10 Brendan Simms, *Three Victories and a Defeat: The Rise and Fall of the First British Empire* (London, 2007), 628.
11 Bemis, *Diplomacy*, 85–86.
12 Dull, *French Navy*, 132–40.
13 Dull, *French Navy*, 146, 159–61.
14 William C. Stinchcombe, *The American Revolution and the French Alliance* (Syracuse, NY, 1969), 77–78.
15 George III to North, 11 June 1779, Fortescue/4, 350–51.
16 North to George III, 10 November 1778, Fortescue/4, 215–16. Pitt's effectiveness as an all-powerful war minister has been questioned by Richard Middleton, *The Bells of Victory: The Pitt-Newcastle Ministry and the Conduct of the Seven Years War, 1757–1762* (Cambridge, 1985), 211–13.
17 George III to North, 15 June 1779, Fortescue/4, 356.
18 N.A.M. Rodger, *Command of the Ocean: A Naval History of Britain, 1649–1815* (New York, 2004), 340.
19 For the Whig interpretation, see Herbert Butterfield, *George III and the Historians* (London, 1957).
20 Cabinet Council Minute, 21 June 1779, Sandwich/III, 256. Piers Mackesy, *The War for America, 1775–1783* (Cambridge, Mass., 1964), 274.
21 A. Temple Patterson, *The Other Armada: The Franco-Spanish attempt to Invade Britain in 1779* (Manchester, 1960), 46–47. Dull, *French Navy*, 140.
22 George III to North, 22 June 1779, Fortescue/4, 370.
23 Estimates for Guards, Garrisons and Plantations, CJ/XXXVII, 17–20.
24 Statutes at Large, 19 Geo III, Chapter 16, XIII, 316–18. Patterson, *Other Armada*, 109–10.
25 Mulgrave to Sandwich, 2 July 1779, Sandwich/3, 33.
26 Parker to Sandwich, 25 April 1778, Sandwich/1, 410. Sandwich to Barrington, 5 August 1779, Sandwich/2, 365.
27 Sir Charles Middleton to Sandwich, 9 July 1779, Sandwich/3, 44.
28 David Syrett, *The Royal Navy in European Waters during the American Revolutionary War* (Columbia, SC, 1998), 65.
29 Quoted in Rodger, *Sandwich*, 161.

30 Middleton to Sandwich, 20 December 1779, Sandwich/4, 413. Ibid., 12 March 1780, Sandwich/4, 414–16.

31 Syrett, *Royal Navy in European Waters*, 65–66.

32 Estimates for Building and Rebuilding the Navy, CJ/XXXVII, 33–34.

33 Number of Seamen Borne, 20 April 1779, Sandwich/2, 265–66. It is difficult to assess the accuracy of these figures, given the frequent discrepancy between the numbers voted by Parliament, seamen enrolled on ships' books, and those actually mustered. See Rodger, *Command of the Ocean*, 636.

34 Mulgrave to Sandwich, 10 June 1779, Sandwich/3, 16–17. Hardy to Sandwich, 13 June 1779, Sandwich/3, 18–19.

35 Lord Thurlow to Sandwich, 21 June 79, Sandwich/3, 26–27.

36 Bowler, *Logistics*, 244–45.

37 Thoughts of Admiral Keppel, 25 February 1779, Fortescue/4, 289–91. Hood to Sandwich, 10 February 1779, Fortescue/4, 270–71.

38 Rodger, *Sandwich*, 257.

39 Middleton to Sandwich, 9 July 1779, Sandwich/3, 42–43. Syrett, *Royal Navy in European Waters*, 62.

40 Syrett, *Royal Navy in European Waters*, 68.

41 Mulgrave to Sandwich, 2 July 1779, Sandwich/3, 33–34. Rodger, *Sandwich*, 258–60.

42 Hardy to Sandwich, 10 July 79, Sandwich/3, 45–46. Sandwich to Hardy, 28 July 79, Sandwich/3, 48–50. For the re-supply of the western squadron in the previous war, see Middleton, "Western Squadron," *Mariner's Mirror*, 75, 349–67.

43 Hardy to Sandwich, 12 August 1779, Sandwich/3, 55–56.

44 T.H. McGuffie, *The Siege of Gibraltar* (London, 1965), 37–47.

45 Dull, *French Navy*, 146–54.

46 Patterson, *Other Armada*, 194. Ibid., 181–85.

47 Mackesy, *War for America*, 290. Estimate for Embodying the Militia, CJ/XXXVII, 23.

48 Mackesy, *War for America*, 291.

49 Commissioner Ourry to Sandwich, 20 August 1779, Sandwich/3, 64–67. General Lindsay to Amherst, 26 August 1779, Sandwich/3, 77.

50 Sandwich to Ourry, 22 August 1779, Sandwich/3, 67–68.

51 Captain Bickerton to Sandwich, 2 September 1779, Sandwich/3, 89–91.

52 Patterson, *Other Armada*, 207–10.

53 Intelligence, 4 September 1779, Sandwich/3, 94–95.

54 Dull, *French Navy*, 157. Rodger, *Sandwich*, 256–60. Hargreaves-Mawdsley, *Spain*, 132.

55 Dull, *French Navy*, 158.

56 John Ferling, *Almost a Miracle: The American Victory in the War of Independence* (New York, 2007), 375–79. Syrett, *Royal Navy in European Waters*, 79–80.

57 North to Sandwich, 23 November 1779, Sandwich/3, 107.

58 Thoughts upon Naval Measures, 14 September 1778, Fortescue/4, 441–42. There is another copy of this document in Sandwich/3, 164–71. Sandwich conveniently did not compare the numbers of frigates and smaller cruisers then in the Royal Navy.

59 Thoughts upon Naval Measures, 14 September 1779, Fortescue/4, 441.

60 Thoughts upon Naval Measures, 14 September 1779, Fortescue/4, 440.

61 Memorandum from Sir Charles Middleton, circa September 1779, Sandwich/3, 172–77.

62 Middleton to Sandwich, 15 September 1779, Sandwich/3, 177–81.

63 Estimates for Naval Building and Rebuilding, 2 February 1780, CJ/XXXVII, 549–51. The sum allocated for new building and major repair amounted to £633,000 compared to £520,000 in 1779.

64 Alfred T. Mahan, *The Major Operations of the Navies in the War of American Independence* (Boston, 1913), 61. John Brewer, *The Sinews of Power: War, Money and the English State, 1688–1783* (New York, 1989), 197–98.

65 Germain to the Commissioners, 15 October 1778, DDAR/XV, 217–18.

66 Proposal for reducing the Country as the British Army passes through it, January 1779, Fortescue/4, 245–47.

67 Amherst to George III, January 1779, Fortescue/4, 249–50.

68 Memorandum on the Mode of Making War in America, January 1779, Fortescue/4, 250–53.

69 Germain to Clinton, 23 January 1779, DDAR/XVII, 43–45.

70 Ibid.

71 Germain to the Commissioners, 4 November 1778, DDAR/XV, 238–39. Germain to Clinton, 4 November 1778, DDAR/XV, 240–41.

72 Germain to Clinton, 23 January 1779, DDAR/XVII, 46–47. For the earlier awarding of equal rank, see Middleton, *Bells of Victory*, 55.

73 Ira D. Gruber, *The Howe Brothers and the American Revolution* (New York, 1972), 344. North to George III, 10 May 1779, Fortescue/4, 337.
74 Washington to Mason, 27 March 1779, WGW/14, 298–302.
75 Washington to Jay, 23 April 79, WGW/14, 435.
76 Washington to Lafayette, 8 March 1779, WGW/14, 222.
77 Washington to Putnam, 18 January 1779, WGW/14, 20.
78 Washington to Gerard, 1 May 1779, WGW/14, 470.
79 Washington to Laurens, 5 May 79, WGW/14, 499–501.
80 Clinton to Germain, 4 April 1779, DDAR/XVII, 96–97.
81 Clinton to Germain, 14 May 1779, CAR, 405–6.
82 Clinton to Germain, 13 May 1779, DDAR/XVII, 123–4.
83 Collier to Germain, 22 May 1779, DDAR/XVII, 130.
84 Collier to Sandwich, 3 April 1779, Sandwich/3, 125.
85 Collier to Sandwich, 19 April 1779, Sandwich/3, 127–28. Clinton to Germain, 5 May 1779, DDAR/XVII, 117–18.
86 Collier to Clinton, 16 May 1779, CAR, 406. Collier to Germain, 22 May 1779, DDAR/XVII, 130–32.
87 Mathew to Clinton, 24 May 1779, DDAR/XVII, 133.
88 Clinton to Germain, 18 June 1779, DDAR/XVII, 144–45.
89 Ibid.
90 Tryon to Clinton, 20 July 1779, DDAR/XVII, 162–65.
91 Ibid., 164–65.
92 Washington to Lafayette, 30 September 1779, WGW/16, 374.
93 Wayne to Washington, 1 July 1779, CAR, 411. Ferling, *Almost a Miracle*, 356–57.
94 Washington to Lincoln, 30 July 1779, WGW/16, 16–18.
95 General Orders, 29 August 1779, WGW/16, 202–3.
96 Clinton to Germain, 25 July 1779, DDAR/XVII, 168–70.
97 M. Le Comte de Lapeyrouse Bonfils, *Histoire de la Marine Française*, 3 vols. (Paris, 1845), III, 92–96. Admiral Parker to Stephens, 26 August 1779, DDAR/XVII, 191–92.
98 Germain to Clinton, 3 March 1779, DDAR/XVII, 72–73.
99 Germain to Clinton, 2 September 1778, DDAR/XV, 193–94. Paul H. Smith, *Loyalists and Redcoats: A Study in British Revolutionary Policy* (Chapel Hill, 1964), 175–77.

100 Brigadier MacLean to Germain, 26 August 1779, DDAR/XVII, 192–96.
101 Collier to Clinton, 19 August 1779, CAR, 416–17. Brigadier Francis MacLean to Germain, 26 August 1779, DDAR/XVII, 192–96.
102 George III to Sandwich, 13 September 1779, Sandwich/3, 135.
103 The obstacles to Collier's promotion are discussed in Rodger, *Sandwich*, 172.
104 William B. Willcox, *Portrait of a General: Sir Henry Clinton in the War of Independence* (New York, 1964), 284–85. Syrett, *Royal Navy in American Waters*, 120–21. For a more favorable assessment of Arbuthnot, see Rodger, *Sandwich*, 283–86.
105 Germain to Clinton, 5 May 1779, DDAR/XVII, 116–17.
106 Alfred T. Mahan, *Major Operations*, 105–12. Dull, *French Navy*, 159–60. The fleets of D'Estaing and Byron are listed in Bonfils, *Marine Française*, III, 93–95.
107 Clinton to Germain, 20 August 1779, DDAR/XVII, 188–89. Ibid., 21 August 1779, DDAR/XVII, 189–90.
108 Gambier to Germain, 29 September 1779, DDAR/XVII, 225–29.
109 Washington to General Armstrong, 10 August 1779, WGW/16, 69–70.
110 Washington to Gates, 24 August 1779, WGW/16, 159–60. Washington to Stirling, 28 August 1779, WGW/16, 190–94.
111 Washington to Governor Trumbull et al., 27 Sept 1779, WGW/16, 344–45.
112 Washington to d'Estaing, 4 October 1779, WGW/16, 409.
113 Dull, *French Navy*, 161. Bonfils, *Marine Française*, III, 103–5. Henri Doniol, *Histoire de la participation de la France à l'établissement des États-Unis d'Amérique: Correspondence diplomatique et documents*, 5 vols. (Paris, 1886–1892), 4, 161–62.
114 Arbuthnot to Clinton, 6 October 1779, CAR, 424. Clinton to Germain, 26 October 1779, DDAR/XVII, 236. Arbuthnot to Sandwich, 30 October 179, Sandwich/3, 136–38.
115 Washington to Benjamin Harrison, 25 October 79, WGW/17, 20–22. For the Patriot campaign against the Iroquois, see Chapter 8, section "The devastation of Iroquoia".
116 Arbuthnot to Commodore Peter Parker, 20 October 1779, DDAR/XVII, 234.
117 Washington to Trumbull, 16 November 1779, WGW/17, 107–8.
118 Prevost to Germain, 1 November 1779, DDAR/XVII, 241–50.
119 For d'Estaing's account of the siege, see Doniol, *Participation de la France*, 303–7.

120 Order of Troop Cantonments, November 1779, WGW/17, 209–11.
121 George III to Sandwich, 13 Sept 1779, Fortescue/4, 432–33.
122 T.H. McGuffie, *The Siege of Gibraltar* (London, 1965), 38–46.
123 Thoughts upon Naval Measures, 14 September 1779, Fortescue/4, 436–37.
124 Proposal for the relief of Gibraltar, circa 1 November 1779, Sandwich/3, 186–87. Cabinet Minute, 4 November 1779, ibid., 187–88. Syrett, *Royal Navy in European Waters*, 84.
125 Sandwich had to make special arrangements so that Rodney could not profit from the sale of stores, as he had done previously; Syrett, *Royal Navy in European Waters*, 82.
126 Admiralty to Rodney, 8 December 1779, Rodney Papers/2, 261–63.
127 Rodney to Stephens, 9 January 1780, Rodney Papers/2, 304–5.
128 Dull, *French Navy*, 170–71, 173. Hargreaves-Mawdsley, *Spain*, 133.
129 Rodney to Sandwich, 27 January 1780, Sandwich/3, 193–95. Ibid., 200–202, 16 February 1780.
130 Rodney to Stephens, 27 January 1780, Rodney/2, 320–21.
131 Rodney to Sandwich, 16 February 1780, Sandwich/3, 200–202.
132 Digby to Sandwich, 2 March 1780, Sandwich/2, 202–4.
133 Sandwich to Rodney, 8 March 1780, Sandwich/3, 205.
134 North to the King, 6 March 1780, Fortescue/5, 27. For the previous war see Middleton, *Bells of Victory*, 206, 213.
135 George III to North, 7 March 1780, Fortescue/5, 30.
136 See above, Chapter 6, section "Britain faces invasion".
137 Estimates for Guards, Garrisons and Plantations, CJ/XXXVII, 473–76. Estimate for New Corps, CJ/XXXVII, 480.

CHAPTER 7

Changing strategies, 1780

The Bourbon powers alter their focus

The year 1779 had been a disappointing one for France and Spain in both Europe and America. Little had been effected in the western hemisphere, while the invasion of Britain had failed to produce any result. One reason had been the poor performance of the Spanish Navy off the coast of Britain. But the attempt had also exposed the difficulties of launching an invasion across the Channel. Among the more pertinent obstacles were the uncertainties of the weather and the lack of suitable ports along France's northern coasts to shelter the fleet and provide bases for embarking the army. Although Spain wanted to renew the invasion plan, Vergennes and Sartine determined to direct their resources in 1780 to the Caribbean and North American theatres. The capture of the British West Indian islands would damage Britain's ability to finance the war, while a successful campaign in North America would fulfill France's principal aim of dismantling her rival's empire. The result would be a devastating double blow for the enemy. The most that Vergennes would contemplate in home waters (therefore) was a naval demonstration at the western end of the Channel.[1]

A new flotilla was accordingly prepared for the West Indies under Admiral Count de Guichen, consisting of 17 ships of the line and a large convoy of merchantmen and transports carrying 4,400 troops. De Guichen was one of the French Navy's most respected officers, having distinguished himself in various engagements since joining the navy in the 1740s. His orders were to reinforce France's principal base at Martinique before seizing Britain's remaining possessions in the eastern Caribbean, the most important being Barbados, St Lucia and Antigua.[2]

Regarding North America, Vergennes and Sartine recognized that temporary deployments from France or the West Indies were not enough to alter the course of the war there. A more permanent military and naval presence was needed, a point made by Lafayette, who had returned home in 1779 to serve in the French regular army.³ However, the Council of Ministers was nervous of antagonizing the local population, as had happened in 1778 on d'Estaing's departure from Newport. The danger was that another such episode might induce the collapse of the alliance. Nevertheless, the need to do something effective was clear. The decision was accordingly taken to dispatch seven ships of the line under Admiral Charles d'Arsac, Chevalier de Ternay with 6,000 troops under the command of the General Jean Baptiste Donatien, Comte de Rochambeau.⁴ Both were experienced officers, though Ternay was advanced in years and of an acerbic temperament. Another problem was that neither man spoke English, making cooperation awkward since few Americans understood French.⁵ However, both men were free of the normal airs and graces of French courtiers and had a better chance of adjusting to the informality of colonial life.⁶

Spain necessarily had to accept these changes in French strategy, being the weaker partner in the alliance. However, Vergennes agreed to assist in the blockade of Gibraltar to placate his ally for abandoning the invasion of Britain. France would also help Spain in the West Indies, once de Guichen had finished his operations in the eastern Caribbean. Admiral du Chaffault was accordingly to join Cordoba at Cadiz with the remaining ships at Brest, while 2,000 French troops from Martinique assisted in the capture of Pensacola in West Florida. Finally, de Guichen would return to Cadiz rather than Brest at the start of hurricane season to provide additional support for the siege of Gibraltar.⁷

These were remarkably generous proposals from Vergennes, though they reflected France's need for Spanish help to maintain naval superiority over Britain. Nevertheless Charles III and Floridablanca were not pleased about the change of strategy and the consequent abandonment of the plan to invade Britain. Hence, it was not until the end of February 1780 that they agreed to cooperate, several weeks after de Guichen's departure from Brest. Help in the reduction of Gibraltar was certainly welcome as was French support in the Western Hemisphere. The Spanish court accordingly proposed to strengthen their forces there by the dispatch of 12 battleships and 11,000 troops under Commodore Jose Solano. These were to sail to the French island of Guadeloupe before proceeding northwards with de Guichen to the Gulf of Mexico.⁸ Nevertheless the delay meant that Solano was unlikely to leave Cadiz before early May. Until then the battle for control in the eastern Caribbean would fall exclusively on France.

The struggle for mastery in the West Indies

As already noted, the North ministry had already decided to strengthen Britain's own forces in the Caribbean by dispatching Rodney with five battleships, once Gibraltar had been relieved. Rodney reached Carlisle Bay in Barbados on 17 March 1780, a week after de Guichen arrived at Fort Royal Bay, the principal anchorage in Martinique. This meant that the two fleets were of equal strength, comprising 23 ships of the line.[9] De Guichen, however, had no interest in an engagement, as befitted French naval doctrine, since his mission was strictly one of supporting the amphibious operations of the French and Spanish land forces. He accordingly declined to engage when Rodney first appeared off the island in early April. However, Rodney's chance came when de Guichen set off for Barbados, the first of several hoped-for conquests suggested by Vergennes. This slowed de Guichen's fleet because of the need to escort the troops under General Bouille. Rodney's plan on 17 April 1780 was to strike the French center and rear divisions rather than the entire French line. Unfortunately he failed to clarify his intentions that each ship should engage the first available enemy vessel rather than waiting to take its correct position in the line, as laid down in the Fighting Instructions.[10] The captains previously under Parker in consequence misunderstood his order, resulting in considerable confusion. Since de Guichen had ordered his ships to fight in the traditional defensive manner by running with the wind, they were able to inflict considerable damage on Rodney's vanguard, similar to that experienced by Keppel at Ushant and Byron at Grenada. The only consolation was that de Guichen abandoned his attempt on Barbados to return to Guadeloupe to await Solano's arrival.[11]

Rodney had no doubt about the cause of his failure to win a decisive engagement. It was the result of "barefaced disobedience to [his] orders and signals," not least by his three flag officers, Rear Admirals Joshua Rowley and Hyde Parker, and Commodore William Hotham. Nevertheless he was sensible enough to recognize that his system of communicating orders had broken down. In future he would transfer his flag to a frigate, clear of the smoke that enveloped naval actions, where his signals could be more readily observed.[12] However, two further attempts to engage the French fleet on 17 and 19 May 1780 were equally unsuccessful, since Guichen persisted in avoiding an engagement. He was able to do so because many of the French vessels either had copper bottoms or were faster through the water because of their shallower hulls.[13]

Despite Rodney's lack of success, he remained for the moment indispensable to British plans in the West Indies. Sandwich therefore had no option but to replace Hyde Parker, with a new second in command. Such was Rodney's querulous reputation that several senior officers refused the appointment. Eventually Sandwich persuaded the semi-retired 56-year-old commissioner of Portsmouth Dockyard, Sir Samuel Hood, who had once served as midshipman under Rodney, to take the assignment. Hood's career, like that of Collier, had been blighted through lack of connections.[14] Nevertheless, he was a talented and ambitious officer. His appointment was to prove one of Sandwich's best.

Rodney's inability to strike a decisive blow appeared doubly unfortunate now that Solano's flotilla was approaching, after leaving Cadiz on 28 April 1780. Rodney quickly recognized the need to intercept Solano before he could join de Guichen, despite the poor state of his ships following the action on 17 April.[15] He decided to station himself off Martinique in the mistaken belief that this was the intended rendezvous, even though de Guichen had already gone to Guadeloupe after his abortive attempt against Barbados. The union of the two allied fleets was accordingly uncontested on 9 June 1780. Rodney was momentarily in despair, telling General Vaughan "what to do I know not."[16] Fortunately for the British, the Spanish fleet was wracked by disease which soon spread to de Guichen's squadron. The two commanders were also unable to agree whether to make Martinique or Cuba their main base of operations.[17] By the time these difficulties had been surmounted it was too late to begin operations in Florida as the hurricane season was approaching. Solano accordingly headed for Havana while de Guichen returned to Europe to assist the blockade of Gibraltar.[18] The Bourbon allies had missed a golden opportunity to inflict a decisive defeat on the British. The latter's remaining islands were still intact while Rodney had survived to fight again, as had Clinton in North America, for whom a French naval victory would have been disastrous.

Britain looks southwards: The campaign for the Carolinas

Vergennes and his colleagues were not alone in changing their views about the conduct of the war in 1780. The British too had determined on a new strategy with respect to America. Instead of concentrating on the northern colonies, the ministry decided that more should be done to recover the southern provinces. For whatever Britain's difficulties in Europe and the West Indies, the crushing of the rebellion remained the primary reason for the war.

Until the expedition to Georgia at the end of 1778 the British had paid little attention to the South, since the center of rebellion appeared to be in New England and the Middle Colonies. Apart from Virginia, the South had made little contribution to the revolutionary cause. However, after the debacle at Saratoga, the region began to seem more important. The lower south had several valuable commodities which helped pay for the Patriot war effort. If British authority could be re-established there, the rebellion elsewhere might fizzle out. Lastly, governors like William Campbell continued to assert that the inhabitants were only waiting "an opportunity of showing their loyalty," as had been initially demonstrated on the army's arrival in Georgia.[19] Germain accordingly ordered Clinton at the end of March 1779 to consider dispatching a force to South Carolina once his own operations in the north had ended in October. The only proviso was that any such force must enjoy "the assistance of the loyal inhabitants."[20]

The minister's enthusiasm for a southern campaign based on popular support for once coincided with the views of Clinton, following the collapse of his attempts to destroy Washington's army on the Hudson. The approach of cooler weather made operations there less hazardous to the health of the army. Clinton could therefore switch his forces for a winter campaign until it was time to make another attempt to bring Washington to battle in the following summer. But another reason was Clinton's conviction, as he told Germain on 21 August 1779: "if we do not conquer South Carolina, everything is to be apprehended for Georgia." The army was accordingly set to work "to perfect the defenses" of New York in order to release more men for the field. Similar reasoning prompted the withdrawal from Verplancks and Stony Point.[21] Finally additional troops would be available once the withdrawal from Rhode Island had been completed. With New York secure, a major offensive in the south was now possible.

Clinton decided to command the expedition himself, perhaps conscious that this was the last chance to enhance his military reputation, following his request to be superseded by Cornwallis.[22] Initially he hoped to sail for Charleston in early October. However, the arrival of d'Estaing at Savannah meant that nothing could be done until the French fleet departed at the end of the hurricane season.

The task force for South Carolina finally left New York on 26 December 1779, comprising 90 transports and 14 warships. On board were 8,000 troops, including several Loyalist units from the middle colonies. Bad weather buffeted the convoy which only reached the Savannah River after a month at sea. Before advancing on Charleston, Clinton dispatched 1,800 men to Augusta to secure the frontier region. Unfortunately they had to be recalled almost immediately because Clinton feared that he would not have enough men for the main attack.[23] It was yet another example of British insensitivity to local opinion, since it left Georgia exposed once again to Patriot incursions from South Carolina. This in turn forced Governor Wright to abandon his plan for holding elections, further undermining Germain's hope that the calling of an assembly would reassure the inhabitants about the ending of military rule.[24]

Despite recalling the troops from Augusta, Clinton still feared that he would have insufficient men for the investment of Charleston, following intelligence that Washington was sending 2,000 Virginian Continentals to Lincoln's assistance. He accordingly ordered Knyphausen to send as many men as possible from New York, consistent with the town's defense. In the event, Knyphausen was able to dispatch 5,000 men, following an appeal for the townsmen to form a local militia. Such was their enthusiasm that over 2,600 answered the call.[25]

Charleston's seaward defenses consisted primarily of two forts, Moultrie and Johnson, which guarded the entrance to the outer harbor. Both works were in a state of disrepair. The only other protection from a seaborne attack was a sand bar which prevented the larger warships of war from entering the Ashley and Cooper Rivers. Unfortunately the defenses were no stronger on the landward side. Across the neck of Charleston there was a line of trenches with just one fort of 18 guns. These too were either in disrepair or incomplete.

For the defense of Charleston, Lincoln had approximately 2,400 Continental troops and some 2,000 North and South Carolina militia. Lincoln himself had served creditably at Boston and Saratoga and had successfully contained Prevost in Georgia. Nevertheless he had relatively little experience in siege warfare and mistakenly believed that Clinton would storm the town at the junction of the Cooper and Ashley Rivers. He accordingly made the defense of Charleston from the seaward direction his principal objective, believing perhaps, like Washington at New York, he could engineer a successful retreat should he be outflanked.

Clinton had no such intention, being resolved to attack from the land side to the rear of the town rather than make a frontal assault on the harbor. Unlike Howe at New York, he wanted to capture not just the town but the Patriot Army too.[26] But first Arbuthnot had to get some frigates over the sand bar to control the navigation around the city. This was done with relative ease, allowing Clinton on 25 March to advance with his main force over the Ashley River 12 miles above Charleston. By 1 April he was ready to begin a formal siege against the vulnerable northern side of Charleston's defenses, though not before a force of cavalry and infantry under Colonel James Webster had advanced inland to prevent help reaching the beleaguered Patriots from the other side of the Cooper River. The trap was finally closed on 14 April 1780 when a regiment of provincial cavalry, commanded by Banastre Tarleton, surprised a rebel force under General Huger at Monck's Corner.[27]

The method of conducting a siege in the eighteenth century was by digging parallel trenches and diagonal walkways to get progressively closer to the enemy lines. Each new parallel was then strengthened by the construction of redoubts for cannon. Essentially this part of the siege was an artillery duel in which the attackers attempted to silence their opponents' fire and breach their defenses as the prelude to an assault. The guns on the first parallel opened fire on 8 April, the second similarly on 19 April, the day after Knyphausen's reinforcement appeared from New York. Their arrival meant that Clinton had 14,000 regulars at his disposal, giving him an advantage of three to one.[28]

Mercifully for those inside, no final assault was necessary. With the town in flames Lincoln accepted the inevitable, not least because of pressure from the civilian population. Clinton's terms were that the Continental troops became prisoners of war until exchanged for Burgoyne's men. The militia in contrast would be paroled and allowed to go home, though still technically prisoners.[29] On 11 May 1780, 2,570 Continentals and 1,800 militia surrendered. The Patriots also lost a huge arsenal of weapons The casualties were relatively modest, being some 250 killed and wounded on each side, though another 200 died when an ammunition store exploded accidentally.[30] This was the biggest Patriot defeat of the war, considerably greater than the one suffered at Fort Washington.

The loss of Charleston was a dreadful blow to the American Patriots, especially in the tidewater area of South Carolina, since it shattered the confidence of the ruling elite. According to James Simpson, the former attorney general, the South Carolina planter class was divided into four groups. The largest class seemed favorable to the restoration of royal government, the second appeared reconciled to it, yet more believed their cause was just but no longer sustainable, while a small minority opposed submission "without the general consent of America." As for the lower sort, Simpson was convinced they would follow the example of their betters and "quietly submit." Nevertheless, he warned that "time and address" would be required before the old order was restored.[31]

The submission of Charleston allowed Clinton to attend to the rest of the province. As he later wrote in his narrative: "Nothing appeared to be wanting toward the entire suppression of rebellion but the occupying a few strong posts in the upper country, and the putting arms into the hands of the King's friends." Three columns were accordingly dispatched into the interior. The largest one under Cornwallis marched to Camden to seal off the main route into North Carolina; another under Colonel Balfour took post at Ninety Six, and a third under Thomas Brown secured the Savannah River at Augusta.[32]

Initially all three met little resistance. The only remaining hostile force in South Carolina was a regiment of Virginia Continentals under Colonel Abraham Buford which had arrived too late for the siege of Charleston and was now retreating towards the North Carolina border. Cornwallis quickly ordered Tarleton and his Tory legion in pursuit. The Legion had originally been recruited in Pennsylvania by Howe and placed under Tarleton, a regular cavalry officer. Tarleton was the son of a Liverpool merchant and lacked the aristocratic credentials normally essential for advancement. Taking command of a provincial unit, therefore offered him a route to promotion and military prowess. Still under 26 years of age, he was handsome, ambitious, arrogant and fearless, qualities often productive of recklessness.[33]

Tarleton set off from Camden on 27 May 1780, covering the 100 miles to Waxhaws in just two days. Tarleton offered Buford terms similar to those granted to the Charleston garrison. However, Buford determined to resist, whereupon Tarleton charged the Patriot line. In the heat of the engagement, a number of the Continentals were killed after they had surrendered, giving rise to the odious phrase "Tarleton's Quarter." It was the beginning of a cycle of violence in which one atrocity was matched by another.[34]

Clinton meanwhile had started to consolidate British control by the formation of a militia. This was to comprise two kinds of unit; one for local defense and another for the protection of the region. He had clearly taken Germain's strictures about developing loyalist support to heart. The local militia was to be recruited from "those who have families," who were "occasionally to assemble in their own district, when required, under officers of their own choosing, for the maintenance of peace and good order." The province-wide militia, on the other hand, were to be recruited from "those who have no families and can be conveniently spared ... [to] assist His Majesty's troops in driving the rebel oppressors" from the province. They "were to be ready to assemble when required, and serve with the King's troops for any six months of the ensuing twelve." They could choose their own company officers and receive pay, ammunition, and provisions like the royal troops. To quell fears that they might be drafted into the regular service, each man would receive a certificate that he was to serve only within the borders of the two Carolinas and Georgia.[35]

Clinton placed the formation and training of the new militias under an inspector, Major Patrick Ferguson of the 71st Highland regiment. Each man in the provincial militia was to be issued with ammunition, material for a "rifle shirt," and arms where practicable. Those who were "averse to serve on foot" could "do so on horseback at their own expense." Finally Ferguson was "to restrain the militia from offering violence to innocent and inoffensive people," especially "the aged and infirm" and "women and children of every denomination."[36] The wining of hearts and minds was as important as victory on the field of battle.

The defeat of Buford on 29 May led Clinton to believe that the whole province was now subdued. On 3 June he accordingly issued a proclamation declaring that earlier militia paroles on the surrender of Charleston would "be null and void" after 20 June. Hereafter everyone must return to being British subjects and were obliged to assist the army and civil officers of the Crown. Those who refused would be treated as rebels and subject to the forfeiture of their lives and property.[37] Clinton made these changes after Loyalists like Governor Wright complained that the Patriots would not only escape any penalty for their treason, but would be free to undermine royal government from within. Many Loyalists, in contrast, remained destitute and unable to contribute to the work of reconstruction.[38] The consequences of these unilateral changes in the status of the former rebels were quickly revealed.

However Clinton was oblivious to any problem, believing that he had completed the pacification of South Carolina. He was encouraged in his view by an address on 5 June 1780 from 200 leading Charleston inhabitants, congratulating Clinton on the restoration of Royal Government.[39] Seemingly the strategy of reclaiming America one colony at a time, starting in the south, was beginning to work. Accordingly on 8 June Clinton handed the command to Cornwallis and took ship with 4,500 men for New York, having received intelligence that Ternay was on his way from Europe with ten battleships and 5,000 troops. It was time to return northwards, the likelihood being that Ternay would first occupy Rhode Island before attacking New York.[40] Accompanying Clinton was Arbuthnot with most of the warships, Charleston being considered safe from an enemy fleet because of the sand bar and strength of the fortifications on Sullivan's Island which were being rebuilt. Remaining behind with Cornwallis to continue the work of pacification were six regiments of British regulars, a battalion of Hessians, and six battalions of northern loyalists, totaling 8,500 men.

Cornwallis first came to America in 1776 as one of Howe's major generals but he had returned to England in November 1778 on the news of his wife's illness, to whom he was much attached. Her death led him to resume active service, though he commented to his brother that he was not returning to America "with views of conquest and ambition", since "nothing brilliant can be expected in that quarter."[41] His career in New Jersey and Pennsylvania had marked him out as an able corps commander, where his affable and dignified demeanor made him popular with the troops. He was certainly fearless in the pursuit of an objective. The question was whether he had the vision to act successfully as an independent commander.[42]

The orders to Cornwallis of 1 June were to pacify the rest of the Carolinas before entering Virginia. However, he must first ensure that South Carolina and Georgia were secure, since consolidation was the key to establishing the King's authority. There must be no more erratic advances which lacked Loyalist support. After this Cornwallis was to establish a post at Wilmington on the Cape Fear River to supply the army as it advanced northwards. Such a base would also assist the forthcoming operations in the Chesapeake, which Clinton intended to undertake "as soon as we are relieved from our apprehension of a superior fleet and the season would admit." This was likely to be in September or early October 1780.[43]

This was a huge task. Although the army had seemingly crushed the resistance of the tidewater planter class, Cornwallis was aware that further resistance awaited him to the north. Nevertheless Cornwallis had learnt that the caution of the Howe brothers had not produced the collapse of the rebellion and he was determined not to follow such policy now. For too long he had had to take orders from unimaginative superiors. Now he was his own master, since Clinton was too far away in New York to direct the southern army himself. Cornwallis would come under his command again only once their forces united in Virginia.

Clearly his first task was to secure South Carolina so that it could be returned to civilian rule. Here the recruiting and training of Ferguson's militia and provincial units was an essential building block. Instructions were accordingly sent to the commanders of the recently established posts to facilitate their formation. The principal bases were Savannah, Beaufort, Charleston, and Georgetown on the coast; Augusta on the Savannah River; Ninety Six close to the Saluda River; Rocky Mount and Camden on the Wateree River; and Cheraw on the Pee Dee. All were connected by roads, with access by water, giving Cornwallis seeming control of 15,000 square miles. By 20 June three provincial units of 500 men had been formed, along with numerous local militias.[44]

This suggested that Cornwallis could contemplate his next move, the invasion of North Carolina where he had been assured of Loyalist support. He outlined his views to Clinton on 30 June. "I think that with the force at present under my command (except there should be a considerable foreign interference) I can leave South Carolina in security and march with a body of troops into the back part of North Carolina with the greatest probability of reducing that province to its duty." The rebel forces there currently comprised 1,000 militia at Cross Creek, and another 500 militia with 300 Virginians at Salisbury. Two thousand Maryland and Delaware Continentals were also said to be on their way to Hillsborough under General Johann De Kalb. However, Cornwallis believed that none of these posed a serious threat, while such advance would provide South Carolina and Georgia with a more "effectual barrier" than if he remained on the border. If Clinton approved, Cornwallis proposed to begin his operations in late August, once the navy had forwarded supplies via Cape Fear.[45]

Unfortunately for Cornwallis, the situation was not quite as he described. In the first place the new militias were far from ready. This was partly due to Ferguson's inattention to his duties. He had formed several volunteer units in the region of Ninety Six, numbering over a thousand men, but had insisted on commanding them himself, ignoring his responsibilities for the rest of the province.[46] Difficulty was also experienced finding suitable officers and equipment. As a result many of these poorly armed and disciplined units quickly disintegrated on facing their first challenge. A prime example was the militia of Colonel Mills at Cheraw which mutinied once the regulars under Major McArthur withdrew. McArthur had left his sick behind, resulting in the capture of over 100 men of the 71st Highlanders. At the start of August Cornwallis had to confess that since this episode "the whole country between the Pedee and the Santee has ever been in an absolute state of rebellion." "Every friend of Government has been carried off and his plantation destroyed."[47]

The main reason for the resumption of hostilities in South Carolina was Clinton's proclamation of 3 June 1780. It was one thing for those who surrendered at Charleston to re-acknowledge the authority of the Crown. It was quite another to take up arms against their former colleagues, as they were now required to do. The erstwhile Patriots believed that Clinton had arbitrarily changed the terms of their parole, which they assumed would allow them to remain neutral.[48]

Among those leading the resurgent opposition were several members of the lesser gentry, like Francis Marion, Thomas Sumter, and Andrew Pickens. Marion was a former store keeper who had established himself as a successful planter along the Santee River close to Eutaw Springs. He first saw service in the war against the Cherokee in 1761, rising to colonel of one of the South Carolina provincial regiments at the start of the Revolution. However, injury meant that he was not present during the siege of Charleston. But the debacle there did not lessen his determination to fight for the Patriot cause. After attempting to liaise with the Continental forces in North Carolina, he began recruiting bands of partisan militia between the Santee and Pee Dee Rivers, where the Scots Irish settlements along the Black River proved fertile ground.[49]

Equally active was Thomas Sumter, a former frontiersman, storekeeper and justice of the peace, who rallied the Patriots in the region north of Camden. He was one of those moved by a sense of injustice following Clinton's proclamation of 3 June 1780. By mid-July he had some 1,500 militia between Waxhaw and the Catawba River.[50] Finally, Andrew Pickens was another Patriot who had accepted Clinton's surrender terms only to be forced to take up arms again, following Loyalist attacks on his plantation at Long Canes near Ninety Six.[51]

Unfortunately for Cornwallis, the situation was no better in North Carolina. At the start of June he invited the Crown's supporters there to "remain quiet until" he could "give them effectual support." He repeated his plea two weeks later, urging sympathizers to "remain at home and get in their harvest," since a "premature rising" would ruin all our plans for the reduction of North Carolina.[52] However, many Loyalists had other ideas, especially along the border. After years of persecution, they were determined on revenge. Within days of Cornwallis's second plea, a large force of 1,300 North Carolina Loyalists under Colonel John Moore had gathered at Ramsour's Mill only to be surrounded by the better-armed North Carolina militia. For a couple of hours the Loyalists held their own, but eventually weakened and ran for safety, suffering heavy losses in the process.[53] News of the engagement then prompted a further 800 Loyalists under Colonel Samuel Bryan in Rowan County to flee down the Yadkin River to the protection of McArthur's regulars.[54] It was a severe setback to British hopes of quelling North Carolina.

Despite these disappointments, Cornwallis was not downhearted, since they confirmed his belief that the answer to the violence in both provinces was an offensive into North Carolina. De Kalb's arrival with his Continentals at Hillsborough had prompted the neighboring militia to advance to the

Deep River while Sumter took post near the Catawba settlements. To Cornwallis it was clear: "Their plan is not only to defend North Carolina, but to commence offensive operations immediately." Hence "the most effectual means of keeping up the spirits of our friends and securing the province" was to follow the plan which he had outlined to Clinton on 30 June. To this end he began moving supplies to Camden while the senior naval officer at Charleston prepared to ferry goods via the province's different rivers.[55] Cornwallis admitted in a further letter to Clinton on 6 August that the renewed violence in South Carolina made some doubt whether a further advance was prudent. Cornwallis was not one of them. The "assurances of attachment" in North Carolina were "as strong as ever," while the Highlanders around Cross Creek had "offered to form a regiment as soon as we enter the country." Nevertheless, "an early diversion" by Clinton "in Chesapeake Bay" would "be of the greatest . . . advantage to my operations."[56] Four days later he was on the road to execute his plan.

Meanwhile Congress had been attempting to repair the damage caused by the loss of Charleston. It had already accepted Washington's proposal to reinforce Lincoln's army with the Maryland and Delaware Continentals under De Kalb.[57] However, Lincoln's surrender meant that a new commander was required. In this crisis Congress turned to Gates, the victor of Saratoga. Gates was more than eager for the task, feeling sidelined since accepting a position on the Board of War. However, few additional troops were available, given Washington's weak situation. As a result Gates found just 1,400 Continental troops when he joined his command on 25 July 1780, though he was expecting several thousand North Carolina and Virginia militia to join him, which would raise his total to at least 5,000 men. Sumter was also planning a diversion below Camden.[58]

This seemed more than adequate for an offensive. Gates accordingly set off for Camden where Lord Rawdon commanded the advanced guard. However, in his haste he took a route through a sparse countryside devoid of provisions. This unnecessarily tired the men, a situation which he compounded on the last day by giving his men a meal which caused much diarrhea. Finally Gates committed himself to a night march, his self-confidence inflated by a belief that he was attacking only a relatively small force under Rawdon. As a result, he failed to discover that Cornwallis had now arrived at Camden with a substantial reinforcement. Gates in consequence would be attacking his opponent's army, which in terms of regular troops was the same as his own, though with far fewer militia.[59]

Cornwallis momentarily considered retiring before Gates's superior numbers, since he was aware that Sumter was advancing down the Wateree

River to attack his supply line below Camden. A retreat, however, would mean abandoning his sick and a considerable quantity of stores. It would also mean the loss of the backcountry, "forfeiting all pretensions to future confidence from our friends in this part of America." Cornwallis accordingly resolved to march on the night of 15 August to attack the Continental line early next morning. It was while carrying out this maneuver that his vanguard collided with the advancing Patriots, compelling both to halt. The situation, however, favored Cornwallis since Gates's freedom of movement was severely restricted by two swamps, which prevented him from using his superior numbers to best effect.[60]

Gates's final error on the morning of 16 August was to order the Virginia militia to attack the British right wing, believing his enemy had yet to form a line of battle. The poorly trained militia in consequence confronted Cornwallis's regulars, advancing in strict order with fixed bayonet. The militia, on discovering their predicament, took flight, exposing the Continental troops to a flank attack. Unsurprisingly after "an obstinate resistance of three-quarters of an hour, they too fell into confusion" and were forced "to give way in all quarters." The lead was given by Gates who rode from the field, not stopping until he reached Charlotte, 60 miles to the north. His leaderless men followed as best they could, harassed for 20 miles by Tarleton's cavalry. The Patriot army suffered 1,900 killed, wounded, and captured, compared to 325 casualties for the British. Barely 700 men remained when Gates reassembled his forces at Hillsborough in North Carolina.[61]

Another setback quickly followed. As the battle ended, news arrived that Sumter had attacked a convoy destined for Camden. Cornwallis immediately ordered the Tory Legion in pursuit. Tarleton caught up with his prey on the morning of 18 August at Fishing Creek a few miles northwest of Camden. Although Sumter had 700 men to Tarleton's 350 cavalry and mounted infantry, he was totally unprepared for the attack which took place at midday just as his men were preparing their lunch. The Patriots lost 150 men killed and wounded, and another 300 captured. Two hundred and fifty Loyalist and regular prisoners were also liberated.

Cornwallis wrote reassuringly to Germain: "The internal commotions and insurrections in the province will now subside."[62] To ensure this, he determined to deal severely with those who had broken their oaths of loyalty and taken up arms a second time. For the planter elite this meant imprisonment on an island off the Carolina coast and the distribution of their property to "those persons who have been plundered and oppressed by them." Ordinary militiamen, however, who had "borne arms with us and had afterwards joined the enemy should be immediately hanged." Everywhere "the most vigorous measures" were to be taken "to extinguish the rebellion."[63]

If Cornwallis thought that his victory over Gates would induce a general collapse of the Patriot cause in the south, he was soon disappointed. Most notably there was no remission in the efforts of Marion and his adherents to threaten the communication to Charleston.[64] Cornwallis in consequence had to dispatch Major James Wemyss to disarm the country between the Santee and Pee Dee, with orders to punish severely all those who had taken and broken their oaths. But most disappointing was the lack of any upsurge of Loyalist sentiment in North Carolina, following the battle of Camden. Cornwallis had promptly "dispatched proper people into North Carolina with directions to our friends there to take arms and assemble immediately." They could act this time with confidence since he would be marching "without loss of time to their support."[65] But within two weeks of Camden, Cornwallis admitted to Clinton that the Tories "do not seem inclined to rise until they see our army in motion." "The severity of the rebel government has so terrified and totally subdued the minds of the people that it is very difficult to rouse them to any exertions."[66] It was now that the consequences of Moore's and Bryan's premature uprisings were really felt.

Nevertheless there still seemed enough potential support to justify a march into North Carolina. Hillsborough might be a suitable place where he could form "a very large magazine for the winter, of flour and meat from the country, and of rum, salt etc from Cross Creek" on the Cape Fear River. However, he reminded Clinton that much would "depend on the operations which your excellency may think proper to pursue in the Chesapeake, which appears, next to the security of New York, to be one of the most important objects of the war."[67]

Cornwallis accordingly set off on 8 September, making for Charlotte via Waxhaw. However, little support was evident among the population. Indeed on approaching Charlotte on 26 September the vanguard was ambushed by partisans, providing one more demonstration that the countryside was not teeming with Loyalists. Cornwallis accordingly halted while he issued another proclamation calling on the inhabitants to surrender their arms in exchange for the King's protection. The situation was everywhere menacing, for news arrived that Augusta was under siege by the partisans of Elijah Clarke.[68] Fortunately Colonel John Cruger had been able to send relief from Ninety Six. In accordance with Cornwallis's new punitive policy, he ordered the hanging 13 prisoners who had broken their parole. He also sent patrols into the countryside to destroy the homes of anyone suspected of serving with Clarke.[69]

Then a more devastating blow hit Cornwallis. He had previously allowed Ferguson, against his better judgment, to march into Tryon County in the northwest corner of South Carolina to protect the army's left flank as it advanced northwards.[70] Ferguson's arrival, however, threatened the backcountry settlements on the other side of the mountains along the Watauga and Holston Rivers. The inhabitants' fears were not assuaged when Ferguson threatened their leaders, Isaac Shelby, John Sevier, and William Campbell, that he would hang them and "lay their country waste with fire and sword" if they persevered in their disloyalty.[71]

The over-mountain area, like the rest of the backcountry, was dominated by small farmers, mostly Presbyterian and other dissenters, who had initially been cool to the tidewater planter class, given its Episcopalian religion and aristocratic composition. But now that their own homes were threatened, they rallied to the revolutionary cause in a determined effort to rid themselves of the Tory threat. As Cornwallis subsequently acknowledged to Clinton: "a numerous and unexpected enemy came from the mountains. As they had good horses, their movements were rapid."[72] By the end of September 800 volunteers had gathered at Sycamore shoals on the Watauga River. Most had little training even as militia. What they did have were rifles and a determination to repulse the threat now posed by Ferguson. In the words of one of their ministers, the Reverend Samuel Doak, it was time to wield "the sword of the Lord and of Gideon."[73]

What followed was a classic demonstration of two very different kinds of warfare. Ferguson's provincials had been trained in orthodox tactics, advancing in a line, ready to use their bayonets after firing their muskets. The backcountry Patriots had no such organization. Each man fought as an individual, using the trees as cover while firing their rifles to good effect. Ironically Ferguson earlier in his career had developed a breech loading rifle only to have it rejected by the Ordnance Board as too innovative. Had it been adopted, the outcome of the ensuing battle might have been different.[74]

Ferguson, on hearing of the Patriot advance, began retreating towards the main army. He did, however, suggest to Cornwallis that "three or four hundred good soldiers, part dragoons, would finish the business." Perhaps in expectation of such reinforcement, he halted for two days on top of King's Mountain, astride the border of North and South Carolina. As he informed Cornwallis in a final dispatch on 6 October 1780: "I arrived today at King's Mountain and have taken a post where I do not think

I can be forced" whatever the numbers of the rebels.[75] Here on 7 October he attempted to fight a European-style battle, sending his troops down the slopes in serried ranks to force the frontiersmen back. Initially this was accomplished with ease, as the mountain men fell back after firing their rifles. However, they quickly returned after reloading, all the time taking a deadly toll of their opponents, who provided an easy target on top of the ridge in their bright clothing, since Ferguson had neglected to provide any entrenchments or fallen trees as cover. Within an hour it was all over, after Ferguson was killed attempting one final charge. What followed was a partial massacre, as the mountain men surged forward, shouting "Tarleton's Quarter," referring to the summary execution of Buford's men at Waxhaw. Nor did the killing stop there, for several captured militia officers were unceremoniously hanged a few days later at Gilbert Town.[76]

The battle is often portrayed as evidence of the superiority of the backcountry method of fighting. In reality this is far from the case. At King's Mountain the backwoodsmen were in their element, using their rifles with deadly effect. However, had they faced the regular light infantry, more familiar with open order tactics, the outcome would probably have been different. The backwoodsmen in any case were of little use in the more open coastal areas, against an army equipped with cannon. The same was true of siege operations. It was for this reason that Washington never wavered in his belief in regular troops.[77] But as King's Mountain demonstrated, in hilly wooded areas, the irregulars could be very effective.

Clinton retrospectively described the defeat at King's Mountain as the southern equivalent of the Hessian defeat at Trenton.[78] Although no posts were lost, their garrisons in future were rarely able to emerge with safety, thus undermining the plan to consolidate British authority. The partisans of Marion and Sumter were especially active between Charleston and the interior, where isolated detachments of the British were frequently mauled. In these circumstances even Cornwallis recognized the futility of advancing further. He accordingly pulled back to Winnsboro, 30 miles north-west of Camden, to secure the frontier. Here he temporarily handed over responsibility to Rawdon, while he recovered from a fever, which was also affecting many of his soldiers.[79] It was little enough to show for all his efforts to re-establish royal authority.

The bloody killings at King's Mountain led to mutual recriminations as to what had happened. Washington suggested that the British were responsible because of their execution of prisoners after the battle of Camden. Cornwallis preferred to cite the "shocking barbarity" shown to Ferguson's men, especially "the hanging of poor old Colonel Mills at

Gilbert town." He warned that if the killings did not stop, justice to the Loyalists would require him to retaliate. No one had been executed, unless guilty either of "bearing arms after having given a military parole to remain quietly at home" or of "enrolling themselves in our militia" and then "taking the first opportunity of joining our enemies." The only persons hanged at Camden "were two or three of the latter description, who were picked out from above 30 convicted of the like offence."[80]

Shortly after the disaster to Ferguson, Cornwallis learnt that Clinton was sending Major General Leslie with 2,500 men to Virginia to "make a diversion" in his favor as he had requested. Leslie's orders were "to proceed up the James River . . . to seize or destroy any magazines the enemy may have at Petersburg, Richmond or any of the places adjacent," from which they supplied their forces in North Carolina. After this he was "to establish a post on the Elizabeth River" as a base for future operations, subject to such orders as he received from Cornwallis.[81]

Clinton issued these instructions before the battle of King's Mountain was known, making any further advance into North Carolina inadvisable. This meant that Leslie would be too distant to support Cornwallis's immediate operations. In these circumstances Cornwallis thought it better if Leslie embarked for the Cape Fear River to open a communication via Cross Creek.[82] This would then give the Loyalists a perfect opportunity to show their support. If they still failed to respond "we must leave them to their fate and secure what we have got."[83]

Leslie needed no prompting to comply. On entering the Chesapeake, he had found a population that was uncooperative after their abandonment by Collier and Mathews, knew nothing of Cornwallis's advance, and had erected numerous batteries to oppose him. The navigation of the James River was also uncertain, given a want of pilots. It was clear that Portsmouth must first be developed as a base before any operations were undertaken in Virginia.[84] He was more than happy to redeploy his forces around Cape Fear.

While awaiting a response from Leslie, Cornwallis attempted to deal with the deteriorating situation in South Carolina. At Ninety Six the militia was so disheartened by Ferguson's defeat that barely a hundred remained.[85] Morale was equally low on the upper Santee where a company of Colonel Samuel Tynes had been surprised by Marion on 25 October 1780 and disarmed.[86] The lack of support was easily explained, as Cornwallis informed Clinton subsequently: "Marion had so wrought on the minds of the people, partly by the terror of his threats and cruelty of his punishments and partly by the promise of plunder, that there was scarce an inhabitant between the Santee and Pee Dee that was not in arms against us." Some parties had even "carried terror to the gates of Charleston." In response, Cornwallis dispatched Tarleton to search out the partisan leader along the Black River. Unfortunately an attempted ambush was thwarted when the inhabitants warned Marion of his presence. Tarleton then torched 30 homes to show "the inhabitants that there was a power superior to Marion, who could likewise reward and punish." In consequence "the greatest part of them have not dared openly to appear in arms against us."[87] It was success of a kind for the policy of severity, though very short-term as it proved.

Indeed, as fast as Cornwallis dealt with one threat, another appeared elsewhere. He had ordered the sixty-third regiment under Wemyss to patrol the Broad River northwest of Camden to protect the army's corn mills. Early in November he received news that Sumter with 300 men was 40 miles away at Moore's Plantation. Wemyss set off with a mixed force of dragoons and infantry and succeeded in surprising Sumter at Fishdam Ford on 9 November 1780. Unfortunately for Wemyss, he was wounded on the verge of victory, leaving an inexperienced junior in command, who ordered a retreat. This setback, as Cornwallis acknowledged to Clinton, encouraged "the whole country" to come "in fast to join Sumter."[88] Cornwallis then attempted to rectify the situation by sending Tarleton in pursuit. Tarleton caught up with Sumter two weeks later at Blackstock's Plantation, but impetuously attacked without waiting for his infantry and artillery, suffering heavy casualties in consequence. The tally of British misfortune was completed on 1 December 1780 when 100 militia under Colonel Henry Rugeley surrendered without firing a shot to a detachment of cavalry under Colonel William Washington. This was despite the protection of a formidable blockhouse, the nearby presence of the Camden garrison, and the Patriot lack of artillery. Cornwallis could only explain Rugeley's actions as those of a traitor.[89]

Hence although Cornwallis reported to Clinton at the beginning of December that the army was healthy and well placed for protecting the northern frontier, the situation was by no means promising. The Patriots were gathering again along the border following the arrival of Continental reinforcements and were everywhere in arms. Cornwallis had accordingly ordered Leslie to come to Charleston, since cooperation "even at the distance of the Cape Fear River" would be difficult. After so many setbacks, the prospects for the next campaign were uncertain. Nevertheless Leslie's force was greater than expected and offered the possibility of decisive action. But everything depended on events.[90]

Congress meanwhile was endeavoring to revive the Continental army, since the partisans alone had no chance of ending the war. After

Camden, a new commander was clearly needed and Congress now accepted Washington's choice of Nathanael Greene.[91] Since the events of 1776, Greene had grown in maturity. Like Washington, he had learnt the key lesson about keeping the army in being. That meant knowing when to attack and when to fight "a fugitive war." But he also knew that an army had to be properly armed and clothed. By the time of his appointment to the southern army, Greene was well versed in such matters, having been Washington's Quarter Master General since March 1778. It was invaluable experience.

Few reinforcements would be available for Greene. Washington himself was desperately short of men. The only available corps was Henry Lee's Virginian legion of cavalry and mounted infantry. Greene would therefore have to make do with the remains of Gates's army and such other men as the southern states could raise, whom Steuben was to train.[92] Greene would also have the services of Morgan, who had been prevented by illness from joining Gates. But the situation was grim as Greene passed through Richmond, the Virginia state capital, where the business of government was at a standstill for want of money. Few wagons were available for Greene's army and no clothing for many of the 3,500 men then being raised as Continentals. The men, unsurprisingly, were deserting in shoals. Greene in desperation ordered Steuben to remain in Richmond until some discipline had been established.[93]

Greene reached the remnants of his army at Charlotte in early December 1780, where he found some 700 Maryland and Delaware Continentals, with a similar number of militia, all clothed in rags, devoid of shoes and hungry. The lack of clothing was especially serious, since it rendered most of the army "unfit for any kind of duty." Equally distressing to Greene, a former Quaker, was the nature of the war now being waged. "The whole country was in danger of being laid waste by the Whigs and Tories, who pursue each other with as much relentless fury as beasts of prey." Hundreds of genteel families were destitute.[94]

Nevertheless, the distress of the population was the least of Greene's worries. He confessed to a colleague: "I am so hedged in with difficulties ... that I can neither fight nor run away; and yet I am afraid I shall be obliged to do part of both." The problem was that "our numbers are by far too small to fight and our means of retreating are so incompetent to the business that it is next to impossible" to escape "an enemy of superior force." He was also plagued by the local militia who went to war on horseback, devastating the countryside by their need to forage and desire to plunder. Only a well ordered army of 6–7,000 men could save the situation.[95]

Greene accordingly spent the first few weeks trying to educate his southern colleagues on how the war must be fought. As he told the governor of North Carolina, Abner Nash: "It is in vain to collect large bodies of irregular troops with the expectation of driving the enemy out of the country; they cannot long be subsisted in the field, nor can they oblige the enemy to fight them, unless it is upon their terms." "Regular troops are not more brave or better men than irregular, but as method and order drives success in business, so discipline and a knowledge of tactics give force and efficacy to an army." Unfortunately, "people not acquainted with military matters believe that numbers are all that is required [for success], but unless these numbers are properly clothed, armed and equipped, numbers merely add to the distress." One had only to look at the present state of the south to see this.[96]

Ironically Cornwallis had the opposite problem to Greene. He had the regular troops, but wanted sufficient militia to maintain control after the former had moved on.

The lack of Continental troops meant that Greene necessarily had to rely on both the militia and partisan forces of Sumter and Marion. Indeed Greene's own forces would have to fight "a kind of partisan war" until a larger and better force was available.[97] In the latter task Virginia had a key role. Like Maryland, it had been relatively unscathed by the war and was the most populous state in the confederacy, with considerable reserves of men and supplies. It was these resources that Greene hoped Steuben could mobilize to balance Leslie's imminent appearance.

To help feed his men, Greene decided to send Morgan with part of the army to the west side of the Catawba River while he moved to Cheraw on the Pee Dee River. From here Greene could watch Cornwallis at Winnsboro while Morgan threatened the British at Ninety Six. Morgan's force was to consist of the light infantry, some militia and Washington's light dragoons, and was in effect to be a mobile "flying corps."[98] As Green informed the new President of Congress, Samuel Huntington, the object of Morgan's detachment was "to straighten the enemy's limits on that quarter, keep up the spirits of the people, give protection to the well affected, collect the provisions and form it into magazines."[99] The disadvantage was that the army was now divided. However, Greene's new rubric meant that each corps could run if necessary to ensure its survival. In preparation for just such an emergency, Greene began surveying all the rivers, noting the location of fords and other features. He also ordered the construction of boats of an especially shallow draught to facilitate the transporting of supplies.[100] The value of these precautions was shortly revealed.

But the outlook was still unpromising, as Greene surveyed the scene from "his camp of repose" at the end of 1780. His lack of troops meant that he could not advance on Charleston, even though the road was open, since the army had to avoid being trapped on ground not of its choosing. Everywhere the Tories appeared strong while the Whig population diminished. Seemingly the strategy of Clinton and Cornwallis was working. "Gold, aided by public distress and loyal feeling, has been too successful in promoting the project of making one conquest the stepping stone to another." The British were "in possession of all the fertile and populous parts of South Carolina." Until circumstances allowed Greene to enter the coastal plain "we shall have to operate in a country that has been exhausted and depopulated by swarms of mounted militia."[101] It was a daunting and frustrating prospect, for unlike Washington, Greene could not expect any French help. Except for Charleston, the Carolinas had few if any accessible ports, shielded as these provinces were by the outer banks and swampy rivers. In contrast to the conflict in the north, the southern war was being waged deep in the interior, where naval power was seemingly irrelevant. Providing the British held Charleston and received their supplies, the tidewater of the lower south was likely to remain in their grasp.

Northern impasse: The bankruptcy of Congress

Despite the halting of Cornwallis, 1780 was in many respects the low point for the Patriots in their struggle for independence, since their situation in the north was proving even less promising.

As in previous years, Washington's problems started while his forces were still in winter quarters. The previous November he had renewed his request that Congress abandon its preference for short-term enlistments in favor of compulsory drafting from the state militias.[102] Congress's response was the formation of another committee, which recommended a cut in the number of the regiments. Washington believed the decision was the result of mistaken notions about an imminent peace rather than concern for economy. He reminded the members of the new "Committee for the Reduction of the Army" that since "the beginning of the contest," such notions had not only caused "great expense," but had been "the means of protracting the war." Congress should understand that peace was best secured by being "well prepared to meet an enemy." This was essential to convince France and Spain of the Patriots' determination to continue the struggle.[103]

The problems of both Washington and Greene stemmed mainly from a lack of money. In the first few years Congress had raised some $24 million through the sale of bonds or loan notes. It had also been able to print currency. But as the number of bonds increased, the population became increasingly reluctant to buy further issues for fear that they would not be redeemed. This led to heavy discounting of the existing bonds. The same depreciation affected the currency. Paper money had to be convertible into specie if confidence was to be retained. Unfortunately, Congress had little gold or silver specie except for the occasional shipment from France. The problem would not have been so severe had Congress had the power to support the currency through taxation. In lieu of this it had to continue printing unsupported notes, resulting in spiraling inflation. The problem first became serious in mid-1777. However, the most spectacular falls occurred at the end of 1778 when Washington reported that the currency was sinking by 5 percent a day.[104] A proposal was then made to redeem the existing notes at a ratio of 40 to 1, but this was merely issuing new notes for old ones in the absence of specie.[105] The only solution to these financial difficulties was to give Congress authority to tax, which would allow the payment of interest on the bonds and restore confidence in the convertibility of the currency. However, this was something that the states were not prepared to concede.

Congress thus had to rely on the requisition system whereby each state contributed according to a quota based on its population. This was highly ineffective since states often missed the deadline or made only partial payment. They also used their own depreciated currencies or offered goods in kind. These were very inefficient ways of meeting the demands of the army. However, Congress's only response in February 1780 was another reduction in the nominal size of the Continental army, this time to 60 battalions totaling just 36,200 men.[106] But even that modest target was beyond the reach of the confederacy, especially when several states resolved to fill their ranks through voluntary enlistments rather than drafting from the militia, as Washington wanted.[107] By the end of March 1780 the army at Morristown and West Point numbered barely 10,000 and the terms of service for a quarter of these would expire shortly.[108]

The result of this lack of money was dissatisfaction in every branch of the service, as Washington informed Huntington in early April 1780. Most unsettling was the disparate treatment accorded by the states to their respective units. Some members "furnish their troops pretty amply ... others supply them with some necessaries, but on a more contracted scale; while others have it in their power to do little or nothing at all."

This naturally created much bitterness among those for whom little provision had been made. "An Army must be raised, paid, subsisted and regulated upon an equal and uniform principle" otherwise endless confusion and discontents must be the result. "Little less than the dissolution of the army would have been long since the consequence of a different plan, had it not been for a spirit of Patriotic virtue, both in officers and men." Nevertheless there were limits to the patience of the army. Many officers were resigning their commissions while the men, denied that option, "brood over their discontents, and have lately shown a disposition to enter into seditious combinations." The only solution was to ensure that "everything relating to the army" was "conducted on a general principle under the direction of Congress."[109]

But not everything was bleak. At the end of April 1780 Lafayette returned with news that France was dispatching an army and fleet to America.[110] There was also good news from Ireland where the Dublin Parliament was demanding legislative independence. The Irish were attempting, like the Patriots, "to remove those heavy and tyrannical oppressions" in order to restore "to a brave and generous People their ancient Rights and Freedom." This could only "promote the cause of America." Washington promptly made St Patrick's Day a holiday, adding the cautionary hope that "the celebrations . . . will not be attended with the least rioting or disorder."[111]

Washington had several times warned Congress that the patience of the army was limited and at the end of May a serious breakdown of discipline occurred in the Connecticut line. The men had for several days had no meat. But equally hurtful was Congress's decision to give them their back-pay in depreciated currency. On 27 May 1780 two regiments seized their arms and threatened to march into the countryside to take food at the point of the bayonet. Fortunately the appeals of the officers and assistance of the other units induced the men to return to their quarters.[112]

The incident nevertheless gave Washington "more concern than any thing that has ever happened." As he informed Reed in Philadelphia, the country seemed "in a state of insensibility and indifference to its interests" at the "decisive moment" of the war, when France was "making a glorious effort for our deliverance." He warned: "If we disappoint its intentions by our supineness, we must become contemptible in the eyes of all mankind." The French might not make another such effort, forcing America to submit to Britain's maritime and financial strength. "In modern wars the longest purse must chiefly determine the event." It was essential, therefore, that the states make one last attempt to secure an honorable peace based on independence.[113]

Nevertheless, the news of an approaching French army and fleet prompted Washington to consider plans for an attack on New York. He informed his officers on 6 June 1780 that the army currently had 8,000 men, though this would rise to 24,000 once the states completed their battalions. The British at New York had perhaps 8,000 regulars, plus 5,000 militia, but only one ship of the line.[114] But despite this, the officers were not optimistic that anything could be done, given the impossibility of knowing "what force we shall have in the field, how they will be appointed, and when they will be collected." The same was true of provisions and supplies."[115] Moreover, Clinton was likely to return from Charleston with part of his army and Arbuthnot's battleships, thus making any operation difficult, even with the help of the French.

For the moment such discussions were academic, since news arrived that the British were advancing into New Jersey. The Connecticut mutiny had encouraged Knyphausen to believe that Washington's men would either desert or be incapable of defending the stores and equipment at Morristown. The population would then hopefully greet the British as liberators.[116] In the event, Knyphausen's calculations proved hopelessly optimistic, as he confessed to Germain after crossing the Hudson in mid-June. "The disposition of the inhabitants" was "by no means such as I expected; on the contrary they were everywhere in arms; nor did I find that spirit of desertion amongst their troops which it was represented to me existed amongst them."[117] For a second time Washington commended the behavior of the New Jersey militia.[118] Nevertheless, it showed that the British could act with impunity even against the Continental army. They had ravaged "a fine country" and would do so again until the states filled their quotas of men.[119] The latter's inertia made Washington doubtful of being able to cooperate even with the French army and fleet.[120] As it was, he had been reduced to "removing our stores from place to place to keep them out of the way of the enemy instead of driving that enemy from our Country."[121]

Ternay and Rochambeau finally arrived at Rhode Island on 10 July 1780 with seven ships of the line and 4,500 regular troops, much to the surprise of the local population. Nevertheless, once the inhabitants had got over the initial shock of a foreign army in their midst, they ensured a cordial reception, encouraged by Rochambeau's friendly demeanor and the good discipline of his troops.[122] Relations were also helped by his readiness to pay hard cash for the goods and services required by his army and Ternay's ships. The orders to Rochambeau stated that his troops were to act as auxiliaries to the Patriot army, meaning that they would be under Washington's command in a distinct body. Ternay was similarly "enjoined to support with all his power all operations in which his co-operation" was required. No specific objectives were laid down, since these could be decided only once the expedition had arrived. The first task was necessarily ensuring that the ships and troops were secure in their new anchorage and camp at Newport.[123]

Unfortunately for the allies, the appearance of Ternay and Rochambeau coincided with the arrival of a British reinforcement of six battleships under Admiral Thomas Graves, giving Arbuthnot a slight superiority in capital ships. The number of troops with Rochambeau was also disappointingly small. However, the French officers reported that a second division was on its way from Brest, there having been insufficient shipping to transport all the soldiers in one embarkation.[124] This was sufficiently encouraging for Washington to order provisions and other supplies for a combined army of 40,000 men, even though he had barely 9,000 Continentals in his camp. He also suggested to Ternay and Rochambeau that New York should be the allied objective rather than Quebec or Charleston, as some were suggesting. But before anything could be attempted, it was essential that the allies achieved naval superiority around the city.[125]

Hence, until the second French division arrived, it was the British who temporarily held the initiative. The need to preempt their enemy was not lost on Clinton and Arbuthnot, who had now returned to New York. Clinton accordingly proposed two variants for an attack on Rhode Island before the French could consolidate their position at Newport. One was for a blockade of the harbor while Clinton with 5,000 men sailed up the Sakonnet Passage to attack from behind. The second was for a more direct advance by the fleet and army through Narragansett Sound. If either was successful, it would not only reduce any threat to New York or Charleston, but would also end the danger of a French invasion of Canada, about which there had been rumors.[126]

However, Arbuthnot had no stomach for either plan, in part because it would mean working with Clinton, from whom he had become estranged following the siege of Charleston. Arbuthnot, like Howe, preferred to fight the French fleet, unencumbered by the army. Thus when Clinton made a special journey through Long Island to Gardiner's Bay, he found that Arbuthnot had already left on the excuse that the French were about to sail.[127] The real reason was that he considered Clinton's schemes impracticable. "The enemy was in great force" at Newport, "covered with a vast artillery, strongly fortified," with the adjacent New England colonies "ready to support them." In these circumstances "a regular siege" would only be possible if Clinton had an army of at least 18–20,000 men.[128] This was clearly not the case.

Clinton unburdened himself once again to Germain, complaining that the arrival of the French had revealed "the utter impossibility of prosecuting the war in this country without reinforcement." It was pointless to expect miracles from the Loyalists, since any hopes of a substantial contribution from them were "visionary," unless the country was permanently occupied by the army. But it would help if the fleet had a commander "whose views with respect to the conduct of the war are similar to my own and whose cooperation with me as commissioner and commander-in-chief is cordial, uniform, and animated." Nevertheless, with adequate naval support "the Peninsula between Chesapeake and Delaware might be reduced to obedience."[129]

Any hopes of undertaking that operation were dashed a few days later by the receipt of Cornwallis's request of 6 August for "a diversion" in Chesapeake Bay. This "new drain" on the army would necessarily impose "a very strict defensive" on Clinton, despite the readiness of the people of New York to assist.[130] The pity was that "this southward business had [not] been adopted three years" earlier when there was no danger of French interference. Nevertheless, he remained confident that once the southern and middle colonies were occupied, the New England provinces could be reduced by expeditions "alone against their seaport towns." But in a moment of self pity, he told a confidant: "I have no money, no provisions . . . nor admiral that I can have the least dependence on, [and] no army. In short I have nothing left but the hope for better times and a little more attention."[131]

Meanwhile the situation of Washington's army remained as precarious as ever, despite the efforts of the Ladies of Philadelphia to buy a shirt for every soldier.[132] In the middle of August Washington asked Congress to make another appeal to the states for recruits, since the Continental battalions still wanted 10,400 men to complete their ranks. He was equally concerned about the lack of provisions.[133] For five days the units in northern New Jersey had no meat and barely any flour, resulting in widespread marauding by the troops.[134] Every day proved the necessity for a more effective supply system. To ease the situation, Washington sent home most of the militia, even though they might shortly be required on the appearance of the French second division.[135]

Washington also had the army's future requirements to consider. Half of the Continental enlistments would expire in early 1781 and without replacements the nation would have the humiliation of depending on foreigners to defend it. Congress must abandon its notion that the war would end shortly, since peace was as far away as ever. Britain had pacified Ireland by concessions to the Dublin Parliament, while its financial resources flourished despite the size of the debt. Hence America must look to its own resources. This brought Washington back to the issue of short-term enlistments which he believed had caused most of the difficulties since 1775.[136] Tackling this issue was all the more important given the news that the second French division was still in Brest, blockaded by the British Channel fleet. Unless the French and Spanish flotilla at Cadiz intervened, the reinforcements for America were unlikely to arrive before the end of the campaign.[137]

It was in this gloomy environment that Washington held a council of war on 6 September, informing his officers that the army now numbered just over 10,000 Continentals and 400 militia. Even with Rochambeau's men, the forces around New York could do little, unless the second division arrived.[138] One possibility was that the French might send their West Indian squadron to help. Washington had accordingly written to de Guichen informing him of the allies' bleak situation: Arbuthnot was blockading Ternay in Rhode Island, Clinton controlled much of New York, the Indians were ravaging the northern frontier, while Cornwallis held most of South Carolina and Georgia. However, if de Guichen could turn the tables in North America, the Patriots could then help France in the West Indies.[139]

While awaiting a reply, Washington met Rochambeau and Ternay on 22 September at Hartford in Connecticut. Here the allies agreed that no campaign could be undertaken without naval superiority, especially against New York. Hence if de Guichen arrived before 1 October and defeated Arbuthnot, a combined expedition should be launched against that city. Alternatively, if that was deemed too difficult, an operation might be undertaken in the south. But whatever was decided, a troop superiority of two to one was required. To ensure this, both allies would have to increase their forces, the French by as many as 10,000 men. Washington then suggested that Rochambeau march on New York to prevent Clinton from reinforcing Cornwallis. Rochambeau refused, however, because Ternay still felt vulnerable at his anchorage at Newport, and he insisted that the French troops remain there as security while Arbuthnot remained nearby in Gardiner's Bay with a superior fleet. This left Washington with nothing more than vague hopes for an effective campaign in 1781, unless de Guichen or the second French division arrived.[140]

In reality neither of these outcomes was possible. De Guichen had already returned to Europe with most of his fleet to assist in the siege of Gibraltar, while at Brest the French ministry had decided to redeploy the second division on other objectives, even though the British Channel fleet returned to port in September. Unfortunately, no one in the French government had attempted to inform either its own commanders or Patriot allies about the change of plan.[141] To remedy this lack of communication, Rochambeau agreed to dispatch his son to Paris to inform the ministry of the decisions made at Hartford: that a reinforcement of 10,000 French troops would be needed and an appropriate number of warships provided to ensure a successful campaign against New York in 1781.[142]

The failure of the French second division to arrive was not the only setback at this time, since Washington returned to West Point in late September 1780 to the shocking discovery that Arnold, one of his most able commanders, had attempted to commit treason by handing over the Highland forts. The reasons for Arnold's treachery are not entirely clear. During his career he had been slighted in his claims to high command, notably in the spring of 1777 when he was passed over for promotion to Major General, even though he was the most senior brigadier. The omission was partially rectified a few weeks later at Washington's insistence, but he was still junior to those already promoted, thus affecting his right to a senior field command.[143] After being wounded at Saratoga, he was placed in charge of the garrison at Philadelphia, only to be accused of peculation and other irregularities. He was eventually court-martialed and found guilty of abusing his position for personal benefit.[144] This undoubtedly added to Arnold's sense of alienation, though the tipping point may have been the military setbacks and general malaise affecting the cause of independence.[145] Ironically it was at this moment that Washington offered Arnold command of the left wing of his army, thus giving him the military recognition that he craved. Arnold declined on the grounds that his wounds were not yet healed, though it is likely that his negotiations with Clinton had gone too far to be withdrawn. Washington then sent him to take charge at West Point.[146]

This was the opportunity that Arnold was perhaps awaiting, having already contacted the British during an intelligence-gathering operation. The agreement required Arnold to assist in the capture of the Highland forts in return for being made a Brigadier General in the British army.[147] Unfortunately for the conspirators, their plan was exposed when Clinton's emissary, Major John André, was detected carrying incriminating plans of the Highland forts.[148] Arnold escaped to the British lines, but André was not so fortunate. Since he had been caught in disguise, carrying a pass with a false name, and confidential papers concealed in his boots, he was treated as a spy, despite Clinton's assertions that he was acting under a flag of truce.[149] Washington may have adopted his harsh stance because of the earlier treatment of one of his officers, Captain Nathan Hale, who had been caught by the British in similar circumstances while gathering intelligence. André was publicly hanged on 1 October for having breached "the law and usage of nations."[150] Nevertheless, Arnold's defection was a shock to Patriot morale. Until this point he had embodied so much that was dear to the Revolutionary cause: a man of energy, courage, vision, and commitment, who had taken up arms in 1775 as the virtuous citizen. Now he was portrayed as the blackest of villains.[151] The British, however, kept their word, giving Arnold a commission as a provincial brigadier and a command shortly in the field.

The detection of the plot was a blow for Clinton since he had put the capture of the Hudson forts ahead of further cooperation with the navy. Consequently when Rodney arrived unexpectedly with ten battleships from the West Indies seeking shelter during the hurricane season, Clinton declined his suggestion for an attack on Rhode Island, arguing that the French were now too well entrenched and easily reinforced by Washington.[152]

As a result the summer and autumn of 1780 passed with almost nothing to show either for the British, French, or Patriots. The British were perhaps most sanguine about the course of the northern war at this point. Robertson assured Germain that "the anarchy, tyranny and exactions exercised among the rebels" were making the population desirous for a restoration of British rule.[153] Arnold supported these assumptions, affirming that control of the Hudson River would deprive Washington of his supplies and lead to the disintegration of his army.[154] The war could seemingly be won by avoiding disaster for a few more months. Nevertheless, Clinton's lack of activity astonished Rodney, especially when he found the officers amusing themselves with theatrical performances instead of striking a decisive blow against a manifestly inferior enemy.[155]

Patriot morale in contrast was low. Even before the revelation of Arnold's treachery, confidence had been damaged by Gates's rout at Camden. To Greene the disaster showed the utter weakness of the Patriot system of government. "The two points which should have been the great objects of governmental attention have been in a manner totally neglected. One is the establishment of the army for the war and the other the business of finance." But instead of forming a regular army, the states preferred the short-term expediency of embodying the militia. This was a false economy since it required many more men to effect what a smaller disciplined body of troops could do. The same unenlightened attitudes to finance had been equally destructive of the government's credibility. "The prostitution of National honor and National faith in matters of finance has given such universal disgust that there is hardly remaining the shadow of confidence in Government." The failure to support the currency in particular had destroyed the credit of Congress and led to the ill-fated "plan of transferring the whole business to the states for them to furnish supplies and establish proper funds." In reality only a Congress with proper constitutional powers could rectify the situation.[156]

Washington could only agree with Greene's sentiments, telling one of his brigadiers: "We have no magazines, nor money to form them, and in a little time we shall have no men, if we had money to pay them. We have lived upon expedients till we can live no longer. In a word the history of the war is a history of false hopes and temporary devices, instead of system and of economy." Only the supine conduct of the British commanders had prevented disaster.[157] However, many felt that the problems were not simply the lack of a strong government. General Jeddah Huntington believed the people had forgotten the ideals of 1775, having given way to pride, greed and luxurious living. The nation must "revive the feelings . . . in the commencement of the war . . . when every man considered the fate of his country as depending on his own Exertions."[158]

In reality the Patriot cause was not as weak as many believed, in part because the British were not as strong as they assumed. By the fall of 1780 Clinton had a provisioning crisis of his own. The majority of victuals for his forces came from Britain and Ireland. This long supply chain was vulnerable to disruption by the French navy and Patriot privateers. The situation became especially critical when Arbuthnot misdirected three victual transports to Halifax.[159] This left the army in New York just two weeks' supplies of key items, Clinton informed Germain at the end of October 1780.[160] Until 1779 the Treasury had shipped the army's provisions in single armed ships. However, the Navy Board was then made responsible for this task. Its chosen method was to use unarmed merchantmen sailing under convoy. Unfortunately the decision was taken without establishing whether the Admiralty had sufficient frigates for such a system. The consequence was perhaps predictable. The victuallers were constantly stranded for "the want of regular and sufficient convoys from Europe." However, following a meeting at the Treasury between North and Middleton, steps were taken to ensure a more dependable supply.[161]

Another weakness in the British position was their continued inability to use the Loyalists effectively, among whom discontent was rife, not least because of Clinton's refusal to give them any significant role in New

York. In 1779 a group of prominent supporters had formed the Board of Associated Loyalists to undertake their own military operations. However, when William Franklin, the former Governor of New Jersey, and his colleagues attempted to secure assistance they were sent on a wild goose chase from one official to another.[162] The reason for their treatment was clear. The British "cannot think of letting us have a separate establishment or of making us independent of any military department." Franklin concluded "we could raise and employ a considerable body of men and do the enemy an infinite deal of mischief... were we not so shackled by forms of office and other restraints." The lack of any meaningful role meant that by the end of January 1781 the Board still had only 400–500 members and most of these had no weapons or other equipment.[163] A vital resource for the reconquest of the colonies lay unused.

The war in Europe: The League of Armed Neutrality

While the Royal Navy struggled to hold its own in the West Indies and North America, it was not without its problems closer to home, even though the French and Spanish had abandoned their plans for an invasion across the English Channel. The trade still had to be protected, as was demonstrated when Cordoba and du Chaffault intercepted an East India convoy on 9 August 1780 off the Portuguese coast, resulting in the loss of cargoes valued at one-and-a-half million pounds, together with 1,500 sailors and a similar number of troops.[164] However the main concern of Sandwich and his colleagues in 1780 was the flow of naval stores from the Baltic. Without such supplies, the Bourbon fleets would be unable to challenge British attempts to reconquer America. The principal products from the Baltic region were sawn timber for the hulls of warships, tall pines for masts, linen for sails, hemp for ropes, and tar for making ships watertight.

Neither the French nor Spanish had ready access to these commodities because of British control of the Channel. However Swedish, Danish, Dutch, and Russian merchants were keen to act on their behalf. This was something that the British could not accept, since the trade in naval stores would allow France and Spain to equip their fleets more easily. The law of nations traditionally limited military contraband to arms and ammunition, but Britain now defined it to include anything of use in wartime like naval stores. To mollify neutral opinion, Britain usually paid for such cargoes to supply its own dockyards. Nevertheless, such action threatened serious consequences because both the Baltic states and Holland insisted on the doctrine of "free ships making free goods," meaning that all neutral trade was permitted except for weapons and ammunition.[165]

In the case of Holland, the situation was complicated by the Anglo-Dutch Treaty of 1674 which specifically excluded naval stores from the list of contraband materials. It also included an article that if one signatory was at war with a third party, the other could trade with both combatants. However, the Dutch were also bound by the Treaty of 1678 which required them to render assistance in the event of war with France or Spain. Britain, by way of compromise, offered to forego her entitlement to military assistance, provided Holland accepted the British interpretation of contraband. The Dutch declined to do so as the trade in naval stores was too valuable, whatever their obligations under the 1678 Treaty.[166]

Accordingly, from the summer of 1778 the Royal Navy began a close watch on shipping passing down the Channel towards the French coast and beyond. The Dutch responded by organizing a convoy system which the British initially respected. However, as the size and number of these flotillas increased, the North ministry ordered the commander of the Downs squadron in late December 1779 to inspect a convoy of 27 vessels, even though it was escorted by five Dutch warships. The Dutch commander refused to comply and shots were exchanged, though the Dutch soon hauled down their colors.[167]

The bullying tactics of the British annoyed not only the Dutch but the Swedes, Danes, and most importantly, Russia. Russia was now a major power in Eastern Europe and anxious to be given recognition. She was also a producer of naval stores. The empress Catherine the Great accordingly saw an opportunity to assert her influence by championing the cause of the neutral powers. In the spring of 1780 she proposed to Denmark and Sweden the formation of an Armed Neutrality League to protect their interests. The League had five principles, the most important being the right of neutrals to trade with all combatants, except in articles narrowly defined as contraband. Furthermore, any blockade had to be effective, meaning the establishment of a tight cordon round a specific port, not the random stopping of ships on the high seas as practiced by the British.[168] Not long afterwards, other north European states, including Austria and Prussia, decided to join the League, angered by similar harassment of their commerce.[169]

North's colleagues might have asked themselves whether the America war was worth continuing, given the extent of the hostility to Britain. Nevertheless, the Cabinet ordered the Admiralty on 10 August 1780 to ensure that the Downs squadron was suitably reinforced to intercept

Dutch convoys, with or without an escort.[170] However, the situation was not as critical as it might have been. None of the Baltic nations had a navy of consequence, while the Dutch ability to fight a major European war was undermined by divisions among its seven provinces. Nevertheless sufficient pride remained for the States General in November 1780 to apply for membership of the League in the hope of securing assistance. It also began equipping 16 ships of the line in case hostilities escalated.

The British were in no mood to acquiesce with this development, which was seen as a hostile act. The war was seemingly going Britain's way in North America with the fall of Charleston, while in Europe the Bourbon powers had suffered a serious setback following the defeat of Langara and relief of Gibraltar. With no threat in the Channel, the North ministry had been able to hold a general election in the summer of 1780, which had preserved its existing majority in Parliament. It was thus able to contemplate an outbreak of hostilities with the Dutch with relative equanimity, the only uncertainty being that if Holland joined the League before war was declared, its members would be obligated to help the Dutch. A convenient excuse for pre-empting such outcome was soon provided when a British warship intercepted a Patriot vessel taking Henry Laurens to France as one of Congress's peace commissioners. Among his papers was a draft treaty between the American states and the merchants of Amsterdam. Although it was not an official government document, it provided Britain with a casus belli that the Dutch were planning an alliance with the American rebels.[171] The British quickly responded with a declaration of war and a close blockade of the Dutch coast. Plans were also made to attack the Dutch islands in the West Indies, notably St Eustatius and Curaçao.[172] Nevertheless, it was one more demand on Britain's overstretched resources, especially if the League came to Holland's aid. Even if the League retrained from hostilities, the likelihood was that the forces of Clinton and Arbuthnot in America would be even more starved of reinforcements with consequences that were as yet incalculable.

Notes and references

1 Jonathan Dull, *The French Navy and American Independence: A Study of Arms and Diplomacy, 1774–1787* (Princeton, 1975), 154–55.

2 Dull, *French Navy*, 187.

3 Lafayette to Laurens, 13 October 1778, Stanley J. Idzerda, ed., *Lafayette in the Age of the American Revolution: Selected Letters and Papers, 1776–1790*, 5 vols. (Ithaca, 1976–83), II, 190. Dull, *French Navy*, 154–55.

4 Henri Doniol, *Histoire de la participation de la France à l'établissement des États-Unis d'Amérique: Correspondence diplomatique et documents*, 5 vols. (Paris, 1886–1892), vol. 4, 280–83, 308–20.

5 Lee Kennett, *The French Forces in America, 1780–1783* (Westport, Conn., 1977), 6–14.

6 Arnold Whitridge, *Rochambeau: America's Neglected Founding Father* (New York, 1965), 49, 52–53.

7 Dull, *French Navy*, 179–89.

8 Dull, *French Navy*, 179–80.

9 Dull, *French Navy*, 187–88.

10 N.A.M. Rodger, *Command of the Ocean: A Naval History of Britain, 1649–1815* (New York, 2004), 345.

11 Rodney to Stephens, 26 April 1780, Rodney/2, 470–73.

12 Rodney to Sandwich, 26 April 1780, Sandwich/3, 211–12. Ibid., 31 May 1780, 214–18.

13 Rodney to Stephens, 31 May 1780, Rodney/2, 527–30.

14 David Hannay, ed., *Letters written by Sir Samuel Hood in 1781–1783* (Navy Records Society, 1895), xi–xii.

15 Rodney to Stephens, 31 May 1780, Rodney/2, 530.

16 Rodney to Vaughan, 14 June 1780, Rodney/2, 563. Rodney to Stephens, 21 June 1780, Rodney/2, 583–87.

17 W.N. Hargreaves-Mawdsley, *Eighteenth Century Spain, 1700–1788: A Political, Diplomatic and Institutional* History (London, 1979), 133. M. Le Comte de Lapeyrouse Bonfils, *Histoire de la Marine Française*, 3 vols. (Paris, 1845), III, 148–50.

18 Dull, *French Navy*, 188–89. Doniol, *Participation de la France*, vol. 4, 498–99.

19 Memorial of William Campbell and other southern Governors, August 1777, DDAR/XIV, 182–84.

20 Germain to Clinton, 31 March 1779, DDAR/XVII, 89–90.

21 Clinton to Germain, 21 August 1779, DDAR/XVII, 189–91.

22 Clinton to Germain, 20 August 1779, DDAR/XVII, 188.

23 Clinton to Germain, 9 March 1780, DDAR/XVIII, 53–55. Paul H. Smith, *Loyalists and Redcoats: A Study in British Revolutionary Policy* (Chapel Hill, 1964), 127–28.

24 Germain to Wright, 19 January 1780, DDAR/XVIII, 37–39. Wright to Germain, 24–28 March 1780, DDAR/XVIII, 67.

25 Pattison to Germain, 22 February 1780, DDAR/XVIII, 50–53. Germain to Clinton, 3 May 1780, DDAR/XVIII, 82–84.

26 Clinton to Germain, 9 March 1780, DDAR/XVIII, 53–55.

27 Robert D. Bass, *The Green Dragoon: The Lives of Banastre Tarleton and Mary Robinson* (Orangeburg, 1973), 74. Clinton to Germain, 13 May 1780, DDAR/XVIII, 86–89.

28 Clinton to Germain, 13 May 1780, DDAR/XVIII, 86–89.

29 *Clinton's Narrative*, CAR, 171.

30 John Ferling, *Almost a Miracle: The American Victory in the War of Independence* (New York, 2007), 427–28. David Syrett, *The Royal Navy in American Waters, 1775–1783* (Aldershot, 1989), 139–40.

31 Simpson to Clinton, 15 May 1780, DDAR/XVIII, 94–95.

32 *Clinton's Narrative*, CAR, 175–76. Clinton to Germain, 4 June 1780, DDAR/XVIII, 101–2.

33 Bass, *Green Dragoon*, 46–48.

34 Tarleton to Cornwallis, 30 May 1780, Ross/1, 45. Bass, *Green Dragoon*, 79–83.

35 Handbill distributed by Sir Henry Clinton, 12 May 1780, CAR, 440–41. Smith, *Loyalists*, 136–37.

36 Instructions of Major Ferguson, 22 May 1780, CAR, 441.

37 William B. Willcox, *Portrait of a General: Sir Henry Clinton in the War of Independence* (New York, 1964), 321.

38 Wright to Clinton, 3 February 1780, DDAR/XVIII, 45–47. Ibid., 24–28 March 1780, 67–68.

39 Humble Address of Diverse Inhabitants of Charleston, 5 June 1780, DDAR/XVIII, 102–4.

40 Clinton to Germain, 4 June 1780, DDAR/XVIII, 101–2. *Clinton's Narrative*, CAR, 191.

41 Franklin and Mary Wickwire, *Cornwallis and the War of Independence* (London, 1971), 115–16.

42 The best biography remains that cited above. For an extremely hostile assessment of Cornwallis, see Hugh F. Rankin, "Charles Lord Cornwallis: Study in Frustration," in George Athan Billias, ed., *George Washington's Generals and Opponents: Their Exploits and Leadership* (New York, 1994), 193–232.

43 *Clinton's Narrative*, CAR, 186–87. Wickwire, *Cornwallis*, 133–35.

44 Cornwallis to Clinton, 30 June 1780, Ross/1, 485–88.
45 Cornwallis to Clinton, 30 June 1780, Ross/1, 485–88.
46 John S. Pancake, *This Destructive War: The British Campaign in the Carolinas, 1780–1782* (Tuscaloosa, 1985), 93–94.
47 Cornwallis to Clinton, 6 August 1780, Ross/1, 53–54. Simpson to Germain, 13 August 1780, DDAR/XVIII, 137–38.
48 Willcox, *Portrait of a General*, 321.
49 Robert D. Bass, *Swamp Fox: The Life and Campaigns of General Francis Marion* (Orangeburg, 1959), 33–34.
50 Cornwallis to Clinton, 14 July 1780, Ross/1, 50–52. Ferling, *Almost a Miracle*, 454.
51 James Simpson to Knox, 28 July 1781, DDAR/XX, 200. Simpson was a former Royal Attorney General of South Carolina, who acknowledged retrospectively the damage done by loyalist mistreatment of Pickens and other former rebels after the surrender of Charleston.
52 Cornwallis to Clinton, 2 June 1780, Ross/1, 45. Cornwallis to Colonel Innes, 16 June 1780, Ross/1, 47.
53 Cornwallis to Rawdon, Charleston, 29 June 1780, Ross/1, 49.
54 Cornwallis to Clinton, 14 July 1780, Ross/1, 50–52. Smith, *Loyalists*, 143–44.
55 Cornwallis to Clinton, 14 July 1780, Ross/1, 50–52.
56 Cornwallis to Clinton, 6 August 1780, Ross/1, 52–54.
57 Washington to Huntington, 2 April 1780, WGW/18, 197–200.
58 Pancake, *Destructive War*, 99–101.
59 Ibid., 100–103.
60 Cornwallis to Germain, 20 August 1780, DDAR/XVIII, 144–48. Pancake, *Destructive War*, 101–3.
61 Cornwallis to Germain, 21 August 1781, DDAR/XVIII, 148–51.
62 Ibid., 151.
63 Cornwallis to Colonel Cruger, 18 August 1780, Ross/1, 56–57.
64 Bass, *Green Dragoon*, 109.
65 Cornwallis to Germain, 21 August 1780, DDAR/XVIII, 152.
66 Cornwallis to Clinton, 29 August 1780, Ross/1, 58.
67 Cornwallis to Clinton, 23 August 1780, Ross/1, 57–58.
68 Cornwallis to Germain, 21 September 1780, DDAR/XVIII, 172–73.

69 Wright to Germain, 27 October 1780, DDAR/XVIII, 211. J. Cashin, *The King's Ranger: Thomas Brown and the American Revolution on the Southern Frontier* (Athens, Ga., 1989), 114–18.
70 Cornwallis to Clinton, 29 August 1780, Ross/1, 58–59.
71 Pancake, *Destructive War*, 116–17.
72 Cornwallis to Clinton, 3 December 1780, Ross/1, 497–500.
73 Wickwire, *Cornwallis*, 208–9.
74 W.J. Wood, *Battles of the Revolutionary War, 1775–1781* (New York, 1995), 188.
75 Ferguson to Cornwallis, 6 October 1780, CAR, 456. This letter is inaccurately dated 6 September 1780.
76 Ferling, *Almost a Miracle*, 461–63.
77 Washington to Huntington, 16 September 1780, WGW/20, 49–50.
78 *Clinton's Narrative*, CAR, 221.
79 Rawdon to Clinton, 29 October 1780, Ross/1, 62–63.
80 Cornwallis to Smallwood, 10 November 1780, Ross/1, 67.
81 Clinton to Leslie, 12 October 1780, CAR, 467.
82 Rawdon to Leslie, 24 October 1780, Ross/1 ,495–97.
83 Cornwallis to Leslie, 12 November 1780, Ross/1, 68–69.
84 Leslie to Clinton, 4 November 1781, CAR, 472–73.
85 Rawdon to Clinton, 29 October 1780, Ross/1, 62–63.
86 Bass, *Swamp Fox*, 75–77.
87 Cornwallis to Clinton, 3 December 1780, Ross/1, 498.
88 Ibid., 498–99.
89 Ibid., 500. Cornwallis to Rawdon, 3 December, Ross/1, 71–72.
90 Cornwallis to Clinton, 3 December 1780, Ross/1, 500.
91 Washington to Greene, 14 October 1780, NGP/6, 385.
92 Washington to Greene, 22 October 1780, NGP/6, 424–25.
93 Greene to Washington, 19 November 1780, NGP/6, 485/87. Greene to Steuben, 20 November 1780, NGP/6, 496–97.
94 Greene to Huntington, 28 December 1789, NGP/7, 7–8. Greene to Catherine Greene, 12 January 1781, NGP/7, 102.
95 Greene to General Cornell, 29 December 1780, NGP/7, 20–21.
96 Greene to Governor Nash, 7 January 1781, NGP/7, 61–65.

97   Greene to Marion, 4 December 1780, NGP/6, 519–20.
98   Greene to Morgan, 16 December 1780, NGP/6, 589–90. Greene had first suggested the idea of a "flying corps" to Washington, 31 October 1780, NGP/6, 447–49.
99   Greene to Huntington, 28 December 1780, NGP/7, 7–8.
100 Greene to Stevens, 1 December 1780, NGP/6, 512–13. Washington had also suggested to Greene that the boats be sufficiently light to facilitate their transportation from one river to the next, 8 November 1780, NGP/6, 469–70.
101 Greene to Anon, 1/23 January 1781, NGP/7, 175–76.
102 Washington to Huntington, 18 November 1779, WGW/17, 125–28.
103 Washington to Elbridge Gerry, 30 January 1780, WGW/17, 462–64.
104 Washington to Benjamin Harrison, 18 December 1778, WP/RWS/18, 450.
105 Ferling, *Almost a Miracle*, 399–400.
106 Washington to Robert Howe, 7 March 1780, WGW/18, 82. Washington to Greene, 9 March 1780, WGW/18, 96–98.
107 Washington to Huntington, 28 March 1780, WGW/18, 170–71.
108 Council of War, 27 March 1780, WGW/18, 166.
109 Washington to Huntington, 3 April 1780, WGW/18, 208–9.
110 Washington to Lincoln, 15 May 1780, WGW/18, 363. Vergennes to Lafayette, 5 March 1780, Idzerda, *Lafayette*, II, 364–67.
111 General Orders, 16 March 1780, WGW/18, 120.
112 Washington to Huntington, 27 May 1780, WGW/18, 428–31.
113 Washington to Reed, 28 May 1780, WGW/18, 434–40.
114 Proceedings of a Council of War, 6 June 1780, NGP/6, 7. Ibid., WGW/18, 482–85.
115 Greene to Washington, 6 July 1780, NGP/6, 64–69.
116 Robertson to Germain, 1 July 1780, DDAR/XVIII, 107–9.
117 Robertson to Germain, 1 July 1780, DDAR/XVIII, 107–9. Knyphausen to Germain, 3 July 1780, DDAR/XVIII, 110–11.
118 General Orders, 16 June 1780, WGW/19, 17–18.
119 Washington to Trumbull, 11 June 1780, WGW/18, 510–11.
120 Washington to Huntington, 20 June 1780, WGW/19, 34–36.
121 Washington to Fielding Lewis, 6 July 1780, WGW/19, 130–32.
122 Whitridge, *Rochambeau*, 87–88.

123 Vergennes to Lafayette, 5 March 1780, Idzerda, *Lafayette*, II, 364–67.
124 Bonfils, *Marine Française*, III, 166–67. Washington to Greene, 19 July 1780, NGP/6, 127. Kennett, *French Forces*, 15.
125 Memorandum for concerting a plan of operation, 15 July 1780, WGW/19, 174–76.
126 Clinton to Arbuthnot, 15 July 1780, CAR, 443–44.
127 Clinton to Arbuthnot, 18 August 1780, CAR, 451. Willcox, *Portrait of a General*, 333–35.
128 Arbuthnot to Clinton, 18 August 1780, CAR, 451–52.
129 Clinton to Germain, 25 August 1780, DDAR/XVIII, 152–54.
130 Clinton to Germain, 30 August 1780, DDAR/XVIII, 154–55.
131 Clinton to William Eden, 1 September 1780, CAR, 456.
132 Washington to Esther Reed, 14 July 1780, WGW/19, 167. The Ladies of New Jersey and Maryland made similar gestures.
133 Washington to Committee of Cooperation, 17 August 1780, WGW/19, 391–94.
134 Circular to the States, 27 August 1780, WGW/19, 449–51.
135 Washington to Huntington, 20 August 1780, WGW/19, 402–13.
136 Ibid.
137 Washington to Reed, 26 August 1780, WGW/19, 440.
138 Council of War, 6 September 1780, WGW/20, 5–8. As was now his practice, Washington asked for the views of the council in writing so that he could consider them privately.
139 Washington to de Guichen, 12 September 1780, WGW/20, 39–42.
140 Conference at Hartford, 22 September 1780, WGW/20, 79–80. Doniol, *Participation de la France*, vol. 4, 381–84.
141 Kennett, *French Forces*, 89. Washington heard about the decision only in late December 1780, Washington to Lafayette, 26 December 1780, WGW/21, 17. However, as Kennett points out, the French ministry was equally in the dark about events in America.
142 Whitridge, *Rochambeau*, 102–3.
143 Washington to Hancock, 12 May 1777, WP/RWS/9, 396–97. This was finally rectified in January 1778, Washington to Arnold, 20 January 1778, WP/RWS/13, 288.
144 Washington to Arnold, 20 April 1779, WGW/14, 418. General Orders, 6 April 1780, WGW/18, 222–24.

145 This was certainly Arnold's view after his defection, Rodney to Sandwich, 10 October 1780, Sandwich/3, 254.

146 Washington to Arnold, 3 August 1780, WGW/19, 309.

147 Clinton to Germain, 11 October 1780, DDAR/XVIII, 183–86.

148 Details of the plan are given in Greene to Governor Greene, 2 October 1780, NGP/6, 328–29. See also Clinton to Germain, 11 October 1780, DDAR/XVIII, 183–86.

149 Washington to Clinton, 30 September 1780, WGW/20, 101.

150 Richard M. Ketchum, *Victory at Yorktown: The Campaign that won the Revolution* (New York, 2004), 59, 65–66. General Orders, 1 October 1780, WGW/20, 109–10.

151 Greene to Governor Greene, 2 October 1780, NGP/6, 328–29.

152 Clinton to Rodney, 18 September 1780, CAR, 457–58.

153 Robertson to Germain, 1 September 1780, DDAR/XVIII, 160.

154 Arnold to Germain, 28 October 1780, DDAR/XVIII, 211–15.

155 Rodney to Germain, 22 December 1780, HMC, Stopford-Sackville, II, 191–95.

156 Greene to General Lewis Morris, 14 September 1780, NGP/6, 283–85.

157 Washington to Cadwalader, 5 October 1780, WGW/20, 221–23. Washington to the States, 18 October 1780, WGW/20, 206.

158 Quoted in Charles Royster, *A Revolutionary People at War: The Continental Army and American Character, 1775–1783* (New York, 1979), 284.

159 Clinton to Arbuthnot, 29 October 1780, CAR, 469. Arbuthnot replied jocularly that he would happily share his last biscuit with Clinton, 1 November 1780, CAR, 471.

160 Clinton to Germain, 31 October 1780, CAR, 470–71. Bowler, *Logistics*, 135–36.

161 North to George III, 29 September 1780, Fortescue/5, 137. Norman Baker, *Government and Contractors: The British Treasury and War Supplies, 1775–1783* (London, 1971), 91–95. Bowler, *Logistics*, 131–34.

162 Board of Loyalists to Clinton, 1 December 1780, DDAR/XVIII, 239–44.

163 Governor Franklin to Galloway, 28 January 1781, DDAR/XX, 49–51.

164 Dull, *French Navy*, 193–94, Piers Mackesy, *The War for America, 1775–1783* (Cambridge, Mass., 1964), 357.

165 David Syrett, *The Royal Navy in European Waters during the American Revolutionary War* (Columbia, SC, 1998), 100. H.M. Scott, *British Foreign Policy in the Age of the American Revolution* (Oxford, 1990), 277–84.

166 Syrett, *Royal Navy in European Waters*, 96–98, 106–7. Scott, *British Foreign Policy*, 284–86.

167 Cabinet Minute, 19 November 1779, Sandwich/3, 106. Captain Fielding to Sandwich, 31 December 1779, Sandwich/3, 113–14.

168 Dull, *Diplomatic History*, 129. Syrett, *Royal Navy in European Waters*, 119–21.

169 Brendan Simms, *Three Victories and a Defeat: The Rise and Fall of the First British Empire* (London, 2007), 642–44.

170 Cabinet Minute, 10 August 1780, Fortescue/5, 107–8.

171 Scott, *British Foreign Policy*, 305–8.

172 Germain to the Admiralty, 20 December 1780, DDAR/XVIII, 258–59.

CHAPTER 8

The North American frontier, 1775–82

The southeastern mosaic

The war of American Independence affected not only the eastern seaboard of the United States but its internal frontiers too, stretching from the Great Lakes to the Gulf of Mexico. The participants included not only Britain, Spain, and the United States but numerous American Indian nations. All had diverse aims. The Indian peoples sought the preservation of their lands and way of life. The Patriots wished to protect both their frontier settlements and the possibility of future expansion. Spain wanted to recover East and West Florida, while Britain sought to protect her existing influence with the native peoples, especially regarding trade.

At the start of hostilities in 1775, both Britain and Congress indicated a desire for peace with their Indian neighbors, affecting to believe that the employment of "savages" was something that Christian powers should not do. However, both were anxious to ensure that their opponents did not take advantage of any such neutrality. In this contest for Indian support, the British generally had the stronger hand. Whatever their past misdemeanors, they were not threatening to settle Indian lands. They also had a wider range of trade goods, providing they could get them across the Atlantic. The Patriots, in contrast, had much less to offer, especially in terms of arms and ammunition. They also posed a much greater threat to Indian territorial sovereignty.

John Stuart, the British Superintendent for the southern region, welcomed his government's initial protestations about peace, fearing that any attack on the white settlements would lead to the shedding of innocent blood. His deputy David Taitt accordingly advised the Creek Indians in

August 1775 to stay at home to avoid provoking the Patriots. However, this was not what many Indians wanted to hear. Apart from threats to their lands, the southern nations were exasperated at the Virginians' failure to supply them gun powder. The chiefs threatened that they could not be responsible for their young warriors should the Patriot embargo continue.[1] Their restlessness coincided with reports from Gage that the rebels were employing Indian marksmen at Boston. Seemingly the Patriots had crossed the threshold. It was time for the British to retaliate by unleashing the native peoples against the rebel backcountry.[2]

Accordingly at the end of December 1775 Stuart received instructions to employ the southern Indians "to distress His Majesty's rebellious subjects by all means practicable." The ministry was especially anxious to enlist Indian help for Clinton Parker expedition to the southern backcountry.[3] Stuart replied that the Cherokee were eager to assist. However, the Creek would not engage until they had settled some differences with the Choctaw. Once those matters were resolved, Stuart believed both the Choctaw and Chickasaw would be "absolutely at our disposal." Unfortunately the Creek, who were much closer to the fighting, remained enigmatic as to their true intentions.[4]

The Cherokee in contrast needed little encouragement to take up arms under Chief Dragging Canoe. They had a long tradition as allies of the British, though the relationship had been severely tested in 1759 and 1761 when British regulars twice invaded their homelands. But this had been more than assuaged by the growing threat of white intruders, which the British were seemingly ready to limit. The first targets in July 1776 were the Watauga settlements in eastern Tennessee, which were close to the Cherokee upper and middle towns and in breach of the 1767 boundary agreement in the Treaty of Hard Labor.[5] The main group of 700 warriors under Dragging Canoe accordingly swept down on the principal post at Eaton's Station. Here on 20 July they attempted to storm the defenses but were eventually repulsed in close fighting. A second group simultaneously attacked a fortified post at Sycamore Shoals a few miles higher up the Watauga River. This too was unsuccessful. The Cherokee then suffered a third setback, when the lower towns attacked Lyndley's Fort on the Savannah River. Despite the assistance of some Tories, they too were repulsed.[6]

Unfortunately for the Cherokee, their attacks merely galvanized the southern states into action. This was at a time when the British were experiencing difficulty getting supplies to the frontier. The Cherokee were also isolated in terms of Indian support. Although the Delaware and Shawnee shared their grievances about settlers, none of the other major southern tribes felt sufficiently threatened to join a pan-Indian war, despite Stuart's efforts to enlist them.[7] In retaliation for the attack on Lyndley's Fort, South Carolina sent Colonel Andrew Williamson with 1,800 men in August 1776 against the lower towns. The South Carolinians were then joined by 2,500 North Carolina militia under General Griffith Rutherford to ravage the middle towns. Finally a force of 4,000 Virginians and North Carolinians under Brigadier Andrew Lewis advanced from the Holston and Watauga River settlements to attack the upper towns. Although the Cherokee capital of Chota survived, little remained of the other settlements, forcing their inhabitants to seek protection among the Creeks.[8] The plight of the Cherokee was heightened by the decision of the Upper Creek to refrain from hostilities following the failure of the Clinton Parker expedition to Charleston. This was despite Stuart's assistance in arranging a peace for them with the Choctaw.[9]

The lower and middle towns consequently had to sign a peace treaty in May 1777, ceding all their lands east of the Blue Ridge Mountains and north of Nolichucky River. But the campaign was also a setback for the British. Not only had the Cherokee failed to inflict any significant damage, their deployment had discredited the British cause in many backcountry areas, where fear of the Indians outweighed dislike of the Patriots. In this respect the Cherokee were more useful as enemies than friends.[10] Finally the defeat of the Cherokee was damaging to Britain because it alerted the other southern nations about what might happen to them if they entered the war as their allies.

British weakness was further exposed early in 1778 when a detachment of Virginians under James Willing came down the Mississippi from Pittsburgh to secure the arms and ammunition which had been secretly promised by Spain in 1776.[11] The Choctaw and Chickasaw were supposed to warn Stuart about such intrusions and check their progress. Willing's force comprised a mere 100 men. Nevertheless the Indians made no attempt to stop him, resulting in the surprise of the British settlements on the east bank of the Mississippi at Natchez and Manchac. Willing then set off for New Orleans, where he was warmly welcomed by the new Spanish Governor, the energetic Bernardo de Galvez.[12]

Stuart and Governor Chester of West Florida subsequently recovered the two settlements on the Mississippi, following the dispatch of some volunteers from Pensacola.[13] They were thus well placed to intercept Willing as he returned from New Orleans. This time it was the Patriots who were totally surprised in the battle of the White Cliffs, 15 miles below Natchez on 16 April 1778.[14] The news was sufficiently encouraging for

Germain to order the building of a new fort near Iberville, large enough for 300 men. Armed row galleys were also to be constructed for patrolling the Mississippi.[15] These measures together with a further substantial reinforcement would hopefully prevent a repetition of these events.

But before these orders could be carried out, a new threat appeared in East Florida where a force from South Carolina and Georgia invaded the province in early July 1778. The Patriots had some 800 men in armed galleys and another 2,500 men marching by land. They got as far as the St John's River, where they were temporarily halted by Brown's Loyalist rangers. This time 500 Lower Creek or Seminoles responded to the British call for help, recognizing the danger to their lands. Although the Patriots successfully crossed the St John's River, constant harassing by the Indians caused them to relinquish their design.[16]

Elsewhere the Creek and other southern native peoples remained neutral, in no small part due to the influence of George Galphin, Congress's Indian Commissioner. He distributed presents with a liberality that Stuart was unable to match, isolated as he was in West Florida. Galphin in contrast had copious supplies from the French and Spanish authorities in the Caribbean.[17] Not that the Creek intended to fight for the Patriots, for as Chester commented, they accepted presents from anyone prepared to give them. Certainly no dependence could be placed on their periodic offers to support Britain. This was hardly surprising, for as one old Creek chief told Stuart, he was tired of hearing about British help which never arrived. His nation would not suffer the fate of the Cherokee who had rushed into war unaided.[18]

However, in the spring of 1779 a number of the upper Creek did take up arms following the arrival of Campbell and Prevost in Georgia. Here was the kind of support desired by all the nations. The British responded by inviting the chiefs to Savannah to participate in their forthcoming operations. But most of the warriors preferred to attack the backcountry, where they could operate in small parties to plunder the inhabitants and carry off their cattle. Only 12 remained with Prevost. The South Carolinians quickly responded by dispatching mounted detachments to surprise the raiders. The Creek then returned to their own country, recognizing that the anticipated British support was unlikely to be realized.[19]

Meanwhile hostilities were about to break out once more with the Cherokee. Many upper townspeople, led by Dragging Canoe, had refused to accept the May 1777 peace treaty, preferring to retreat over the mountains to the Chickamauga River. Here they built a temporary settlement until a suitable opportunity occurred to return home.[20] They did not lack encouragement from Alexander Cameron, another of Stuart's agents, especially on the news of Prevost's advance on Charleston. Dragging Canoe and his warriors accordingly responded in May 1779 by marching towards the Georgia frontier. Unfortunately they left their own settlements unguarded, allowing the Virginians and North Carolinians from the Holston River to launch a surprise attack. Though most of the women and children escaped, the Chickamauga habitations were destroyed.

Despite this setback, the Cherokee resolved to continue the struggle, after being joined by Cameron with a company of Loyalist refugees. However, they were soon confronted in late August 1778 by a large force of South Carolinian cavalry and mounted infantry under Williamson. He offered the Cherokee a pact of neutrality provided they surrendered Cameron and his companions. The Cherokee refused to do this. Williamson then burnt six of their towns, forcing the population to flee to the woods to live on nuts and berries until Cameron arranged a supply of corn.[21]

Many British observers blamed Stuart for the ineffectiveness of the southern Indians in the first four years of war. His death in May 1779, accordingly, allowed a reorganization of his department. Cameron was given responsibility for the Choctaw and Chickasaw, while Brown took charge of the Creek, Cherokee, and Catawba.[22] With Spain about to enter the war, the friendship of the Choctaw and Chickasaw was especially important, given the danger of a Spanish offensive against the British settlements on the Mississippi and Gulf of Mexico.

For once the British seemed ready to provide the Indians with the support they desired. In October 1778 Clinton implemented Germain's orders to reinforce the garrison in West Florida by the dispatch of 1,000 regulars under Brigadier John Campbell. His instructions were to rebuild the fort at Manchac to guard the navigation of the lower Mississippi. He was also to consider an attack on New Orleans, once Spain's entry into the war was confirmed.[23] Unfortunately these plans proved hopelessly optimistic. Most of Campbell's troops were of poor quality, since Clinton had sent the least desirable elements in his army. Campbell also lacked wagons, boats and carpenters to build the new fort. Another problem was that Manchac was subject to flooding.[24] In these circumstances an attack on New Orleans was impossible.

The initiative accordingly passed to the Spanish, who were ready to launch an offensive for the recovery of West Florida, following the arrival earlier of large reinforcements.[25] The assault was to be led by Galvez, with a force of 1,800 Spanish regulars and militia and as many Indians as could be mustered. After recognizing American Independence on 20 August

1779, Galvez began his campaign by attacking the British settlements on the east bank of the Mississippi.[26] These were quickly compelled to surrender long before Campbell had time to organize a counter-attack from Pensacola. Indeed he required all his forces for his own defense, not having a single Royal Navy ship to assist him.[27]

Early in 1780, Galvez launched the next stage of his offensive, an assault on Mobile, after receiving reinforcements from Havana. Galvez had approximately 1,400 men. The garrison numbered just 300 and surrendered after two days, being destitute of naval support.[28] However, Pensacola, the center of British power in West Florida, proved more formidable, especially after the arrival of several frigates from Jamaica. Campbell was also aided by a large body of Seminole warriors who had previously assembled for the defense of St Augustine.[29] The Creeks had long memories of Spanish cruelty stretching back to the sixteenth century.

While Galvez considered this check to his plans, the final battle was being fought between the Patriots and the Cherokee. Until this point the Cherokee had been isolated from the main fighting between the British and their Patriot opponents. However, Cornwallis's victory at Camden in August 1780 and the advance of Ferguson into the backcountry meant that a more effective cooperation was now in prospect. But the hopes of the Cherokee were no sooner raised than they were dashed. First Ferguson's force was destroyed at King's Mountain. Then a detachment of 250 riflemen under John Sevier routed a war party near the Holston River, opening the way for another force of 650 Virginians from Watauga to attack the Overhill towns. This time Chota fell without resistance, leaving the population dispersed and starving in the mountains.[30] The chiefs once more had to seek a peace, surrendering their lands east of the Appalachian Mountains. Although Dragging Canoe continued a desultory resistance, the power of the Cherokee was broken.[31] Never again would they be able to challenge the white men militarily.

The crushing of the Cherokee also coincided with a renewed attempt on Pensacola by Galvez. Once again he was thwarted, this time by a storm. Nevertheless, he was not to be deterred, following his promotion as Lieutenant General of the region. In March 1781, Galvez successfully assembled a Franco Spanish force in Cuba of 7,000 troops and 15 ships of the line. This time he laid siege to Pensacola with overwhelming odds. The garrison of 1,600 men under Campbell did their best until one of the principal redoubts blew up, making further resistance hopeless.[32] Although several hundred Creek and Choctaw arrived in support, they were unable to oppose such a powerful force.[33] The capture of Pensacola in May 1781 meant that the British presence in East and West Florida was reduced to one post, the town of St Augustine. For Britain, the war on the southern frontier was effectively over.

The success of Spain in West Florida, though unwelcome to the southern Indians, was less threatening than it would have been in the sixteenth century when Spanish power was at its height. Indeed, the southern Indians, with the exception of the Cherokee, had retained their lands almost intact. However, the growing white population in the Carolinas and Georgia meant that a new wave of settlement was in the offing, should the Patriots prevail in their struggle with Britain. Much would depend on Spain's ability to maintain the balance of power in the region to provide a counterweight to the territorial ambitions of the English-speaking inhabitants.

The struggle for the Ohio and Illinois

Like the southern nations, the native peoples of the Ohio valley were uncertain what course to pursue on the first outbreak of hostilities between Britain and the Colonists in 1775. The latter wanted peace so that they could concentrate on the conflict in the east. Congress accordingly invited the Shawnee, Delaware, and Mingo to a conference at Pittsburgh in July 1775 to negotiate a mutually beneficial neutrality. The difficulty was that the Ohio peoples were by no means united on the matter. Most Delaware were content to stay out of the conflict, especially the Moravian mission villages along the Tuscarawa River. The Shawnee and Mingo in contrast were more hostile because of their recent losses during Dunmore's War in 1774, when the Shawnee had been compelled to cede the southern bank of the Ohio River.[34] But all the Ohio nations were restrained by the interruption of supplies from Britain, following the invasion of Canada by Montgomery and Arnold.

The Patriot retreat from Canada and resumption of supplies accordingly tilted the balance in favor of the British. However, it was not until February 1777 that the Shawnee were ready to open hostilities, after the murder of their chief, Cornstalk. He had ironically been attempting to restrain the war party in his nation and had actually gone to warn the settlers of their danger. The Shawnee were not long in being joined by the Wyandot, Ottawa, and Ojibwa from Great Lakes. Although not directly threatened by white settlement, these nations had been close allies of the Ohio peoples during Pontiac's War.[35] They were encouraged to take up arms now because the British wanted support for the armies of Burgoyne and Howe. The commander at Detroit, Colonel Henry Hamilton, accordingly, was to employ as many Indians as possible "in making a diversion and exciting alarm upon the frontiers of Virginia and Pennsylvania."[36] The only proviso was that Hamilton was to ensure that proper persons were in charge of the natives "to restrain them from committing violence on the well affected and inoffensive inhabitants" as they headed eastwards towards the British armies. The Shawnee, however, preferred to make Boones Borough on the Kentucky River, and Fort Henry near the mouth of Wheeling Creek, below Pittsburgh, their main objectives. But all attempts to capture these key posts were unavailing.[37]

These assaults by the Ohio and Great Lakes nations prompted Congress to consider an attack on Detroit in 1778 as the key to curbing British influence in the region and bringing peace to the frontier. To expedite matters, Congress decided to create two new frontier regiments.[38] Washington simultaneously ordered General Lachlan McIntosh to take command at Pittsburgh. McIntosh was an officer in whom Washington had great confidence.[39] However, McIntosh quickly found that he had insufficient men and supplies even for an advance on the Wyandot settlement at Sandusky. It was as much as he could do to protect the inhabitants in the vicinity of Fort Pitt.[40]

While the plans of Congress were failing, Virginia was making its own arrangements to subdue the Indians. The state had long claimed the Ohio region as part of its territory. It now enlisted George Rogers Clark, an officer in the Kentucky militia, to make good those claims, seeing this as the best way of protecting the white inhabitants.[41] Clark has been traditionally portrayed as the authentic frontier hero who secured the Ohio and Old North West for the emerging democracy of the United States. In reality he was a settler who sought to consolidate white control of Kentucky by extirpating the native peoples. As he subsequently told Hamilton, "for his part he could never spare man, woman or child" of the Indians "on whom he could lay his hands."[42]

Clark recognized that Detroit might be a step too far for his limited resources. Instead he turned his attention to the Illinois country. He calculated that its French-speaking inhabitants would welcome him now that France was the ally of the United States. Clark was accordingly authorized by Governor Patrick Henry to proceed with his scheme. He set off down the Ohio in May 1778 with 175 volunteers, his plan being to travel to Massac near the junction with the Mississippi, before completing his journey on foot to avoid detection. As Clark had predicted, the British presence in the Illinois was minimal and Kaskaskia, the principal settlement, was quickly occupied on 5 July 1778, with the seeming approval of its French inhabitants. The latter then assisted in the peaceful occupation of Vincennes on the Wabash River.[43]

News of these proceedings immediately prompted Hamilton at Detroit to attempt a counter-attack in October 1778. He accordingly assembled a similar force of regulars and French Canadians, anticipating that he would be joined by several hundred Shawnee. His plan was to attack Vincennes before proceeding to Kaskaskia, where Clark was stationed with most of his men. Vincennes in consequence had only a small detachment of Patriot soldiers, who were quickly forced to surrender on 17 December 1778. Since winter had arrived, Hamilton decided against continuing to the Illinois.[44] Winter was the Indian hunting season. He accordingly allowed his native allies to disperse while he strengthened Vincennes' defenses. The recapture of the Illinois could wait until reinforcements arrived from Canada in the spring.[45]

In reality Hamilton had underestimated the dangers facing him, since Clark quickly organized a new offensive to recapture Vincennes, despite the severity of the season. His force consisted of just 130 men, many being recruits from the French population. Nevertheless, Clark reached Vincennes on 25 February 1779, where he completely surprised Hamilton. Before the surrender negotiations were completed, a small party of Indians returned to Vincennes ignorant of Clark's arrival. He promptly executed the newcomers to terrorize his opponents, both red and white alike. On this occasion his tactics worked. Hamilton was quickly induced to capitulate.[46] He and his principal officers were then dispatched in irons to jail in Virginia. Clark justified such treatment on the grounds that his captives had encouraged Indian massacres of white settlers in Kentucky.[47]

Clark's success at Vincennes coincided with news that another Virginian force under Colonel John Montgomery was advancing to join him with 500 men, thus raising the possibility of an expedition to Detroit in 1779.[48] Unfortunately for Clark, Montgomery arrived with a mere 150 men, after the majority of his party decided to attack the Shawnee settlement of Chillicothe instead. This left Clark no option but to abandon the projected attack on Detroit. It was time to secure what had already been won. Montgomery was accordingly left to hold the Illinois while Clark returned to Kentucky to organize its defenses and recruit more men.

These checks to Clark encouraged the British and their allies to renew their attacks in the spring of 1780. Two offensives were planned. The first under Captain Emanuel Hesse, comprising 1,000 Great Lakes Indians, was to advance from Lake Michigan down the Mississippi to restore British authority in the Illinois. The second, a diversionary raid, was designed to draw Clark back to the defense of the Kentucky settlements. Hesse duly reached his objective, but discovered Clark still in the Illinois and too well entrenched at Cahokia to be dislodged. Hesse then turned his attention to the Spanish settlement at St Louis. However, he found his enemy similarly well prepared. Long sieges were alien to Indian warfare and Hesse's native allies soon began to desert. He accordingly retreated back down the Illinois River to Lake Michigan. This allowed Clark to return to Kentucky to meet the second British offensive while Montgomery remained in command in the Illinois.[49]

The remit of the second British force under Captain Henry Bird, consisting of 150 Tories and 1,000 Delaware and Shawnee warriors, was to threaten the settlements south of the Ohio. Bird began his advance in early June 1780 via the Maumee and Miami Rivers into the Licking River valley in northern Kentucky. Here he captured two isolated posts, Ruddle's and Martin's stations, seizing 100 prisoners. Some of the latter were summarily executed by the Indians, demonstrating the ferocity of the conflict now being waged. The Indians then began to disperse, ignoring the danger that Clark might return, which he did on receiving news of Bird's foray. Clark quickly recruited several hundred Kentuckian riflemen and crossed the Ohio. His objective this time was Chillicothe, the principal Shawnee village, which he duly burnt. After this he advanced on Piqua, where the Shawnee had assembled their main force. Clark had close to 1,000 men, the Shawnee only 350. The Kentuckians were now as adept as the Indians in bush fighting and completely routed their enemy. No prisoners were taken though the casualties on both sides were modest.[50]

Clark's destruction of Chillicothe inevitably prompted the Shawnee to make a fresh appeal to their allies for help in exacting revenge. A conference was accordingly held at Detroit in April 1781 where it was agreed to launch a new offensive. Present was Joseph Brant, the noted Mohawk warrior.[51] The allies first assembled their forces at Sandusky before setting off in June 1781 for the Ohio in search of Clark, who had meanwhile been attempting to organize a new expedition against Detroit. Clark initially hoped to get assistance from Washington. However, the commander-in-chief had no troops to spare, though he did make some supplies available.[52] Clark then turned to the Virginian State government which gave him a commission to raise an army of 2,000 men from the western militias. Such numbers were totally unrealistic given the exhaustion of the frontier settlements. Nevertheless Clark set off once more down the Ohio in early August 1781 with 400 men, intending to go as far as the Ohio Falls before marching overland to the western end of Lake Erie. In his haste he left 100

Pennsylvanians behind with instructions to catch up on route. They never arrived, being ambushed on 24 August 1781 at the mouth of the Miami River by Brant, with the loss of almost the entire detachment.[53] This setback ended Clark's ambition of getting to Detroit, since he was both short of supplies and outnumbered by the Ohio and Great Lakes nations. He accordingly retreated back across the Ohio at the end of October 1781. Washington tersely noted that disappointment was usually the fate of such militia ventures.[54]

Even before these setbacks, Clark had found it expedient to abandon the Illinois country. Few volunteers were available to recruit the garrisons at Kaskaskia, Cahokia, and Vincennes and supplies were equally unobtainable following the invasion of Virginia by Cornwallis. In addition the French inhabitants were becoming increasingly discontented with Patriot military government. The Spanish at St Louis were more than ready to fill the resulting political and military vacuum, if only to strengthen their claims to the territory east of the Mississippi. This left Louisville at the falls of the Ohio as the furthest westward Patriot outpost.[55]

Nevertheless fighting along the Ohio during 1782 did not slacken, though hostilities were coming to a close in the east, following the British defeat at Yorktown. The prospect of peace was not improved when some Pennsylvania militia under Colonel David Williamson murdered over 100 Moravian Delaware at their settlement of Gnadenhutten. Williamson's party had been searching for the killers of a white family on 8 March 1782 when they stumbled on the Moravians. Despite piteous appeals for mercy the Delaware were butchered as they sang hymns. As with all such incidents, revenge was not long in coming, especially when Williamson and Colonel William Crawford launched another attack across the Ohio with 300 Pennsylvanian troops. Their intention was to destroy the settlements on the Sandusky River. The Shawnee and Wyandotte soon anticipated the expedition's purpose and surprised the Pennsylvanians on 4 June 1782 close to their objective, capturing a number of prisoners, including Crawford. Although he had not participated in the Gnadenhutten massacre, the Delaware had no hesitation in administering their sense of justice by burning him slowly to death.[56]

The success at Sandusky encouraged the Ohio and Western Indians to renew their attacks, following a new wave of settlement in Kentucky. The Loyalists were ready to support them in the hope that they too could retrieve something from the war. At a joint conference in June 1782 at Wapatomica, a Shawnee village on a branch of the Great Miami River, the native peoples and their loyalist allies agreed to make one last assault on the Kentucky settlements. Simon Girty, a former Seneca captive from Pennsylvania, who had thrown in his lot with the British, suggested that the Indians first threaten the Patriot post of Bryan's Station near present-day Lexington. His intention was to provoke the frontiersmen into to sallying forth in order to lure them into a trap set by the Tory rangers of Captain William Caldwell.

The plan worked perfectly. After an initial skirmish at Bryan's Station, 200 frontiersmen dashed off in pursuit, thinking that they could overtake the retreating Indians. This was despite the advice of Daniel Boone not to do so. Boone's caution was fully vindicated on 19 August 1782, when the frontiersmen were ambushed by 300 Tories and Indians near Blue Licks on the Licking River. The Kentuckians lost half their force.[57] Nevertheless, the raid had effects quite contrary to those intended, since it merely prompted Clark to cross the Ohio River once more with 1,000 mounted frontiersmen to strike the Shawnee villages. Unable to summon the Wyandot or other more distant allies to their aid, the Shawnee had to witness the second destruction of their villages.[58]

All the efforts of the Ohio and Western Indians and their Tory allies had done little to reverse the defeat suffered in Dunmore's War. Kentucky and Eastern Tennessee were still in white hands, and the number of settlers was increasing. Indeed, the war with the Patriots had brought nothing but death and destruction for the native participants, unless Britain won the peace, which was now unlikely. Admittedly, the native peoples had forced Clark to retreat across the Ohio as well as vacate the Illinois. Unfortunately, this counted for nothing when the peace negotiations opened in Paris. What Clark had been unable to effect by force of arms, the British relinquished by a stroke of the pen without thought for their native allies. The scene was thus set for the next confrontation with the settlers, this time for the lands north of the Ohio.

The devastation of Iroquoia

The Six Nation Iroquois confederacy, like the Ohioan peoples, had remained neutral for the first two years of hostilities. This was despite British orders in July 1775 to Guy Johnson, the son of the former northern superintendent, to engage them "to take up the hatchet against His Majesty's rebellious subjects."[59] The Patriots, in contrast, recognizing their relative lack of influence, made no such attempt. When the confederacy met General Schuyler at Albany in August 1775, he told them that Congress wanted only their neutrality. This suited the Iroquois, since they were keen to avoid any disadvantageous entanglement. They accordingly declared "that as it was a family quarrel, they would not interfere, but remain neuter."[60] In reality the Iroquois hoped to play off the two sides, as in earlier wars between France and Britain. The Patriots were accordingly able to invade Canada without opposition from the Iroquois, though some Canadian Mohawk assisted in the defense of St Johns.[61]

For most of 1776 the truce between the Patriots and the Iroquois held, though British agents like John Butler and the Johnson family did their best to win over the confederacy. The magistrates at Albany responded by attempting to arrest Sir John Johnson, the head of the family, forcing him to flee to Canada.[62] Among Johnson's followers was Joseph Brant, the brother of Molly, Sir William Johnson's partner in his latter years. Joseph had been educated at the Indian school of the Reverend Eleazar Wheelock and his relative sophistication was one reason why Guy Johnson, now northern superintendent, took Brant to London in November 1776. Here he had become convinced of the justice of the British cause, especially when Germain implied that Indian lands would be protected.[63]

The British, however, found it difficult to obtain active support from the Iroquois in the first 18 months of the war because of their military weakness. The evacuation of Boston prompted the Iroquois to visit Washington at New York and then Congress in Philadelphia.[64] Butler in response could only tell a conference at Niagara in June 1776 that the Patriots would cheat them out of their lands, if they did not support the Great King. Kiashuta, who had played a leading role in Pontiac's War, replied that it was the British who were "mad, foolish, crazy and deceitful." The Patriots had given them good advice to stay out of the white man's quarrel.[65] But this was before the Indians learnt of Schuyler's occupation of Fort Stanwix, which he had secretly planned during further talks that summer at Albany.[66] The garrison was a substantial one, numbering 900 men, and was close to Onondaga where the Confederacy had its council chamber.

This was a nasty shock for the Iroquois and increased the pressure on them to join St Leger's expedition down the Mohawk valley which was being planned as part of Burgoyne's offensive. Despite this the majority of the Iroquois still resisted open support for the British, fearful that it would expose the eastern members of the confederacy to attack by the Patriots. Butler accordingly had to organize another conference in July 1777 at Irondequoit, distributing liberal quantities of rum and other presents to persuade the majority to take up the hatchet. Even then most of the Oneida and Tuscarora refused to join the expedition. The Oneida were heavily influenced by their minister, Samuel Kirkland, who was from Boston and a strong Patriot.[67]

St Leger's force eventually comprised 300 regulars, 350 New York Loyalists, 100 Canadian axe men, and 1,000 Six Nation Indians led by Blacksnake, a Seneca chief, and Brant. The allies first gathered at Oswego before setting off on 26 July for Fort Stanwix, where Schuyler had 500 Continentals working on the defenses. To his surprise, St Leger found the fort stronger than expected when he arrived on 3 August, leaving him in a dilemma, since he had insufficient artillery for a formal a siege.[68] This gave General Herkimer and 800 Tryon County militia time to march to the relief of the fort. They were accompanied by 60 Oneida.

News of the relief force was given to the besiegers by Molly, who was still at the Mohawk town of Canajoharie.[69] St Leger decided that his best course was to ambush the relief column before it could reach the garrison. John Johnson and Butler took charge of the Tory rangers while Brant and Blacksnake led the Iroquois. The allies soon found a place along the river where the road passed through a ravine. Initially the battle at Oriskany on 6 August 1777 went well for the allies, despite some premature fire from the Iroquois. But the momentum was lost when many of the warriors plundered Herkimer's wagon train. This allowed the main Patriot body to extract itself from the ravine. The fighting then became indiscriminate, with heavy casualties on both sides.[70] The Indian tactic was to lure individual militiamen into the trees where they could be tomahawked. But Herkimer had ordered his men to fight in pairs. As one man took aim the other reloaded. At this critical moment news arrived that the garrison had launched a counter-attack on the Indian camp. The warriors immediately rushed back to protect their women and belongings. This forced the Loyalists to desist, despite support from St Leger and a few regulars. But Herkimer was in no condition to exploit the situation. One hundred and sixty of his men were dead or wounded, and he sensibly retreated to German Flats.[71]

St Leger then resumed his siege of Fort Stanwix, though with little effect, given his lack of artillery. Nevertheless the situation was sufficiently desperate for Schuyler to ask Gates for help, even though Burgoyne was advancing towards Albany. In this crisis, Arnold offered his services, which Schuyler quickly accepted. Twelve hundred men eventually set off, though Arnold wisely spread rumors about the true strength of his detachment. The ploy worked, since the Tories and Indians were badly shaken by the slaughter at Oriskany and unwilling to face a new foe. St Leger in consequence had little option but to retreat to Oswego. Arnold then re-supplied Fort Stanwix before returning to Albany to join the fight against Burgoyne.[72]

The battle had a number of consequences. Firstly, the Iroquois confederacy was now hopelessly divided, with the Mohawk, Seneca, Onondaga, and Cayuga supporting the British, while the Oneida and Tuscarora allied with the Patriots. But unlike previous disagreements within the confederacy, the differences this time were absolute: the league organized by Dekanawidah and Hiawatha four centuries earlier was no more. Blood had been shed, demanding a response according to the mourning war ritual. The pro-British nations accordingly struck the nearby Oneida village of Oriska, burning the houses, destroying the crops, and carrying off the cattle. The Oneida then retaliated by forcing Molly and her Mohawk neighbors to flee to Niagara. This was followed by the destruction of the lower Mohawk settlement of Caughnawaga, compelling its inhabitants to escape similarly destitute to Montreal. Inevitably retaliation was not long in coming. After an impassioned speech by Molly in the grand council chamber at Onondaga, the four remaining members of the confederacy attacked the main Oneida settlements, forcing them to seek refuge at Albany.[73]

The year 1777 had not been a happy one for the Six Nations, given their losses at Oriskany, the consequent civil war, and the defeat of Burgoyne. Nevertheless, Butler reported from Niagara that the majority of the confederacy remained strongly in favor of cooperation with Britain.[74] This was fortunate for the British since they needed their allies to help defend the frontiers. Frederick Haldimand, the new Governor of Canada, of necessity had to keep most of his forces in the St Lawrence because of the uncertain loyalty of the Canadians following the entry of France into the war. The main operations on the western frontier of New York in 1778, therefore, were devoted to Indian rather than British objectives. Brant was to win back the Mohawk valley while Seyenqueraghta, the leading Seneca warrior, struck the Wyoming Valley in North Eastern Pennsylvania, an area long claimed by his nation.[75]

To counter these threats, the Patriots similarly sought help from their Indian friends. Schuyler hosted a conference in March 1778 with the Oneida and Tuscarora, promising them that a fort would be constructed at Oriska to protect their families while they went to war.[76] However, the Patriots were too weak to do more. As Washington commented to Laurens, the British had too many presents to tempt the native peoples to change sides. He could only hope that news of a French alliance might dissuade the Iroquois from further hostilities.[77]

The initiative, therefore, lay with the British and their Six Nations allies. Brant was the first to start hostilities. After assembling a force of 300 Tories and Iroquois at the end of May 1778, he attacked the settlement of Cobleskill Creek, 20 miles west of Albany, before ambushing a detachment of Continentals and militia sent to its relief. He was greatly helped by the ineffectiveness of the Patriot forts, which allowed him to move freely from one target to another south of the Mohawk River.[78] This emboldened him to attack German Flats in September, though he failed to carry the nearby stockades of Forts Herkimer and Dayton where the inhabitants had sought refuge. Nevertheless he was able to burn numerous houses, barns, and grist mills before eluding the Tryon County militia. Haldimand was especially complimentary about Brant, "whose attachment to the government, resolution and personal exertion, makes him a character of a very special kind." However, when Germain proposed making him Colonel of the Indians, Haldimand demurred. Brant was only a relatively junior warrior and did not have the standing of other chiefs. Such notice would make him more enemies than friends.[79]

Meanwhile Butler, with a mixed force of 110 Loyalist rangers and 450 Seneca and Cayuga warriors under Seyenqueraghta and Cornplanter, another Seneca Chief, had advanced on Wyoming valley. Here on 3 July 1778 he persuaded two of the smaller forts to surrender without bloodshed, indicating that the war had not yet descended to the savagery many feared. He then learnt that a force of 500 Patriots was advancing to attack. Butler set fire to the two forts to make it appear that he was in retreat, thus luring his opponents into an ambush. This time the surprise was total. As a consequence the allies routed their foe after half an hour, losing just one Indian and two rangers. The Patriot losses in contrast were severe, comprising 227 scalps and only five prisoners, though most of survivors managed to escape.

The remaining stockades then surrendered with no further bloodshed, due to Butler's restraining efforts. Indeed, he told his immediate superior: "In the destruction of this settlement not a single person has been hurt of the inhabitants but such as were in arms; to those indeed the Indians gave no quarter." As to the battle itself, Butler ascribed the high casualties to Indian anger after their losses at Oriskany. The refusal to take prisoners in battle was not uncommon in conflicts between Indians and Whites.[80] Nevertheless, a bloody precedent had been set which both sides blamed on the other. Neither would quickly forget the battle of Wyoming.

The Patriots had one success on 9 October 1778 when a detachment of Continentals from Schoharie destroyed the Tory settlement of Unadilla.

They also occupied Brant's former base at Oquaga, though it was now abandoned.[81] But retaliation was not long in coming when a mixed Indian and Loyalist force led by Walter Butler, John Butler's son, and Brant struck the settlement of Cherry Valley. The inhabitants were ill prepared, despite a warning from the Oneida. The situation was not helped by feuding between the defending troops from Massachusetts and the local inhabitants, many of whom were Presbyterian Scots Irish.[82] The Massachusetts commander, Colonel Alden, compounded his difficulties by taking quarters outside the fort. Many of the defenders were in consequence easily surprised when Brant and Butler attacked at dawn on 11 November 1778. Meeting little resistance, the Indians began indiscriminately killing the inhabitants, despite Brant's efforts to restrain them. Among the dead were several Tories. The Indians justified their actions because the rebels had made false accusations about their conduct at Wyoming, which Butler commented "has much exasperated them." The Iroquois were equally angered by the conduct of the men spared at Wyoming, who shortly afterwards were "marching into their country intending to destroy their villages." They resolved that "they would no more be falsely accused or fight the enemy twice."[83]

The events at Cherry Valley and Wyoming were also a parting of the ways for the Patriots regarding the war on their northern frontiers. Henceforth they believed only the wholesale destruction of the Iroquois homeland would bring peace to the region.[84] Congress had voted for some such operation in May 1778, only for Washington to assert that the resources were not available. The best way of controlling the Indians was by conquering Canada.[85] Congress then suggested a joint attack on Canada with the French, but Washington again vetoed the idea, this time because the plan was "not only too extensive and beyond our abilities" but unnecessarily "complex."[86] Nevertheless Congress persisted in its determination to combat the Indians by proposing a more limited strike against Niagara and Detroit. For a third time Washington affirmed that his resources were insufficient even for this less ambitious target. Instead he suggested the army conduct "some operation on a smaller scale against the savages and those people who have infested our frontier," meaning the Six Nations and their Tory allies.[87]

The command of the expedition was entrusted to Sullivan. Five thousand men were to take part, the vast majority being Continentals.[88] Washington agreed to their deployment in the belief that Clinton would be too preoccupied by the French naval threat to New York to undertake any immediate operations up the Hudson valley. The plan was for the army to advance in three columns. The main force under Sullivan, comprising

3,000 men, was to move up the Susquehanna River from Wyoming, while the second under General James Clinton, comprising 1,000 men, marched from the Mohawk River for a meeting with Sullivan at Tioga on the eastern branch of the Susquehanna. A third detachment of 500 men under Brigadier Daniel Brodhead would then ascend the Allegheny River from Pittsburgh to strike the Iroquois from the rear. The aim of the expedition was "the total destruction and devastation of their settlements and the capture of as many prisoners of every age and sex as possible." The holding of hostages was "the only kind of security to be depended upon" for their good behavior.[89] Only the villages of the Oneida and Tuscarora were to be spared.

But first a subsidiary force of 500 men was dispatched to Onondaga from Fort Stanwix. The Six Nations had for some time wanted the British to fortify Oswego as a base to counter the Patriot threat to Onondaga. Haldimand acknowledged the desirability of this but believed he was already overstretched defending the St Lawrence Valley and posts at Niagara and Detroit.[90] Hence no help was at hand on 20 April 1779 to prevent the destruction of the Council Longhouse, though most of the inhabitants managed to flee. Colonel Bolton at Niagara ominously warned Haldimand that unless troops were sent to Oswego the Iroquois would be forced to make peace.[91] But the Patriots did not have everything their own way in these opening exchanges, since Brant killed 60 militiamen who tried to ambush him after a foraging expedition to Minisink in north west New Jersey.[92]

This engagement made no difference to Sullivan's plans, though supply difficulties meant that the main Patriot offensive began only at the end of August, when the two principal divisions of Sullivan's army met at Tioga on the eastern branch of the Susquehanna River. By now the intention of the Patriots was abundantly clear. Since the garrison at Niagara had no spare men, the defense of Iroquoia was left to John Johnson, the two Butlers, and Brant with a force of 300 Loyalists and some 600 Seneca under Sayenqueraghta and Cornplanter. This gave the Patriots a numerical advantage of almost four to one. They also had artillery.[93] Despite this, the Indians and their Tory allies determined to make a stand at the Seneca village of Newtown, hoping to reduce the odds through an ambush. Unfortunately the Seneca changed their position at the last moment, which not only revealed their presence but also exposed them to a flank attack. The result was an easy victory on 29 August 1779 for the Patriots, leaving their opponents to flee for their lives.[94]

The battle of Newtown now opened the way for Sullivan to advance on the Seneca villages as far as the Genesee River. After destroying these, he dispatched 500 men to punish similarly the Cayuga to the east. By early October 40 towns had been destroyed, leaving the majority of the Seneca, Cayuga, and Onondaga homeless and without food to face one of the coldest winters in memory.[95] Five thousand sought refuge at Niagara. Not since the French invasion of 1687 had the Seneca seen such devastation. Haldimand reluctantly acknowledged Sullivan's achievement, especially his marching through such an extensive tract of Indian country without losing a single man, despite the efforts of Brant.[96]

Sullivan had originally hoped to capture Niagara, even though it was not in his orders. However, the long line of communication meant that his army was short of supplies, especially after the destruction of the Indian cornfields. He accordingly returned to Tioga, followed by Johnson with 400 Indians and rangers, who had been ordered by Haldimand to harass the invaders' rear. But Sullivan's forces retreated in the same good order as they had advanced and reached their destination untroubled.[97]

Unfortunately for the Iroquois, the trail of destruction was not yet ended, for Sullivan's assault coincided with the third leg of the Patriot offensive from Pittsburgh. This was directed against the Mingo settlements on the upper Allegheny River. Like their Seneca relatives, the Mingo, led by Kiashuta, pleaded for help from Niagara, and equally without result.[98] Little resistance was offered during Brodhead's advance on Venango, where the Patriots discovered an extensive and prosperous settlement.[99] Ten settlements were now destroyed, along with 500 acres of corn and vegetables.[100]

The final act in the destruction of Iroquoia was performed by the Tryon County Militia, who drove the last Mohawks from their settlement at Caughnawaga. Here too the prosperity of the native inhabitants was noticed. As Colonel Gansevoort commented: "This castle is in the heart of our settlements, and abounding with every Necessary so that it is remarked that the Indians live much better than most of the Mohawk River farmers, their houses very well furnished with all necessary household utensils, great plenty of grain, several horses, cows and wagons." The spoils of war were shared with the surrounding white farmers to compensate them for previous losses.[101]

When the destruction was over, Haldimand acknowledged to Germain the futility of what had been done. "These small strokes, although they alarm and partially distress the people, only serve to exasperate them." The activities of Brant and Butler had done nothing to further the British cause. However, the cost to the native peoples had been high, since the raids had "been the cause of the rebels making a campaign in the Indian country." As a result Iroquoia now lay in ruins.[102]

Despite their losses, the Six Nations determined to continue the struggle to recover their homeland. Many had no option since they were now totally dependent on the British for food and clothing. Returning to the warpath was the price for receiving aid. The same was true for the Loyalists. Brant, Sayenqueraghta, Cornplanter, together with Butler and Johnson, accordingly launched a number of raids in the summer of 1780, the most important being that of Johnson with 700 men against Schoharie and Stone Arabia. The destruction included "two hundred dwelling houses, a proportionate number of barns and out houses, about two hundred thousand bushels of grain of various sorts, and a hundred horses and oxen." However, Johnson's raid nearly ended in disaster when the Tryon County militia caught him as he was about to cross the Mohawk River on his return to Canada. Fortunately for him, the various Patriot units failed to recognize each other, thus allowing Johnson to escape in the confusion.[103]

By the fall of 1780 Patriot control along the Mohawk extended little further than Schenectady, where the Oneida and Tuscarora lodged in miserable circumstances, following another raid by Brant. Some 50 miles of a once fertile valley had been destroyed, putting further pressure on Washington's precarious food supplies, as he readily acknowledged.[104] The situation was little better north of Albany. The dismal condition of New York was described by its governor in an appeal to Congress. "A great portion of our most valuable and well inhabited territory" had been destroyed, hundreds of its inhabitants killed and many more hundreds carried into captivity, and thousands ruined by the need to seek refuge. "The frequent calls on the militia have capitally diminished our Agriculture in every part of the State." As a result "we are not in a condition to raise troops for the defense of our frontier."[105]

However, the Six Nations had fared little better. Though the Mohawk valley had been largely cleared of white settlers, it was not safe for the Iroquois to return. Indeed few native settlements remained east of the Genesee River. Nevertheless Brant and the other chiefs were buoyed by reports that the rebels were being chastised by the great warrior chief, Cornwallis. Consequently they dispatched over 60 raiding parties during 1781 in the hope of reoccupying their lands. These forced the Patriots to evacuate Fort Stanwix in May 1781, making Fort Herkimer their most advanced post. The year finished with yet another Loyalist and Indian raid on the Mohawk valley under Major John Ross, during which he came within 12 miles of Schenectady, destroying a hundred farms, three mills, and numerous stock. Ross did, however, suffer casualties on his retreat after being pursued by some Continentals and militia under Colonel Marinus Willett. Among those killed was the younger Butler.[106]

Despite Cornwallis's defeat at Yorktown, the British and Six Nations continued the hostilities in 1782. The British wanted to strengthen their position in Canada while the Indians remained determined to recover their lands. Haldimand accordingly dispatched Ross to rebuild Fort Ontario at Oswego before unleashing Brant and a company of regulars down the Mohawk valley. However, attempts to take Forts Herkimer and Dayton proved fruitless and the expedition achieved little except the killing of a few inhabitants and some livestock. Shortly afterwards the party was recalled, following news that peace was in prospect.[107]

For the British the frontier warfare had been a sideshow. As Haldimand had earlier confessed to Germain: "I should be sorry the little excursions of rangers or Indians, so overrated in the public papers, were considered of material consequences to the success of the war."[108] For the Patriots the struggle had been more important and more costly, though the recovery of their backcountry settlements was rapid once independence was secured. But for the Iroquois the war had been a disaster. The loss of land and population meant that their ability to protect themselves as a free nation had been irrevocably damaged. Their reduced status was indicated by the lack of any provision for them in the subsequent treaties ending the war between the white peoples. As Haldimand acknowledged, the peace fell "far short" of what they had been led "to expect, deprived of their Lands and driven out of their country." The consequence for most Iroquois was either a reservation in western New York or permanent exile in Canada, leaving their once vast country to white settlement.[109]

Notes and references

1. David Taitt to John Stuart, 1 August 1775, DDAR/XI, 61–62.
2. Gage to Stuart, 12 September 1775, DDAR/XI, 105. Gage had clearly mistaken the Virginian and Pennsylvanian riflemen for Indians.
3. Stuart to Cameron, 16 December 1775, DDAR/XI, 210–11.
4. Stuart to Clinton, 15 March 1776, DDAR/XII, 76–79.
5. Henry Stuart to John Stuart, 7 May 1776, DDAR/XII, 130–33.
6. John Richard Alden, *The South in the Revolution, 1763–1789* (Baton Rouge, 1976), 272.
7. John Stuart to Germain, 23 August 1776, DDAR/XII, 188–91. Henry Stuart to John Stuart, 25 August 1776, DDAR/XII, 191–208.

8   Alexander Cameron to John Stuart, 23, September 1776, DDAR/XII, 229–30. Stuart to Germain, 24 November 1776, DDAR/XII, 253–54.

9   Stuart to Germain, 26 October 1776, DDAR/XII, 239–42. Stuart to Howe, 13 April 1777, DDAR/XIV, 68–69. Stuart to Germain, 6 October 1777, DDAR/XIV, 192–95.

10 Rachael N. Klein, *Unification of a Slave State: The Rise of the Planter Class in the South Carolina Backcountry, 1760–1808* (Chapel Hill, 1990), 94–95.

11 Samuel Flagg Bemis, *The Diplomacy of the American Revolution* (Bloomington, 1961), 90–91. See above, Chapter 2, section "Congress widens the conflict: Canada."

12 Stuart to Germain, 5 March 1778, DDAR/XV, 55–56. Chester to Germain, 14 April 1778, DDAR/XV, 98–99.

13 Stuart to Germain, 13 April 1778, DDAR/XV, 94–95.

14 Chester to Germain, 7 May 1778, DDAR/XV, 118–19. Hutchins to Germain, 21 May 1778, DDAR/XV, 123–26.

15 Germain to the Commanding Officer, 1 July 1778, DDAR/XV, 150–51.

16 Tonyn to Germain, 24 July 1778, DDAR/XV, 168–69.

17 Alden, *South in the Revolution*, 275. Norman Baker, *Government and Contractors: The British Treasury and War Supplies, 1775–1783* (London, 1971), 199–200.

18 Chester to Germain, 24 August 1778, DDAR/XV, 186–88. Stuart to Knox, 9 October 1778, DDAR/XV, 211–14.

19 James Prevost to Germain, 14 April 1779, DDAR/XVII, 101–4. Charles Shaw to Germain, 7 August 1779, DDAR/XVII, 183–85.

20 Stuart to Germain, 4 December 1778, DDAR/XV, 284–85.

21 Cameron to Germain, 18 December 1779, DDAR/XVII, 268.

22 Germain to Cameron and Brown, 25 June 1779, DDAR/XVII, 154–55. Cameron was not pleased with this arrangement, claiming that he knew little about his new assignees, Cameron to Germain, August 1780, DDAR/XVIII, 157–60.

23 Clinton to Germain, 8 October 1778, DDAR/XV, 209–10. Germain to Brigadier Campbell, 25 June 1779, DDAR/XVII, 153–54.

24 Campbell to Clinton, 10 February–21 March 1779, DDAR/XVII, 54–65.

25 John Lynch, *Bourbon Spain, 1700–1808* (Oxford, 1989), 319.

26 Campbell to Germain, 14 September 1779, DDAR, XVII, 216–18.

27 Campbell to Germain, 15 December 1779, DDAR/XVII, 260–67.

28 Campbell to Germain, 24 March 1780, DDAR/XVIII, 64–67.
29 Campbell to Germain, 15 May 1780, DDAR/XVIII, 92–94.
30 Col. Arthur Campbell to Greene, 8 February 1781, NGP/7, 258.
31 Commission to Treat with the Cherokee and Chickasaw Nations, 26 February 1781, NGP/7, 351–52.
32 Campbell to Germain, 7 May 1781, DDAR/XX, 136–38. Ibid., 12 May 1781, DDAR/XX, 138–42.
33 Cameron to Germain, 27 May 1781, DDAR/XX, 149–51.
34 Eric Hinderaker, *Elusive Empires: Constructing Colonialism in the Ohio Valley, 1673–1800* (Cambridge, England, 1997), 207–9.
35 Richard Middleton, *Pontiac's War: Its Causes, Course and Consequences* (New York, 2007), 83–90.
36 Germain to Carleton, 26 March 1777, DDAR/XIV, 51–52. Proceedings of Governor Hamilton from November 1777 to June 1781, HMC, Stopford-Sackville, II, 223. Lowell H. Harrison, *George Rogers Clark and the War in the West* (Lexington, KY, 1976), 11.
37 Dale Van Every, *A Company of Heroes: The American Frontier, 1775–1783* (New York, 1962), 117–46.
38 Laurens to Washington, 3 May 1778, WP/RWS/15, 22–23.
39 Ibid., 12 May 1778, 108–10.
40 Andrew Lewis to Washington, 8 August 1778, WP/RWS/16, 272–75.
41 Harrison, *Clark*, 17–18.
42 Quoted in Richard White, *The Middle Ground: Indians, Empires, and Republics in the Great Lakes Region, 1650–1815* (Cambridge, Eng., 1991), 368.
43 Hamilton to Germain, July 1778, DDAR/XV, 175–76. Harrison, *Clark*, 23–36.
44 Hamilton to Haldimand, 18–30 December 1778, DDAR/XV, 288–93.
45 Hamilton to Haldimand, 24 January 1779, DDAR/XVII, 48.
46 Harrison, *Clark*, 57–60.
47 Hamilton Proceedings, HMC, Stopford–Sackville, II, 237–41.
48 Bolton to Haldimand, 2 April 1779, DDAR/XVII, 95. Van Every, *Company of Heroes*, 210.
49 Harrison, *Clark*, 72.
50 Harrison, *Clark*, 75.

51 Isobel Thompson Kelsay, *Joseph Brant, 1743–1807: Man of Two Worlds* (Syracuse, NY, 1984), 309–10.

52 Washington to Jefferson, 10 October 1780, WGW/20, 148–49. Washington to Brodhead, 29 December 1780, WGW/21, 33. Washington to Clark, 8 June 1781, WGW/22, 184–86.

53 Haldimand to Germain, 23 October 1781, DDAR/XX, 248–49. Kelsay, *Brant*, 312–13.

54 Washington to Irvine, 18 December 1781, WGW/23, 396–97.

55 Van Every, *Company of Heroes*, 271, 290–92. Harrison, *Clark*, 79.

56 Van Every, *Company of Heroes*, 309–10. Washington responded to the incident by advising General Irvine that none of his men "should allow themselves to be taken alive," 6 August 1782, WGW/24, 474.

57 Theodore P. Savas and J. David Dameron, *A Guide to the Battles of the American Revolution* (New York, 2006), 337–41.

58 Van Every, *Company of Heroes*, 322. Harrison, *Clark*, 90–92.

59 Dartmouth to Guy Johnson, 24 July 1775, DDAR/XI, 55–56.

60 Schuyler to Washington, 27 August 1775, WP/RWS/1, 367.

61 Barbara Graymont, *The Iroquois in the American Revolution* (Syracuse, 1972), 71–80.

62 Schuyler to Washington, 21 May 1776, WP/RWS/4, 362.

63 Graymont, *Iroquois* 104–8. Kelsay, *Brant*, 172–73.

64 Message from the Six Nations, 16 May 1776, WP/RWS/4, 319–20.

65 Graymont, *Iroquois*, 97–9. For Kiashuta's role in Pontiac's War see Middleton, *Pontiac's War*, 35–42, 97, 145, 175–81.

66 Schuyler to Washington, 11 June 1776, WP/RWS/4, 504–5.

67 Graymont, *Iroquois*, 120–22. For details of Kirkland's ministry, see ibid., 34–40.

68 Claus to Knox, 16 October 1777, DDAR/XIV, 221–24. Claus (an officer in the Indian department), claimed he had warned St Leger about the size of the garrison and the consequent need for artillery.

69 Kelsay, *Brant*, 203.

70 Claus to Knox, 16 October 1777, DDAR/XIV, 219–24.

71 Schuyler to Washington, 15 August, 1777, WP/RWS/10, 624–25. Schuyler to Washington, 17 August 1777, WP/RWS/10, 654. Graymont, *Iroquois*, 135–36.

72 Schuyler to Washington, 17 August 1777, WP/RWS/10, 654. St Leger to Carleton, 27 August 1777, DDAR/XIV, 171–74. Claus to Knox, 16 October 1777, DDAR/XIV, 222–23.

73 Claus to Knox, 6 November 1777, DDAR/XIV, 249–51. Kelsay, *Brant*, 207–9.
74 Butler to Carleton, 14 December 1777, DDAR/XIV, 274–75.
75 Graymont, *Iroquois*, 160.
76 Washington to Indian Commissioners, 13 March 78, WP/RWS/14, 167–68. Schuyler to Washington, 22 March 1778, WP/RWS/14, 276–77.
77 Washington to Laurens, 3 May 1778, WP/RWS/15, 20–21.
78 Commissioners for Indian Affairs to Washington, 9 June 1778, WP/RWS/15, 360–61.
79 Haldimand to Germain, 24 October 1778, DDAR/XV, 229–31. Ibid., 13 September 1779, DDAR/XVII, 211–13.
80 Butler to Colonel Bolton, 8 July 1778, CAR, 386–88.
81 Kelsay, *Brant*, 228. Stark to Washington, 18 October 1778, WP/RWS/17, 448.
82 Alden to Washington, 4 November 1778, WP/RWS/18, 37–38.
83 Graymont, *Iroquois*, 185–90.
84 Washington to Laurens 16 November 1778, WP/RWS/18, 169–70.
85 Washington to Board of War, 3 August 1778, WP/RWS/16, 226–29.
86 Committee for Foreign affairs to Washington, 27 October 1778, WP/RWS/17, 597–98. Washington to Laurens, 11 November 1778, WP/RWS/18, 94–105.
87 Washington to Schuyler, 18 January 1779, WGW/14, 18–20.
88 Washington to Sullivan, 4 May 1779, WGW/14, 492.
89 Instructions to General Sullivan, June 1779, WGW/15, 189. Christopher Ward, *The War of the Revolution*, 2 vols. (New York, 1952), II, 639.
90 Haldimand to Clinton, 26 May 1779, DDAR/XVII, 135.
91 Bolton to Haldimand, 16 August 1779, DDAR/XVII, 187.
92 Washington to Sullivan, 1 August 1779, WGW/16, 29–31. Kelsay, *Brant*, 250–51.
93 Graymont, *Iroquois*, 197, 205.
94 Kelsay, *Brant*, 261–62.
95 Ward, *War of Revolution*, II, 644.
96 Haldimand to Germain, 3 October 1779, DDAR/XVII, 231–32.
97 Haldimand to Germain, 1 November 1779, DDAR/XVII, 238–39.
98 Bolton to Haldimand, 16 August 1779, DDAR/XVII, 187.

99 Graymont, *Iroquois*, 218–19.
100 Graymont, *Iroquois*, 218–19. General Orders, 18 October 1779, WGW/16, 480–81.
101 Graymont, *Iroquois*, 219.
102 Haldimand to Germain, 1 November 1779, DDAR/XVII, 239.
103 Colonel Hay to Greene, 26 October 1780, NGP/6, 434–35.
104 Haldimand to Germain, 25 October 1780, DDAR/XVIII, 208–9. Washington to Governor George Clinton, 5 November 1780, WGW/20, 295–96.
105 Quoted in Graymont, *Iroquois*, 240.
106 Haldimand to Germain, 23 November 1781, DDAR/XX, 262–63.
107 Kelsay, *Brant*, 324–28.
108 Haldimand to Germain, 1 November 1779, DDAR/XVII, 239.
109 Kelsay, *Brant*, 334.

CHAPTER 9

No daylight at the tunnel's end, 1781

France seeks a resolution

Three campaigns had passed since the entry of France into the war without the expected victory. Some Patriots suspected that the French were deliberately prolonging the war to weaken the other combatants. John Adams was one such person, telling Vergennes in July 1780 that a French fleet must be kept in American waters to avoid these suspicions.[1] Vergennes vigorously rejected the charge, pointing out that Ternay and Rochambeau had been ordered to "to act as they shall judge proper for the relief of the United States." This included staying in North America during the winter despite the lack of dockyard facilities. Hence, Louis XVI was "far from abandoning the American cause."[2] But as Luzerne, the French minister, indicated to Greene in January 1781, the French too had complaints. The states must act "as if they did not expect any foreign assistance," hinting at a lack of Patriot commitment.[3]

Nevertheless, it was recognized in Paris that the war must not drag on beyond the next campaign, since France's finances would not permit it. As Vergennes told the Spanish ambassador; "The war has gone too slowly; it is a war of hard cash, and if we drag it out the last shilling may not be ours."[4] French naval expenditure was approaching 175 million livres, an unparalleled sum. Certainly the fleet was as strong as at any time, comprising some 250 warships of which 80 were battleships, manned by 50,000 officers and men.[5] But such expenditure could not be sustained indefinitely, as the finance minister Jacques Necker was privately warning.[6]

Another problem for Vergennes was that it was by no means obvious where France should deploy her resources. It was clear that the British would try to regain the initiative in the West Indies, following de Guichen's failure in 1780 against Barbados and the other islands in the Lesser Antilles. The Spanish too were certain to demand assistance in the recapture of Gibraltar. Help was also needed for the French posts in India. Finally Rochambeau's son had arrived at the end of December 1780 with a request for "money, ships and men" following the conference with Washington and Ternay at Hartford. This would mean an extra 10,000 troops for a successful attack on New York. In view of France's straitened finances, Vergennes concluded that another assault on Britain might be the best way of achieving a quick and decisive end to the war.[7]

Vergennes and the Marquis de Castries, the new French minister of Marine, accordingly offered their Spanish colleagues two plans in early February 1781: one a full-scale invasion of Britain, the second a more limited deployment in the Channel to divert British attention from the other theatres of the war.[8] However, a memorandum by Castries made it clear that the Spanish would have to play a more prominent role, since the French did not have sufficient transports for an invasion force of 30,000 troops. Unless Spain provided half the shipping, the allies would be restricted to short coastal raids with troops carried on board the warships. As to timing, Castries suggested that the two fleets should prepare to enter the Channel at the beginning of June and remain there until mid-September 1781. After this, some French ships would be needed in the West Indies, where the Council of Ministers was planning a further offensive at the end of the year.[9]

The Spanish eventually ruled out an invasion of Britain when they replied to Castries' memorandum in early March. The main reason was that they too did not have the requisite shipping. They were equally cool to the idea of coastal raids. On the other hand, a short cruise in the Channel would divert British attention from the Mediterranean, where the Spanish were meditating an assault on Minorca. Nevertheless, Floridablanca asserted that the Spanish King needed more time before making such decision.[10] The only certainty regarding the war in Europe was Spain's determination to continue the siege of Gibraltar.[11]

The Spanish were similarly equivocal about operations in the western hemisphere, where they were awaiting the outcome of Galvez's siege of Pensacola. Success there would make Jamaica the next logical target. However, they accepted that this could wait until the French had completed their other operations across the Atlantic. For the moment Floridablanca merely asked that the French commanders in the West Indies liaise with their Spanish counterparts before sending their naval forces away at the start of the hurricane season.[12]

This response cleared the way for Vergennes and de Castries to proceed with their plans for the East and West Indies which were already advanced at Brest. The flotilla for the East Indies was to comprise five battleships and 2,000 troops under the command of Admiral Pierre André, Baille de Suffren. The larger task force for the West Indies was to comprise 21 battleships and 4,000 troops under Admiral François Joseph Paul, Comte de Grasse. The two flotillas would initially sail into the Atlantic until it was safe to separate, leaving Suffren to head for the Cape of Good Hope while de Grasse proceeded to the West Indies. Here he was to attack Britain's remaining islands in the Lesser Antilles, notably Barbados, St Lucia, and Antigua. After this de Grasse was to meet Galvez at Cape Français to ascertain Spanish plans in the Caribbean. But whatever the Spanish decided to do, de Grasse was to send at least half of his fleet to end Arbuthnot's blockade of Ternay at Rhode Island. He could then consult with Rochambeau and Washington about a suitable joint venture, since Vergennes and Castries were anxious to give their commanders as much latitude as possible. However, if Washington's army had disintegrated, as reports suggested, de Grasse was to evacuate Rochambeau's corps and return to the West Indies.[13]

The uncertain situation in North America meant that there would be no reinforcement for Rochambeau, despite his request for 10,000 men. Vergennes had earlier been advised that it would be cheaper to subsidize the Patriot forces than to send French troops. Rochambeau accordingly would receive just 600 recruits to fill the depleted ranks of his regiments. Otherwise, until de Grasse arrived, the war effort in North America would have to rely on French money and local manpower. Louis XVI, accordingly, informed Franklin on 6 March 1781 that France was giving Congress six million livres, supplemented by a further loan of four million livres to help equip Washington's army.[14]

De Grasse sailed on 22 March 1781 with 26 ships of the line and 6,000 troops, including Suffren's detachment for India.[15] Despite Vergennes' hopes of striking a decisive blow, it was by no means clear that anything effective could be done across the Atlantic, since the season was late for operations in the Caribbean while the situation in North America was distinctly discouraging. Indeed, the diplomatic and military position seemed so unpromising that Vergennes felt obliged to tell the Patriot commissioners in Paris that they might have to accept a recent offer of mediation by Russia and Austria. The two central European powers were proposing a general ceasefire for one year on the basis of *uti possidetis*, or possessions in hand. This would mean Britain's continued occupation of New York and the Carolinas.[16] The ceasefire would in due course lead to a peace conference in Vienna, by which time it was hoped that combatants would have resolved their differences. This of course was totally contrary to the aspirations of the Patriot commissioners. Adams could only protest that no such congress would be acceptable to the United States without prior recognition of its independence and the evacuation of its soil by Britain.[17] Fortunately for both allies, the mediation project collapsed because Britain refused to accept its terms. The Austrian ambassador in London was informed that "the King of England would recognize the independence of the colonies when the French were masters of the Tower of London," while possession of Madrid would be the only acceptable equivalent for the handing over of Gibraltar.[18]

Washington's darkest hour: The Continental mutiny

Louis XVI was right to make contingencies in case of a Patriot collapse, since Washington's army was about to experience its worst of many crises. Food was especially short, following Brant's raids along the Mohawk valley. The settlement of Schoharie had previously provided 80,000 bushels of wheat, but not now. The situation was doubly serious in that supplies could no longer be expected from Maryland and Pennsylvania, given the state of the winter roads. By mid-December Washington warned that the army had been "several days past with but a small pittance from their rations." In these circumstances it was impossible to be confident of holding "the important posts on this river, or even to assure myself the troops can be kept together from one day to another."[19] Mutiny was a distinct possibility.

The tipping point came on the night of 1 January 1781 when the Pennsylvania Line at Morristown refused to obey orders. As with previous mutinies, the reason stemmed directly from the inability of Congress to pay, feed, and clothe the men.[20] But an additional grievance was that many of the Pennsylvanian Continentals believed they had enlisted for three years rather than the duration of the war, as the authorities claimed. Their detention was all the harder when compared to the lot of men from other states who were entitled to an annual bonus on re-enlisting. After killing several officers, the mutineers set off with several pieces of artillery for Philadelphia to put their case to Congress. They were followed at a discreet distance by Wayne, who repeatedly called for calm. Washington wanted to pursue the mutineers himself but feared his absence from West Point might provoke a similar uprising there.[21]

News of the eruption was not long in reaching Clinton in New York, prompting him to dispatch emissaries offering the mutineers money if they enlisted in the British army. He simultaneously moved units to Staten Island to assist their desertion.[22] He was encouraged by Arnold, who had earlier advocated compensating the men with a promise of land if they surrendered or joined the King's army. Money in America was always a more "forcible argument than arms."[23]

Initially the men refused Wayne's entreaties, but at Trenton cooler heads prevailed after Congress promised to pay part of the arrears and allow those who wished to leave the service to do so. The mutineers then handed over Clinton's emissaries. Washington himself wanted the ringleaders to be executed while simultaneously recognizing the men's grievances. However, the Pennsylvania government insisted on a negotiated compromise whereby those who had served their full term were entitled to leave. About half chose to do so, resulting in the temporary dissolution of the Pennsylvanian line.[24] Washington consoled himself with the thought that those departing were not from the "native" population, meaning that they were either Germans or Scots Irish. Hopefully "the rest of the army (the Jersey troops excepted) being chiefly composed of natives . . . will continue to struggle under the same difficulties they have hitherto endured."[25]

However, as Washington feared, the placatory ending of the mutiny set an example for others to follow. On 20 January 1781 the New Jersey line similarly erupted. This time Washington determined to preempt any intervention by the civil authorities. He had previously gathered an elite detachment of New Englanders under Major General Robert Howe at West Point in case the negotiations at Trenton failed. Howe was now ordered to end the mutiny by insisting on "unconditional submission" and the arrest of the ringleaders.[26] This was despite Washington's doubts whether the New Englanders would obey their orders. However, he "thought it indispensable to bring matters to an issue" whatever the dangers, since unless "this dangerous spirit is suppressed there will be an end to all discipline." Fortunately Howe's men fulfilled their responsibilities by surprising the mutineers early in the morning of 27 January. Two of the principals were then shot by a firing squad and the rest pardoned.[27]

The mutiny of the Pennsylvania Line produced one of Washington's most gloomy assessments of the struggle. Essentially the war seemed to be beyond the capacity of the country, considering "the diffused population of these states, the consequent difficulty of drawing together its resources, the composition and temper of a part of its inhabitants [the Loyalists], the want of a sufficient stock of national wealth as a foundation for revenue, and the almost total extinction of commerce." Clearly "the efforts we have been compelled to make ... have exceeded the natural abilities of this country." The currency in consequence had depreciated, undermining support for the army, which in turn had driven men beyond the limits of endurance to mutiny. Unless France increased her support, the cause of Independence would fail.[28]

The need for French assistance was the reason for the dispatch of Colonel John Laurens to Paris early in the New Year. The weak condition of the United States indicated that only two things could save her from defeat, Washington told the new envoy. The first was an injection of money "to revive public credit and give vigor to future operations." The second was a decisive effort in "the ensuing campaign, to effectuate once for all the great objects of the alliance; the liberty and independence of these states." Only France could realize these objectives. Ideally a reinforcement of French troops should be sent, since their "perfect discipline and order" would be an invaluable addition "to the corps already here." However, Washington feared that more French troops might mean less financial aid. On balance he preferred money for the Continental army.[29] Laurens was accordingly to seek a loan rather than further land forces.

The crippling shortage of money led Congress to discuss plans for a permanent revenue through a tax on imports. However, as one Congressman advised Greene, such a bold step required the consent of the individual state governments and would be a "thing of time."[30] In the meantime Congress attempted to improve its administrative arrangements by replacing its cumbersome committee system with departmental heads. The most important posts were the superintendent of finance and the secretaries of state for war and foreign affairs. Washington welcomed these proposals, which he believed should "soon lead us to system, order and economy," providing the posts were filled by able men with "proper powers." He was also encouraged by Virginia's decision to drop its claims to lands west of the Allegheny Mountains, which finally persuaded Maryland to sign the Articles of Confederation. Hopefully the states would now be disposed to give Congress more authority.[31] In the meantime preparations for an offensive would continue. The plan was for 20,000 Patriot and 10,000 French troops to simultaneously attack Manhattan and Brooklyn.[32]

But the optimism did not last. Two months later none of the new administrative positions had been filled. Nor was there any agreement about a permanent revenue. Moreover, only 400 of the new levies for the army had arrived.[33] Depressingly many states were again resorting to the old expedient of short-term enlistments. Early in April 1781 Washington warned John Laurens: "We are at the end of our tether, and now or never our deliverance must come" from the French.[34] Not the least of Washington's problems was the old one of bread, the staple item for avoiding starvation. New York and New Jersey were bare of provisions. Indeed, the exactions of the army had prompted the formation of local associations to resist its demands.[35] Another reason for the shortage was that the states south of Pennsylvania were now supplying Greene's army. Only New England could seemingly fill this gap.[36] The lack of food was one reason why Washington declined Rochambeau's offer to join him at New York. Such move would require the mobilization of 3,000 New England militia to protect the French fleet at Newport, an insupportable burden at this point.[37]

Meanwhile the ministers in London were assessing the situation in the light of France's recent dispatch of troops and ships across the Atlantic. Their own plan for America was still basically one of wearing down the Patriots, though hopes were high that Cornwallis would be successful in the south. Regarding the movements of the French fleet, Germain affected to be unconcerned should de Grasse leave the Caribbean for North America during the hurricane season. He reassuringly told Clinton on 4 April 1781: "As Sir George Rodney's force is but little inferior to him, and he will be watchful of his motions, I am not apprehensive he will give him time to do you any material injury before he comes to your succor."[38] Accordingly, no additional ships were being sent to North America, though in reality the ministers were making a virtue out of necessity. Extra ships were simply not available. Not until early June 1781 did the Cabinet agree to the dispatch of three more battleships. These were to be commanded by Admiral Robert Digby, who was to replace Arbuthnot in a belated attempt to improve relations between Clinton and the navy.[39]

Unfortunately for Clinton, ships were not the only things in short supply. Recruits for the army were proving hard to find in Britain, even in wintertime when men traditionally turned to the colors. The regular army in consequence was not expected to exceed 104,500 men, an increase of just 6,000 men on the previous year.[40] The demand for troops in contrast continued to grow. The East India Company was calling for help following Suffren's recent departure.[41] If Spain attacked Portugal, Britain's oldest ally, a military commitment would be required on the Iberian Peninsula, as in 1762. Hence Clinton should not expect any sizable reinforcement, since the ministry had few spare troops. The best that Germain could do was the dispatch of just 1,000 recruits for the existing regiments.[42]

Nevertheless, Germain and his Cabinet colleagues were still optimistic about the war in America. They had for some time been aware of the parlous state of France's finances, leading George III to declare in September 1780 that "this war like the last will prove one of credit."[43] This view had been reinforced by the receipt of a confidential letter from Necker, suggesting a truce on the basis of *uti possidetis*.[44] It now seemed clear that the Patriots would not be able to continue the war unless the French rescued the Continental currency, and that appeared unlikely in view of France's own difficulties.[45] The financial weakness of the enemy contrasted sharply with North's success in securing yet another loan of 12 million pounds, despite the hostilities with the Dutch who were normally big investors in British funds.[46] The ministers were also heartened by the possibility that Vermont might secede from the rebellion, following informal contacts from its leaders who opposed incorporation into New York. Their secession might prompt an even wider collapse.[47] The policy of attrition looked increasingly promising. The only fly in the ointment was the continued criticism of the American war by the opposition in Parliament, which encouraged the rebels to believe that they could tire out Great Britain. The King, however, was confident that, with divine providence, it would be the enemy who first sued for peace, for at issue was the question whether Britain was "to rank among the great powers of Europe or be reduced to one of the least considerable."[48] George III had no doubt what the nation expected or what the result would be.

The Royal Navy bids Europe defiance

Despite renewed optimism about the war in North America, the British ministry still had major problems to surmount in Europe if it was to emerge unscathed. The country now had to fight a war with Holland. A new convoy was also urgently needed for the relief of Gibraltar and Minorca. Although Rodney had resupplied both fortresses at the start of 1781, the Spanish were continuing their attempt to starve the former into surrender. The defenders were on short rations and were suffering from scurvy due to a lack of fresh vegetables. The Spanish were also constructing lines at the northern end of the peninsula in preparation for an assault. Although no attempt had yet been made to land on Minorca, the garrison of 1,700 men was also clearly vulnerable. A relief convoy was urgently needed.[49]

Gibraltar was the easier of the two missions, given Minorca's deeper location inside the Mediterranean. This led the ministry momentarily to consider offering Minorca to Russia in return for barring Dutch entry into the Armed Neutrality League. However, George III disliked such territorial concessions. The plan in any case was unrealistic since the Russians had little interest in the offer.[50] The ministry accordingly had to consider the relief of both fortresses. The plan, as previously with Rodney, was for the western squadron under Admiral George Darby to escort the two convoys down the west coast of France past Cadiz to Gibraltar, where the fleet of Cordoba could be expected to mount a challenge. Providing that was successfully accomplished, the convoy for Minorca could then proceed with a smaller escort, since the Bourbon powers had few vessels in the Mediterranean itself. However the use of the Channel fleet for this purpose meant that there would be no squadron to intercept de Grasse and Suffren on their departure from Brest.

The flotilla left Portsmouth at the end of February 1781, consisting of 29 battleships and over 100 supply vessels and merchantmen. Before sailing into the Bay of Biscay, Darby first collected some victuallers at Cork.[51] He finally reached Gibraltar in early April without incident, despite the presence of a Spanish fleet of 30 battleships at Cadiz. For the moment Cordoba declined another confrontation following Langara's defeat.[52] But any joy among the defenders at the approaching relief was quickly extinguished by the opening of a thunderous cannonade by the besiegers. The arrival of Darby had persuaded the Spanish that a continuous bombardment at the northern end of the Rock was the only way to reduce their enemy. The town was soon on fire and the inhabitants forced to seek shelter along the cliffs. However, Darby's sole concern was the safe delivery of supplies for the garrison. After dispatching the Minorca flotilla, he set off home for the western approaches, having received information that a French squadron of eight battleships was in the Bay of Biscay under Admiral La Motte-Piquet.[53]

Unfortunately for the North ministry, La Motte-Piquet had already returned to Brest, though not before intercepting a valuable convoy from the West Indies.[54] This underlined the desirability for a more continuous presence in the western approaches. But any hopes of filling this void were quickly extinguished with the news in mid-May 1781 that the Dutch fleet was at sea, forcing the Admiralty to scramble every remaining vessel in the Downs.[55] The demand for ships was the main reason why the Cabinet declined to send a more substantial reinforcement to North America when it reviewed the situation in early June.[56] Fortunately, the report about the Dutch proved premature. Nevertheless the wisdom of not sending more ships to North America was seemingly demonstrated in early July when a Dutch fleet of eight warships did sail from Texel. Soon the British North

Sea squadron under Admiral Hyde Parker was in pursuit. This time the Dutch stood their ground, resulting in a four-hour battle off Dogger Bank in which both sides lost over 100 men.[57] Eventually the Dutch retreated to Texel while their diplomats requested urgent help from the League of Armed Neutrality. In this they were to be disappointed since Catherine of Russia had little to gain from protecting the Dutch. Nevertheless the threat posed by the Texel fleet meant that ships had to be stationed not only along the coast of Holland but off the Shetland Isles to prevent enemy vessels sailing down the west coast of Scotland.[58]

These were burdens that the Royal Navy could have done without, since reports arrived shortly that the French and Spanish were threatening the Channel approaches once more, with a combined force of some 49 battleships under Cordoba and de Guichen. The allied fleet had gathered at Cadiz according to the plans agreed by Vergennes and Floridablanca, though it only left the rendezvous on 21 July 1781. The intention was to sail via the Azores towards Britain. The result was a repeat of what had happened in 1779. Darby's fleet of 30 ships was in the western approaches when news reached him that the French and Spanish squadrons were off the Scilly Isles. Darby immediately made for Torbay where he formed a defensive line in readiness for the enemy's appearance, confident that the greater speed of his ships and knowledge of the coast would prove decisive should the enemy seek a battle. Nevertheless, such a station did not eliminate the risk that Cordoba and de Guichen might pass up the Channel and threaten the dockyards at Portsmouth. Another danger was that they might join the Dutch or assist an invasion of Ireland.[59]

Faced by such dangers, Sandwich could only advise Darby to remain at Torbay until the situation was clearer, leaving frigates to warn inward convoys about the need to make a detour round Scotland. In the event Sandwich was vindicated in not taking any undue risks. The allied timetable required their fleets to leave the Channel by mid-September for operations elsewhere. The Spanish accordingly returned to Cadiz on 5 September to strengthen the blockade of Gibraltar and prevent access to the Mediterranean via the nearby Straits. The French similarly recalled their fleet to prepare for operations in the East and West Indies at the start of 1782. Unlike the British, the French had the resources to take a longer view of what was operationally desirable. The downside was that for a second time the allies had failed to exploit their superiority in British waters.[60]

Even so, the incursion into the Channel had allowed the Spanish to disembark 14,000 troops unimpeded on Minorca, commanded by the Duc de Crillon, one of France's most distinguished officers, who was now in the Spanish service. The landings on 20 August 1781 forced the British garrison of 1,700 men under General James Murray to take shelter in Fort St Philip, the principal base guarding the approach to Port Mahon. This was a formidable structure which had been greatly strengthened since its previous capture in 1756. Indeed Vergennes and Castries doubted that it could be reduced.[61] Despite this the British ministry immediately recalled Darby to prepare a squadron of seven battle ships and a regiment of foot for dispatch to the Mediterranean.[62] Seemingly there was no end to the demands on the Royal Navy. Then fortune intervened, for Murray shortly afterwards informed the ministers that the best time for reinforcing Minorca would be after Christmas when enemy vessels would have difficulty maintaining their station.[63] Hence no immediate reinforcement was needed. This was some relief.

But the lull was only temporary, since intelligence indicated that another large armament was being prepared at Brest, most likely for an attack on Jamaica.[64] Although the Royal Navy now had 400 ships in commission, including 90 of the line, and almost 100,000 seamen, the resources of the nation seemed truly stretched.[65] Nevertheless the ministry recognized "that it would be of the greatest consequence to intercept or . . . retard this squadron." Sandwich was accordingly to recommend at the next cabinet meeting "the most effectual method of carrying this service into execution."[66]

The British ministry was right to be concerned, since the French were preparing a second major reinforcement for both the East and West Indies to ensure overwhelming force in those two areas. In addition they were intending a further strengthening of the Spanish blockade of Gibraltar. The plan of Vergennes and Castries, was for de Guichen to escort the East and West Indian convoys into the Atlantic with 19 battleships. Ten of these with accompanying transports and merchantmen would proceed to the Caribbean under Admiral Vaudreuil, while another battleship with several frigates and transports set sail for India. De Guichen would then take his remaining eight battleships to join Cordoba in the Straits of Gibraltar.[67]

When the Cabinet met on 22 October, Sandwich presented his ideas for dealing with the new threat. The worsening weather meant that the navy's large three-deck battleships of over 80 guns would have difficulty remaining at sea. Sandwich accordingly adopted an earlier suggestion of Lord Mulgrave, one of his Admiralty colleagues, for sending Kempenfelt to patrol the western approaches with a "flying squadron" of smaller more seaworthy two-deck 64- and 74-gun battleships. Copper-bottoming meant that such a squadron would be swift enough to evade the main French battle fleet but still strong enough to disrupt an enemy convoy, however well protected.[68] The proposal was well received by Sandwich's colleagues, who readily agreed to the recalling of the western squadron under Darby so that an appropriate "detachment" could be prepared for dispatch to Ushant to prevent "the sailing of the French convoy from Brest."[69]

Kempenfelt received his orders on 22 November 1781, though his ships were not ready to leave until early December. He reached his station off Ushant on 12 December 1781 just after de Guichen had emerged from Brest with his two convoys. At the time of sighting, de Guichen was to the leeward of the merchantmen, not expecting a British force so late in the year. This allowed Kempenfelt to attack the unprotected side of the convoy, seizing 20 transports and over a thousand troops before de Guichen could come to the rescue. The British commander then used his superior speed to withdraw.[70] The engagement proved more important than it initially appeared, since it was followed by a storm which drove most of de Guichen's ships back to port. Only three battleships and a few transports continued their journey with Vaudreuil, thus reducing French strength in the Caribbean for the 1782 campaign. French plans for India were similarly disrupted. Nevertheless George III, on learning of Kempenfelt's retreat, ungraciously commented that every Admiral appeared unwilling to fight unless commanding an equal number of battleships. He despaired of ever seeing a decisive blow struck.[71] He was wrong, for by this time such a blow had been struck across the Atlantic. Unfortunately it was delivered by a French admiral rather than a British one.

Britain's southern strategy unravels

One reason for British optimism about the war in early 1781 was their confidence that they now had a winning strategy in America. British authority was to be consolidated in one province at a time, starting in the south, until all the colonies outside New England had been subdued.[72]

The war in the Carolinas had seen a short lull at the end of 1780 while Cornwallis awaited Leslie's reinforcements, leaving Greene and Morgan to keep watch from their respective camps on the border of North and South Carolina. However, early in the New Year, Cornwallis determined to resume his advance. He was tired of the "perpetual uprisings" in South Carolina and the inability of the Loyalists to protect themselves.[73] Perhaps he would have better success if he first subdued North Carolina, whither his orders directed him to proceed. It was clear that the rebels in

South Carolina were being sustained by their friends in the neighboring province. Denying Sumter, Marion, and Pickens that support might cause the rebellion in South Carolina to collapse, which in turn would assist the consolidation of British authority in Georgia and Florida.[74] Cornwallis was further encouraged to resume his advance into North Carolina by the news that Clinton was sending a further 1,500 men under Arnold to intercept Greene's supplies from Virginia. As he observed to Rawdon, the arrival of these forces would allow them to "make a great change in the southern colonies in these next four months," providing the French did not appear.[75] Cornwallis accordingly ordered 300 men under Major James Craig to occupy Wilmington to provide an alternative line of supply into the interior of North Carolina via the Cape Fear River.[76]

Cornwallis had one other inducement to resume operations, which was his desire to exploit Morgan's separation from Greene. The need to do something was emphasized on 27 December 1780 when Morgan's cavalry destroyed a unit of 250 Loyalists at Hammond's Store, barely 30 miles from Ninety Six.[77] The danger was that Morgan would march on that important stronghold, thus threatening Georgia too. Cornwallis was accordingly receptive to Tarleton's suggestion that he advance with an elite force, either to "destroy Morgan's corps, or push it . . . over the Broad River" into the path of the rest of the army.[78] The only objection to this plan was that to make Tarleton's force respectable, Cornwallis would be left with just 700 men. Nevertheless, Leslie's approach offered the prospect of a substantial reinforcement. Accordingly, while Cornwallis marched slowly northward, Tarleton with 1,100 men from his British Legion and two Highland regiments sped westward in a wide circle to drive Morgan into the trap.[79]

Since the action at Hammond's Store, Morgan had been uncertain whether "to retreat or to move into Georgia," given his lack of "forage and provisions." However, he believed "a retreat would dampen the spirit which now begins to pervade the people and call them into the field." Greene agreed about the need to avoid a retreat, but did not approve an invasion of Georgia which would drive an even greater wedge between the two wings of the Patriot army. Greene accordingly advised Morgan to "hold your ground if possible." Should Tarleton pay him a visit, Greene did not doubt that "he will have a decent reception and a proper dismissal."[80]

In the event Morgan had the decision taken for him, since late on 14 January 1781 he received news that Tarleton was approaching with a superior force. Morgan immediately abandoned his camp on the Pacolet

River and retreated towards Greene's Army. However, he soon realized that he would not be able to outrun Tarleton. He accordingly took up a position at Hannah's Cowpens, an isolated farmstead on the west side of the Broad River, a few miles from Cherokee Ford.[81]

Morgan's force consisted of the Delaware and Maryland Continentals, plus various militia units from Virginia, North Carolina, and Georgia, totaling 800 men. His position superficially appeared weak, since he had the Broad River in his rear and open country in front, which offered no cover for his timorous militia, thus seemingly favoring Tarleton's cavalry. However, the site was well chosen in one respect, comprising rising undulating ground which helped conceal the true nature of his dispositions. Morgan was about to deploy some novel tactics that would shortly serve Greene equally well. He recognized that it was folly to expect the militia to withstand regular soldiers on the field of battle, even with ground advantage. He accordingly arranged his army in three lines, the first consisting of riflemen skirmishers, the second the Georgia and North Carolina militias, and the third the Continentals and Virginia militia. His instructions were that the riflemen and less well seasoned militia from Georgia and North Carolina were to fire two volleys with their muskets and rifles, after which they were to retreat behind the Continentals, where they were to reform their ranks. They would be encouraged to do so by William Washington's cavalry.[82]

This maneuver was largely successful when the two armies came together on the morning of 17 January 1781, following a night march by Tarleton. By the time Tarleton's advancing infantry reached the Continental forces, they had suffered considerable casualties. Now, unexpectedly, they faced a third line of battle. It was at this point that Tarleton committed his reserves, the 71st regiment of Highlanders. Unfortunately for the British, they found that the entire Patriot line had reformed, just beyond the crest of the hill, luring them into a dreadful fire. With the British advance stalled, Morgan sent his remaining forces, including the reformed militia, to encircle the enemy. After attempting one last charge with his mounted infantry, in which he exchanged blows with Washington, Tarleton fled from the field, leaving 100 dead and 800 prisoners. This time quarter was offered. Nevertheless, Morgan had given the hated Tory Legion "a devil of a whipping."[83]

But there was no time for celebrations. Within hours Morgan was on the road, conscious of the need to avoid the other jaw of the trap, namely the army of Cornwallis, which was now just 25 miles distant. Cornwallis was certain to attempt a counter-attack, once he had been joined by Leslie, if only to retrieve the captives. Morgan accordingly made a rapid march towards Greene's army, sending the prisoners northwards along backcountry roads into Virginia. He was helped by faulty intelligence which led Cornwallis initially westwards in the wrong direction. The loss of Tarleton's cavalry was a serious blow in this respect, since it had been the ears and eyes of the British commander. The detour allowed Morgan to escape across the Catawba River before heavy rain delayed Cornwallis from doing the same.[84]

Cornwallis now had to decide whether to continue his advance into North Carolina or retire back to Camden. Although Leslie's arrival more than offset Tarleton's losses, Cornwallis's situation was full of menace, as he confessed to Rawdon, who had gone to reinforce Ninety Six. "I see infinite danger in proceeding, but certain ruin in retreating." He would therefore continue "unless some misfortune should happen to you, which God forbid."[85] Not everyone welcomed the decision. One objector was Governor Wright of Georgia. He observed to Germain that the operations of Cornwallis and Tarleton had "fallen far short of just expectations." The danger was that a rebel army would come in behind Cornwallis "and throw us into the utmost confusion and danger, for this province is still in a defenseless state."[86] Sadly, neither the punishment "so deservedly inflicted on those who had taken up arms again" nor any of the other measures had yet "quelled the spirit of rebellion." This was disappointing since a new Georgia assembly was passing laws inspired by a dutiful sense of loyalty.

Nevertheless, Cornwallis determined to persevere in his scheme. Recognizing that speed was essential, he jettisoned most of his baggage and ordered the army to live off the land, a dangerous procedure given the lack of habitation and distance from the coast. It was also questionable since it was likely to alienate the local population. For the next few weeks the army would have no wagon train "except those loaded with hospital stores, salt and ammunition and four reserved for the sick or wounded."[87] Cornwallis's only insurance against starvation was his occupation of Wilmington in the hope that he could be supplied up the Cape Fear River to Cross Creek. The desperate nature of his gamble was well described by General O'Hara in a subsequent letter: "In this situation, without baggage, necessaries, or provisions of any sort for officer or soldier, in the most barren inhospitable, unhealthy part of North America, opposed to the most savage, inveterate, perfidious, cruel enemy, with zeal and with bayonets only, it was resolved to follow Greene's army to the end of the world."[88]

Greene was privately delighted at these developments, believing that Cornwallis's "mad scheme of pushing through the country" must result in his destruction.[89] By luring the British towards Virginia, he could turn the tables on his opponent, since Greene could expect growing support, while Cornwallis experienced an ever-lengthening line of communication. Greene might even be able to do to Cornwallis what Gates had done to Burgoyne at Saratoga. Nevertheless, he knew the dangers of being overconfident, telling the chairman of Congress's southern committee: "Our prospects are gloomy notwithstanding these flashes of success." He feared that Morgan's victory would be used as an excuse not to send desperately needed men and supplies. But to prepare for any eventuality, Greene left his main force on the River Pee Dee to consult Morgan, Sumter, and Pickens about their future operations.[90]

But before this, Greene had to deal with Cornwallis, who had resumed his march from Ramsour's Mills on 28 January 1781. Fording the Catawba was successfully accomplished, despite the opposition of the local militia under General Davidson. Fortunately for Greene he had now been joined by Morgan's corps. Nevertheless, he was still inferior in numbers to Cornwallis, though superior in cavalry. In this situation he again appealed to the state militia for help while urging Steuben to complete the Continental enlistments and other detachments in Virginia.[91] He also wrote to the victors who had defeated the Tories at King's Mountain. He told William Campbell that the loan of 1,000 of his brave "mountain militia" for a month would greatly help thwart Cornwallis's invasion of North Carolina.[92]

The two armies now played cat and mouse as Cornwallis attempted to ensnare the Continental army as it retreated towards the River Dan and the border with Virginia. However, the Patriots were able to elude their pursuer because of their familiarity with the countryside and knowledge of the fords over the region's numerous rivers. Greene strengthened his advantage by making sure that boats were available when the rivers were too swollen to ford. But it would be touch and go whether the troops could reach their destination safely, as Greene told the Governor of North Carolina.[93] The army still had only 1,420 infantry, many of whom were poorly armed militia.[94] To improve their chances, Greene requested Sumter and Pickens to create a diversion along the borders of South Carolina to threaten Cornwallis's line of communication.[95]

To protect the army on its retreat, Greene formed an elite corps of light horse and infantry under Colonel Otho Williams and Lee to harass the van of Cornwallis's army and slow his advance.[96] This was essential because Cornwallis's "movements are so rapid that few or no militia" could keep up. "He marches from twenty to thirty miles a day and is organized to move with the same facility as a light infantry corps. Should he continue to push us, we must be finally ruined without reinforcement." Nevertheless, aided by his knowledge of the rivers, Greene finally crossed the Dan River into Virginia at Irwin's Ferry on 14 February 1781, with "several hundreds of soldiers tracking the ground with their bloody feet."[97] Here he could expect supplies and further reinforcement.

At this point Cornwallis abandoned the pursuit. His line of communication was dangerously fragile, leaving his rear open to the attacks of Sumter and Pickens. He had in any case achieved his objective of forcing Greene out of North Carolina. It was time to re-establish order in the province. He accordingly returned to Hillsborough to issue a new proclamation on 22 February 1781, inviting "all such faithful and loyal subjects to repair without loss of time, with their arms and ten days provisions, to the Royal Standard." This would allow the implementation of "effectual measures for suppressing the remains of the rebellion in this province, and for the re-establishment of good order and constitutional government."[98] But the proclamation had a mixed reception. More inhabitants came to look than participate, perhaps intimidated by the proximity of Lee's cavalry and Pickens' partisans. The danger posed by the Patriots was soon demonstrated when 300 Loyalists under Colonel John Pyle attempted to join Cornwallis. On arriving at Haw's Field the Loyalists mistook Lee's force for that of Tarleton, since both units wore green uniforms. Before they could rectify their mistake, 90 were dead and another 150 laid low with fearsome saber wounds.[99]

Cornwallis's proclamation ironically had one unanticipated effect in that it prompted Greene to re-cross the Dan River. The reports of Loyalists flocking to the Royal standard persuaded Greene that he must reassert the authority of Congress by advancing once more into North Carolina. He was encouraged to do so by the assembling of the neighboring militia, though it was unclear whether they would join him in the field. Some 400 Continentals were also expected from Virginia where Steuben had been working hard to recruit and discipline them. Greene, in any case, resolved not to await the arrival of these reinforcements, though he was still not confident of a confrontation with Cornwallis. For the moment he positioned himself at High Rock Ford not far from the Dan River in case another retreat became necessary.[100]

In early March the militia finally began to appear, along with Steuben's Continentals, though disappointingly Campbell brought only 60 of his mountain rifle men. Nevertheless, Greene's army was for the first time numerically superior.[101] He now felt confident of advancing towards Cornwallis, though he recognized that a general action would have to be on ground of his choosing, where he could fight the type of defensive engagement that had served Morgan so well at Cowpens. During the retreat to the Dan River Greene had camped briefly at Guilford Court House and noted its defensive capabilities. Accordingly, on 12 March the army advanced towards its new position, arriving two days later.[102]

Since issuing his appeal to the loyal people of North Carolina, Cornwallis had been attempting to open a communication with Cross Creek, since the troops were "in the greatest want of shoes and other necessaries" following the pursuit of Greene. He also asked Rawdon to send three regiments recently arrived from Ireland by way of Cape Fear to counter Greene's increasing strength.[103] However, Cornwallis was not about to deny himself the opportunity of a battle with Greene which he had been seeking since entering North Carolina in early January. As he subsequently informed Germain: "I was determined to fight the rebel army if it approached me, being convinced that it would be impossible to succeed in the great object of our arduous campaign, the calling forth the numerous Loyalists of North Carolina, whilst a doubt remained" about "the superiority of our arms."[104]

Greene deployed his men along a ridge on which the court house stood overlooking the settlement below. The terrain was partially wooded, making it difficult for the British to appreciate the nature of the task facing them. Greene, impressed by Morgan's dispositions at Cowpens, determined to adopting a similar defense in depth, with three separate lines of battle. The first line consisted principally of 1,000 North Carolina militia. Their task, as at Cowpens, was to deliver two volleys before retiring. Three hundred yards behind was the second line, containing 1,200 Virginia militia, with a similar mission of firing two volleys before retreating. Lastly at the top of the hill was Greene's main force of Virginian and Maryland Continentals, some 1,400 men. However, to protect the flanks of his army, Greene also had two "corps of observation," one on the right comprising Washington's cavalry and a regiment of riflemen, the other on the left under Lee with a similar force of cavalry and marksmen.[105]

Cornwallis meanwhile was advancing with 1,900 regulars and Loyalists on a 12-mile night march to be sure of catching his foe. Among his units were two elite Guards battalions. He arrived on the morning of 15 March 1781 at the foot of the valley, to be greeted by Greene's artillery after which he formed his line of battle, while Lee and Tarleton exchanged blows. The main action began, as Greene anticipated, with a British frontal assault on the North Carolinian Militia and supporting units. Not all of them fired their two rounds, but those with rifles did serious damage to a regiment of Highlanders. Nevertheless they were forced to retire, bringing the British to Greene's second line of defense, which was partially concealed behind trees. This line too gave way, though only after causing more damage to the hungry if enraged regulars. Finally the British had to confront Greene's third line, comprising the Virginian and Maryland Continentals. At this point Cornwallis's light infantry on the left wing were driven back after several volleys and a bayonet charge by Greene's men. But they soon rejoined the rest of the British line in a final effort to drive the Patriots off the ridge. With both sides locked in hand-to-hand fighting, Cornwallis ordered his artillery to fire grape shot into the melee of bodies. The two lines then separated but it was the British who reformed more quickly for another charge, having as Greene admitted "only gained their point by superior discipline." Nevertheless, they were now poised to complete the encirclement of "the whole of the Continental troops." In these circumstances Greene "thought it advisable to order a retreat," having designated Speedwell's iron works ten miles from Guilford as a suitable rallying point. The Patriots had to abandon their artillery, ammunition wagons, and wounded, but otherwise retired in good order. The British regulars were too exhausted to follow beyond the Reedy Fork River.[106] Nor were they able to resume their offensive the next day, with so many wounded and "the total want of provisions in an exhausted country."[107]

From the British viewpoint the battle was meaningful only if Cornwallis had destroyed Greene's army. This he had failed to do. Indeed it was his own army that was close to destruction, having lost a third of his men on the field of battle, some 600 killed and wounded. Hence although Cornwallis had technically won the battle, it was a pyrrhic victory, as was soon to be revealed.

His first setback was the lack of any Loyalist support following the battle, despite the issue of another proclamation on 18 March that it was time for "all loyal subjects to stand forth and take an active part in restoring order and government."[108] Cornwallis described the response to Clinton: "Many of the inhabitants rode into camp, shook me by the hand and said they were glad to see us and to hear that we had beat Greene, and then rode home." Cornwallis "could not get more than 100 men in all the Regulator country to stay with us, even as militia."[109] The reasons were not hard to find, for as one resident explained, the inhabitants "had been so often deceived in promises of support ... that the people were now afraid to join the British army, lest they should leave the province." For should that happened "the resentment of the revolutionaries" would be inflicted with even "more cruelty," especially against those with relatives in the army.[110]

With a third of the army sick and wounded and the rest "without shoes and worn down with fatigue," Cornwallis recognized "it was time to look for some place of rest and re-fitment" before resuming the campaign. He accordingly marched by easy stages to Cross Creek where he hoped supplies would be ready from Wilmington. But here a second disappointment awaited him, for "contrary to all former accounts . . . it was impossible to procure any considerable quantity of provisions" or forage. "The navigation of Cape Fear River," about which he had received such optimistic reports, "was totally impracticable, the distance from Wilmington by water being 150 miles." Furthermore, the breadth of the river was seldom more than 100 yards, the banks were "generally high and the inhabitants on each side almost universally hostile," making a regular supply of stores impossible. This left Cornwallis no option but to retreat to Wilmington itself. Here he could attend to his sick and wounded and procure the necessary materials "to put the troops into a proper state to take the field."[111]

In the interim Greene prepared his men for another engagement which he promised them would "eventually secure victory." He was buoyed by the conviction that had the North Carolina militia done their duty "we should certainly have ruined the British army."[112] Within a few days he was ready to advance in the hope of attacking Cornwallis as he marched towards the sea.[113] Unfortunately the old problem of militia enlistments reappeared, so that his forces dwindled as rapidly as they had grown. Once again he might have to look for safety in flight.[114]

In this situation Greene adopted a radical change of plan. Instead of confronting Cornwallis, he would "carry the war into South Carolina." This would force Cornwallis either to follow him or give up his posts. If he followed Greene, it would lead to the evacuation of North Carolina which could then mobilize its resources more effectively. The plan was risky, since Greene's forces were likely to consist of little more than his 1,200 Continentals while the British under Rawdon had twice that number of regulars, even if Cornwallis did not return to South Carolina. But "all things considered" he told Washington, "I think the movement is warranted by the soundest reasons, both political and military."[115] He accordingly asked Sumter, Marion, and Pickens to attack the British outposts as the prelude to a general assault in South Carolina.[116] He also urged the governors of Maryland, Virginia, and North Carolina to fulfill their earlier promises to raise troops. In particular Greene wanted authority to conscript the militia in an emergency.[117] Finally he informed the Board of War that his troops were almost naked and in desperate need of shoes, if a march to the south was to be undertaken.[118]

Cornwallis was similarly considering his options after arriving at Wilmington on 7 April. He too had only 1,400 men fit for duty, though by mid-April this number had increased to 2,180.[119] But this was still too few to protect both North and South Carolina. He also knew that General William Philips had joined Arnold in Virginia with another 2,000 men, all of them technically under his command. In a letter to Philips, Cornwallis commented: "I am quite tired of marching about the country in quest of adventure." If an offensive war was intended, "we must abandon New York and bring our whole force into Virginia." This would then give Britain "a stake to fight for," while "a successful battle may give us America." On the other hand, "if our plan is defensive, mixed with desultory expeditions, let us quit the Carolinas . . . and stick to our salt pork at New York, sending now and then a detachment to steal tobacco etc." Clearly Cornwallis was not attracted by this mode of warfare. He still believed in the possibility of victory on the battlefield in the south. If the three regiments from Ireland arrived, he would be able to march by land to join Philips, though he was still doubtful whether he would have enough men "for a war of conquest." By this "I mean to possess the country sufficiently to establish a militia and some kind of mixed authority of our own." It was for this reason that he wanted to move the army from New York to Virginia. However, Cornwallis was not the Commander in Chief. Such change of direction was a matter for Clinton to decide.[120]

Cornwallis accordingly wrote to Clinton to suggest that the war be moved from New York to Virginia. His reason for so drastic a step was that "until the Virginia is in a manner subdued, our hold on the Carolinas must be difficult, if not precarious. The rivers in Virginia are advantageous to an invading army" while "North Carolina is, of all the provinces in America, the most difficult to attack . . . on account of its great extent and numberless rivers and creeks and the total want of interior navigation."[121]

The letters to Philips and Clinton reflect the bankruptcy of Cornwallis's ideas. The strategy of posts and the formation of local militias had failed in North Carolina and was perilously close to collapse in South Carolina too. Nothing suggested that Virginia would be any different, despite the navigability of its rivers. And although Virginia was important for the supply of men and supplies to Greene, there was little indication that its control would be decisive in the overall context of the war. The abandonment of

New York, on the other, hand would be a huge blow to British prestige and the Loyalist cause in the north.

Nevertheless, he wrote two further letters to Clinton outlining his thoughts. He also wanted to hear from Rawdon before committing himself irrevocably to an advance into Virginia, conscious that the posts in South Carolina were "so distant from each other and his troops so scattered as to put him into the greatest danger of being beat in detail." He accordingly began a leisurely advance towards Halifax near the Virginia border while awaiting news from either New York or Charleston. There he heard on 12 May that Rawdon had defeated Greene at Hobkirk's Hill near Camden. South Carolina was for the moment seemingly safe. It was the green light that Cornwallis had been waiting for even though he had not received permission from Clinton. The next day he crossed the Roanoke and headed for Petersburg in Virginia.[122]

Cornwallis did not wait for a response from New York because he knew that Clinton wanted to retire. If that happened, Cornwallis would be his successor, allowing him to direct the war as he wished, subject to Germain's approval. Ironically Clinton acknowledged on 13 April "the propriety" of Cornwallis's "coming to Chesapeake Bay." However, he was assuming that Cornwallis had won a decisive victory at Guilford Court House and had completed the pacification of the Carolinas.[123] Once he realized this was not the case he made his disapproval clear, asserting that Cornwallis's move was "likely to be dangerous to our interests in the southern colonies."[124]

The dangers envisaged by Clinton were not long in being realized. Even before Guilford Court House, Wright had warned how small rebel parties from South Carolina were assassinating known Loyalist magistrates and militia officers in Georgia. Wright had been unable to stop these incursions since the killers quickly retreated on horseback. Now even the communication between Savannah and Charleston had been severed. Wright believed a fatal error had been committed in not securing one district at a time. The Loyalists would then have flocked to the King's standard, providing the necessary support and protection for the army to resume its advance.[125]

However, this picture of Loyalist collapse and Patriot dominance was not entirely accurate. Sumter reported on 7 April that his forces were still scattered, as were those of Pickens, though he expected to have 600–700 men shortly. Ironically he too was suffering from the inconveniencies of short-term enlistments. To keep his men together he was rewarding each recruit with a slave confiscated from the Tory plantations. In reality the scheme was little more than plundering and did nothing to improve discipline or morale among a "dissolute" population, as Sumter acknowledged.[126]

Nevertheless within a few weeks of Guilford Court House, the partisans set about capturing the outlying British posts. Among the first objectives was Fort Watson on the Santee River which Marion invested in early April 1781 with support from Lee. However, the reduction of Fort Watson proved more arduous than expected since the Patriots had no artillery to breach the defenses. The problem was overcome only when Major Hezekiah Mahan built a log tower, which allowed sharpshooters to fire down on the now vulnerable defenders.[127] The fort finally surrendered on 22 April.

Greene meanwhile had advanced on Camden where Rawdon had his main force. He was hopeful that with Sumter's support he could invest the town successfully, especially if Cornwallis failed to return to South Carolina.[128] However, he discovered that the garrison in Camden was larger than expected. He also found the surrounding countryside strongly Tory in sentiment, forcing him to provide escorts for the smallest task. Seemingly, the constant depredations of the partisans had alienated the inhabitants.[129] Among the worst offenders was a Colonel Culp who not only burnt and destroyed "every kind of property" but "tortured with the most cruel death" anyone to whom he took exception.[130] Greene's frustration with the partisans was completed when they failed to prevent a Loyalist regiment from Ninety Six entering Camden to strengthen the garrison.[131] The only option left to Greene was to retire in the hopes of inducing Rawdon to sally forth. He accordingly positioned himself on the well-wooded Hobkirk's Hill, one mile from Camden.[132]

This ploy succeeded rather sooner than Greene expected. Until this point Rawdon "was so weak in troops" that he could "not risk men to harass him [Greene] as he advanced." His orders in any case were to retire behind the Santee River if the enemy appeared in force. But Rawdon, like Cornwallis, believed in taking the initiative, especially when he heard that Greene's army was not as numerous as first believed. Rawdon had the remnants of six regiments of regulars, and by "arming our musicians, our drummers and in short everything that could carry a firelock, I mustered above nine hundred for the field." He accordingly set off early on the morning of 25 April to attack Greene abreast Hobkirk's Hill.[133] On this occasion Greene believed he had sufficient force to surround the British. It proved an unwise decision, since the Patriot army was still unable to resist a determined push by the British veterans. Two regiments of Maryland Continentals gave way, throwing the Patriot line into confusion. However, William Washington's cavalry limited the pursuit to just three miles, after which the Continentals reformed their line. Washington then retook Hobkirk's Hill after routing a detachment of dragoons which Rawdon had left as a covering force on his return to Camden.[134]

Tactically the British had won yet another engagement, but as at Guilford Court House, their success was illusory. Although Rawdon received a reinforcement under Colonel Watson and confronted Greene once more on 8 May 1781, his ploy proved unsuccessful. Greene this time kept to his entrenchments.[135] Meanwhile the partisan leaders were finally making inroads against the smaller posts protecting the roads between Charleston, Camden, and Augusta. Rawdon accordingly abandoned Camden on 10 May 1781 for the safety of the Santee, while ordering the evacuation of the other inland posts, including Ninety Six.[136] Only Augusta was to be retained in the backcountry.

The wisdom of retreating was confirmed on the march towards the coast. The countryside everywhere was in partisan hands, the population sullen, and supplies unobtainable. Balfour at Charleston informed Clinton that the defection was "so universal that I know of no mode short of depopulation to retain it."[137] Rawdon finally halted at Moncks Corner, 30 miles from Charleston, to await the three regiments from Ireland. By this time it was clear that the orders to vacate the smaller posts were too late, since Sumter had captured Orangeburg on 11 May, Marion had taken Fort Motte on the 12 May, and Fort Granby had fallen to Lee and Sumter on 15 May 1781.[138] Only Augusta and Ninety Six remained in Loyalist hands and both were dangerously isolated.

Despite these successes, considerable discontent prevailed in the Patriot ranks. Sumter was annoyed that Lee had directed the siege of Fort Granby, because he was a Continental officer.[139] But even the partisan commanders were sufficiently discouraged about their men to wish to retire. The first was Marion, who asked to be relieved of his command, since he could do little "with such men as I have, who leave me very often at the very point of executing a plan." Five days later Sumter similarly requested leave to resign his command because of the "discontent and disorder among the militia."[140]

Greene was in no position to accept either resignation, whatever his past criticism of the partisan leaders and their men, since much still remained to be done before South Carolina and Georgia were free of the enemy. Since the end of April, Pickens had encircled Ninety Six while Clarke laid siege to Augusta. Greene now decided to send Lee to Augusta while he went to the aid of Pickens at Ninety Six.[141] This placed Rawdon in a quandary, since he did not have enough troops to relieve both posts simultaneously, even with the reinforcement from Ireland. As Greene succinctly observed: "If they [the British] divide their forces they will fall by detachments and if they operate collectively they cannot command the country."[142] It was an insidious situation.

In the event Rawdon resolved to go to the aid of Ninety Six, perhaps recognizing that it was too late to save Augusta. The defenders at Ninety Six comprised two Loyalist regiments from New Jersey and New York under Cruger, totaling about 600 men.[143] Fortunately for Rawdon, Greene and Pickens were finding the siege a tough proposition. Greene had only a skeleton force of Continentals, and was still awaiting 2,000 Virginians promised by Jefferson. He told one senior officer in frustration: "I wish the [state] legislatures would" either "give effectual support to the army or give up the dispute." As it was, they were merely prolonging the misery for everyone. The miracle was that although the army had "been beaten again and again," its perseverance had resulted in the capture of all the enemy posts except Charleston, Savannah, and Ninety Six.[144]

The siege of Ninety Six was now in its twentieth day and Greene's army was on the verge of success, with just one rampart to breach. To allow more time, Greene requested Marion and Sumter to harry Rawdon's advance while Pickens and Clarke joined him so that they could fight a battle should the British appear.[145] But an attempt to storm the principal redoubt was without success, not least because the partisans failed to answer Greene's call. He told Lee bitterly: "Marion is below, Pickens I can get no account of, and Sumter wants to make a tour of Monk's Corner." Nothing that Greene could "say would induce them to join his army."[146] Had Sumter and Pickens joined him he could have taken Ninety Six before Rawdon arrived or defeated him on his approach.

Greene, accordingly, had to retire on 19 June 1781 before Rawdon's superior force, leaving him once more facing a disagreeable situation. The region around Ninety Six still had many Tories, making the reduction of the countryside uncertain. Indeed he expected Rawdon to readopt the plan "to conquer with British troops and garrison with the militia or Tories."[147] In desperation he again appealed to Shelby to bring 1,000 mountain riflemen to drive the British back towards Charleston.[148] It was still uncertain which side would capitulate first.

Rawdon finally reached his destination on 21 June 1781. Here he gave the Loyalists the option of either remaining with a reinforced garrison or of accompanying him back to the low country where they could resettle in the relative safety of Charleston and its environs between the Edisto and Santee Rivers. Almost all opted for the latter. However, on hearing that Greene was only 16 miles away, Rawdon determined to try once more the fortunes of a battle. But after advancing 40 miles, he decided that further pursuit was not only fruitless but dangerous, given his lengthening supply chain and the collapse of the British cause elsewhere. Rawdon accordingly spent the next three weeks at Ninety Six while the Loyalists gathered up their families and movable possessions for the long march to Monck's Corner.[149]

Rawdon's decision to relieve Ninety Six meant that Augusta was left to fend for itself. The town was garrisoned by 600 Loyalists under Thomas Brown. Brown was particularly hated, not least for his hanging of various Patriots after they had broken their paroles. He was also accused of encouraging the Indians to commit outrages on the frontier.[150] The siege itself began on 15 May with the arrival of Pickens's South Carolina partisans and the Georgia militia of Clarke. Not surprisingly, the Loyalists put up a desperate resistance, refusing several calls to surrender from Lee. Their principal defense was Fort Cornwallis which Brown had turned into a formidable structure. As at Fort Watson, the Patriots built a Mahan tower so that their snipers could fire into the cramped quarters of the garrison.[151]

With Rawdon still far away, Brown finally agreed terms on 5 June. These were relatively generous, given the circumstances.[152] Lee, a Continental professional from another state, appreciated the skill and courage of his opponent. He also agreed with Greene about the need to avoid a bloodbath by the local partisans, who "exceed the Goths and Vandals in their schemes of plunder, murder and iniquity," which they perpetrated "under the pretence of supporting the virtuous cause of America." Lee accordingly protected Brown though he was unable to save some of those implicated in the earlier hangings following Cruger's relief of Augusta in September 1780.[153] Nevertheless, by mid-June 1781 the whole of Georgia between Ebenezer and Augusta was in Patriot hands.[154]

The situation was no better for the British in South Carolina, where Rawdon had placed his army at Orangeburg, on the north branch of the Edisto River. Here he was watched by Greene from the High Hills of the Santee, while Marion, Lee, and Sumter attacked the coastal settlements as far as Dorchester, just a few miles from Charleston.[155] By the end of July 1781 the British held just two enclaves in the south around Charleston and the town of Savannah. It was eloquent testimony to the failure of Britain's southern strategy of progressively reducing the country one state at a time. It also called into question the advisability of Cornwallis's advance into Virginia. Nevertheless, the Patriots had still not won the war while the British held these bastions. Something else was needed to realize the Patriot's dream of independence.

Notes and references

1 Adams to Vergennes, 13 July 1780, Gregg L. Lint ed., *Papers of John Adams*, Series III, *General Correspondence*, IX (Cambridge, Mass., 1996), 526–76.

2 Vergennes to Adams, 20 July 1780, ibid., X, 16.

3 Chevalier Luzerne to Greene, 21 January 1781, NGP/7, 167–68.

4 Piers Mackesy, *The War for America, 1775–1783* (Cambridge, Mass., 1964), 386.

5 Lee Kennett, *The French Forces in America, 1780–1783* (Westport, Conn., 1977), 25.

6 In his published statement, *Comte Rendu au Roi*, February 1781, Necker painted an entirely positive picture of France's financial situation to encourage investors to lend money to the government.

7 Kennett, *French Forces*, 77. Jonathan Dull, *The French Navy and American Independence: A Study of Arms and Diplomacy, 1774–1787* (Princeton, 1975), 205. Arnold Whitridge, *Rochambeau: America's Neglected Founding Father* (New York, 1965), 130.

8 Dull, *French Navy*, 216–18.

9 Dull, *French Navy*, 217–18.

10 Dull, *French Navy*, 220. Ibid., 228–34.

11 T.H. McGuffie, *The Siege of Gibraltar* (London, 1965), 63–64.

12 Dull, *French Navy*, 227.

13 Dull, *French Navy*, 216–23. Mackesy, *War for America*, 387. Henri Doniol, *Histoire de la participation de la France à l'établissement des États-Unis d'Amérique: Correspondence diplomatique et documents*, 5 vols. (Paris, 1886–1892), 548–50.

14 Kennett, *French Forces*, 77, 88–91. Dull, *French Navy*, 239. William C. Stinchcombe, *The American Revolution and the French Alliance* (Syracuse, NY, 1969), 87–89, 146.

15 Dull, *French Navy*, 216–24.

16 Orville T. Murphy, *Charles Gravier, Comte de Vergennes: French Diplomacy in the Age of Revolution, 1719–1787* (Albany, 1988), 331. Doniol, *Participation de la France*, vol. 4, 500–504.

17 Samuel Flagg Bemis, *The Diplomacy of the American Revolution* (Bloomington, 1961), 180–87.

18 Quoted in H.M. Scott, *British Foreign Policy in the Age of American Revolution* (Oxford, 1990), 314.

19 Washington to Governor Clinton, 10 December 1780, WGW/20, 452.
20 Washington to the Governors of New England, 5 January 1781, WGW/21, 61–62.
21 Washington to Governor Clinton, 4 January 1780, WGW/21, 58–59. Washington to Huntington, 6 January 81, WGW/21, 64–66.
22 Clinton to Germain, 25 January 1781, DDAR/XX, 43.
23 Arnold to Germain, 28 October 1780, DDAR/XVIII, 211–15.
24 Washington to Greene, 2 February 1781, WGW/21, 172. Washington to Steuben, 6 February 1781, WGW/21, 192–93.
25 Washington to Rochambeau, 20 January 1781, WGW/21, 120–21.
26 Washington to Robert Howe, 22 January 1781, WGW/21, 128–29.
27 Washington to Huntington, 23 January 1781, WGW/21, 135–36. Washington to Livingston, 27 January 1781, WGW/21, 148–49.
28 Washington to Colonel Laurens, 15 January 1781, WGW/21, 105–10.
29 Ibid.
30 John Mathews to Greene, 10 February 1781, NGP/7, 275.
31 Washington to Schuyler, 20 February 1781, WGW/21, 261.
32 Washington to Knox, 10 February 1781, WGW/21, 209.
33 Washington to Lincoln, 4 April 1781, WGW/21, 412–13.
34 Washington to Huntington, 8 April 1781, WGW/21, 429–31. Washington to Laurens, 9 April 1781, WGW/21, 437–39.
35 Washington to Livingston, 31 January 1781, WGW/21, 163–65.
36 Washington to Huntington, 16 April 1781, WGW/21, 475–77.
37 Washington to Rochambeau, 7 April 1781, WGW/21, 426–28.
38 Germain to Clinton, 4 April 1781, DDAR/XX, 98–100.
39 Cabinet Minute, 2 June 1781, Fortescue/5, 243.
40 Letter to Amherst, 18 December 1780, Fortescue/5, 164. Estimate for Guards, Garrisons, CJ/XXXVIII, 33–35.
41 Cabinet Minute, 23 April 1781, Fortescue/5, 222–23.
42 Germain to Clinton, 3 January 1781, DDAR/XX, 30.
43 George III to North, 26 September 1780, Fortescue/5, 136.
44 George III to North, 18 December 1780, Fortescue/5, 163. Andrew Stockley, *Britain and France at the Birth of America* (Exeter, 2001), 14–15.
45 George III to North, 30 April 1781, Frtescsue/5, 224.

46 North to George III, 17 December 1780, Fortescue/5, 162–63. Peter D.G. Thomas, *Lord North* (London, 1976), 102.

47 The mainly New England population of Vermont was opposed to incorporation into New York.

48 George III to North, 13 June 1781, Fortescue/5, 247.

49 McGuffie, *Gibraltar*, 63–92.

50 Cabinet Meeting, 1 January 1781, Fortescue/5, 177. Ibid., 7 January 1781, Fortescue/5, 179. Brendan Simms, *Three Victories and a Defeat: The Rise and Fall of the First British Empire* (London, 2007), 650–51.

51 David Syrett, *The Royal Navy in European Waters during the American Revolutionary War* (Columbia, SC, 1998), 140–42.

52 Sir Charles Petrie, *King Charles III of Spain* (London, 1971), 195. John Lynch, *Bourbon Spain, 1700–1808* (Oxford, 1989), 316.

53 Darby to Sandwich, 22 April 1781, Sandwich/4, 34–36. Cabinet Minute, 19 May 1781, Sandwich/4, 39.

54 Darby to Sandwich, 19 May 1781, Sandwich/4, 29. Mackesy, *War for America*, 392–93.

55 Sandwich to George III, 15 May 1781, Fortescue/5, 229.

56 Cabinet Minute, 2 June 1781, Fortescue/5, 243.

57 Sandwich to George III, 9 August 1781, Fortescue/5, 262. Syrett, *Royal Navy in European Waters*, 130–31.

58 Syrett, *Royal Navy in European Waters*, 129–32. For the details of the North Sea squadron, see Cabinet Minute, 17 February 1781, Sandwich/4, 84.

59 Darby to Sandwich, 31 August 1781, Sandwich/4, 50. Mulgrave to Sandwich, 31 August 1781, 50–51.

60 Sandwich to George III, 1 September 1781, Fortescue/5, 272. Alfred T. Mahan, *The Major Operations of the Navies in the War of American Independence* (Boston, 1913), 188–89.

61 Petrie, *Charles III*, 198. Dull, *French Navy*, 232.

62 Cabinet Minute, 27 September 1781, Sandwich/4, 67.

63 Ibid., 1 November 1781, Sandwich/4, 296.

64 Cabinet Minute, 20 October 1781, Sandwich/4, 70–71. Ibid., 22 October 1781, 72.

65 Abstract of Ships in Commission, November 1781, Sandwich/4, 428–30.

66 Cabinet Minute, 20 October 1781, Fortescue/5, 290. Syrett, *Royal Navy in European Waters*, 148–49.

67 M. Le Comte de Lapeyrouse Bonfils, *Histoire de la Marine Française*, 3 vols. (Paris, 1845), III, 229.

68 Mulgrave to Sandwich, 3 September 1781, Sandwich/4, 56–58. The plan to use only two-deck battleships was supported by Darby, see Darby to Sandwich, 12 November 1781, Sandwich/4, 74–75.

69 Cabinet Minute, 22 October 1781, Fortescue/5, 291.

70 Syrett, *Royal Navy in European Waters*, 149–50.

71 George III to Sandwich, 18 December 1781, Sandwich/4, 77–78.

72 Germain to Clinton, 2 May 1781, DDAR/XX, 131–32.

73 Cornwallis to Clinton, 6 January 1781, CAR, 485.

74 Two centuries later American commanders in South Vietnam would similarly argue that the Vietcong guerillas were being sustained by supply lines through neighboring Cambodia.

75 Cornwallis to Rawdon, 30 December 1780, Ross/1, 76–77.

76 Franklin and Mary Wickwire, *Cornwallis and the War of Independence* (London, 1971), 252. Craig to Balfour, 4 February 1781, DDAR/XX, 54–56.

77 Morgan to Greene, 31 December 1781, NGP/7, 30–31.

78 Tarleton to Cornwallis, 4 January 1780, printed in Robert D. Bass, *The Green Dragoon: The Lives of Banastre Tarleton and Mary Robinson* (Orangeburg, 1973), 144–45.

79 Cornwallis to Clinton, 18 January 1781, Ross/1, 81.

80 Morgan to Greene, 4 January 1871, NGP/7, 50–51. Greene to Morgan, 7 January 1781, NGP/7, 72. Ibid., 13 January 1781, 106.

81 Morgan to Greene, 19 January 1781, NGP/7, 152–54. Don Higginbotham, *Daniel Morgan: Revolutionary Rifleman* (Chapel Hill, 1961), 130–31.

82 Morgan to Greene, 19 January 1781, NGP/7, 153.

83 Ibid., 154–55. Cornwallis to Clinton, 18 January 1781, Ross/1, 82. Higginbotham, *Morgan*, 142.

84 Morgan to Greene, 23 January 1781, NGP/7, 178–79. Greene to Huntington, 31 January 1781, NGP/7, 225–26. Higginbotham, *Morgan*, 145–47.

85 Quoted in Wickwire, *Cornwallis*, 275.

86 Wright to Germain, 25 January 1781, DDAR/XX, 45–46.

87 Cornwallis to Germain, 17 March 1781, Ross/1, 502–6.

88 Quoted in Wickwire, *Cornwallis*, 277–78.

89 Greene to Huger, 30 January 1781, NGP/7, 220.
90 Greene to Mathews, 23 January 1781, NGP/7, 174. Greene to Lee, 26 January 1781, NGP/7, 202–3.
91 Greene to Salisbury Militia, 31 January 1781, NGP/227–28. Greene to Steuben, 3 February 1781, NGP/7, 242–43.
92 Greene to Campbell, 30 January 1781, NGP/7, 218–19.
93 Greene to Nash, 9 February 1781, NGP/7, 263–65. W.J. Wood, *Battles of the Revolutionary War, 1775–1781* (New York, 1995), 234–35.
94 Council of War, 9 February 1781, NGP/7, 261–62.
95 Greene to Pickens, 3 February 1781, NGP/7, 241–42. Greene to Sumter, 3 February 1781, NGP/7, 245–46.
96 Greene to Washington, 9 February 1781, NGP/7, 267–68.
97 Greene to Washington, 15 February 1781, NGP/7, 287. Greene to Steuben, 15 February 1781, CAR, 487.
98 Proclamation, Hillsborough, 20 February 1781, Ross/1, 91–92.
99 Lee to Greene, 25 February 1781, NGP/7, 347. Cornwallis to Germain, 17 March 1781, Ross/1, 505.
100 Greene to Steuben, 29 February 1781, NGP/7, 374–76.
101 Greene to Jefferson, 10 March 1781, NGP/7, 419–20.
102 Greene to Steuben, 11 March 1781, NGP/7, 427.
103 Cornwallis to Rawdon, 21 February 1781, Ross/1, 84.
104 Cornwallis to Germain, 17 March 1781, Ross/1, 502–6.
105 Greene to Huntington, 16 March 1781, NGP/7, 433–34.
106 Ibid., 434–35. For Cornwallis's account see his letter to Germain, 17 March 1781, Ross/1, 507–10.
107 Cornwallis to Clinton, 10 April 1781, CAR, 508.
108 Quoted in Wickwire, *Cornwallis*, 314–15.
109 Cornwallis to Clinton, 10 April 1781, CAR, 508.
110 Quoted in Wickwire, *Cornwallis*, 315.
111 Cornwallis to Clinton, 10 April 1781, CAR, 508–10. See also Cornwallis to Germain, 18 April 1781, Ross/1, 91.
112 General Orders, 16 March 1781, NGP/7, 431–33. Greene to Sumter, 16 March 1781, NGP/7, 442–43.
113 Greene to Lee, 22 March 81, NGP/7, 461.
114 Greene to Huntington, 30 March 1781, NGP/8, 7–8.

115 Greene to Washington, 29 March 1781, NGP/7, 481–82.
116 Greene to Sumter, 30 March 1781, NGP/8, 12. Greene to Marion, 4 April 1781, NG/8, 47.
117 Greene to Nash, 3 April 81, NGP/8, 36–37. Greene to Jefferson, 6 April 1781, NGP/8, 58–59. Greene to Thomas Lee, 7 April 81, NGP/8, 62.
118 Greene to Board of War, 30 March 1781, NGP/8, 3–4.
119 Cornwallis to Germain, 18 April 1781, Ross/1, 91. State of the Army, 15 April 1781, Ross/1, 88.
120 Cornwallis to Philips, 10 April 1781, Ross/1, 87–88.
121 Cornwallis to Clinton, 10 April 1781, CAR, 509–10,
122 Wickwire, *Cornwallis*, 321.
123 Clinton to Cornwallis, 13 April 1781, CAR, 510.
124 Clinton to Cornwallis, 29 May 1781, CAR, 523–24.
125 Wight to Germain, 5 March 1781, DDAR/XX, 73–75. Wright to Germain, 5 May 1781, DDAR/XX, 134–35.
126 Sumter to Greene, 7 April 1781, NGP/8, 66–67. Klein, *Unification of a Slave State*, 103.
127 Greene to Lee, 4 April 1781, NGP/8, 46. Marion to Greene, 23 April 1781, NGP/8, 139–40.
128 Greene to Sumter, 15 April 1781, NGP/8, 100.
129 Greene to Huntington, 22 April 1781, NGP/8, 129–31.
130 Colonel Emmet to Greene, 9 April 1781, NGP/8, 74.
131 Greene to Lee, 24 April 1781, NGP/8, 143.
132 Greene to Huntington, 27 April 1781, NGP/8, 155–57.
133 Rawdon to Cornwallis, 26 April 1781, CAR, 513–15.
134 Greene to Huntington, 27 April 1781, NGP/8, 155–57.
135 Greene to Lee, 9 May 1781, NGP/8, 227–28.
136 Rawdon to Cornwallis, 24 May 1781, CAR, 521–22.
137 Balfour to Clinton, 6 May 1781, CAR, 520.
138 Greene to Huntington, 14 May 1781, NGP/8, 250–51. Lee to Greene, 15 May 1781, NGP/8, 262–63.
139 Sumter to Greene, 14 May 1781, NGP/8, 258–59. William M. Wallace, *Appeal to Arms: A Military History of the American Revolution* (New York, 1951), 241–42.
140 Marion to Greene, 11 May 1781, NGP/8, 242. Sumter to Greene, 16 May 1781, NGP/8, 274.

141 Greene to Lee, 16 May 1781, NGP/8, 272.
142 Greene to Huntington, 14 May 1781, NGP/8, 251.
143 Rawdon to Cornwallis, 5 June 1781, CAR, 527.
144 Greene to Smallwood, 9 June 1781, NGP/8, 371.
145 Greene to Marion, 10 June 1781, NGP/8, 374. Greene to Pickens, 14 June 81, NGP/8, 388–89.
146 Greene to Lee, 24 June 1781, NGP/8, 452–53.
147 Greene to Huntington, 20 June 1781, NGP/8, 419–22. Greene to Lee, 24 June 1781, NGP/8, 452–53.
148 Greene to Shelby, 22 June 1781, NGP/8, 439. Shelby replied that few men would be available before a peace treaty had been signed with the Cherokee, 2 July 1781, NGP/8, 482.
149 John S. Pancake, *This Destructive War: The British Campaign in the Carolinas, 1780–1782* (University of Alabama, 1985), 214–15. Pickens to Greene, 10 July 1781, NGP/8, 518.
150 Edward J. Cashin, *The King's Ranger: Thomas Brown and the American Revolution on the Southern Frontier* (Athens, Ga., 1989), 219–26. Cashin largely absolves Brown of these charges.
151 Pickens to Greene, 25 May 1781, NGP/8, 310–11.
152 Pickens and Lee to Greene, 5 June 1781, NGP/8, 351–52.
153 Lee to Greene, 4 June 1781, NGP/8, 346. Pickens to Greene, 7 June 1781, NGP/8, 359.
154 Wright to Germain, 14 June 1781, DDAR/XX, 161.
155 Balfour to Clinton, 20 July 1781, CAR, 550–52.

CHAPTER 10

Resolution at Yorktown, 1781

The war moves to Virginia

We have seen that the British plan for the war in America in 1781 was essentially a war of attrition until the rebellion collapsed or Cornwallis succeeded in re-imposing the authority of the Crown by force of arms. Germain's main concern at the start of 1781 was a continued presence in Virginia, not only to interdict supplies to Greene's army, but to prevent the French from establishing themselves in the Chesapeake as they had done at Rhode Island. This required a "secure port for our ships to resort to for supplies." But such post was also essential to restore the inhabitants' confidence that they would receive "permanent and effectual succor." Clinton was accordingly to replace Leslie's force as soon as possible.[1]

Clinton for once had already anticipated Germain's request by sending a new corps of 1,200 men under Arnold. Arnold's orders were similar to those of Leslie. First he was to destroy Greene's supply depots at Petersburg. After that he was to establish a post at Portsmouth on the Elizabeth River, offering protection for those wishing to declare for the King. However, Arnold was to limit his appeals to the surrounding countryside, since the rest of the population should not be roused "till such time as you can establish yourself and afford them the like protection."[2] He made no mention of a naval facility.

The choice of Arnold for this assignment proved judicious since within two days of sailing up the James River he had captured Richmond, the state capital. Here, as a gesture of magnanimity, he offered the merchants half the value of their goods. The offer, however, required the consent of Governor Jefferson and he declined to accept the proposal, whereupon

Arnold burnt all public buildings, warehouses, small foundries, and a ropewalk. The tobacco ships in contrast were sent down the river for British use. The defenses of Virginia were so weak that barely a shot was fired during these proceedings.[3] Arnold then fell back down the river to begin the task of establishing a post at Portsmouth.

The operations of Arnold did not go unnoticed by either Washington or the French on Rhode Island, where Captain Destouches had become commander following the death of Ternay. When news was received that Arbuthnot's fleet had been damaged in a storm off Gardiner's Bay and forced to return to New York, Destouches sent three of his ships to attack Arnold's naval escort. This prompted Washington to order Lafayette with 1,200 Continentals to join Steuben who was still in Virginia forwarding men and supplies to Greene. He hoped that Lafayette, with the help of the French fleet and local militia, would be able to encircle Arnold at Portsmouth and destroy the British forces there. Should he be successful, Arnold was to be summarily executed for "treason and desertion."[4] The dispatch of Lafayette meant that Washington would have just enough men to garrison West Point, leaving the communication between the Delaware and Hudson Rivers to be guarded by only two regiments.[5] It was one of Washington's many calculated risks.

Clinton's response to these movements was to order another 2,000 men to Virginia under Philips, requesting Arbuthnot simultaneously to clear the French warships out of the Chesapeake.[6] Philips's first task, like that of Arnold, was the destruction of the rebel depots at Richmond and Petersburg and the establishing of Portsmouth as a refuge for the Loyalists. However, in view of the recent incursion by the French Navy, Philips was to consult with Arbuthnot about a suitable naval base. If Arbuthnot found Portsmouth unsuitable for "large ships," he could select either Yorktown or old Point Comfort, providing he had enough troops. Philips was then to return to New York, leaving a sufficient force at Portsmouth. Clinton was still hoping to win a decisive victory against Washington once the campaigning season began in the north.[7]

Before Philips could embark, news arrived that Destouches had put to sea with his entire squadron, following prompting from Washington.[8] He also had 1,100 troops on board. Fortunately for Clinton, Arbuthnot was ready to depart with an equal number of battleships. Moreover, his ships, being copper-bottomed, were faster so that he was able to overtake Destouches. In the ensuing engagement off the Capes of Virginia on the 16 March 1781 the French again fought a defensive battle, disabling the British vessels by firing at their rigging. Nevertheless it was Arbuthnot who secured the entrance to Chesapeake Bay, opening the way for the dispatch of Philips's reinforcement.[9] This was fortunate, for Arnold was now surrounded by some 4,800 Virginia militia and Continentals under Lafayette and Steuben.[10]

As already noted, Clinton was expecting Philips to return with most of his men for an offensive in the North. However, Germain's letter of 3 January made it clear that a more formidable presence was required in the Chesapeake. Germain expressed his ideas in his usual fashion as comments rather than orders, leaving the final decision to Clinton. Nevertheless they could not but have influence, coming from the minister responsible for the war in America. Clinton responded by asserting "I have ever been sensible of the very great importance of operations in the Chesapeake," despite the risks which were considerable "unless we are sure of a permanent superiority at sea." He had recently been studying a proposal from Colonel William Rankin of Pennsylvania for an operation between the Chesapeake and Delaware River, where loyalist opinion was allegedly strong. But Clinton was utterly opposed to Cornwallis's suggestion of moving operations entirely to Virginia. New York was an essential link with Canada and its abandonment would be a gross betrayal of its 25,000 inhabitants.[11]

The continued presence of the British in Virginia caused much anxiety among the Patriots. The need for more troops was emphasized by the politically influential Benjamin Harrison on a visit to West Point at the end of March. Washington responded that he had no spare men, having barely enough to check the British on Manhattan. Besides he wanted to conserve his forces for an attack on New York, believing that this was the most effective way of helping the southern states.[12] Nevertheless he instructed Lafayette to stay in Virginia with his Continentals, contrary to his initial instructions to return to "the grand army" once the expedition against Arnold had ended. He also permitted the newly reformed Pennsylvania line under Wayne to stay in Virginia rather than immediately joining Greene in the Carolinas, if the latter agreed.[13]

Lafayette for his part could only watch and wait, given the disparity of his forces to those of Arnold and Philips. His Continentals also wanted clothing and equipment, which he tried to provide from his own purse.[14] The redcoats, accordingly, were able to march at will up the James River, destroying several unfinished privateers, before reaching Petersburg where on 26 April 1781 they seized a huge quantity of tobacco. Arnold then burnt several more partially built warships on the Appomattox River, before returning to Manchester, opposite Richmond, where he repeated the work of destruction. Lafayette and his men on the other side of the James River could only act as "spectators of the conflagration."[15]

It was at this point that Cornwallis entered Virginia, reaching Petersburg on 20 May 1781. Arnold was there to greet him, following the death of Philips a few days earlier from a fever. The two forces now comprised some 7,200 fit for action. Cornwallis immediately took charge. Since Clinton had yet to give him new orders, he accepted the instructions to Philips to "dislodge Lafayette from Richmond," while destroying "any magazines or stores ... which may have been collected either for his use or that of General Greene's army." After that he would retire to the Jamestown Peninsula to inspect York as a possible a naval base, Portsmouth now being deemed inadequate because of its poor defensive capabilities, unhealthy site, and lack of protection for "a ship of the line."[16]

On the future conduct of the war, Cornwallis quickly rejected the Rankin plan because it was too similar to those already attempted in North Carolina. Cornwallis had now changed his views on how the war should be conducted. The key was to have "as few posts as possible and that wherever the King's troops are they should be in respectable force." A fast-moving field army was required to convince the rebels of the futility of further resistance. For this reason he dismissed the idea of Philips and Arnold for a descent on Philadelphia, doubting its practicality or utility. "Without an intention of keeping or burning it (neither of which appear advisable) I should apprehend it would do more harm than good to the cause of Britain." His conclusion as before was that "if offensive war is intended, Virginia appears to me to be the only province in which it can be carried on" successfully. However a large army would be necessary, which he tactfully suggested Clinton should command.[17]

Cornwallis, in conformity with his new mode of warfare, first drove Lafayette from Richmond before ordering Simcoe with the Queen's Rangers to advance westwards to attack Von Steuben and his Continentals at Point of Fork, where they were guarding a considerable quantity of stores. Tarleton simultaneously visited Charlottesville on 4 June 1781, forcing the Virginia legislature to flee. He then climbed the steep road to Monticello, giving Jefferson just ten minutes to escape. However, an attempt by Simcoe to seize an important magazine at Albemarle Court House was beaten off, following the arrival of Wayne with 700 Pennsylvania Continentals.[18] Cornwallis then retraced his steps to Richmond on 20 June to investigate the suitability of York as a naval base. Lafayette followed at a discreet distance, deploying a light corps under Wayne to harry the British rear.[19]

The difficulties in Virginia were discussed during a conference at Wethersfield in Connecticut on 22 May, which Rochambeau had called to inform Washington that de Grasse would be coming to North America for a brief visit in the late summer, with an as yet undetermined number of ships. The two men then reaffirmed that New York should be the point of attack, since effective action further south appeared beyond the resources of the allies.[20] As Washington explained to Sullivan on 29 May 1781: "The perplexed, distressed and embarrassed state of our affairs" made New York the only feasible objective. An operation in the south would require a long march in the heat of the summer with all the attendant difficulties of finding supplies. In contrast "the weakness of the garrison of New York," its central "position for drawing together men and supplies, and the spur which an attempt against that place would give" to the allied cause "were among the reasons which prompted" the undertaking. Above all, an attack on New York offered "the fairest promise of success," unless Clinton recalled his forces from Virginia. Should that happen the operation would still bring relief to Greene and Lafayette.[21]

Washington hoped that his plan for "striking the enemy a fatal blow" would energize Congress and "the several states immediately concerned." With this in mind he asked the New England governors to bring their battalions up to strength by 1 July 1781.[22] He also made preparations for raising 300 riflemen to act as sharpshooters, a tactic that Clinton had employed to great effect during the siege at Charleston with his German Jaegers. In the meantime Rochambeau agreed to march to the North River to join Washington in preparation for the attack.[23]

Washington calculated his own field army to be 8,250 strong, after deducting Lafayette's detachment and making provision for the northern frontier and West Point. Nevertheless he advised Rochambeau that these figures were only provisional, since much depended on the states.[24] It was partly for this reason that he wrote to the French minister, Luzerne, suggesting that de Grasse bring a considerable body of troops.[25] Rochambeau wrote similarly, to de Grasse, informing him of the British strength and of Washington's belief that New York was the only practicable target. But he added that de Grasse should also visit Chesapeake Bay to destroy any of Arbuthnot's ships inside, since the prevalent winds would carry him past the entrance without requiring a detour. Washington acknowledged the sense of this proposal, though he still believed that de Grasse should first come to New York. If he appeared without warning, he would "have a very good chance of forcing the entrance before dispositions could be made to oppose him," thus preventing a repetition of events in 1778 when Howe prevented d'Estaing from entering the harbor and linking up with Washington. Then, "should the British fleet not be there, he could follow them to Chesapeake, which is always accessible to a superior force."[26]

By now Clinton had reconciled himself to Cornwallis's advance into Virginia, acknowledging on 29 May that what had been done could not be immediately reversed. Accordingly, Cornwallis was to carry "on such operations as you shall judge best in Virginia" until the climate dictated otherwise.[27] But within two weeks Clinton was ordering the return of six regiments to New York, while Cornwallis took "a defensive station at Williamsburg or Yorktown." Clinton had recently received Germain's warning of 4 April 1781 that a French fleet of 26 battleships and transports with between 7,000 and 12,000 men had sailed for the West Indies and that part of this force would probably come to North America during the hurricane season. Now intercepted letters revealed that Rochambeau intended to join Washington near New York. If the squadron under Count de Barras, Ternay's replacement, did the same, the French and Americans would have a superiority of men and ships, posing a serious threat to New York.[28]

Fortunately, the situation was not as threatening as it seemed, given the strength of Rodney's fleet in the West Indies. But to make sure, Clinton wrote to Rodney himself on 28 June 1781, requesting him to come northwards in person, once de Grasse's intentions were clear. Then "I am persuaded that our combined efforts will not only render all the enemy's attempts abortive, but ensure success to such operations as we may afterward undertake together."[29] The danger that de Grasse might go to the Chesapeake caused Clinton little concern, for as he told Arbuthnot on 17 June, he had advised "Lord Cornwallis to take post at Yorktown," which should be sufficient guard against any French fleet.[30] The possibility that Washington and Rochambeau might join de Grasse for a joint attack did not occur to him. It was to prove a fatal oversight.

Rodney and de Grasse: The naval prelude

By June 1781 the land commanders in North America were all relying on their respective fleets in the West Indies to determine the outcome of the campaign. Much therefore rested on the conduct of Rodney and de Grasse.

At the start of 1781 the British seemingly had a considerable superiority in the West Indies, with 32 ships of the line. The French and Spanish in contrast had just 21 battleships. However, the British superiority was more apparent than real, since the figures did not include de Grasse's armament then preparing at Brest. Eight of Rodney's battleships on the other hand were in a poor condition and due to return to England for a major refit.[31] The balance of naval power was about to swing decisively towards France and Spain, especially as war had now broken out with Holland.

Nevertheless for the moment the initiative remained with Rodney as he received orders to attack the Dutch island of St Eustatius, which was an important source of supplies for the French and Spanish West Indies. The island itself was almost defenseless and fell an easy capture in early February 1781 to the troops under General Vaughan. It proved a rich haul, for in the harbor were two Dutch warships and a convoy worth half a million pounds sterling. A similar quantity of sugar, cotton, and tobacco was in adjacent warehouses, so that the total value of the captures exceeded one million pounds, equivalent to 5 percent of the annual cost of the war.[32]

Sorting out the booty and strengthening the defenses of St Eustatius took Rodney the best part of two months. Eighteenth-century custom allowed the officers and crews to keep a proportion of any capture as prize money, with the largest share going to the respective military and naval commanders. Rodney had been on the verge of being imprisoned for debt on taking up his command in November 1779.[33] Now his creditors could be paid in full. Indeed the success at St Eustatius prompted Rodney and Vaughan to consider making the Dutch Island of Curaçao their next target. Their plans, however, were interrupted with news that de Grasse was on his way across the Atlantic heading for the Caribbean.[34]

Instead of taking immediate command himself, Rodney dispatched Hood, his second in command, with a weakened squadron to deal with de Grasse while he remained at St Eustatius with three battleships, two of which, the *Vigilant* and *Vengeance*, were to escort the convoy with his booty to England.[35] Rodney then compounded his errors by instructing Hood to keep a close blockade of Fort Royal Bay, where four French battleships were at anchor. Rodney was apparently concerned that these warships might escape and intercept the St Eustatius convoy, which was about to sail. Hood protested that such station gave him little chance of engaging the main French fleet. De Grasse only needed a following wind to sail into the safety of Fort Royal Bay, while Hood tacked on a dangerous lee shore. Hood wanted to position his squadron to the windward of Martinique, since this would allow him to converge on the French while de Grasse protected his convoy. But Rodney would have none of it, despite four letters from Hood, in which he stressed the desirability of Rodney taking command himself.[36]

The result of Rodney's capricious decisions was as Hood feared. Although Hood attempted to get to the windward of de Grasse as he approached Martinique on 29 April 1781, it proved impossible. Both the French battleships and transports got safely inside Fort Royal Bay. Hood subsequently formed a line outside the anchorage but de Grasse refused to engage, despite his superiority of 23 battleships to Hood's 18. He had more important tasks than risking a battle with the British navy at this point.[37] Hood despairingly concluded: "Never was a squadron more un-meaningfully stationed, and what Sir George Rodney's motive for it could be I cannot conceive."[38] Rodney had squandered an opportunity to inflict serious damage on the French navy and army in the West Indies. Had that been achieved, the subsequent British inferiority at Yorktown might have been avoided.

The arrival of de Grasse meant that the French could now take the initiative until the onset of the hurricane season. This they duly did by capturing the island of Tobago in early June. Rodney appeared off the island on 5 June the day after it surrendered. However, he had only 20 capital ships to de Grasse's 24 and decided not to fight, despite having the wind in his favor, citing the dangerous navigation as the reason for his caution.[39] But he promised Sandwich that he would seize the first opportunity to engage de Grasse, recognizing that "the fate of the war may depend upon the event."[40]

The approach of the hurricane season meant that both commanders now had to prepare the various trade convoys and make provision for the future dispositions of their fleet. Rodney decided on 9 July 1781 to send three of his battleships the *Sandwich*, *Torbay*, and *Prince William* with a convoy to Jamaica, while he returned on health grounds to England in his flagship the *Gibraltar*. Another two battleships, the *Panther* and *Triumph*, were to convoy the Leeward Island trade to England, leaving 14 battleships to accompany Hood to the safer waters of North America. Admiral Graves, who had temporarily succeeded Arbuthnot, currently had seven battleships at New York with another three coming from England with Digby. This meant that the North American fleet would have 24 battleships, seemingly sufficient for any likely requirements.[41] Rodney did subsequently suggest to Parker that "as the enemy have a very great naval force in North America," he should dispatch "the *Torbay* and *Prince William*" and "every line of battleship you can possibly spare" to that station.[42] But he did not consider the situation sufficiently serious to travel home in a frigate to release the 80-gun *Gibraltar*. Indeed in a dispatch to Arbuthnot on 13 August, Rodney reiterated his earlier views that de Grasse had left the Caribbean with the French trade fleets, sending perhaps just

12 of his 26 ships of the line northwards, though he had no specific information on this point, not having detached any frigates for that service. Rodney still believed the real threat to Britain lay in the Caribbean, it being "certain that the Enemy intend to make an early and vigorous campaign in the West Indies, after the Hurricane months." The movement of their fleet to American waters was simply a holding operation, like his visit the previous year.[43]

No one queried these arrangements. Parker in Jamaica had no doubt that "we shall be at least a match for the French."[44] The assumption was that de Grasse would similarly detach some of his capital ships for convoy duty and necessary repairs. In this Rodney and Parker were initially correct, since de Grasse's orders merely required him to liaise with the Spanish before sending part of his squadron to North America. De Grasse accordingly left Martinique on 5 July with his whole fleet of 26 ships and 200 merchantmen for Cape Français. Here he met Galvez, who was now the senior Spanish military officer in the region, following his successful capture of Pensacola that May. Galvez recognized that no further operations would be possible during the hurricane season, an opinion with which Solano agreed. He accordingly urged de Grasse to sail with his whole force (including three battleships which had helped the Spanish at Pensacola) in order to seek out and destroy the British fleet in North America. He should also take with him the French troops under General St Simon that were currently unemployed on St Domingue. De Grasse could then return to the Caribbean in mid-October to join Galvez for an assault on Jamaica, thus completing the destruction of British power in the western world.[45] When the French Governor of St Domingue expressed concern about the island's defenseless state on the departure of St Simon's troops, Solano offered to provide naval cover until de Grasse returned.[46] The authorities in Havana also agreed to help raise 1,250,000 livres which Rochambeau's army needed to take the field.[47]

Galvez's generosity, combined with the flexibility of Castries' original orders, emboldened de Grasse to accept the proposal. Consequently when he sailed from Cape Français on 5 August 1781 he had not only 29 battleships but 3,500 troops with artillery under St Simon.[48] The scene was thus set for the decisive engagement of the war.

Cornwallis ensnared

Clinton's order of 11 June 1781 to Cornwallis to return six regiments necessarily changed the British campaign in Virginia from an offensive to a defensive one. After establishing himself at Yorktown, Cornwallis was accordingly to limit himself to "desultory" raids against the rebel communications and magazines, until reinforcements from Europe made a more expansive mode of warfare possible.[49]

Cornwallis was not enamored of Clinton's proposals, repeating his view "that until Virginia was to a degree subjected we could not reduce North Carolina, or have any certain hold of the backcountry of South Carolina." However, he would embark the six regiments as ordered and with the rest of his army search for a suitable base, though he was doubtful about York "in that it far exceeds our power consistent with your plans to make safe defensive posts there and at Gloucester." He had still to inspect Portsmouth, but suggested any post in the Chesapeake "will always be exposed to a sudden French attack, and which experience has now shown makes no diversion in favor of the southern army." Cornwallis accordingly requested permission to return to South Carolina where Rawdon's health was giving concern. Cornwallis had come to America to be useful to his country, and did not think he could "render any service in a defensive situation" in Virginia. However he would remain in command until he heard from Clinton.[50]

While awaiting Clinton's reply, Cornwallis continued his search for a base, looking first at Yorktown before opting for Portsmouth on the Elizabeth River. His march from Williamsburg on 4 July required a crossing of the James River, during which he attempted to surprise Lafayette still following in his wake. Cornwallis anticipated that Lafayette would attack his rearguard thinking it was no longer supported by the main body. Lafayette accepted the bait at Green Spring on 6 July 1781 and almost lost part of his corps when Cornwallis launched an unexpected counter-attack. Fortunately a resolute stand by Wayne's brigade and approaching nightfall enabled the Patriots to disengage.[51] Cornwallis then resumed his march to Portsmouth. However, he remained skeptical about his mission, repeating to Clinton on 8 July 1781 that keeping a post in the lower Chesapeake was pointless, since it "cannot have the smallest influence on the War in Carolina" and was "for ever liable to become a prey to a foreign enemy with a temporary superiority at sea."[52]

But Clinton was more than ever resolved on establishing a naval base in Virginia, following a conference with Graves. The navy had for some time been dissatisfied with New York as a port, following the extension of the war to the West Indies and the employment of large three-deck battleships of 90 guns and more. As Graves pointed out, these vessels and even some two-deck 74's could not clear the entrance to New York Harbor without damaging their hulls. Another problem was the danger posed by ice in the river.[53] Clinton accordingly informed Cornwallis on 11 July: "We are both of opinion that it is absolutely necessary we should hold a station in Chesapeake for ships of the line as well as frigates." Graves believed that Old Point Comfort would be the best place, covering as it did the anchorage at Hampton Road. Cornwallis was accordingly to fortify this post. Then Clinton added: "If it be your lordships opinion that Old Point Comfort cannot be held without having possession of York . . . and that the whole cannot be done with less than 7,000 men, you are at full liberty to detain all the troops now in the Chesapeake."[54] Clinton had recovered from his fears for New York, following reassurances about Rodney's strength. As to Cornwallis's request to return to South Carolina, this would have to wait until the current operations were completed.[55]

Cornwallis expressed surprise on receiving these instructions with their "extreme earnestness" about securing "a harbor for ships of the line." There had been no such requirement in the previous orders to Philips. Ships of the line were in any case unnecessary for operations in the Chesapeake. Nevertheless, he had ordered his engineer to inspect Old Point Comfort and visited the site himself with the ships' captains. All agreed it was not a suitable anchorage. Clinton had also mentioned the fortification of Yorktown as an additional protection for the fleet. Cornwallis was not enamored of that idea either, having already considered it while at Williamsburg. Firstly, it would require "a great deal of time and labor to fortify York and Gloucester," both of which were "necessary to secure a harbor for vessels of any burden." But he had other objections also. Even after being fortified, the posts would be dangerously exposed, since both were "accessible to the whole force of this province." Another objection was the lack of any high ground for commanding the surrounding countryside. Nevertheless, he would "take measures with as much dispatch as possible to seize and fortify York and Gloucester, being the only harbor in which we can hope to be able to give effectual protection to line of battle ships."[56] It was to prove a fateful requirement.

On 2 August the army began entrenching itself on the Gloucester side of the York River, while O'Hara evacuated the remaining forces at Portsmouth.[57] Cornwallis had almost 6,000 men fit for duty, with another 1,200 sick and 300 wounded. The warships and transports also had 1,500 sailors and marines, making a grand total of 9,000 men.[58] Even so, constructing the ditches, fascines, and covered ways to withstand a siege for such a large area was a thing of time. By 22 August the works at Gloucester were reasonably advanced, but Cornwallis calculated that another six weeks would "be required to put the intended works" at Yorktown "into a tolerable state of defense." Even then they would not be strong.[59] His lack of confidence in the scheme was reflected in his letter of 20 August 1781 strongly urging Clinton to direct the Chesapeake operations in person. Otherwise Cornwallis must have explicit instructions "on all points that will admit of them."[60]

Until now Washington and Rochambeau had been distant if bemused spectators of the events in Virginia, which were equally baffling to friends of the British cause. As William Franklin the former governor of New Jersey commented: "Every measure of Sir Henry Clinton since he came to the command has been so far beyond the view of vulgar capacity" as to prevent anyone from understanding "his deep laid schemes."[61] The focus of the allies remained on New York, though Washington confessed to Knox at the end of June that he was "more and more dubious" about carrying "into execution the operation which we have in contemplation," especially as Clinton was reported to have received a troop reinforcement from Europe.[62] Early in July he proposed to Rochambeau a joint attack on the northern tip of Manhattan, but soon found the British works too strong without naval support.[63]

Washington was once again reduced to stumbling on, despite constant appeals to Congress and the states for action. Recruits came in so slowly that he despaired of ever having sufficient men. As it was, his numbers were sustained only by the widespread enlistment of northern African Americans.[64] He was also angry about living from hand to mouth for provisions, telling Governor Trumbull of Connecticut that unless the states made more strenuous exertions, the army would have to disband. The situation was doubly frustrating because the country was full of supplies. But without money they were beyond the reach of the army.[65] Another frustration was the lack of any definite plan. Until de Grasse arrived little could be done, since Barras was too weak to force New York harbor, where the British had six ships of the line, two 50-gun vessels and eight frigates. The same was true of the allied army, which comprised 4,400 French but fewer than 3,500 Continentals, once provision had been made for the Highland forts and frontier garrisons.[66] This was far short of what was required.

The situation was accordingly not promising when Washington and Rochambeau conferred together on 19 July. Both men recognized that de Grasse might be too late to do anything effective or might arrive without troops. If that happened the only alternative was for the two commanders to ferry their men to the Chesapeake, "should the enemy still keep a force" in Virginia, which was by no means certain.[67] However, as Washington wrote to de Grasse on 21 July: "I flatter myself the glory of destroying the British squadron at New York is reserved for the King's fleet under your command and that of the land force" gathered thereabouts. The plan agreed at Wethersfield was still the best option.[68] Nevertheless, its implementation seemed ever less likely, as Washington informed Thomas McKean, the incoming president of Congress, at the beginning of August 1781. The lack of money and manpower meant that many of the troops had to be deployed as boatmen, teamsters, and artificers. Bread was also again lacking.[69] Even if an opportunity for military action did arise, the army would not be able to take advantage of it with so many short-term enlistments and poorly trained men. The campaign was seemingly wasting away as in previous years, despite the alliance with France.[70]

Then on 14 August 1781 news arrived that de Grasse had left the West Indies for the Chesapeake, with 29 ships of the line and "a considerable land force" under St Simon.[71] This was larger than anyone had anticipated. The downside was that his stay would be short, since his fleet would be needed in the West Indies by early November to complete the conquest of Britain's remaining islands in the lesser Antilles before assisting a Spanish attack on Jamaica. De Grasse had chosen the Chesapeake because Rochambeau, Washington, Luzerne, and Barras had all indicated that this was the place most likely "to effect the good which you propose."[72] De Grasse's decision to go to the Chesapeake, of course, was not entirely unexpected, following the allied discussions on 19 July 1781. Washington had already asked Robert Morris if shipping would be available to carry the army from Philadelphia or Baltimore. Washington therefore quickly if reluctantly accepted de Grasse's proposal to strike the British in the Chesapeake.[73] The siege of New York was going nowhere and might be unsuccessful even with de Grasse. This plan ensured that the allies would have the necessary superiority by land and sea, if their commanders moved quickly before Cornwallis consolidated his position or retreated into North Carolina.[74]

Initially Washington proposed to entrust the command of the Patriot force of 2,000 Continentals to General Alexander McDougall, while he remained with the rest of the army to guard the Highlands and threaten New York. But within two days Washington had decided that the Chesapeake would be the decisive scene of action and that he should take charge there. He accordingly placed General Heath in command of the New England regiments in the Highlands while the rest prepared for the long march south.[75] Secrecy was essential, especially when the allies began their journey on 21 August with a crossing of the Hudson River. Initially Washington made it appear that the allied forces were preparing an assault on New York via Staten Island. However by the end of August the troops were well on their way to Philadelphia, though Washington remained "distressed beyond expression" in case de Grasse failed to make the rendezvous.[76]

In the event Washington's worries were needless, for de Grasse anchored on 31 August inside the Capes of Virginia. He had taken longer to reach his destination, because of his decision to use the more tortuous Old Bahama Channel on leaving Santo Domingo to avoid alerting the British of his approach. During the next few days he ferried St Simon's 3,300 men up the James River to Williamsburg where Lafayette was stationed to prevent Cornwallis escaping from the Jamestown peninsula.[77] Washington meanwhile wrestled with the logistics of moving the northern forces to their new location 400 miles away. Most important was the need for French naval assistance in ferrying the allied forces down the Chesapeake to the Hampton Roads. It was with this in mind that he had written to de Grasse on 17 August requesting help.[78] As a result Washington and Rochambeau were able to embark from the Head of Elk with minimal delay in the second week of September. By 26 September the entire allied army was on the Jamestown Peninsula near Williamsburg, comprising approximately 7,500 French regulars, 4,500 Continentals and 3,000 Virginia militia. In close support was de Grasse with 20,000 sailors and marines. Cornwallis, with some 7,000 troops and marines, was now trapped with a superior army in front and an enemy fleet behind.[79]

Clinton initially failed to appreciate the significance of Washington's crossing of the Hudson. As late as 27 August he speculated to Cornwallis: "It is possible he means for the present to suspend his offensive operations against this post and to take a defensive station at the old post of Morristown, from whence he may detach to the southward." Alternatively Washington's maneuver might "only be a feint and that they may return to their former position, which they will certainly do if de Grasse arrives." Clinton's attention in any case was focused on Rhode Island, where Barras's seven battleships provided a tempting target."[80]

Clinton's composure in consequence was not disturbed when letters arrived from Hood, warning him that de Grasse was on his way. The reason for his confidence was Hood's assertion that his fleet was "equal fully to defeat any designs of the enemy, let De Grasse bring or send what number of ships he might in aid of Barras."[81] Nor did Hood change these views when he appeared on 28 August with 14 ships of the line. Hood was unsure of the French number but believed it was no more than 12 battleships. In addition he had seen no sign of de Grasse either in the Chesapeake or

Delaware Bay where he had briefly called. Hood's only concern was that if Barras joined de Grasse, the French fleet might be too strong to attack. He told Clinton and Graves accordingly: "whether you attend the army to Rhode Island or seek the enemy at sea, you have no time to lose."[82]

Consequently the alarm still failed to register in New York, where Clinton continued his discussions with Graves for an attack on Rhode Island. Even the news on 30 August that Barras had sailed from Newport in a southerly direction caused no undue concern. The British vessels in New York were all copper-bottomed, making it likely that they would catch Barras before he reached the Chesapeake. In any case there was no reason to believe that the fleet of Hood and Graves could not deal with the combined forces of the French, even though two of Graves's ships of the line, the *Robust* and *Prudent*, and two 50-gun vessels had yet to complete their refitting.[83] As for Washington his movements still indicated an attack on New York, at least until 2 September when his advanced guard crossed the Delaware River into Pennsylvania.

Only now did Clinton advise Cornwallis that Washington and Rochambeau might be moving against him. If this proved the case, Clinton would "either endeavor to reinforce the army under your command," or make a diversion in his favor. The strength of the fleet with Graves and Hood, which had left New York on 31 August, made him confident that Cornwallis would "have little to apprehend from that of the French." In the meantime, Clinton ordered Arnold with 1,500 men on a "small expedition" to New London, "to give the enemy every annoyance."[84]

The true gravity of the situation emerged only when the British fleet arrived off the Chesapeake on 5 September to find de Grasse inside with 24 ships of the line while another three blockaded the York River. Graves and Hood had just 19.[85] They would have been even more shocked had they realized that Barras had yet to appear. Clinton himself began to be enlightened only on 7 September with the receipt of letters from Cornwallis that de Grasse had arrived with 40 battleships and frigates, plus a substantial body of troops.[86] Even then he believed the situation was redeemable, once the navy had cleared the way for Clinton's reinforcements. As he informed Germain on 12 September: "His lordship cannot be easily forced in such a post as York is represented to be ... notwithstanding the numerous army that may be collected against him."[87]

Graves himself recognized that he had little alternative but to attempt a battle with the French despite his inferiority, since it was clear that Cornwallis could not otherwise be relieved. De Grasse decided to accept the challenge to keep the Chesapeake open for Barras. But he still intended to fight defensively in accordance with French naval doctrine when the two fleets engaged on 5 September 1781, recognizing that trapping the British army in Virginia was strategically more important than a victory over the Royal Navy. Hood subsequently believed that Graves could have won the engagement if he had attacked the French fleet as it emerged from Chesapeake Bay.[88] But this would have meant abandoning the traditional order of battle as laid down in the Fighting Instructions.

Graves accordingly ordered his ships to form their line. However, a number in the rear division under Hood were slow to do so because of their decrepit state, which resulted in a gap between them and the rest of the fleet.[89] Attempts by Graves to rectify the situation only increased the confusion, especially when he simultaneously signaled the fleet to remain in line while engaging at close quarters. The French meanwhile constantly tacked before the wind, while firing on the British rigging. Towards evening Graves finally desisted, since his ships in the center and van were too badly damaged to continue the encounter.[90]

For the next few days the two fleets drifted within sight of each other, carrying out repairs in readiness for another battle. However, the decision to engage was de Grasse's since his ships were in better condition.[91] On 9 September de Grasse took advantage of the weather to set sail in a southeasterly direction, prompting Hood to suggest that the British occupy the French anchorage in Lynnhaven Bay. This would then force de Grasse to fight his way back into the Chesapeake. But he made this proposal unaware that Barras had still to arrive.[92] In any case de Grasse regained his anchorage on 12 September just as Barras appeared. It was only at this point that the British learnt the real strength of the French fleet, following the dispatch of some frigates for intelligence. There was now no chance of forcing an entry into the Chesapeake to relieve Cornwallis. Equally clear was the shattered condition of the British fleet, epitomized by the need to destroy the 74 gun *Terrible*. Graves accordingly returned on 13 September to New York for repairs and reinforcements.[93]

Cornwallis's initial reaction on the appearance of de Grasse was to offer Lafayette and St Simon battle. However on 5 September he heard that a British fleet had arrived promising relief. He accordingly decided to concentrate on his defenses so that the army was ready for action once it had been reinforced. Several days passed before he learnt the outcome of the naval battle and that Washington and Rochambeau were advancing down the Chesapeake. This left Cornwallis with one final opportunity of breaking out. He accordingly ordered Tarleton to reconnoiter once more the position of Lafayette and St Simon.[94] The odds however were not promising. The enemy would have at least 8,000 men to his own 5,000 fit for duty. Moreover fighting the battle was only the start of his difficulties, since he would then have to march 400 miles through hostile territory to Camden, without dependable supplies in the face of a superior enemy.

Any inclination to attempt this was countered by the arrival on 14 September of word from Clinton that a naval reinforcement under Admiral Digby was expected from Britain.[95] Relief from his predicament might yet occur. He accordingly wrote to Clinton on 16 September that "as you say Admiral Digby is hourly expected, and promise every exertion to assist me, I do not think myself justifiable in putting the fate of the war on so desperate an attempt." He had six weeks' provision. But one thing was clear: diversionary expeditions would not work: only "by coming directly to this place" could Clinton hope to do anything effective. The following day he repeated his warning: "If you cannot relieve me very soon, you must be prepared to hear the worst."[96]

At Williamsburg, Washington, Rochambeau, and St Simon continued to assemble their forces, though Washington was momentarily alarmed when de Grasse proposed to sail after the British fleet. He feared that this might allow Graves to slip in reinforcements while de Grasse was absent. Fortunately, Washington prevailed on the French admiral to remain in Chesapeake Bay to provide the necessary firepower and logistical support for a successful siege.[97] The need for urgency was increased by reports that a naval force of ten battleships had arrived at New York under Digby, thus making the relief of Cornwallis more plausible. Washington's best hope of success, therefore, was by battering Cornwallis into submission rather than starving him out, which would require more time.[98] The allied armies accordingly advanced briskly on 28 September on Yorktown. Here the French positioned themselves on the left while the Patriots occupied the eastern side of the allied line, opposite the British left. Two days later they began digging their first trenches, 1,100 yards from the British entrenchments.[99]

Cornwallis originally planned to have an outer defense line linked by several large redoubts, and an inner line of entrenchments and small redoubts. However Cornwallis had insufficient time to complete the outer ring, which would have given his army more space and protection from the cannon of a besieging army. Accordingly he decided to abandon his outer line except for two redoubts, number nine and number ten, on the eastern side. The disadvantage was that the inner entrenchments were a mere 400 yards from the shore, leaving his forces in a cramped condition. He was prompted to do this by yet another letter from Clinton promising that a second more powerful relief force would leave New York on 5 October, with 5,000 troops on board the ships of war.[100] By conserving his forces Cornwallis would be better able to take the offensive should relief arrive. Hence he made no further attempts to break out or offer battle. This inactivity puzzled Washington, leading him to conclude: "he either has not the means of defense, or he intends to reserve himself until we approach very near him."[101]

Back in New York the return of the fleet and the arrival of Cornwallis's letter of 17 September finally revealed to Clinton the true gravity of the situation, though he still interpreted "the worst" to mean that Cornwallis would have to retreat from Yorktown. In any event he believed that Cornwallis should have sufficient provision to survive until the end of October. This would allow the fleet to be repaired, Admiral Digby to arrive, and an effective sea-borne rescue organized. In reality hope of the latter had all but disappeared. Although several more battleships appeared, including the *Torbay* and *Prince William* from Jamaica and Digby with his three ships from England, Graves still only had 25 such vessels to face the 36 now with de Grasse and Barras. In addition, the damage incurred in the first encounter was more extensive than initially thought.[102] Clinton's deadline of 5 October accordingly passed. Not until the 19 October were Graves and Hood finally ready to set off again for the Chesapeake.[103]

In the interim Clinton and the senior officers discussed various schemes about how the situation could be remedied, resulting in some sharp exchanges between the two services. At one point Clinton even considered marching overland to attack Philadelphia independently of the navy, though he lacked the logistical support for such an endeavor.[104] Eventually Clinton and Graves agreed that the fleet should carry 7,000 troops on the decks of the battleships and force its way past the blocking French squadron. After this the troops would land in the York River to join Cornwallis for a decisive battle.[105] Quite how the fleet would get past the vastly superior French force was not addressed, nor was proper consideration given to the likelihood of the enemy adopting a defensive formation at the entrance to the Chesapeake, which would allow them to rake the approaching British ships one at a time. Equally fanciful was the lack of consideration as to how the troops were to be fed and supplied once they had joined Cornwallis. The scheme was eloquent testimony to the bankruptcy and desperation of the British commanders.[106]

By now Washington and Rochambeau had begun the process of an orthodox siege, first digging a parallel trench before making a diagonal one leading to the second parallel. In this work the French were the masters, as Washington readily acknowledged, familiar as they were with the principles of the great seventeenth-century engineer Vauban. The first parallel was completed on 6 October some 600 yards from the British lines, allowing the artillery to open fire at 3 pm on 9 October.[107] This continued "without intermission with about 40 pieces of cannon (mostly heavy), and sixteen mortars from eight to sixteen inches." After two days, Cornwallis reported, "we have lost about seventy men, and many of our works are considerably damaged." Several of the navy's ships in the York River were also on fire. On such "disadvantageous ground, against so powerful an attack," the defenders could not "hope to make a long resistance."[108]

The intensity of the bombardment allowed the allies on the night of 11 October to begin their second parallel 300 yards from the British lines, making the two redoubts protecting the British left vulnerable to assault. On the night of 14 October both positions were surprised, number nine being captured by the French and number ten by the Patriots. These were then incorporated into the allied second parallel and turned against the British. As Cornwallis informed Clinton the next day; "We dare not show a gun to their old batteries, and I expect that their new ones will open tomorrow morning . . . The safety of the place is, therefore, so precarious that I cannot recommend that the fleet and army run great risk in endeavoring to save us."[109] However, to give Clinton's relief force more time, Cornwallis ordered a sortie of 350 men against two of the most forward enemy batteries. Both positions were stormed just before daybreak on 16 October and the cannon spiked with broken bayonets. But the work was done hurriedly and the guns were soon in action again.[110]

One faint hope remained, an escape across the York River for a march to the sea or into North Carolina. But after ferrying one division over the river the weather worsened and forced an abandonment of the operation. Cornwallis now recognized that further resistance was useless, since he had no serviceable cannon, his works were ruined, and the French fleet was threatening his communication with Gloucester. "Under these circumstances I thought it would have been wanton and inhuman in the last degree to sacrifice the lives of this small body of gallant soldiers—who had ever behaved with so much fidelity and courage—by exposing them to an assault which, from the numbers and precautions of the enemy, could not fail to succeed."[111] On the afternoon of 17 October he sent an officer to discuss surrender terms.

Initially Cornwallis hoped that his army might be repatriated to Europe and eligible for exchange with persons of similar rank.[112] But Washington would have none of this. The British must accept the same terms as they had imposed on Lincoln at Charleston, becoming prisoners of war until peace was concluded.[113] Discussion then turned to the status of the Loyalists serving with the British. Cornwallis endeavored to insert a clause that "natives or inhabitants of different parts of this country ... are not to be punished on account of having joined the British army." Washington sternly insisted that the fate of the Loyalists was a matter for the civil courts. However, he granted one concession: the sloop, *Bonetta*, might carry dispatches to Clinton without being searched, thereby allowing a few leading Loyalists to escape.[114]

Early on the afternoon of 19 October the British army marched out to surrender. Cornwallis was not among their number, pleading sickness. The ceremony was therefore performed on the British side by O'Hara. But when O'Hara attempted to surrender his sword to Rochambeau, the Frenchman politely directed him to Washington, who in turn pointed to Lincoln, his second in command.[115] After this the British troops and seamen, totaling almost 8,000 men, laid down their weapons and returned to the town until they could be sent into the interior. Despite the bitterness of the conflict, Washington hosted the customary dinner for the senior officers of the three armies, with O'Hara deputizing for Cornwallis. Washington noted privately how the British general appeared "very social and easy." But as the evening progressed it was the British and French who appeared most relaxed, given their social backgrounds and ability to converse, leaving the American Patriots awkward outsiders.[116]

But there was no time to relax. The British fleet might still reappear. Most pressing was the need to secure the spoils of the siege which included seven brass field guns, 140 iron cannon, and 7,320 muskets.[117] Many slaves were also within the British lines attempting to secure their freedom by pretending to be freemen. All were now to be secured: those unable to prove their claims were to be repatriated to their owners.[118] The precautions proved fully justified, for five days after the surrender, the fleet of Graves and Hood appeared off the Capes of Virginia, accompanied by Clinton with 5,000 troops. Escapees from Yorktown soon confirmed Cornwallis's surrender. After a few days at the Bay's entrance, Graves determined to head back with his 25 battleships to New York for fear of a second disaster.[119]

In his general orders for 20 October Washington fulsomely acknowledged the part played by his allies. He well knew that the victory at Yorktown would not have happened without the French army and fleet. Yorktown was essentially a French victory, since four out of five of those engaged were soldiers and sailors of Louis XVI. Even if the 22,000 seamen on de Grasse's fleet are discounted, which is a nonsensical method of assessing the outcome, the French still provided almost twice as many regular soldiers as the Patriots. Nor was this the limit of foreign help, as Washington acknowledged, when mentioning Lafayette, Steuben, and Duportail, the chief engineer. The Patriot contribution, in contrast, had been modest, a fact rarely admitted by American historians, though clearly recognized by Washington. The only Patriots mentioned by him were Lincoln and Knox— the latter for his handling of the artillery. Otherwise he restricted his comments to a commendation of the Virginia militia and an order pardoning "those men belonging to the army who may now be in confinement." He concluded by urging those Patriots not on duty next day to attend divine service to give thanks for "the astonishing interpositions of Providence."[120]

Washington hoped that the success at Yorktown would allow the allies to strike at Charleston. At the very least de Grasse might assist in the capture of Wilmington. He accordingly visited the French admiral on 21 October to put these suggestions to him, thanking him simultaneously for all that he had done.[121] De Grasse initially agreed to help at Wilmington but two days later withdrew his offer, believing it incompatible with his orders to return to the West Indies once the hurricane season was over. Washington therefore had to be satisfied with a vague promise of cooperation against New York or Charleston in 1782.[122] In the interim he had to determine how best to employ the Continental troops during the winter months. Washington eventually decided to send the Pennsylvania, Virginia, and Maryland regiments southwards to join Greene, while the other units returned to winter quarters in New Jersey and the Highland forts.[123] Rochambeau in contrast was to remain at Yorktown until the allies decided whether New York or Charleston was to be the next objective.[124]

It had been an impressive performance by the allies, showing what could be achieved through proper coordination. But as so often, chance had played a huge part in the eventual outcome. Had Galvez decided to undertake immediately further military operations in the Caribbean, the French naval and military presence in North America would have been much smaller and far less decisive. Galvez's readiness to facilitate de Grasse's departure for North America showed remarkable strategic vision, for without the whole French fleet and the troops of St Simon, the Royal Navy was likely to have gained command of the Chesapeake, allowing Cornwallis either to escape or join Clinton for a decisive battle on British terms.

Credit must also be given to de Grasse for choosing the Chesapeake as his objective. Had he gone to New York, as Washington wanted, the allies would have had to deal with an army almost twice as large as that of

Cornwallis, protected by defenses that had been progressively strengthened over five years. The makeshift naval base at Yorktown offered a much more vulnerable target. As it was, de Grasse was able to keep the trap closed on Cornwallis's army, while providing additional men, cannon, and ammunition for the besieging army. Here French expertise in siege warfare was of inestimable value.

Finally, of course there was the contribution of Washington. Yorktown was a reward for all his years of endeavor. He had patiently waited for such a moment, recognizing that a premature move on his part could destroy the Revolutionary cause. Generalship, however, is not solely or even mainly about heroic actions or sudden inspired decisions. The instruments of war first had to be fashioned in the shape of officers, men, and supply services. This required him to act not only as a soldier but as a statesman, politician, and diplomat too as he endeavored to work with the French while coordinating the efforts of Congress and the states. It had been a truly remarkable achievement.[125]

For the British, Yorktown was an unimaginable disaster. As one officer commented at the end of the siege: "Who would have thought a hundred years ago that out of this multitude of rabble would arise a people who could defy kings."[126] But although the British had been fairly beaten by a superior force, this did not prevent recriminations for what had happened. Initially Clinton blamed the ministry for not sending enough ships and troops. He told Germain on 29 October how everyone had been surprised at de Grasse's arrival with 28 ships of the line compared to Hood's 14. "To this inferiority then I may with confidence assert, and to that alone, is our present misfortunate to be imputed."[127] But after receiving Cornwallis's formal report, Clinton began to feel that he too should bear some responsibility for misconstruing his directions regarding a base at Yorktown. He also criticized Cornwallis subsequently for advancing into Virginia without having first subdued the Carolinas.[128]

Cornwallis's response was generally restrained, though he rightly suggested that the disaster was the result of Clinton's insistence on establishing a naval base in the Chesapeake. As he commented in his official account to Clinton on 20 October, a successful defense had been impossible since Yorktown was little more than "an entrenched camp." The site was "in general so disadvantageous that nothing but the necessity of fortifying it as a post to protect the navy could have induced any person to erect works upon it."[129]

In reality Yorktown was a collective failure by the British, reflecting their unrealistic expectations about the war and resources required to win it. However, certain individuals contributed significantly to the outcome. Rodney's misuse of his resources and erratic conduct resulted in several missed opportunities to defeat de Grasse long before his arrival in the Chesapeake.[130] Germain once again failed to give his generals a coherent strategy and must also take some of the blame for the belief that a naval base was necessary in Virginia. However, Clinton must take the primary responsibility for the decision to provide such an elaborate facility, which left Cornwallis's army in a highly vulnerable position. Clinton had previously acknowledged that success in 1781 would "depend in great measure on naval maneuvers and arrangements."[131] Unfortunately he was only thinking of British naval superiority, though he had several times experienced the narrow margin on which the Royal Navy operated in American waters after France entered the war. For him there can be little excuse.

Notes and references

1. Germain to Clinton, 3 January 1781, DDAR/XX, 29–30.
2. Clinton to Arnold, 14 December 1780, DDAR/XVIII, 256.
3. Arnold to Clinton, 21 January 1781, DDAR/XX, 40–43. Steuben to Greene, 8 January 1781, NGP/7, 76–79.
4. Washington to Lafayette, 20 February 1781, WGW/21, 253–55.
5. Washington to Benjamin Harrison, 27 March 1781, WGW/21, 380–82.
6. Clinton to Arbuthnot, 28 February 1781, CAR, 489–90.
7. Clinton to Philips, 10 March 1781, DDAR/XX, 84–85.
8. Washington to Detouches, 22 February 1781, WGW/21, 278.
9. Arbuthnot to Sandwich, 30 March 1781, Sandwich/4, 166–70.
10. Steuben to Greene, 16 March 1781, NGP/7, 443–44.
11. Clinton to Germain, 23 April 1781, DDAR/XX, 113–15. Petition of the Associated Loyalists, 14 October 1780, DDAR/XVIII, 187–89.
12. Washington to Harrison, 27 March 1781, WGW/21, 380–83.
13. Washington to Wayne, 8 April 1781, WGW/21, 433–34. Washington to Lafayette, 11 April 1781, WGW/21, 444–46.
14. Lafayette to Greene, 17 April 1781, NGP/8, 107.
15. Arnold to Clinton, 12 May 1781, Petersburg, DDAR/XX, 142–45.
16. Cornwallis to Clinton, 20 May 1781, Ross/1, 99. Ibid., 26 May 1781, 100–101.

17 Cornwallis to Clinton, 26 May 1781, CAR, 522–23.

18 Lafayette to Greene, 18 June 1781, NGP/8, 411.

19 Lafayette to Greene, 27 June 1781, NGP/8, 468–69. Cornwallis to Clinton, 30 June 1781, Ross/1, 103–5.

20 Conference with Rochambeau, 23 May 1781, WGW/22, 105–7.

21 Washington to Sullivan, 29 May 1781, WGW/22, 131–32. Washington to Greene, 1 June 1781, NGP/8, 336–37.

22 Washington to the Governors of New England, 24 May 1781, WGW/22, 109–11.

23 Washington to Reed, 24 June 1781, WGW/22, 257–58. Washington to Luzerne, 23 May 1781, WGW/22, 103–4.

24 Strength of the Army, 22 May 1781, WGW/22, 102–3. Washington to Rochambeau, 2 June 1781, WGW/22, 154–55.

25 Washington to Luzerne, 13 June 1781, WGW/22, 205–6.

26 Rochambeau to Washington, 12 June 1781, WGW/22, 206. Washington to Rochambeau, 13 June 1781, WGW/22, 207.

27 Clinton to Cornwallis, 29 May 1781, CAR, 523–25.

28 Clinton to Cornwallis, 8, 11 June 1781, CAR, 528–31. Germain to Clinton, 4 April 1781, DDAR/XX, 99.

29 Clinton to Rodney, 28 June 1781, CAR, 532–33.

30 David Syrett, *The Royal Navy in American Waters, 1775–1783* (Aldershot, 1989), 179.

31 Ships of the Line in North America and the West Indies from January to October 1781, Sandwich/4, 126–27. Jonathan Dull, *The French Navy and American Independence: A Study of Arms and Diplomacy, 1774–1787* (Princeton, 1975), 370–71.

32 Rodney to Sandwich, 7 February 1781, Sandwich/4, 148.

33 Syrett, *Royal Navy in European Waters*, 81–83.

34 Rodney to Sandwich, 27 April 1781, Sandwich/4, 152–53.

35 Despite Rodney's precautions, the convoy was intercepted by La Motte Piquet as it approached the Channel, resulting in the capture of most ships; Piers Mackesy, *The War for America, 1775–1783* (Cambridge, Mass., 1964), 392–93.

36 Hood to Sandwich, 4 May 1781, Sandwich/4, 158–60.

37 Dull, *French Navy*, 238. M. Le Comte de Lapeyrouse Bonfils, *Histoire de la Marine Française*, 3 vols. (Paris, 1845), III, 193–95.

38 Hood to Sandwich, 4 May 1781, Sandwich/4, 156.
39 D. Hannay, ed., *Letters Written by Sir Samuel Hood in 1781–1783* (Navy Records Society, 1895), 18–20. Mackesy, *War for America*, 418–19.
40 Rodney to Sandwich, 29 June 1781, Sandwich/4, 162–64.
41 Ships of the Line in North America and West Indies, January to October 1781, Sandwich/4, 126–27.
42 Rodney to Parker, 30 July 1781, Fortescue/5, 259.
43 Rodney to Arbuthnot, 13 August 1781, Fortescue/5, 264–65.
44 Parker to Sandwich, 1 September 1781, Sandwich/4, 165–66.
45 Dull, *French Navy*, 243–44. Henri Doniol, *Histoire de la participation de la France à l'établissement des États-Unis d'Amérique: Correspondence diplomatique et documents*, 5 vols. (Paris, 1886–92), vol. 4, 650–61.
46 Bonfils, *Marine Française*, III, 202–3.
47 Arnold Whitridge, *Rochambeau: America's Neglected Founding Father* (New York, 1965), 171.
48 Dull, *French Navy*, 245–46.
49 Clinton to Cornwallis, 11 June 1781, DDAR/XX, 157–59
50 Cornwallis to Clinton, 30 June 1781, DDAR/XX, 166–68.
51 Ibid., 8 July 1781, 183–84. Lafayette to Greene, 8 July 1781, NGP/8, 507–8.
52 Cornwallis to Clinton, 8 July 1781, DDAR/XX, 183–84.
53 Graves to Sandwich, 4 July 1781, Sandwich/4, 174–75. Ibid., 20 July 1781, 176–77.
54 Clinton to Cornwallis, 11 July 1781, DDAR/XX, 184–85.
55 Clinton to Cornwallis, 15 July 1781, DDAR/XX, 189–90.
56 Cornwallis to Clinton, 27 July 1781, Ross/1, 107–9.
57 Cornwallis to Clinton, 12 August 1781, CAR, 556.
58 Abstract of Forces in Virginia with Cornwallis, 15 August 1781, CAR, 556–57.
59 Cornwallis to Clinton, 22 August 1781, CAR, 560–61. Cornwallis to Leslie, 27 August 1781, Ross/1, 117.
60 Cornwallis to Clinton, 20 August 1781, Ross/1, 113–15.
61 Quoted in Whitridge, *Rochambeau*, 160.
62 Washington to Knox, 28 June 1781, WGW/22, 272–73.
63 Washington to Rochambeau, 30 June 1781, WGW/22, 293–94. Ibid., 3 July 1781, WGW/22, 324–25.

64 Washington to Bland, 8 July 1781, WGW/22, 341. Conway, *American Independence*, 26–27.

65 Washington to Trumbull, 1 July 1781, WGW/22, 311–12. Washington to Reed, 16 July 1781, WGW/22, 390.

66 Washington to de Grasse, 21 July 1781, WGW/22, 400–402. Disposition of His Majesty's ships, 4 July 1781, DDAR/XX, 173–74.

67 Conference at Dobbs Ferry, 19 July 1781, WGW/22, 395–97.

68 Washington to de Grasse, 21 July 1781, WGW/22, 400–402.

69 Washington to McKean, 2 August 1781, WGW/22, 445–46. Washington to Morris, 2 August 1781, WGW/22, 449–50.

70 Washington to Colonel Fitzhugh, 8 August 1781, WGW/22, 480–82.

71 Washington to Lafayette, 15 August 1781, WGW/22, 501.

72 Lee Kennett, *The French Forces in America, 1780–1783* (Westport, Conn., 1977), 130. Luzerne was probably the most influential advocate for de Grasse coming to the Chesapeake, emphasizing the political dangers to the United States should the British subdue Virginia, ibid., 126.

73 Washington to Morris, 2 August 1781, WGW/22, 450–51. For Washington's continued reluctance about the Chesapeake as a proposed objective, see his Diary for 14 August 1781.

74 Washington to de Grasse, 17 August 1781, WGW/23, 7. See also Washington to Greene, 4 September 1781, WGW/23, 84–85.

75 Washington to McDougall, 19 August 1781, WGW/23, 19. Washington to Heath, 19 August, 1781, WGW/23, 20–23.

76 Washington to Lafayette, 2 September 1781, WGW/23, 77.

77 Washington to Luzerne, 5 September 1781, WGW/23, 87. Bonfils, *Marine Française*, III, 203–6.

78 Washington to de Grasse, 17 August 1781, WGW/23, 10–11.

79 Cornwallis to Clinton, 16–17 September 1781, CAR, 571.

80 Clinton to Cornwallis, 27 August 1781, CAR, 562. Clinton to Graves, 24 August 1781, CAR, 561.

81 *Clinton's Narrative*, CAR, 328.

82 William B. Willcox, *Portrait of a General: Sir Henry Clinton in the War of Independence* (New York, 1964), 421. See also Hood to Stephens, 30 August 1781, Hannay, *Letters by Sir Samuel Hood* (Navy Records Society, 1895), 26.

83 Graves to Sandwich. 14 September 1781, Sandwich/4, 181. Hood to Digby, 31 October 1781, Sandwich/4, 199.

84 Clinton to Cornwallis, 2 September 1781, CAR, 563. Clinton to Germain, 4 September 1781, DDAR/XX, 221–22.
85 Graves to Clinton, 9 September 1781, CAR, 567.
86 Cornwallis to Clinton, 2 September 1781, CAR, 563.
87 Clinton to Germain, 7 September 1781, DDAR/XX, 222–23. Clinton to Germain, 12 September 1781, DDAR/XX, 229–31.
88 Hood to Sandwich, 16 September 1781, Sandwich/4, 186–89.
89 An account of the proceedings of the fleet, 5 September 1781, Sandwich/4, 183–86.
90 Graves to Sandwich, 14 September 1781, Sandwich/4, 181–83. Syrett, *Royal Navy in American Waters*, 194–99.
91 Graves to Clinton, 9 September 1781, CAR, 567.
92 Hood to Graves, 10 September 1781, Sandwich/4, 191–92. Hood to Sandwich, 16 September 1781, Sandwich/4, 186–89.
93 Council of War, 13 September 1781, Sandwich/4, 192–93. Graves to Sandwich, 14 September 1781, Sandwich/4, 181–82.
94 Franklin and Mary Wickwire, *Cornwallis and the War of Independence* (London, 1971), 360–61.
95 Clinton to Cornwallis, 6 September 1781, CAR, 564.
96 Cornwallis to Clinton, 16–17 September 1781, CAR, 571.
97 Washington to de Grasse, 25 September 1781, WGW/23, 136–39. Washington to de Grasse, 1 October 1781, WGW/23, 160–64.
98 Washington to Greene, 28 September 1781, WGW/23, 148–51.
99 Washington to Heath, 1 October 1781, WGW/23, 156–58. Cornwallis to Clinton, 3 October 1781, CAR, 580.
100 Clinton to Cornwallis, 24 September 1781, Ross/1, 120. Wickwire, *Cornwallis*, 369–70.
101 Cornwallis to Clinton, 29 September 1781, CAR, 577. Washington to Thomas Lee, 12 October 1781, WGW/23, 209–10.
102 Graves to Clinton, 21 September 1781, CAR, 572–73.
103 George Damer to Germain, 13, 29 October 1781, HMC, Stopford–Sackville, II, 213–15.
104 Clinton to Cornwallis, 30 September 1781, CAR, 578.
105 Council of War, 10 October 1781, CAR, 580–81.
106 Syrett, *Royal Navy in American Waters*, 205–17.
107 Washington to Mckean, 12 October 1781, WGW/23, 213.

108 Cornwallis to Clinton, 11 October 1781, CAR, 581.
109 Quoted in Wickwire, *Cornwallis*, 381–82.
110 Cornwallis to Clinton, 20 October 1781, DDAR/XX, 245–46.
111 Ibid., 246–47.
112 Cornwallis to Washington, 17 October 1781, Ross/1, 514.
113 Washington to Cornwallis, 18 October 1781, Ross/1, 514–15. Ibid., WGW/23, 237–38.
114 Cornwallis to Washington, 18 October 1781, Ross/1, 515. Articles of Capitulation, 19 October 1781, Ross/1, 515–18.
115 Richard Ketchum, *Victory at Yorktown: The Campaign that Won the Revolution* (New York, 2004), 251.
116 Diary for 19 October 1781, Donald Jackson and Dorothy Twohig, eds., *The Diaries of George Washington* (Charlottesville, 1979), III, 433. Ketchum, *Victory at Yorktown*, 254.
117 Washington to Greene, 24 October 1781, WGW/23, 260–61.
118 Washington to David Ross, 24 October 1781, WGW/23, 262. General Orders, 25 October 1781, WGW/23, 264–65.
119 Clinton to Germain, 29 October 1781, DDAR/XX, 252.
120 General Orders, 20 October 1781, WGW/23, 244–47.
121 Washington to de Grasse, 20 October 1781, WGW/23, 248–49.
122 Washington to de Grasse, 28 October 1781, WGW/23, 286–87.
123 Washington to Colonel Pickering, 27 October 1781, WGW/23, 281–82.
124 Whitridge, *Rochambeau*, 242.
125 For a balanced assessment of Washington's strengths and weaknesses as a commander, see Edward G. Lengel, *General George Washington: A Military Life* (New York, 2005), 365–71.
126 Quoted in David K. Wilson, *The Southern Strategy: Britain's Conquest of South Carolina and Georgia, 1665–1780* (Columbia, 2005), v.
127 Clinton to Germain, 29 October 1781, DDAR/XX, 253.
128 Clinton to Germain, 6 December 1781, DDAR/XX, 276–79. Cornwallis to Ross, 15 January 1783, Ross/1, 144.
129 Cornwallis to Clinton, 20 October 1781, DDAR/XX, 244–47.
130 Rodney made a vigorous defense of his conduct, blaming everyone but himself for the superiority of the French on 5 September 1781, Rodney to Jackson, 19 October 1781, Hannay, *Letters of Samuel Hood*, 44–47.
131 Quoted in Willcox, *Portrait of a General*, 444.

CHAPTER 11

End game, 1782

The political and military consequences of Yorktown

The defeat at Yorktown was not necessarily the end of the war. The British still held important posts at New York, Charleston, and Savannah, for which they might extract a price or use as bases to continue the struggle. The Spanish remained committed to regaining both Minorca and Gibraltar, while France, Spain, and Britain had ambitions to fulfill in the Caribbean. Lastly the Patriots had yet to secure their independence, which they could achieve only by forcing Britain to abandon its claims to sovereignty. The one factor restraining all the combatants was their serious financial concerns, which made peace seem increasingly desirable.

French hopes for 1782 were mainly focused on the West Indies the assumption being that after Yorktown the Patriots could look after themselves. Despite the disruption of de Guichen's convoy, Vergennes and Castries still anticipated having a superior force in the Caribbean, especially when their troops and ships were added to those of Spain. First de Grasse was to capture the remaining British islands in the Lesser Antilles, notably St Lucia, Antigua and Barbados. After this he was to join Galvez and Solano for an attack on Jamaica.[1] The allied armada was expected to comprise 45 battleships and 20,000 troops, well capable of completing the destruction of British power in the western hemisphere. As to Europe, Vergennes had few specific objects other than a successful conclusion to the war, which could seemingly be best attained by helping Spain. The Spanish had yet to achieve their principal aim, the recovery of Gibraltar, without which they refused to accept any peace. Vergennes accordingly offered 12,000 troops and a powerful fleet to assist in its capture. He proposed, as in 1781, that the allied fleets should first sail into the English Channel to disable the Royal Navy before returning for a final assault on the Rock of Gibraltar.[2]

While the Bourbons were planning a successful ending of the war, the British were enmeshed in political turmoil following the events at Yorktown. News of the debacle reached London on 25 November 1781. The impact was all the greater because previous reports had given no cause for alarm.[3] Lord North immediately threw his hands in the air, declaring "Oh God, it is all over." Nevertheless he still had a majority in Parliament, while the King remained resolutely opposed to the granting of American Independence. Hence, within a day of hearing about Yorktown, George III asked Germain to draft a paper "on the mode that seems most feasible for conducting the war." He was still convinced that "with the assistance of Parliament" and well concerted measures "a good end may yet be made to this war."[4] For the moment the North ministry was to remain in office. The raising of taxes and voting of 20 million pounds for the army and navy accordingly went ahead. This was six times more than had been voted in the last peacetime budget. Ominously, 65 percent of the money was to be found by new loans.[5]

However, the majority of the nation was beginning to recognize the financial and political folly of continuing the struggle in America. Even Germain accepted that his position was becoming untenable, given the dislike of the war there.[6] Ironically he was constrained from resigning since this would appear to be abandoning the King. The constitutional convention was that the monarch appointed and dismissed ministers, though the informal consent of Parliament was necessary to ensure a working relationship between the executive and legislature. But as the consequences of Yorktown became apparent, even George III accepted by late January 1782 that Germain must go.[7] After six campaigns he had failed to produce an effective strategy or find commanders to implement it. It was his poorly drafted orders that had led to the disasters at Saratoga and Yorktown.

Germain's dismissal of course by no means appeased the Whig opposition in Parliament, led by Rockingham. They now gathered their supporters after Christmas for a decisive series of resolutions. On 20 February 1782 the Whigs narrowly lost a motion condemning Sandwich for his administration of the navy. A week later they carried a resolution against the American war by 19 votes.[8] Then on 4 March 1782, they prompted the Commons to vote for a "restoration of harmony" between Britain and her former colonies, affirming that the House would "consider as enemies to His Majesty and this country" all those still advising or "attempting the further prosecution of offensive war."[9] Finally on 20 March they called for a general removal of the ministers. This motion was never debated, since George III finally accepted that North and his colleagues could not continue without the support of Parliament.[10] Before the debate began, North announced that he had already resigned and that a new ministry would shortly take office. In this moment of humiliation, he alone had a carriage waiting to take him home. As he left the chamber he commented to bystanders: "Gentlemen you see what it is to be in the secret."[11]

George III had several times hinted that he would abdicate rather than "annihilate the rank in which this British Empire stands among the European States."[12] Nevertheless, his sense of duty led him to summon Rockingham to form a new ministry. Rockingham was an old-style Whig who believed in the constitutional settlement of 1688–1689 which had placed government in the hands of the aristocracy rather than "the King's Friends" or "country gentry." But Rockingham was not a great parliamentarian nor did he possess a sharp intellect. He was also physically weak. Nevertheless he had been a consistent opponent to the conflict in America and was ready to accept its independence. Even so he was not strong enough politically to form a ministry on his own. He needed the support of Chatham's former supporters led by the Earl of Shelburne, and another group of Whigs associated with Charles James Fox. Fortunately all these groups agreed on the need to end the American war, if only to concentrate on the struggle with France and Spain.[13]

The new ministry took office on 27 March 1782 and quickly formulated its plans for the new campaign. Carleton was to replace Clinton in America with orders to cease all offensive operations. This would then allow resources to be switched to the Caribbean, where the capture of the French and Spanish sugar islands would compensate Britain for the loss of her continental colonies. Another advantage was that the granting of independence might detach the former colonies from their alliance with France. Although formally outside the British Empire, they would still be attached to it through ties of trade and blood. Indeed, ending the commitment to reconquer America finally gave Britain the potential to seize the initiative, something which had eluded her since the entry of France into the war. There was much to play for before the signing of a final peace.[14]

Orders were accordingly sent to Carleton for the withdrawal of the troops from New York, Charleston, and Savannah and their redeployment in the West Indies. For as Shelburne commented: "the evacuation of New York can never be justified but by active measures elsewhere." Simultaneously an envoy was dispatched to Paris to discuss peace terms with Franklin, while Carleton was ordered to approach Washington about an informal ceasefire.[15]

However, not everything was agreeable to the new ministers. Within a week of taking office, they received news that Minorca had been lost. Murray had previously been confident of holding his position until the spring, such was the formidable nature of the fortifications at Fort St Philip. However, a lack of fresh provisions had resulted in an outbreak of scurvy, which disabled almost the entire garrison, forcing him to surrender on 5 February 1782 with his 1,650 men.[16]

The loss of Minorca in one sense was a blessing since it allowed the Rockingham ministry to concentrate on the defense of Gibraltar and the West Indian sugar islands. Nor was the news all bad. On 20 April Admiral Barrington intercepted a French East Indies convoy, which had originally been part of de Guichen's flotilla the previous December. Barrington had been sent, like Kempenfelt, with a "flying squadron" of 12 battleships in early April, following information of French armaments at Brest. During a running battle he captured two battleships and over 1,000 troops, seriously damaging French plans in India.[17] An honorable peace still seemed a possibility.

The war draws to a close in America

The arrangements of the Rockingham ministry took time to reach America, where Clinton remained in command until the arrival of his successor. A principal concern after Yorktown was the need to reassure the Loyalists that their interests would be protected. They had been deeply shocked at Cornwallis's inability to protect them on the capitulation at Yorktown. Even his draft article that the Loyalists should not be "punished" had caused distress, since it implied they had committed a crime in fighting for the King.[18] Clinton now attempted to reassure them that any future peace would place them on an equal footing with the other subjects of the Crown.[19]

Meanwhile Clinton still had to consider the security of his remaining forces. He had in any case been authorized by Germain on 2 January 1782 to maintain all the existing posts, using any available troops in coastal raids to encourage the Loyalists.[20] Hence in March 1782 he suggested a series of assaults "against the posts and towns upon the seacoasts of the revolted provinces." However his senior officers were not impressed, believing the objective insufficient "to justify the attempt in the present critical situation."[21] Then on 8 May 1782 instructions arrived from the

Rockingham ministry to end all offensive operations in America. Included was the announcement that Clinton was to be replaced by Carleton.[22]

It was a miserable end to Clinton's career, though one that had been long in the making. Except for the capture of Charleston, he had done nothing to change the course of the war, not least because of his obsession with the security of New York. His strategy, if he had one, was that of the "big blow" against Washington's army. But he failed to consider that even if successful, it was unlikely to subdue New England, which would remain a beacon for discontented Patriots elsewhere. However, in contrast to Howe, he recognized his wider responsibilities for the war. The Burgoyne debacle would not have happened had he been commander in chief. But he too readily allowed subordinates like Cornwallis to dictate events rather than impose his own views on the conduct of operations. In reality his readiness to facilitate others became an excuse for doing nothing himself, preferring to blame Germain instead for sending inadequate resources. In short, he saw obstacles when he should have grasped opportunities.

As we have seen, the British position in the south had collapsed even before the debacle at Yorktown. Since the departure of Rawdon in July 1781, the principal British force under Colonel Alexander Stewart remained near Charleston to protect the low country. Greene in response stationed his army in the hills of Santee, except for the occasional partisan foray along the coast. However, early in September 1781 Greene decided to challenge Stewart on learning that Washington and Rochambeau were moving against Cornwallis. Greene had still not won a battle and hoped that victory this time would lead to the capture of Charleston. Stewart was equally ready for an engagement to curtail Patriot attacks on the city. He accordingly moved to Eutaw Springs on the Santee River to face his enemy. Greene's force consisted of 2,400 men, comprising a mixture of Continentals and militia. Stewart's 2,000 men were mainly regulars, though he was inferior in cavalry.[23]

For a time it seemed as though Greene would achieve his aim on 8 September 1781. During a series of attacks, the Continentals used their bayonets as efficiently as the British regulars, forcing them back in confusion. Unfortunately the Patriots started to ransack the British camp, not having breakfasted that day. This allowed Stewart to organize a successful counter-attack. But as at Hobkirk's Hill, the British were unable to exploit their advantage due to a lack of cavalry. They also suffered heavy casualties. Indeed the need to look after the wounded resulted in a rapid withdrawal to Monck's corner.[24] Nor was this all, for Stewart was replaced shortly afterwards by Leslie. He found the army in such poor condition that he decided to retire even further to Goose Creek just north of Charleston.[25]

Although Greene had now restricted the British to the environs of Charleston, he could do little except watch the enemy and intercept their forage parties. His army lacked even basic support. As he told Washington on 25 October 1781: "Our troops have been exceedingly sickly," not least for "want of medicines and hospital stores." As a result "We can attempt nothing further except in the partisan way." The situation would be even worse in December, "when the whole Virginia line" was due to leave.[26] Fortunately Washington was able to send a sizable reinforcement of Pennsylvania, Maryland, and Delaware Continentals in the aftermath of Yorktown.

But in other respects the situation did not improve, as Greene informed Washington in March 1782. "For upwards of two months, more than a third of our men were entirely naked, with nothing but a breech cloth about them." In these unhappy circumstances, a small group from the Pennsylvania line plotted to hand Greene over to the British in return for a reward. The scheme had no chance of success and the ringleader, a sergeant, was summarily hanged. Nevertheless, Greene was again reduced to waiting for the enemy to make a move, for as Washington observed, until the intentions of the British were known it was impossible to "fix the operations of the campaign on our part."[27] In reality the intention of Leslie was to stay behind his defenses, for as he reported to Clinton, although the spirits of his army had revived, "nothing material" was to be gained "from offensive operations."[28] The war had reached a stalemate, unless the French intervened once more.

Although Greene had failed to win a single battle in the South, he had sustained the Patriot cause there in its darkest hour. Like Washington, Greene recognized that the British claim to sovereignty was hollow while Congress had an army in the field, since this facilitated the operations of Sumter, Marion, and Pickens. The southern war had been a perfect demonstration that guerilla and conventional warfare were complementary. Each had its place in a successful war of liberation.

Washington's last year of the war was similar to that of Greene. Initially he believed that the victory at Yorktown would invigorate the Patriot cause. He told Lafayette in January 1782 that Congress favored vigorous preparations. There was consequently to be no reduction in the army. However, the states still had to provide the troops' pay, clothing and provisions.[29] In this respect the situation did not improve. Early in

April 1782 Washington noted that the army was in great need of clothing and shoes. Recruitment was also languishing. When Washington consulted his officers on 15 April about the forthcoming campaign, he reported that the army numbered just 8,000 men, inclusive of guards and garrisons. Even with Rochambeau's 4,000 men, the allies would still barely equal the garrison in New York.[30] Moreover, according to Lafayette, there was little chance of further help from France, the prevalent attitude being that the United States must do more for itself. Only the recruitment of an effective field army would secure additional assistance.[31] The one hope was that the French West Indies fleet might pay another visit to North American waters.

Washington accordingly continued drawing up a list of objectives from New York and Charleston to Halifax and Penobscot while warning his correspondents that the war was still far from won.[32] Since Congress was impotent, he turned to the states for help, pointing out that they had not raised a single dollar of the eight million requested from them. How could they expect an army to operate without money: why did they not see the consequences of doing nothing? France might abandon the cause, giving Britain an opportunity to re-impose its authority, despite the talk of peace in London.[33] But all such pleas were in vain, leaving the army destitute and again on the verge of mutiny, resulting in several executions and a flood of desertions from the Connecticut line. One officer suggested that the only solution was to make Washington a king to avoid relying on "the weakness of republics" for justice.[34]

Washington's warning that the war was not yet won was reinforced by news that de Grasse had been defeated in the Caribbean. Hence, although Rochambeau marched northwards in May to join Washington's army, it was clear when the two commanders met in Philadelphia in July 1782 that nothing could be attempted against either New York or Charleston without naval superiority, and of that there was now little prospect. Washington in lieu suggested an invasion of Canada by land but Rochambeau replied that he had no authority to do this.[35] The situation momentarily brightened when Vaudreuil arrived at Boston from the West Indies with 13 battleships to carry out repairs and replenish their provisions.[36] But any superiority in American waters was likely to be temporary, since British naval reinforcements were on the way. The French Admiral's plans in any case were limited to a raid against Castine on the Penobscot River. After this he was to convoy Rochambeau's troops back to the West Indies in preparation for another French offensive in that region.[37] The campaign accordingly passed with nothing accomplished, despite rumors that the British intended to evacuate their remaining posts. Once more Washington could only reflect that the Patriots appeared locked in a struggle that would never end, unless the European powers acted decisively.

The rumors of an impending British withdrawal, of course, were correct. But as the Rockingham ministry soon discovered, carrying out such plans was impossible without the necessary logistical support. The evacuation of Savannah on 11 July 1782 proved relatively easy since the garrison was small and few Tories remained following the capitulation at Yorktown.[38] However, the forces in Charleston and New York were too large to be taken off without a huge quantity of shipping.[39] As a result, no land forces were available to turn the tide of war in the Caribbean. Everything here depended once more on the fleets of de Grasse and Rodney.

Britain strikes back in the Caribbean

Rodney's strategic perception may have been flawed regarding the course of events before Yorktown, but he was certainly correct that the French intended "to make an early and vigorous campaign in the West Indies" at the end of the hurricane season.[40] The French expectation was that de Grasse would first secure Britain's remaining possessions in the Windward and Leeward islands before joining Galvez and Solano in Cuba for the assault on Jamaica. The aim of the two Bourbon powers was to have at least 40 battleships and 16,000–20,000 troops in place for that operation by March 1782.[41] However, as already noted, the French plan to strengthen their forces had been disrupted by the mishaps to de Guichen's convoy. As a result, de Grasse would have fewer capital ships than planned, threatening the momentum which Vergennes was so anxious to maintain following the victory at Yorktown.[42]

By the time the Rockingham ministry took office in March 1782, it was too late to send reinforcements to the Caribbean. Fortunately for the new ministers, the North ministry had already taken measures to remedy the situation. Initially Sandwich proposed to send Rodney back to the Leeward Islands with eight ships of the line to join the 14 already there with Hood.[43] However, following the news of Yorktown, he calculated that a fleet of at least 30 battleships would be necessary to counter de Grasse. He accordingly ordered a further five battleships from England while Digby in North America was urged to forward as many vessels as possible from his command. Then on 20 December 1781 the North ministry added yet another five battleships, giving Rodney a total fleet of 37 capital ships, once they had all been assembled.[44]

Meanwhile in the Caribbean the rival fleets were preparing once more for action. Hood left New York in mid-November, reaching Barbados on 5 December with 16 battleships.[45] By this time de Grasse was already at Martinique with some 30 battleships, having left the Chesapeake on 7 November 1781.[46] Initially he planned to attack Barbados but he had to abandon the enterprise because of bad weather. He then decided to attempt St Kitts, setting off in early January, with 6,000 troops under General Bouille and 29 ships of the line.[47] The heavily outnumbered British garrison on St Kitts immediately retreated to their principal post on Brimstone Hill to await deliverance. Hood quickly followed, having now 22 ships of the line. He discovered de Grasse in a safe anchorage ten miles from the British fort, and immediately prepared to attack, despite his inferiority. This prompted de Grasse to put to sea so that he could deploy his superiority more effectively. Hood thereupon occupied the French anchorage to facilitate contact with the beleaguered garrison, an action which one of his captains described as "the most masterly maneuver I ever saw."[48] The next day, 26 January 1782, de Grasse twice attacked Hood but was prevented from exploiting his superiority so close to land. Nevertheless, Hood was unable to relieve the garrison on Brimstone Hill despite landing a force of 1,500 marines and soldiers.[49] The defenders finally surrendered on 14 February 1782. Hood then returned to Antigua to await Rodney's arrival, following information that de Grasse had been joined by two additional battleships from Europe. The neighboring British islands of Nevis and Montserrat in consequence had to be left to their fate, being almost defenseless.[50]

Rodney finally reached Antigua on 25 February 1782 with 12 battleships and a further 3 on the way, giving him a total of 37. The British could now think of acting more offensively. Clearly the first task was the interception of Vaudreuil before he joined de Grasse, who had now returned to Martinique following the capture of St Kitts. There were two likely approaches to Fort Royal. The first was via Desirada at the northern end of the island, the other by Point Salines on the southern tip. Unfortunately Rodney was convinced that Vaudreuil would approach via Port Salines and he refused Hood permission to patrol the other side of the island with part of the fleet. Hood believed that the speed of the British copper-bottomed ships would allow the fleet to be divided safely into two equal squadrons of 18 battleships, since they could be quickly reunited if de Grasse emerged to support the approaching reinforcement. The result of Rodney's refusal was that Vaudreuil sailed round the northern coast via Desirada and reached Port Royal Bay unmolested. Hood commented bitterly: "How Sir George could guard one path while leaving another more probable route open is a matter of astonishment." Rodney's "very great unsteadiness" suggested that "nothing short of a miracle can retrieve the nation's affairs in these seas."[51]

During this interlude de Grasse was busy preparing his flotilla for the northward journey to Santo Domingo, where he was to meet Solano and Galvez for the attack on Jamaica. Rodney vacillated whether to sail directly for Jamaica or challenge de Grasse in his passage. He finally chose the latter after consulting Hood.[52] But by the time the British fleet reached Fort Royal, de Grasse had already left. However, the French Admiral was slowed by having to escort the troop transports, thus allowing Rodney to sight this foe on 9 April near the Iles des Saintes, between Guadeloupe and Dominica. Nevertheless, the British fleet got to the windward of the French only on 12 July when Hood exchanged shots with their rear, during which one of the French battleships became separated. De Grasse turned back to rescue the vessel, even though he had only 30 battleships to Rodney's 33. His intention was still to fight defensively, deploying the usual tactics of damaging the British sails and rigging to inhibit further pursuit. The generally light airs, however, limited his maneuverability, allowing the British to engage at close quarters, where their more robust construction and better discipline came into play. By late afternoon five French ships had been forced to surrender, including de Grasse's flagship, the *Ville de Paris*.[53]

Fortunately for the French, Rodney neglected to order a general chase, which allowed the rest of de Grasse's fleet to escape despite considerable damage to some vessels. Rodney then spent the next day securing the *Ville de Paris* and other prizes.[54] When he did send Hood in pursuit, it was with only ten ships of the line. By the time Hood reached the critical Mona Passage on 19 April between Puerto Rica and Santo Domingo, the French had already passed through the previous day with some 26 warships. However, Hood succeeded in overtaking and capturing two French battleships and two frigates, thus adding to the British haul.[55] Nevertheless Hood believed that had a vigorous pursuit been undertaken immediately on the night of 12 April 1782, 20 French battleships would have been captured.[56]

The battle of the Iles des Saintes is invariably presented by British historians as a great victory for the Royal Navy, symbolized by the capture of de Grasse, the victor of Yorktown. In reality the battle was not that decisive and Hood was not alone in thinking that much more might have been done if Rodney had only pursued his enemy more vigorously.[57]

Although the British ended the affair without loss, three battleships had to be taken to Jamaica for repairs. The consequence was that the French under Vaudreuil still had 26 ships of the line in the Caribbean, while Solano's squadron of 12 battleships was untouched. Indeed by the middle of May the allies had some 40 battleships and 20,000 troops assembled on Santo Domingo. Hood could only lament afresh that had Rodney exerted himself following the Iles des Saintes, the danger would have ended "instead of being at this hour upon the defensive."[58] However, the battle did halt the erosion of British power in the West Indies, since Vaudreuil and Galvez decided to abandon the attack on Jamaica in view of de Grasse's defeat. Instead Solano returned to Havana while Vaudreuil sailed to Rhode Island to carry out repairs and to collect Rochambeau's troops for another attempt against Jamaica in the autumn.[59] In reality de Grasse's misfortune strengthened those in Paris who believed France should now seek a diplomatic end to the war, given her straitened finances.

Europe: Final operations

Although Spain had been disappointed in its plan to seize Jamaica, she was still hopeful of taking Gibraltar, following the capture of Minorca. Vergennes, as ever, was ready to facilitate his ally by agreeing to a fresh incursion into the Channel by way of diversion. He also offered the services of 12,000 French troops for the final assault, perhaps reassured that de Crillon would be in overall command, following his success at Minorca.[60]

Rumors about a new French and Spanish entry into the Channel began circulating in England in the early spring. An additional danger for the British was that the Dutch might join the allies, bringing another 12 battleships to the fray. But first a commander had to be found who was politically acceptable to the new ministry, following Keppel's promotion as Rockingham's First Lord of the Admiralty. All those associated with Sandwich and North were deemed unemployable, including Rodney, whose success at the Iles des Saintes was as yet unknown.[61] Keppel wisely chose the one officer who still enjoyed general respect in the fleet, Richard Lord Howe.[62]

The situation facing the Royal Navy in the early summer of 1782 was as threatening as that in 1781, when France, Spain, and Holland had all threatened British control of the Channel. Although the new ministry had inherited a greatly increased program of naval construction, it would require time before these vessels could be delivered. France and Spain were in any case continuing their efforts to retain naval superiority, especially in the construction of three deck ships of 100 guns and more. Even without the Dutch, the Bourbon powers would still have 134 battleships in commission, compared to Britain's 104.[63] This was a substantial superiority.

The most immediate danger proved to be the Dutch squadron at Texel. Howe was accordingly instructed in early May 1782 to sail with ten battleships into the North Sea to strike an early blow. The Dutch, however, were unprepared for battle and soon retired to port, allowing Howe to return to his principal task of guarding the western approaches against the fleets of France and Spain.[64]

The French and Spanish plan, as in 1781, was to disable the British Channel fleet before returning to Gibraltar. At the end of June, news was received in London that the combined fleet under Cordoba and de Guichen had left Cadiz for Brest to pick up the rest of the flotilla. Their timing was propitious since the Royal Navy was once again poorly placed to meet this threat, nearly half of its battleships being overseas in the Leeward Islands and elsewhere. As a result by mid-July 1782 the Bourbon powers had 40 battleships ready for Channel operations compared to 25 under Howe, who had the additional task of shielding a vital convoy from Jamaica. In the event, Howe's tactical skill, the lack of Franco-Spanish coordination, and bad weather once again came to the British rescue. First the convoy succeeded in entering the Channel undetected. Then at the beginning of August 1782 a storm drove the French and Spanish off their station. This setback was sufficient to persuade the Spanish to return home for what they hoped would be the final act in the siege of Gibraltar. But for a third time the Bourbon fleets had failed to benefit from their superiority, having neither intercepted a major convoy nor broken the power of the Channel squadron.[65]

Nevertheless there was no time for the British to celebrate, since news arrived that the Dutch were once again about to sail from Texel, putting at risk several Baltic convoys with vital naval stores for the Royal Navy. Howe was accordingly ordered for a second time to take part of his fleet to search out the Dutch squadron, proceeding as far as the southern tip of Norway for his quarry. But once again the Texel squadron put back to port before doing anything significant.[66]

The withdrawal of the Dutch was fortunate as the situation of Gibraltar was becoming critical. Since Darby's relief of the fortress in April 1781, the Spanish had continued their bombardment of the defenses at the northern end as the prelude to their storming. Progress proved painfully slow, despite the massive number of guns, not least because the Spanish navy again failed to prevent supplies reaching the garrison in late March 1782. To break the deadlock, de Crillon now engaged the services of the Chevalier D'Arcon, one of France's leading engineers. D'Arcon proposed to breach the defenses from the seaward direction by means of 12 floating batteries. These were to be constructed from the hulls of old warships and covered with timber and earth to protect them from the defenders' guns. The intention was to deploy the batteries against the town and old harbor, the weakest point in Gibraltar's defenses.[67]

News of these developments made it clear by the summer of 1782 that without further help Gibraltar was likely to fall. Preparations were accordingly intensified to prepare the necessary relief. The plan, as before, was for the Channel fleet under Howe, comprising 35 ships of the line, to escort three trade convoys and transports, carrying supplies and two regiments for the garrison.[68]

Howe eventually departed from England on 11 September, just as de Crillon and d'Arcon were about to launch their grand assault. D'Arcon's floating batteries had been completed in late August, allowing two weeks to practice maneuvering them. However, they were far from ready for actual deployment when Cordoba and de Guichen arrived on 12 September following their cruise in the English Channel. Nevertheless de Crillon resolved to attack immediately on 13 September to preempt Howe's expected attempt to relieve the fortress. The batteries proved difficult to maneuver, leaving them exposed to a murderous fire from the defenders. Most in consequence were destroyed by red hot shot which lodged in the timbers, causing fires that were hard to extinguish. The final setback was a severe storm which dispersed the blockading fleet. This allowed Howe to anchor safely on 14 October 1782 at Gibraltar without incident.[69] Luck, as on so many occasions, had been with the British.

Howe set off back for England five days later and quickly sighted the combined fleet. Cordoba and de Guichen had 46 battleships to Howe's 35. Despite his inferiority, Howe prepared for battle once he had cleared the Straits. But the French and Spanish were again unable to form an effective line of battle, even though they had the wind in their favor. Shots were eventually exchanged on the evening of 20 October 1782 and some damage was inflicted by both sides. Howe decided not to renew the contest with his water running low.[70] Clearly the Royal Navy was still struggling to compete with the joint fleets of France and Spain. Indeed, it had been fortunate to win one of its three major engagements in 1782 and not lose the other two.

A peace takes shape: The Treaty of 1783

Well before the Spanish failure at Gibraltar, the combatants had been exploring the possibilities of peace, since their views and aspirations were beginning to converge. The Patriots wanted independence, with possession of Canada and a western border along the Mississippi. The French supported American Independence, but not the inclusion of Canada, believing that France's interests would be best served by a balance of power in the western hemisphere.[71] Regarding terms with the British, they accepted the need for flexibility following de Grasse's defeat but still expected some gains, since vigorous efforts were being made to replace the losses in the Caribbean. Nevertheless, as Vergennes told his ambassador in Madrid: "The English have to some degree regenerated their navy while ours has been used up."[72] It was time to talk.

One reason for Vergennes's view was the state of France's finances. Sixty percent of the budget was now devoted to servicing the debt. As Vergennes informed the Spanish Ambassador in Paris in September 1782: "England without doubt is very fatigued, but we are so ourselves." The key question was "whether our credit or that of England will survive." The odds favored Britain, since "its constitution" and other "establishments" like the Bank of England, made available "resources" which were not available to France and Spain. Here was another reason for "honorably terminating" the conflict.[73]

However, the Spanish were still reluctant to recognize American independence for fear of its impact on their colonies. For this reason they wanted to confine the new republics to a boundary well east of the Mississippi River. They were also determined to obtain Gibraltar, despite the failure of their grand assault on 13 September 1782. Diplomacy might yet effect what they had not achieved by force of arms, especially if Jamaica was captured, for which preparations continued to be made.[74]

As for Britain, she too was thinking more positively about peace. Like other combatants she was also experiencing financial constraints. The estimates for 1782 would raise the national debt to £228 million (from £130,000 in 1775), requiring annual interest payments of nearly £8.5 million, more than the peacetime budget of 1774.[75] The constant need to borrow meant that the government was now paying 5½ percent for its money, causing the existing 3 percent stocks to fall to 58 percent of their original purchase price. Such devaluation raised fears that the government would not be able to honor its long-term obligations. Moreover the consequences of such high spending did not end here. There was also the impact of the taxes required to support this burden, amounting to 23 percent of per capita income.[76] The economy was additionally hurt by the loss of 3,000 merchant ships during the war, which adversely affected both the nation's trade and customs revenue.[77] Between 1778 and 1781 the value of imports and exports dropped 18 and 24 percent respectively.[78] The financial if not the political will of the nation was dangerously stretched.

As already mentioned, the Rockingham ministry, despite its warlike aspirations in the West Indies, began the peace process by sending an envoy to Paris in April 1782 to talk to the United States and France on the basis of independence for America and a return to the Treaty of 1763 respecting France. The man chosen for this task was Richard Oswald, a confidant of Shelburne and wealthy merchant, who had lived in Virginia for six years. He arrived in the French capital on 12 April 1782, where he met Vergennes and Franklin for an initial meeting. Here Vergennes readily agreed that negotiations between the Patriots and Britain could proceed in tandem with those of Britain and France.[79] However, Oswald initially made little progress, not having authority to acknowledge independence, on which the American Patriots were insisting as a precondition for talks.[80] Another obstacle was Congress's nomination of four peace commissioners, both to preserve regional balance and to prevent misconduct by any one delegate, as had happened previously. The four negotiators were Franklin, ambassador to France, John Adams, minister to the Dutch republic, John Jay, who was still in Madrid, vainly seeking recognition from Spain, and Henry Laurens, who had only just been paroled from the Tower of London following his capture in 1780. Clearly time would be required to get the negotiators together.[81]

The situation was also complicated on the British side because of rivalries between Shelburne, the colonial secretary, and Fox the foreign secretary. Fox wanted to recognize the United States before any substantive talks, in order to detach the Patriots from their alliance with France. Shelburne on the other hand wished to make the granting of independence part of the general settlement, believing this would give more scope for diplomatic maneuver.[82] Eventually the Cabinet accepted Fox's call for immediate recognition. However, the continuing tensions between Shelburne and Fox led to the sending of two envoys to Paris in May 1782. Oswald was to negotiate with Franklin, Jay, and Adams, while Fox's appointee, Thomas Grenville, discussed terms with Vergennes.[83]

Oswald was well received by Franklin on his return to Paris, now that Britain had conceded the principle of independence. The Patriot envoys were increasingly distrustful of their French allies, following Vergennes's warning in 1781 that a compromise peace might be necessary. Franklin even went so far as to indicate that the Patriots would make a separate peace with Britain without the concurrence of either France or Spain, though contrary in the former case to the Treaty of 1778. Such outcome would be greatly facilitated if Britain ceded Canada to the United States and allowed unrestricted access to the Newfoundland fishery.[84]

This was a step too far for Britain. Nevertheless Shelburne was ready to be generous to the Americans in hopes of restoring the special relationship between the former colonies and mother country. Hence he was prepared to concede the Mississippi as the United States' western limit, even though Clark had been driven out of the Illinois. Shelburne was equally generous regarding the boundary through the Great Lakes.[85]

The terms finally agreed provided for the recognition of the United States with a boundary along the upper St Lawrence, through the Great Lakes and down the Mississippi as far as the 31st parallel. The Americans, principally the New Englanders, would also be admitted to the Newfoundland fishery. Other articles stipulated that all debts incurred before the outbreak of hostilities would be honored and that property taken by either side would be restored. In return Congress would request the states to end the persecution of the Loyalists. The preliminary articles were finally signed by Oswald, Franklin, and Jay at Oswald's residence in Paris on 30 November 1782.[86]

American historians have traditionally presented the terms as a triumph of Patriot honesty over the dark arts of European diplomacy. They argue that although Franklin, Jay and Adams had technically breached the 1778 Treaty by unilaterally concluding their talks, they were justified because France was ignoring America's claims to the Mississippi boundary and Newfoundland fishery. Outsmarted, Vergennes could only express his astonishment and anger on learning these details.[87] However, as recent historians have emphasized, the 1778 Treaty did not prohibit exploratory talks. Indeed Vergennes had agreed to them at his initial meeting with Oswald and Franklin. Admittedly he expected the Patriot negotiators to follow their instructions from Congress "to make the most candid and confidential communications upon all subjects to the ministers of our generous ally the King of France." Nevertheless, the agreement signed in Oswald's apartment in Paris became effective only once Britain and France had reached a settlement. There was therefore no breach of the 1778 alliance, though Vergennes was certainly surprised at the generosity of Britain's concessions to the American states.[88]

The discussions between Britain and France also quickened once Shelburne become the sole responsible minister, following the resignation of

Fox in July 1782. Both sides were ready for peace as autumn approached. Britain had suffered no further defeats since the loss of Minorca and had reversed her decline in the Caribbean. The recognition of American independence meant that she had nothing left to fight for, since there was little prospect of quick gains in the West Indies despite Rodney's victory. Vergennes too was anxious for peace once he was convinced of Shelburne's sincerity. France had achieved its principal objective of reversing the 1763 Peace of Paris. Detaching the American colonies from Britain would surely weaken her old foe, making her less of a threat to France's interests. France on the other hand had lost no colonies and could expect modest gains in the Caribbean. She should also gain a share of America's trade.

The eventual terms between Britain and France were that both powers would share the Newfoundland fishery, though with distinct zones to avoid future conflict. Britain restored St Lucia and also gave up her claim to Tobago. The French in response returned Grenada, Dominica, St Christopher's, Nevis, and Montserrat to Britain, but received in recompense the West African colony of Senegal. As to India, both powers agreed to return to the status quo at the start of the conflict. Lastly, French pride was assuaged by the removal of the restrictions on the port of Dunkirk, which had been imposed by the Treaty of Utrecht in 1713.[89]

The most difficult parts of the negotiations were those involving Spain. These began in earnest only following her repulse on 13 September 1782 at Gibraltar. Nevertheless the Spanish continued to seek possession of that fortress by diplomatic means. The British were equally determined to retain it. Various compromises were proposed and towards the end Vergennes and Shelburne worked together to find an acceptable outcome. Eventually Spain agreed to accept Minorca together with East and West Florida in lieu of Gibraltar.[90] The Preliminaries between Britain, France, Spain, and Holland were finally signed on 20 January 1783 at Versailles.

The terms still had to be ratified by the respective governments. This caused no difficulty for Spain, France, and the United States. However, in Britain a majority in Parliament argued that Shelburne had been too generous to the Bourbon powers. The result was a new ministry led by Fox. But despite six months of diplomatic endeavor, Fox had to accept almost everything that had been agreed in Versailles, since a resumption of hostilities was unthinkable. The definitive articles were finally signed on 3 September 1783, those between the European powers (except Holland) being witnessed at Versailles while Britain and the United States completed their formalities in Paris.[91]

By this time only New York remained in British hands. However, such was the size of the garrison and number of loyalists that three months were required to facilitate the evacuation. Not until 25 November was the city free of British troops, the day that Washington finally entered it. Even then the territorial integrity of the new United States was incomplete, since Britain continued to hold Detroit and several other posts in the Great Lakes as security for the implementation of the treaty. Two issues concerned Britain: one the settlement of pre-war merchant debts, the other the treatment of the Loyalists. The British rightly feared that the latter would not be allowed to return or recover any property, since most states retained their acts of attainder, despite the pleas of Congress. Indeed, within months 100,000 had left their homeland to begin new lives in Canada. These issues were not adjudicated until Jay's Treaty in 1794.

At least the Loyalists were included in the negotiations. The Native American peoples had no such courtesy. Shelburne disowned any obligation to include them despite previous commitments regarding Indian lands and way of life. When the issue was raised in Parliament Shelburne argued disingenuously that the Indians had been "remitted to the care of neighbors, whose interest it was... to cultivate friendship with them." The Indians still owned their lands even though not as sovereign peoples.[92] But the reality was far different, as the Six Nations discovered when they met Congress's commissioners to agree a peace. They were informed that they were a conquered people, since the King had abandoned them and signed away their lands. Those who wished to stay as a tribal group must confine themselves to the five Finger Lakes in western New York and the north-western corner of Pennsylvania. Nor did the Oneida and Tuscarora fare any better, despite their support for the Patriot cause. No attempt was made to restrict white settlement, which quickly undermined their economy and way of life.[93] Most Iroquois like Brant sought refuge in Canada, making new homes on the Grand River in Ontario. Within 15 years a similar westward exodus became necessary for the peoples of the Ohio and south-eastern United States.

Even among the victors there were many losers, notably the veterans of the Continental army. In his farewell address to the army on 3 November 1783, Washington assured his men that the nation would show its gratitude for their glorious exertions. Congress would pay the money and lands owing them.[94] His optimism proved ill-founded. The troops were given three month's leave with pay, resulting in their dispersal and disbandment. The officers, too, had little to show for their efforts other than empty promises of half pay for life. Washington's farewell dinner on

4 December 1783 in New York was thus a somber affair. Nevertheless, he surrendered his commission to Congress on 23 December 1783, ending the threat of military rule for many of his countrymen. America could finally start to become a nation.

Notes and references

1 Jonathan Dull, *The French Navy and American Independence: A Study of Arms and Diplomacy, 1774–1787* (Princeton, 1975), 249–53.

2 Ibid., 264–65.

3 George III to North, 3 November 1781, Fortescue/5, 297.

4 George III to North, 28 November 1781, Fortescue/5, 303–4.

5 Peter D.G. Thomas, *Lord North* (London, 1976), 103.

6 Germain to George III, 16 December 1781, Fortescue/5, 314–15.

7 See I.R. Christie, *The End of North's Ministry* (London, 1958), 291–94.

8 George III to North, 21 February 1782, Fortescue/5, 356. North to George III, 28 February 1782, Fortescue/5, 374–75.

9 North to George III, 4 March 1782, Fortescue/5, 376.

10 North to George III, 19 March 1782, Fortescue/5, 398. Thomas, *North*, 131–32.

11 Christie, *End of North's Ministry*, 368–69.

12 George III to North, 21 January 1782, Fortescue/5, 334–35. The King actually drafted a message abdicating in favor of George, Prince of Wales, March 1782, Fortescue/5, 425.

13 Draft of the New Administration, 27 March 1782, Fortescue/5, 419.

14 Piers Mackesy, *The War for America, 1775–1783* (Cambridge, Mass., 1964), 471–44.

15 Cabinet Minute, 30 March 1782, Fortescue/5, 435–36. Mackesy, *War for America*, 487.

16 Mackesy, *War for America*, 438.

17 Dull, *French Navy*, 278–79. David Syrett, *The Royal Navy in European Waters during the American Revolutionary War* (Columbia, SC, 1998), 154–55.

18 Governor Franklin to Germain, 19 December 1781, DDAR/XX, 255–57. Cornwallis acknowledged that he should have used the word "molested" or persecuted.

19 Council of War, New York, 17 January 1782, CAR, 592–93.
20 Christie, *End of North's Ministry*, 321–22.
21 Council of War, 8 March 1782, CAR, 596. Ibid., 28 March 1782, CAR, 598–99.
22 *Clinton's Narrative*, CAR, 361–62.
23 John Ferling, *Almost a Miracle: The American Victory in the War of Independence* (New York, 2007), 519–20.
24 Stewart to Cornwallis, 9 September 1781, DDAR/XX, 226–29. John S. Pancake, *This Destructive War: The British Campaign in the Carolinas, 1780–1782* (University of Alabama, 1985), 217–22.
25 Leslie to Clinton, 1 December 1781, DDAR/XX, 267–68.
26 Quoted in Christopher Ward, *The War of the Revolution*, 2 vols. (New York, 1952), II, 836–38.
27 Ibid., II, 840. Washington to Greene, 23 April 1782, WGW/24, 152–53.
28 Leslie to Clinton, 29 January 1782, CAR, 594–95.
29 Washington to Lafayette, 4 January 1782, WGW/23, 429–30. Washington to the Governors, 22 January 1782, WGW/23, 458–60.
30 Washington to Lincoln, 15 April 1782, WGW/24, 110–12. Council of General Officers, 15 April 1782, WGW/24, 121.
31 Washington to Robert Livingston, 23 April 1782, WGW/24, 155.
32 Memorandum on the Conduct of the War, 1 May 1782, WGW/24, 194–211.
33 Washington to the Governors, 4–8 May 1782, WGW/24, 234–38.
34 Washington to Morris, 17 May 1782, WGW/24, 289. Washington to Colonel Nicola, 22 May 1782, WGW/24, 272–73.
35 Conference with Rochambeau, 19 July 1782, WGW/24, 433–35.
36 Dull, *French Navy*, 299. Washington to Vaudreuil, 10 August 1782, WGW/24, 497–500.
37 Washington to Vaudreuil, 10 August 1782, WGW/24, 497–500. Lee Kennett, *The French Forces in America, 1780–1783* (Westport, Conn., 1977), 161–62.
38 Colonel Clarke to Clinton, Savannah, 20 December 1781, CAR, 591.
39 Mackesy, *War for America*, 475–76. David Syrett, *The Royal Navy in American Waters, 1775–1783* (Aldershot, 1989), 223–26.
40 Rodney to Arbuthnot, 13 August 1781, Fortescue/5, 264–65.
41 Dull, *French Navy*, 251–52.

42 Dull, *French Navy*, 262–63.

43 Cabinet Minute, 22 October 1781, Fortescue/5, 291.

44 Cabinet Minute, 1 December 1781, Sandwich/4, 204–5. Ibid., 20 December 1781, Sandwich/4, 227–28.

45 Hood to Stephens, 10 December 1781, David Hannay, ed., *Letters written by Sir Samuel Hood in 1781–1783* (Navy Records Society, 1895), 48–51.

46 Washington to Greene, 16 November 1781, WGW/23, 346–47.

47 M. Le Comte de Lapeyrouse Bonfils, *Histoire de la Marine Française*, 3 vols. (Paris, 1845), III, 244–46.

48 Lord Robert Manners to the Duke of Rutland, 8 February 1782, Hannay, *Letters of Hood*, 78–80.

49 Hood to Sandwich, 7 February 1782, Sandwich/4, 233–38.

50 Hood to Sandwich, 20 February 1782, Sandwich/4, 238–42.

51 Hood to Sandwich, 31 March 1782, Sandwich/4, 243–46.

52 Hood to Sandwich, 3 April 1782, Sandwich/4, 249–50.

53 Bonfils, *Marine Française*, III, 289–300. Mackesy, *War for America*, 457–58. Hood to Jackson, 16 April 1782, Hannay, *Letters of Hood*, 101–3.

54 Hood to Sandwich, 13 April 1782, Sandwich/4, 250–51.

55 Hood to Sandwich, 22 April 1782, Sandwich/4, 260. Hood to Rodney, 22 April 1782, Sandwich/4, 261–63.

56 Hood to Jackson, 16 April 1782, Hannay, *Letters of Hood*, 103–8. Rodney claimed by way of explanation that the center and the rear divisions of his fleet were too badly damaged to chase immediately, Rodney to Sandwich, 19 April 1782, Sandwich/4, 258.

57 Shelburne to George III, 19 May 1782, Fortescue/6, 34–35.

58 Hood to Jackson, 30 April 1782, Hannay, *Letters of Hood*, 135–37.

59 Dull, *French Navy*, 283–88.

60 Dull, *French Navy*, 280–81. Sir Charles Petrie, *King Charles III of Spain* (London, 1971), 195. John Lynch, *Bourbon Spain, 1700–1808* (Oxford, 1989), 199.

61 Cabinet Minute, 26 April 1782, Fortescue/5, 488. The ministry had to hastily arrange a peerage for Rodney and Hood, George III to Shelburne, 18 May 1782, Fortescue/6, 33–34.

62 Keppel to George III, 1 April 1782, Fortescue/5, 438. David Syrett, *Admiral Lord Howe: A Biography* (Annapolis, MD, 2006), 100.

63 Commodore Stewart to Sandwich, 29 September 1781, Sandwich/4, 409. Dull, *French Navy*, 286–87, 373–76.

64 Cabinet Minute, 7 May 1782, Fortescue/6, 11. Ibid., 23 May 1782, Fortescue/6, 43. Syrett, *Howe*, 100–101.

65 Cabinet Minute, 17 July 1782, Fortescue/6, 88–89. Syrett, *Royal Navy in European Waters*, 157–59.

66 Cabinet Minute, 14 August 1782, Fortescue/6, 101–2. Syrett, *Howe*, 103–4.

67 Petrie, Charles III, 201–2. T.H. McGuffie, *The Siege of Gibraltar* (London, 1965), 139.

68 Cabinet Minute, 23 August 1782, Fortescue/6, 113–14. Syrett, *Howe*, 104–5.

69 Dull, *French Navy*, 307–8. Petrie, *Charles III*, 202–3. Mackesy, *War for America*, 483–84.

70 Syrett, *Howe*, 105. Bonfils, *Marine Française*, III, 273–77.

71 Andrew Stockley, *Britain and France at the Birth of America: The European Powers and the Peace Negotiations of 1782–1783* (Exeter, 2001), 33–49.

72 Dull, *French Navy*, 316–17. Bonfils, *Marine Française*, III, 305.

73 Quoted in Dull, *French Navy*, 304. Stockley, *Britain and France*, 88–92.

74 Stockley, *Britain and France*, 60. Dull, *French Navy*, 318–19.

75 Public Debts, 5 July 1783, CJ/XXXIX, 805. Unfunded debt, 1 October 1783, CJ/XXXIX, 821. Account of Money given for the Service of 1774, CJ/XXXV, 286–87.

76 Stephen Conway, *The British Isles and The War of American Independence* (Oxford, 2000), 50–55.

77 Paul Kennedy, *The Rise and Fall of British Naval Mastery* (London, 1976), 128.

78 Conway, *British Isles*, 70.

79 Stockley, *Britain and France*, 37–38. Orville T. Murphy, *Charles Gravier, Comte de Vergennes: French Diplomacy in the Age of Revolution, 1719–1787* (Albany, 1988), 321–22.

80 Samuel Flagg Bemis, *The Diplomacy of the American Revolution* (Bloomington, 1961), 207–9.

81 Ferling, *Almost a Miracle*, 549. William C. Stinchcombe, *The American Revolution and the French Alliance* (Syracuse, NY, 1969), 153–69. Laurens appeared only at the end of the negotiations.

82 H.M. Scott, *British Foreign Policy in the Age of the American Revolution* (Oxford, 1990), 320–22. Stockley, *Britain and France*, 37–42.

83 Cabinet Minute, 25 April 1782, Fortescue/5, 488. Shelburne to George III, 26 April 1782, Fortescue/5, 488.

84 Fox to George III, 21 May 1782, Fortescue/6, 40–41. Bemis, *Diplomacy*, 196.

85 Stockley, *Britain and France*, 52–57. Scott, *British Foreign Policy*, 327–28. The lack of impact by Clark and others on the negotiations in Paris is acknowledged by Lowell H. Harrison, *George Rogers Clark and the War in the West* (Lexington, KY, 1976), 97–98.

86 Stockley, *Britain and France*, 63–66. For the text of the treaty, see Bemis, *Diplomacy*, 259–63.

87 Bemis, *Diplomacy*, 239–42. Stinchcombe, *French Alliance*, 195–96.

88 Stockley, *Britain and France*, 65. Murphy, *Vergennes*, 393. Congress's instructions to its envoys are printed in Henri Doniol, *Histoire de la participation de la France à l'établissement des États-Unis d'Amérique: Correspondence diplomatique et documents*, 5 vols. (Paris, 1886–1892), vol. 4, 604–6.

89 Scott, *British Foreign Policy*, 335.

90 Cabinet Minute, 11 December 1782, Fortescue/6, 182. Stockley, *Britain and France*, 113–129.

91 Terms between Britain and Holland were completed only on 20 May 1784, Scott, *British Foreign Policy*, 335–37. The delay was caused by Dutch attempts to include neutral rights and the restoration of all their colonial territories.

92 Quoted in Barbara Graymont, *The Iroquois in the American Revolution* (Syracuse, 1972), 262.

93 Ibid., 290–91.

94 Farewell Orders to the Armies, Princeton, 2 November 1783, Saul K. Padover, *The Washington Papers: Basic Selections from the Public and Private Writings of George Washington* (New York, 1955), 257–61.

Conclusions and consequences

Nineteenth- and twentieth-century historians have customarily assumed that the outcome of the War for Independence was pre-ordained: that the victors, despite their humble origins, were destined to become a free and powerful people. However, as this book has tried to show, this was far from the case. For much of the war the cause of independence hung by a thread, sustained by little more than Washington's indomitable courage and resolve.

In assessing the reasons for the war's outcome, the contribution of France must be emphasized. After six campaigns, Britain and the United States were like two exhausted boxers. Neither was able to inflict a decisive blow on the other, as evidenced by the campaigns of Washington and Clinton. Washington was too weak to leave his fortress defenses while Clinton lacked the resources to search him out. It required a third combatant, France, to end the stalemate, a fact too often neglected by American writers, though something privately acknowledged by Washington as early as March 1779 in his darker moments.

The same neglect has been true of Spain. It has been fashionable to deride Spain's military and naval power. But though her officers and crews may have been inferior, her warships were as good if not better than their equivalents in the Royal Navy. Her entry into the war consequently widened the conflict, diverting Britain's resources from recovering the colonies. Seventy percent of her war effort, consequently, went on areas not directly related to that objective. From 1778 France and Spain set the war's agenda, forcing Britain to respond as best she could, while the Patriots waited to profit from her misfortunes, with or without the help of the Bourbon powers. In these circumstance Britain was lucky not to suffer more defeats. Only the incompetence of the Bourbon high command prevented worse misfortunes.

Among the other reasons for the war's outcome was the Patriots' persuasive ideology. As the loyalist historian Charles Stedman subsequently acknowledged: "their councils were animated by liberty."[1] But in securing their freedom the Patriots had a number of practical advantages. Most important was the nature of the countryside, as one of Rochambeau's aides commented. "Though the people of America might be conquered by well disciplined European troops, the country of America could not", as Cornwallis discovered.[2] This was fortunate given the Patriots' lack of an effective federal government.

However, the contribution of individuals was important too. Vergennes's diplomatic vision ensured that France could give her undivided attention to the maritime war, something that she had not been able to do for 120 years. Washington kept the Patriot cause alight when all seemed lost. He was frequently criticized for his caution and lack of battlefield success, especially between July 1779 and August 1781 when he undertook no military initiative worthy of the name. However, he had no alternative but to adopt a defensive stance, given the weakness of Congress and shortsightedness of the states. By making the preservation of the army his prime objective, he provided a focus for the revolutionary cause and a reassurance to the Patriots everywhere. Had the Continental army dissolved, it is likely that the middle and southern states would have returned to British rule. New England might eventually have won its independence, though it is difficult to determine the breaking point when societies abandon their ideology in favor of survival. But whatever the end result, it would not have been the United States as it emerged in 1783.

The British, in contrast, had a poor understanding of the conflict. They acted as though the interests of the imperial center were the only matters of importance. They had no concept of a popular war that was supported by a society which was not innately monarchical. Above all, they failed to realize that it was a political war that had to be fought against the potent ideology of popular rights. In that struggle the values of an *ancien régime* were found wanting.

This lack of understanding was demonstrated by the inability of the British to formulate a winning strategy. At heart they faced the conundrum posed by all civil wars: whether to conciliate the rebels or repress them. The Howe brothers adopted the first course, believing that they would alienate the population if they adopted severe methods. Cornwallis in contrast opted for repression after he found that oaths of allegiance were broken as soon as they were made. The outcome was as the Howe brothers feared. The infliction of summary punishment merely began a cycle of violence in which one side outdid the other in committing atrocities.

However, the British might have fared better if they had supported the Loyalists more effectively, especially at the start of the conflict. More than a year passed before the army intervened in force. This gave the Patriots time to establish their ideas and institutions. Even then the British declined to use the Loyalists, believing that the army must first restore order. Hence no sustained attempt was made to enhance their role until the campaign in South Carolina, five years after the start of the rebellion. But perhaps they were right not to see the Loyalists as the basis for a winning strategy. The supporters of the Crown were too few in number in most areas and the passive nature of their loyalty made them ill-suited to a country where a new political and social order was being developed.

But there were other reasons for the British failure too. Not least was the insufficiency of Britain's resources. In the first three years this was due to her cumbersome methods of mobilization. The dislike of standing armies ruled out rapid expansion through conscription. Howe, Carleton and Burgoyne consequently lacked the troops to impose British authority by force of arms. Lack of resources was also true of the war at sea, though the deficiency was made worse by North's ill-judged economy before 1778. The Royal Navy never had enough frigates and cruisers in the period 1775–1777 to destroy the colonial economy and prevent supplies reaching the Patriot forces. Thereafter the entry of France and Spain into the conflict made the task of reconquering America virtually impossible. Instead of dictating events, the British army and navy had to respond to them. The Channel Fleet, for example, was constantly being diverted from one task to another, making it impossible to blockade France's Atlantic ports in the manner that had served Britain so well during the Seven Years War. Yorktown in these circumstances was a disaster waiting to happen.

Britain in reality lacked the population to be both a world-class naval and military power. This inherent weakness was exposed ironically by the magnitude of Britain's success in the previous war. As Sandwich pointed out before leaving office, Britain's empire might have expanded to the four corners of the globe by 1763, but so had her commitments. The consequence was that "these distant dominions" had "lessened the security arising from our situation as an island" nation.[3] She was constantly having to "punch above her weight," not a good position for any boxer, whatever the assertions of a recent British Prime Minister.

Nevertheless, some historians imply that Britain might have succeeded had she been blessed with a more efficient bureaucracy.[4] They argue that the main departments were too steeped in traditional methods to produce the men and ships for ultimate victory. Planning was always done on the basis of what had been previously achieved, not what was currently necessary. Widespread profiteering was another bar to efficiency, though this is prevalent in most societies, whether at war or at peace.[5] In addition too much reliance was placed on birth and status rather than merit in the making of appointments. However, there is no indication that Britain was overall less effective in the management of her resources. Indeed, compared to France and Spain, the British state was infinitely more efficient, though the war did reveal the need for the subsequent "economical reforms" of the younger Pitt. France in contrast required a bloody revolution to change her social and political structures.

Finally historians have suggested that Britain lacked the right political leadership. Nineteenth-century Whig historians in particular blamed George III for the war's outcome, accusing him of acting unconstitutionally in the governance of the country. Above all, he insisted on a policy of repression in America. However, except for the invasion crisis in 1779, he did not attend meetings of the Cabinet and almost invariably accepted the advice of his ministers.[6] His determination to regain the colonies was supported by the vast majority of the nation until the debacle at Yorktown. However, his refusal to search for a minister who could take responsibility for military and naval matters seriously undermined the effective conduct of the war. North showed great political skill in managing Parliament and raising money, demonstrating the same skills as the Duke of Newcastle during the Seven Years War. However, such qualities were not enough in a wartime leader, as Newcastle discovered, when the departments of state had to be synchronized in the pursuit of an effective strategy. The problem for Newcastle was finally solved when he formed a coalition with William Pitt. North never had that opportunity due to George III's obstinacy. As a result, the two key war ministries of Sandwich and Germain were frequently at odds with each other. This was crucial, given their conflicting priorities regarding the war in America and the defense of Britain. In this respect the French Council of ministers, chaired by Louis XVI, was a more effective institution of government.[7] The same was true of Spain following the appointment of Floridablanca as Charles III's leading minister.[8] But although the decision-making process of the Bourbon powers may have been more efficient, the execution of those decisions left much to be desired because of the failings of the bureaucracy and incompetence of the military and naval commanders.

On the day of Cornwallis's surrender, his soldiers allegedly marched to a tune called "The world turned upside down." Contemporaries everywhere agreed with such sentiments regarding Britain. The emperor Joseph II of Austria believed that the war had reduced her to the rank of a second-class state like Denmark or Sweden. Frederick the Great thought similarly. Horace Walpole in London confessed that he saw "little or no prospect of England ever being a great nation again." Another pundit exclaimed: "Unhappy England, bankrupt in genius" without a single person "capable of preserving the Empire."[9]

But however dramatic the spectacle, the impact of Yorktown proved less epochal than assumed. Britain was not reduced to the status of a second-class power. Indeed the reduction of her empire seemingly introduced an era of economic growth as the Industrial Revolution gathered pace. Vergennes' hopes that the loss of the colonies would reduce Britain's power and influence were not realized. The war merely jolted the governing elite into a series of reforms, making merit rather than lineage the criterion for office. Vigorous steps were also taken to ensure that Britain achieved a two-power naval standard for the first time in its history.[10] The effect of these changes meant that the country was able to meet the challenges of the French Revolutionary and Napoleonic Wars.

French interests, in contrast, were not significantly advanced by her intervention in the War of American Independence. Most of America's trade resumed its old channels, while the balance of power in Europe stayed much as before. Indeed the effects of the conflict were almost all detrimental to France, showing the weakness of her economy and oppressive nature of her social and political structures.[11] The consequences were revealed with the outbreak of Revolution of 1789 and the destruction of the *ancien régime*. The execution of Louis XVI was more truly symptomatic of a world turned upside down.

Spain too experienced a decline in fortune. The war restored some pride following the capture of Minorca and West Florida. However, it did nothing to halt her fundamental decline because of her inability to accept political, economic, and social change. Like France, she became swallowed up in the vortex of war and revolution. Although the Bourbon monarchy was restored in 1814, her once mighty empire did not survive the rhetoric of the Jacobins and example of an independent America.

American historians like to quote Ralph Waldo Emerson's epitaph for the Concord Monument: "Here once the embattled farmers stood, and fired the shot heard around the world." In reality the shot fired at Lexington was not much heard beyond North America. The United States after 1783 sat awkwardly on the outer fringes of Europe, a maverick entity little admired by other nations. No outbreak of republican fervor occurred as a result of the American Revolution. The world was not turned upside down by the infant state until the growth of the United States as an economic super power. However, the War of Independence did start the transformation of a continent with epochal consequences for all.

Notes and references

1 C. Stedman. *The History of the Origins, Progress and Termination of the American War*, 2 vols. (London, 1794), II, 447.

2 Piers Mackesy, *The War for America, 1775–1783* (Cambridge, Mass., 1964), 510.

3 Ibid., 355.

4 J.E.D. Binney, *British Public Finance and Administration, 1774–1794* (Oxford, 1958). R. Arthur Bowler, *Logistics and the Failure of the British Army in America, 1775–1783* (Princeton, 1975). Norman Baker, *Government and Contractors: The British Treasury and War Supplies, 1775–1783* (London, 1971). David Syrett, *Shipping and the American War, 1775–1783: A Study in British Transport Organization* (London, 1970).

5 Bowler, *Logistics*, 167–211.

6 Peter D.G. Thomas, "George III and the American Revolution," *History*, LXX (1985), 16–31.

7 Jonathan Dull, *The French Navy and American Independence: A Study of Arms and Diplomacy, 1774–1787* (Princeton, 1975), 5, 48, 108–9.

8 John Lynch, *Bourbon Spain, 1700–1808* (Oxford, 1989), 296.

9 H.M. Scott, *British Foreign Policy in the Age of the American Revolution* (Oxford, 1990), 337–39. Mackesy, *War for America*, 516–17.

10 Naval construction exceeded £1,000,000 in both 1783 and 1784, CJ/XXXIX, 164–67, 897–901.

11 Dull, *French Navy*, 343–44. Orville T. Murphy, *Charles Gravier, Comte de Vergennes: French Diplomacy in the Age of Revolution, 1719–1787* (Albany, 1988), 397–404.

APPENDIX

Washington on the art of command

Letter to Colonel William Woodford, 10 November 1775, W.W. Abbot, ed., *The Papers of George Washington, Revolutionary War Series* (Charlottesville, 1987), Volume 2, 346–47.

The inexperience you complain of is a common case, and only to be remedied by practice and close attention. The best general advice I can give, and which I am sure you stand in no need of, is to be strict in your discipline; that is to require nothing unreasonable of your officers and men, but see that whatever is required be punctually complied with. Reward and punish every man according to his merit, without partiality or prejudice; hear his complaints; if well founded, redress them; if otherwise, discourage them, in order to prevent frivolous ones. Discourage vice in every shape, and impress upon the mind of every man, from the first to the lowest, the importance of the cause, and what it is they are contending for. For ever keep in view the necessity of guarding against surprises. In all your marches, at times, at least, even when there is no possible danger; move with front, rear and flank guards, that they may be familiarized to the use; and be regular in your encampments, appointing necessary guards for the security of your camp. In short, whether you expect an enemy or not, this should be practiced; otherwise your attempts will be confused and awkward, when necessary. Be plain and precise in your orders, and keep copies of them to refer to, that no mistakes may happen. Be easy and condescending in your deportment to your officers but not too familiar, lest you subject yourself to a want of that respect, which is necessary to support a proper command.

Bibliography

Printed primary sources

W.W. Abbot et al., *The Papers of George Washington: Revolutionary War Series*, 19 vols. (Charlottesville, 1985–).

G.R. Barnes and J.H. Owen, eds., *The Private Papers of John, Earl of Sandwich, First Lord of the Admiralty, 1771–1782* (Navy Records Society, 1933–38, LXIX, LXXI, LXXV and LXXVII).

F.E. Chadwick, ed., *The Graves Papers and other Documents relating to the Naval Operations of the Yorktown Campaign, July to October 1781* (New York, 1916, reprinted 1968).

Clarence E. Carter, *The Correspondence of General Thomas Gage, 1763–1775*, 2 vols. (Yale, 1931).

William Bell Clark, ed., *Naval Documents of the American Revolution*, 10 vols. (Washington, 1964–).

K.G. Davies, ed., *Documents of the American Revolution, 1770–1783: Colonial Office Series*, 21 vols. (Shannon, 1972–81).

John C. Fitzpatrick, ed., *The Writings of George Washington from the Original Manuscript Sources, 1745–1799*, 39 Vols. (Washington DC, 1931–44).

Sir John Fortescue, ed., *The Correspondence of King George the Third from 1760–1783*, 6 vols. (London, 1927–28).

Historical Manuscripts Commission, *Report on the American Manuscripts in the Royal Institution of Great Britain*, 4 vols. (London, 1904–9).

Historical Manuscripts Commission, *Report on Manuscripts in Various Collections*, VI: *The Manuscripts of Miss M. Eyre Matcham, Captain H.V. Knox, Cornwallis Wykeham-Martin* (London, 1909).

Historical Manuscripts Commission, *Report on the Manuscripts of Mrs Stopford-Sackville of Drayton House*, 2 vols. (London, 1904–10).

Historical Manuscripts Commission, *Report on the Manuscripts of the Late Reginald Rawdon Hastings*, 3 vols. (London, 1928).

Otis G. Hammond, ed., *Letters and Papers of Major General John Sullivan, Continental Army*, 3 vols. (Concord, NH, 1930–39).

D. Hannay, *Letters Written by Sir Samuel Hood, 1781–1783* (Navy Records Society, London, 1985).

William Howe, *Narrative of Lieutenant General Sir William Howe in a Committee of the House of Commons* (London, 1780).

Stanley J. Idzerda et al., eds., *Lafayette in the Age of the American Revolution: Selected Letters and Papers, 1776–1790*, 5 vols. (Ithaca, 1976–83).

Sir J.K. Laughton, *Letters and Papers of Charles, Lord Barham, Admiral of the Red, 1758–1813*, 3 vols. (London, NRS, 1906–10).

New York Historical Society Collections, vol. 5, *Papers of Charles Lee, 1776–1778* (New York, 1873).

Howard C. Rice and Anne S.K. Brown, *The American Campaigns of Rochambeau's Army, 1780–1783*, 2 vols. (Princeton, 1972).

Charles Ross, ed., *Correspondence of Charles, First Marquis of Cornwallis*, 3 vols. (London, 1859).

Richard K. Showman et al., *The Papers of Nathanael Greene*, 13 vols. (Chapel Hill, 1976–2005).

Benjamin Franklin Stevens, ed., *The Campaign in Virginia, 1781: An Exact Reprint of Six Rare Pamphlets on the Clinton-Cornwallis Controversy*, 2 vols. (London, 1888).

David Syrett, *The Rodney Papers: Selections from the Correspondence of Admiral Lord Rodney*, Vol. 2, *1763–1780*, Navy Records Society (Aldershot, 2007).

Banastre Tarleton, *A History of the Campaigns of 1780 and 1781 in the Southern Provinces of North America* (London and Dublin, 1787).

W.B. Willcox, ed., *The American Rebellion: Sir Henry Clinton's Narrative of his Campaigns, 1775–1783, with an Appendix of Original Documents* (New Haven, 1954).

Reference works

Mark M. Boatner III, *Encyclopedia of the American Revolution* (New York, 1976).

Jack P. Greene and J.R. Pole, *A Companion to the American Revolution* (Oxford, 2000).

Theodore P. Savas and J. David Dameron, *A Guide to the Battles of the American Revolution* (New York, 2006).

Secondary sources

John Alden, *A History of the South*, Vol. 3, *The South in the Revolution, 1763–1789* (Baton Rouge, 1976).

Rodney Atwood, *The Hessians: Mercenaries from Hessen-Kassel in the American Revolution* (Cambridge, 1980).

Bernard Bailyn, *The Ideological Origins of the American Revolution* (Cambridge, Mass., 1967).

Norman Baker, *Government and Contractors: The British Treasury and War Supplies, 1775–1783* (London, 1971).

Thomas Balch, *The French in America during the War of Independence of the United States, 1777–1783* (Philadelphia, 1891).

Robert D. Bass, *The Green Dragoon: The Lives of Banastre Tarleton and Mary Robinson* (Orangeburg, SC, 1973).

Robert D. Bass, *Swamp Fox: The Life and Campaigns of General Francis Marion* (Orangeburg, SC, 1974).

Samuel Flagg Bemis, *The Diplomacy of the American Revolution* (Bloomington, 1961).

Hugh Bicheno, *Robels and Redcoats: The America Revolutionary War* (London, 2010).

George Bilias, ed., *George Washington's Generals and Opponents: Their Exploits and Leadership* (New York, 1994).

Jeremy Black and Philip Woodfine, *The British Navy and the Use of Naval Power in the Eighteenth Century* (Leicester, 1988).

M. Le Comte de Lapeyrouse Bonfils, *Histoire de la Marine Française*, 3 vols. (Paris, 1845).

R. Arthur Bowler, *Logistics and the Failure of the British Army in America, 1775–1783* (Princeton, 1975).

Kenneth Breen, "Graves and Hood at the Chesapeake," *Mariner's Mirror*, 66 (1980), 53–65.

Timothy Breen, *American Insurgents, American Patriots: The Revolution of the People* (New York, 2010).

John Brooke, *King George III* (London, 1972).

Gerald S. Brown, *The American Secretary: The Colonial Policy of Lord George Germain, 1775–1778* (Ann Arbor, 1963).

John Buchanan, *The Road to Guilford Court House: The American Revolution in the Carolinas* (New York, 1997).

John Buchanan, *The Road to Valley Forge: How Washington Built the Army that Won the Revolution* (New York, 2004).

Richard Buel, *In Irons: Britain's Naval Supremacy and the American Revolutionary Economy* (New Haven, 1998).

Colin G. Calloway, *The American Revolution in Indian Country: Crisis and Diversity in Native American Communities* (New York, 1995).

Edward J. Cashin, *The King's Ranger: Thomas Brown and the American Revolution on the Southern Frontier* (Athens, Georgia, 1989).

I.R. Christie, *The End of North's Ministry, 1780–1782* (London, 1958).

W.S. Coker and R. Rea, *Anglo-Spanish Confrontation on the Gulf Coast during the American Revolution* (Pensacola, 1982).

Stephen Conway, *The War of American Independence, 1775–1783* (London, 1995).

Stephen Conway, *The British Isles and the War of American Independence* (Oxford, 2003).

Patrick Crowhurst, *The Defence of British Trade, 1689–1815* (Folkestone, 1977).

Edward E. Curtis, *The Organization of the British Army in the American Revolution* (New York, 1926).

Thomas Desjardin, *Through a Howling Wilderness: Benedict Arnold's March to Quebec, 1775* (New York, 2006).

Henri Doniol, *Histoire de la participation de la France à l'établissement des États-Unis d'Amérique: Correspondance diplomatique et documents*, 5 vols. (Paris, 1886–1892).

Jonathan Dull, *The French Navy and American Independence: A Study of Arms and Diplomacy, 1774–1787* (Princeton, 1975).

John Ferling, *John Adams: A Life* (New York, 1992).

John Ferling, *Almost a Miracle: The American Victory in the War of Independence* (New York, 2007).

John Ferling, *Independence: The Struggle to Set America Free* (London, 2011).

James T. Flexner, *George Washington in the American Revolution* (Boston, 1967).

David Hackett Fischer, *Paul Revere's Ride* (New York, 1994).

David Hackett Fischer, *Washington's Crossing* (New York, 2004).

Sir John Fortescue, *A History of the British Army*, 13 vols. (London, 1899–1930).

Douglas Southall Freeman, *George Washington: A Biography*, 7 vols. (New York, 1948–57).

Robert Gardiner, ed., *Navies and the American Revolution, 1775–1783* (London, 1996).

Don R. Gerlach, *Proud Patriot: Philip Schuyler and the War of Independence, 1775–1783* (Syracuse, 1987).

Terry Golway, *Washington's General: Nathanael Greene and the Triumph of the American Revolution* (New York, 2005).

Louis Gottschalk, *Lafayette and the Close of the American Revolution* (Chicago, 1941).

Barbara Graymont, *The Iroquois in the American Revolution* (Syracuse, 1972).

Robert Gross, *The Minutemen and their World* (New York, 1976).

Ira D. Gruber, *The Howe Brothers and the American Revolution* (New York, 1972).

W.N. Hargreaves-Mawdsley, *Eighteenth Century Spain, 1700–1788: A Political, Diplomatic and Institutional History* (London, 1979).

Lowell H. Harrison, *George Rogers Clark and the War in the West* (Lexington, KY, 1876).

Don Higginbotham, *Daniel Morgan: Revolutionary Rifleman* (Chapel Hill, 1961).

Don Higginbotham, *George Washington Reconsidered* (Charlottesville, 2001).

W. Robert Higgins, ed., *The Revolutionary War in the South: Power, Conflict and Leadership: Essays in Honor of John Richard Alden* (Duke, 1979).

Ronald Hoffman and Peter J. Albert, *Diplomacy and Revolution: The Franco American Alliance of 1778* (Charlottesville, 1981).

Ronald Hoffman and Peter J. Albert, eds., *Peace and the Peacemakers, The Great Powers and American Independence* (Charlottesville, 1986).

Paul M. Kennedy, *The Rise and Fall of British Naval Mastery* (London, 1976).

Lee Kennett, *The French Forces in America, 1780–1783* (Westport, 1977).

Richard M. Ketcham, *Saratoga: Turning Point of America's Revolutionary War* (New York, 1997).

Richard M. Ketchum, *Divided Loyalties: How the American Revolution came to New York* (2002).

Richard Ketcham, *Victory at Yorktown: The Campaign that Won the Revolution* (New York, 2004).

Georges Lacour-Gayet, *La Marine Militaire de la France sous le règne de Louis XVI* (Paris, 1905).

Robert Stansbury Lambert, *South Carolina Loyalists in the American Revolution* (Columbia, 1987).

Edward G. Lengel, *General George Washington: A Military Life* (New York, 2005).

Bruce Lenman, *Britain's Colonial Wars, 1688–1783* (London, 2001).

Charles Lee Lewis, *Admiral de Grasse and American Independence* (Annapolis, MD, 1945).

J.C. Long, *Lord Jeffery Amherst, Soldier of the King* (New York, 1933).

John F. Luzader, *Saratoga: A Military History of the Decisive Campaign of the American Revolution* (El Dorado Hills, CA, 2008).

John Lynch, *Bourbon Spain, 1700–1808* (Oxford, 1988).

Brendan McConville, *The King's Three Faces: The Rise and Fall of Royal America, 1688–1776* (Chapel Hill, 2006).

T.H. McGuffie, *The Siege of Gibraltar, 1779–1783* (London, 1965).

Piers Mackesy, *The War for America, 1775–1783* (Cambridge, Mass., 1964).

Piers Mackesy, *The Coward of Minden: The Affair of Lord George Sackville* (London, 1979).

Peter J. Marshall, ed., *The Oxford History of the British Empire, Volume II, The Eighteenth Century* (Oxford, 1998).

Peter J. Marshall, *The Making and Unmaking of Empires: Britain, India and America, c. 1750–1783* (Oxford, 2005).

David Mattern, *Benjamin Lincoln and the American Revolution* (Columbia, SC, 1995).

James Kirby Martin, *Benedict Arnold: Revolutionary Hero* (New York, 1997).

Robert Middlekauf, *The Glorious Cause: The American Revolution, 1763–1789* (Oxford, 1982).

Richard Middleton, *The Bells of Victory: The Pitt Newcastle Ministry and the Conduct of the Seven Years War, 1757–1762* (Cambridge, Eng., 1985).

Richard Middleton, "British Naval Strategy, 1755–1762: The Western Squadron," *Mariners' Mirror*, 75 (1989), 349–67.

Richard Middleton, *Pontiac's War: Its Causes, Course and Consequences* (New York, 2007).

Richard B. Morris, *The Peacemakers: The Great Powers and American Independence* (New York, 1965).

Orville T. Murphy, *Charles Gravier, Comte de Vergennes: French Diplomacy in the Age of Revolution, 1719–1787* (Albany, 1982).

Paul David Nelson, *General Horatio Gates: A Biography* (Baton Rouge, 1976).

Paul David Nelson, *Anthony Wayne: Soldier of the Early Republic* (Bloomington, 1985).

William R. Nester, *The Frontier War for American Independence* (Mechanicsburg, Pa., 2004).

James H. O'Donnell, *Southern Indians in the American Revolution* (Knoxville, 1973).

Andrew J. O'Shaughnessy, *An Empire Divided: The American Revolution and the British Caribbean* (Philadelphia, 2000).

Francisco Morales Padron, *Spanish Help in American Independence* (Madrid, 1952).

R.R. Palmer, *The Age of the Democratic Revolution: A Political History of Europe and America*, 2 vols. (Princeton, 1959–64).

John S. Pancake, *1777: The Year of the Hangman* (Tuscaloosa, 1977).

John S. Pancake, *This Destructive War: The British Campaign in the Carolinas, 1780–1782* (Tuscaloosa, 1985).

A. Temple Patterson, *The Other Armada: The Franco Spanish Attempt to Invade Britain in 1779* (Manchester, 1960).

Howard H. Peckham, *The Toll of Independence, Engagements and Battle Casualties of the American Revolution* (Chicago, 1974).

James Breck Perkins, *France in the American Revolution* (Boston, 1911).

Charles Petrie, *King Charles III of Spain: an Enlightened Despot* (London, 1971).

Louis W. Potts, *Arthur Lee: A Virtuous Revolutionary* (Baton Rouge, 1981).

Benjamin Quarles, *The Negro in the American Revolution* (Norton, 1973).

N.A.M. Rodger, *The Insatiable Earl: A Life of John Montagu, 4th Earl of Sandwich* (New York, 1993).

N.A.M. Rodger, *The Command of the Ocean: A Naval History of Britain, 1649–1845* (New York, 2004).

Charles Royster, *A Revolutionary People at War: The Continental Army and American Character, 1775–1783* (New York, 1979).

Charles Royster, *Light Horse Harry Lee and the Legacy of the American Revolution* (New York, 1981).

Barnet Schecter, *Battle for New York: The City at the Heart of the American Revolution* (2002).

Hamish M. Scott, "The Importance of Bourbon Naval Reconstruction to the Strategy of Choiseul after the Seven Years War," *International History Review*, 1 (1979), 17–35.

Hamish M. Scott, *British Foreign Policy in the Age of the American Revolution* (Oxford, 1990).

Hal T. Shelton, *General Richard Montgomery and the American Revolution* (New York, 1994).

Brendan Simms, *Three Victories and a Defeat: The Rise and Fall of the First British Empire* (London, 2007).

Paul H. Smith, *Loyalists and Redcoats: A Study in British Revolutionary Policy* (Chapel Hill, 1964).

David Spinney, *Rodney* (London, 1969).

Mathew H. Spring, *With Zeal and With Bayonets Only: The British Army on Campaign in North America, 1775–1783* (Norman, Oklahoma, 2010).

Charles Stedman, *The History of the Origin, Progress and Termination of the American War*, 2 vols. (London, 1974).

William C. Stinchcombe, *The American Revolution and the French Alliance* (Syracuse, 1969).

Andrew Stockley, *Britain and France at the Birth of America: The European Powers and the Peace Negotiations of 1782–1783* (Exeter, 2001).

David Syrett, *Shipping and the American War, 1775–1783: A Study in British Transport Organization* (London, 1970).

David Syrett, *The Royal Navy in American Waters, 1775–1783* (Aldershot, 1989).

David Syrett, "Home Waters or America? The Dilemma of British Naval Strategy in 1778," *Mariner's Mirror*, 77 (1991), 365–77.

David Syrett, *The Royal Navy in European Waters during the American Revolutionary War* (Columbia, SC, 1998).

David Syrett, *Admiral Lord Howe: A Biography* (Annapolis, MD, 2006).

John E. Talbott, *Pen and Ink Sailor: Charles Middleton and the King's Navy, 1778–1813* (London, 1998).

Alan Taylor, *The Divided Ground: Indians, Settlers and the Northern Borderland of the American Revolution* (New York, 2006).

Theodore Thayer, *The Making of a Scapegoat: Washington and Lee at Monmouth* (Port Washington, 1976).

Evan Thomas, *John Paul Jones: Sailor, Hero, Father of the American Navy* (New York, 2003).

Peter D.G. Thomas, *Lord North* (London, 1976).

Peter D.G. Thomas, "George III and the American Revolution," *History*, 70 (1985), 16–31.

B.P. Thompson, *Spain: Forgotten Ally of the American Revolution* (North Quincy, Mass., 1976).

Nicholas Tracy, *Navies, Deterrence and American Independence: Britain and Seapower in the 1760's and 1770's* (Vancouver, 1988).

William Wallace, *Appeal to Arms: A Military History of the American Revolution* (New York, 1964).

Christopher Ward, *The War of the Revolution: A Military History of the American Revolution*, John R. Alden, ed., 2 vols. (New York, 1952).

Gavin K. Watt, *Rebellion in the Mohawk Valley: The St Leger Expedition of 1777* (Toronto, 2002).

Richard White, *The Middle Ground: Indians, Empires, and Republics in the Great Lakes Region, 1650–1815* (Cambridge, Eng., 1991).

Peter Whiteley, *Lord North: The Prime Minister who lost America* (London, 1996).

Arnold Whitridge, *Rochambeau: America's Neglected Founding Father* (New York, 1965).

Franklin and Mary Wickwire, *Cornwallis and the War of Independence* (London, 1971).

William B. Willcox, *Portrait of a General: Sir Henry Clinton in the War of Independence* (New York, 1964).

David K. Wilson, *The Southern Strategy: Britain's Conquest of South Carolina and Georgia, 1775–1780* (Columbia, SC, 2005).

W.J. Wood, *Battles of the Revolutionary War, 1775–1781* (New York, 1995).

Index

Adams, John, 16, 43, 78, 237
  peace negotiations, 54, 240, 312–3
Admiralty
  shipping and transports, 44, 47
  convoys, 92–3, 199
  relations with other departments, 91–2
  see also Britain (Royal Navy) and Sandwich
African Americans, 15, 32, 35
  recruitment by Patriots, 27, 33, 281
  service with British, 289
Albany, 17, 223
  British objective, 70, 71, 72, 75, 83, 84–5, 86–7, 88, 89
Allen, Ethan, 23
American colonies
  differences with Britain, 3–5
  regional differences, 16–7
  collapse of royal government, 12, 19–20
  and independence, 16, 31–2, 34–5
American Indians
  see Native Americans and individual nations
American Loyalists
  persecution of, 10, 20, 23, 31, 45, 63, 122–3, 131, 183, 186–7, 289
  numbers and location, 41–5, 183, 255–56, 258, 260, 261–62
  British attitude towards, 45, 62–3, 151–2, 199–200, 301, 323
  provincial units and militias, 74, 128–9, 130, 174, 176–7, 178–9
  after Yorktown, 305, 313, 315
American Patriots
  areas of support, 41–45
  geographical advantages, 21, 322
  attitude to Britain, 6–7, 16, 31–2, 52, 177, 179–80, 182–3, 321
  antipathy to standing armies, 4, 16, 21, 106
  provincial congresses, 9–10, 12, 30–1, 43
  and loyalists, 10, 131
  independence, 16, 31–2
  attitude to French Canadians, 9, 23, 25, 32
  and the French, 29–30, 31, 104–5, 237
  lack of morale, 198–9, 199
  attitude to Indians, 23, 211–2, 231
  see also American States, Continental Congress
American states
  population, 15
  constitutions and bills of rights, 34–5
  state rivalries, 16–17, 49
  recruiting of Continental army, 73–4, 121, 159, 191–2, 242–3, 303–4
  see also American Patriots, Continental Congress, Washington and Greene
Amherst, General Sir Jeffery, 71
  favours maritime measures, 107, 150, 151
  at cabinet meetings, 110
  defence of Britain, 147–8
André, Major John, 197–8
Anson, Admiral Lord,
  benchmark achievements, 113, 114, 149
Antigua, 306
Aranjuez, Treaty of, 141–2

Arbuthnot, Admiral Marriot, 157, 158, 167 footnote 104
  relations with Clinton, 194, 209 footnote 159
  naval operations, 174, 177, 194, 196, 271–2
Arcon, Chevalier d', 310
Armed Neutrality League, 201–2
  Britain's attitude to, 244–5
  see also Holland, Russia
Arnold, Benedict, 23, 241
  campaigns, 25–6, 28–9, 58, 82, 85–6, 224–5
  treason and subsequent career, 197–8, 270–3, 284
Augusta, 129–30, 173–4, 176
  Patriot siege, 183, 260, 262
Austria, 103, 105
  Offer of Mediation, 239

backcountry
  northern, 231
  southern, 42–3, 44, 184–5, 269 footnote 148
Balfour, Colonel Nesbitt, 176, 260
Barbados (Carlisle Bay), 171, 306
Barras, Commodore Comte de, 275, 282, 284, 285
Barrington, Lord William, 25, 90
Barrington, Admiral Samuel, 127–8, 301
Baum, Colonel Friedrich, 83–4
Beaumarchais, Pierre Augustan, 29, 30, 74
Bennington, Vt., 83–4
Bird, Captain Henry, 220
Blue Licks, battle of, 221–2
Blackstock's Plantation, battle of, 187
Boston, 5–7, 8, 9
  siege and evacuation, 11, 12–13, 19, 32–3, 34
  French fleet at, 125, 304
Bouille, General, Marquis de, 171, 306
Bourbon Powers (France and Spain), 105
  naval forces, 141, 309
  plans to invade Britain, 142, 143, 147–8
  other joint operations, 246, 275–8, 305, 309, 310
  impact on Britain's resources, 321
  see also France and Spain
Brandywine Creek, battle of, 78–9
Brant, Joseph, Mohawk Warrior, 221, 224
  campaigns, 221, 224, 225, 226, 228, 230, 231
  and peace, 315
Brant, Molly [Mary], 223, 225
Brest, 111–2, 148, 239
  British attempts to blockade, 114–5, 146, 162, 245, 247–8
Britain (army)
  recruitment and strength, 2, 18, 24–5, 46, 70, 106–7, 144, 147, 150–1, 162, 43, 323
  discipline and tactics, 37 footnote 18, 79, 255
  deployment in America, 32–4, 44–5, 50–63, 72, 75–89, 121–4, 128–32, 152–7, 172–87, 193–4, 223–4, 248–62, 270–5, 278–89, 301–2
  in West Indies, 127–8, 276, 306
  casualties and losses, 12, 20–21, 87, 155, 289
  supplies, 59, 63, 73, 77, 80
  relations with civilians, 43, 56, 77, 126, 155, 193, 198, 260
  see also Gibraltar, Minorca
Britain (ministry)
  legacy of Seven Years War, 15, 47
  Treasury and finance, 1–2, 15, 299, 310–11
  value of the colonies, 1–3, 6–10, 17–18, 111, 301, 323
  attitude to Patriots, 7–8, 9, 15–16, 17–18, 23, 24, 243, 322–3
  and Loyalists, 23, 44, 45, 152, 199–200, 315, 323
  and Native Americans, 211–12, 213, 222, 225, 315
  military and naval resources, 15, 24–5, 46–8, 70, 162, 321, 243, 323–4
  attitude to France, 92–3, 109, 111, 240, 243
  attitude to Spain, 141, 240,
  attitude of other European powers, 19, 201, 244, 324–5

Britain (ministry) (*continued*)
  strategy and view of the American war, 18–19, 31–2, 44–8, 69, 88, 106–08, 110, 150, 172–3, 198, 244, 248, 262, 270, 298, 300
  lack of a war minister, 109–10, 143, 324
  West Indies, 18, 110, 127, 159, 305
  Holland and neutral trade, 200–2, 244
  peace commissioners and negotiations, 24, 111, 130–1, 300–1, 310–15
  assessment of, 63, 96, 322–4
  consequences of the war, 325
Britain (Royal navy)
  North American squadron, 90–5, 111, 156, 194, 202, 243, 277, 283–5, 287, 289
  support of the army in America, 31–2, 44, 90
  blockade enforcement, 19, 90–2, 93, 95–6
  convoys and supplies to the army, 199, 200
  privateers, 27, 90–1, 93, 148
  merchant losses, 93, 95, 150
  mobilization and size of fleet, 90–1, 92, 145, 149, 247
  manpower, 145, 164 footnote 33
  ship construction, 94–5, 145, 150, 165 footnote 63, 308–09
  coppering and other technical improvements, 115, 144–5, 284, 306
  lack of frigates, 91, 92, 94–5, 117, 149, 199
  lack of battleships and naval supremacy, 113–14, 162, 247, 291–2, 323
  Channel fleet, 112, 114–17, 164 footnote 42, 245, 309–10
  West Indies, 127–8, 157, 171–2, 216, 275–78, 305–8
  North Sea, 200–2, 309, 245
  tactics (Fighting Instructions), 116, 144, 161, 285
  divisions among officers, 116–17, 161
Brodhead, Brigadier Daniel, 228, 229
Brooklyn, NY, 49
  battle of, 52–3

Brown, Colonel Thomas, 176, 262
  Indian responsibilities, 215, 262, 269 footnote 150
Brunswick, Principality of
  hire and deployment of troops from, 46, 83–4
Brunswick, NJ, 58, 62
Buford, Colonel Abraham, 176
  "Tarleton's Quarter," 185
Bunker Hill, battle of, 20
  influence on Patriot military tactics, 26, 33, 52, 54, 78
Burgoyne, General John, 20, 71, 84
  campaign plans and orders, 70, 71, 72, 84, 88
  strength of army, 81, 85, 87
  Saratoga campaign, 80–7, 88, 89
  assessment of, 89
Butler, John, 224, 226
Byron, Admiral John, 112, 125, 128, 157

Cadiz, 141, 142, 148, 159, 160, 196, 245, 246, 309
Camden, 259
  battle of, 181–2
Cameron, Alexander, 215, 232 footnote 22
Campbell, Colonel Archibald, 128–31
Campbell, Brigadier John, 215–16
Campbell, Colonel William, 184, 252
Campbell, Governor William, 43, 44, 173
Canada
  French speaking population, 2, 18
  relations with Patriots, 23, 28, 29
  Patriot plans and campaigns, 23–4, 28–9, 49, 126–7
  French attitude to, 30, 104, 106, 304, 311
Cape Fear River, 186, 249, 256
Cape Français, 278
Cape St Vincent, battle of, 161
Caribbean,
  see West Indies
Carleton, General Sir Guy, 23, 47
  Canadian campaigns, 58, 70, 81, 88–9
  commander-in-chief in New York, 300–1
Carlisle, Lord,
  peace Commission, 110, 122–3

Castine, Me, 156–7, 304
Castries, Marquis de, 238, 239, 298
Catherine, Empress, 46, 201
  see also Russia
Caughnawaga, NY, 225, 229
Channel (English)
  navigation hazards, 144, 169
  French and Spanish incursions into, 147–8, 246, 308, 309
Channel Fleet (Western Squadron)
  defence of the Channel, 114–16, 146–8, 164 footnote 42, 245–8, 323
  relief of Gibraltar, 160–2, 245, 310
Charles III, King of Spain, 140–1, 170
Charleston, SC, 45, 131, 262
  capture by British, 174–5, 177
  evacuation, 300, 305
Chatterton's Hill, NY, battle of, 57
Cherokee, 212
  campaigns against the Patriots, 212–13, 214–15, 216,
Cherry Valley, NY, 227
Chesapeake
  British attempts to patrol, 91, 93, 95–6
  British interest in, 178, 183, 272
  military and naval operations, 77, 270–5, 278–89
  British plans for a naval base, 186, 271, 273, 279–80
Chickasaw Indians, 212, 213, 215
Choiseul, Etienne, Duc de, 1, 19, 103
Choctaw Indians, 212, 213, 215, 216
Clark, George Rogers, 218–22
  attitude to Indians, 218, 219
  influence on Peace terms, 313, 320 footnote 85
Clarke, Colonel Elijah, 183, 260, 262
Clinton, General Sir Henry, 11, 44–5, 59–60, 108, 281
  orders from Germain, 108–9, 110, 150–1, 153, 157, 173, 243, 270, 292, 301
  lack of reinforcements, 151, 156, 157, 195, 199, 202, 215, 243
  view of the war, 195, 197–8, 241
  campaigns in the north, 86–7, 108, 110, 122–3, 126, 153–9

southern operations, 44–5, 128, 153, 173–7, 179, 195, 249, 258
  and loyalists, 44–5, 128, 153, 178, 195, 199–200, 280, 301
  and Royal Navy, 154, 156, 194, 195, 198, 275
  plans to attack Rhode Island, 125, 194, 198, 283, 284
  and the Chesapeake, 178, 186, 195, 272
  concern for New York, 177, 272, 275
  Yorktown campaign, 270, 271, 272, 275, 278–80, 283–4, 286, 287, 291
  contemporary and historical assessment of, 281, 292, 302
Collier, Sir George, 167 footnote 103
coastal raids, 94, 154–5, 156–7
Concord, Ma, battle of, 11–2
Confederation, Articles of, 35–6
  western lands, 36, 242
Connecticut,
  Loyalists, 10, 31, 83–4
  Continental troops, 192
  see also New England
Continental army
  formation and terms of service, 11–12, 55–6, 315
  numbers, 53, 60, 62, 73, 81–2, 85, 86, 121, 129, 132, 154, 179, 181, 188, 191, 193, 195, 196, 252, 290, 302
  recruitment, 21–2, 27–8, 33, 121, 127–8, 190, 195–6, 303–4
  equipment and supplies, 22, 50, 118–20, 127, 152, 195, 240, 242–3, 303–4
  discipline and training, 22, 48–50, 78, 120–1
  winter quarters, 127, 152, 159, 290
  plundering by troops, 56–7, 77, 195
  interstate jealousies, 49, 50, 82
  British view of, 46, 76, 88
  morale, 50, 53, 63, 127, 155, 191–2
  mutinies by, 152, 192, 240–1, 304
  officer dissatisfaction, 119, 120, 121, 192, 315–16
  casualties, 20, 53, 57, 129, 175, 182
  see also Washington, Greene, Gates

Continental Congress (First, 1774), 9, 17
Continental Congress (Second, 1775–1783), 12
  powers under Articles of Confederation, 35–6
  military appointments by, 18, 85, 181, 188
  Indian relations, 211, 217, 222–3, 227, 315
  attitude to Canada, 23–4, 49
  French alliance, 29–30, 105–6, 313
  independence, 31-2, 34–5
  fears of a standing army, 55, 119, 316
  control of the army, 61, 79, 118, 190, 242
  recruitment of the army, 12, 17, 27–8, 56, 190, 242
  appeals to the states (requisition system), 35–6, 191
  currency and financial difficulties, 17, 152, 191, 242
  peace terms and negotiations, 54, 310, 311, 312–3
  see also American Patriots, Articles of Confederation, Washington and Greene
Continental navy, 60, 93, 117, 143, 148
  privateers, 27, 90–5, 104
Conway, Thomas, 90
coppering of ships, 115, 144, 271
Cordoba, Admiral don Juan, 147, 148, 161, 200, 245, 246, 309, 310
Cornplanter, warrior chief, 226, 228, 230
Cornwallis, Charles, Earl, 178, 204 footnote 42
  early campaigns, 58–9, 61–2
  orders from Clinton, 178, 249, 257–8, 273
  criticism of Clinton, 279, 280, 291
  treatment of prisoners and paroles, 182–4, 185–6
  Loyalist appeals and proclamations, 183, 186, 253, 255
  military operations in the Carolinas, 176, 177–87, 248–58
  advance into Virginia, 257–8, 273–5, 278–80
  Yorktown, 280–81, 283–4, 285–7, 288–9, 291, 316 footnote 18

counterfactual history, 125–6
Cowpens, battle of, 249–50
Crawford, Colonel William, 221
Creek Indians, 211–217
Crillon, Duc de, 246–7, 308, 310
Cross Creek, NC, 179, 183, 186, 251, 254, 256
  Highland Loyalists, 180
Cruger, Colonel John, 183–4, 261

Danbury, Conn, 73
Darby, Admiral George, 245, 246, 266 footnote 68
Dartmouth, Lord, 8, 47
Deane, Silas, 30, 104
Delaware Indians, 212, 217, 221
Delaware River, 77
  forts, 79–80
Detroit, 3, 315
  Patriot plans against, 218, 219, 220
  British operations from, 219, 220
Dickinson, John, 24, 60
Digby, Admiral Robert, 161, 162, 286, 305
Dominica, 127, 128, 142, 314
Dogger Bank, battle of, 246
Dragging Canoe, warrior chief, 212, 214–15, 216
Dunmore, Lord, 32, 43

East India Company, 7, 8, 243, 314
  convoys, 92–3, 200
Ebenezer, Ga., 129
Elk River, 77, 98 footnote 43
Estaing, Admiral, Comte d'
  operations in America, 111–12, 124–6, 128, 159
  West Indies, 157
Eutaw Springs, SC, battle of, 302

Falmouth, Me, 31
Ferguson, Major Patrick
  South Carolina militia, 177, 178, 179
  King's Mountain, 184–5
Fishdam Ford, SC, 187
Fishing Creek, SC, 182
Florida
  Spanish Claims to, 140, 314
  East Florida, 2, 110, 217, 314
  West Florida, 213–14, 215–16

Floridablanca, Count, 140, 170, 238, 324
Fort Edward, NY, 81–2
Fort George, NY, 82
Fort Lee, NJ, 57, 58
Fort Pitt, *see* Pittsburgh
Fort Royal Bay, *see* Martinique
Fort St Johns, Canada, 25, 28–9, 88, 229
Fort St Philip (Minorca), 247, 301
Fort Stanwix, NY, 223, 224, 225
Fort Washington, NY, 51, 56–8
Fox, Charles James, 312, 313–14
France (army)
    strength and European deployment, 105, 112
    army in America, 193–4, 239, 304, 308
    engineers, 287–8, 290
    French officers in American service, 74, 104
    Attitude to Patriot military ability, 125
France (ministry)
    political and strategic aims, 30, 103–4, 112, 141–2, 169–70, 237–8, 298–9, 305
    relations with Britain, 19, 103, 104–5
    early contacts with Patriots, 29–30, 104–5
    American alliance, 105–6, 170, 237, 304, 313
    military supplies to Patriots, 30, 74, 104, 142, 239, 248
    Bourbon alliance (with Spain), 105, 141–2, 169–70, 309–10
    dispatch of forces to America, 170, 192, 194, 196–7, 208 footnote 141
    West Indies, 106, 142, 169–70, 237–8, 239, 298–9
    financial constraints, 103, 311
    peace moves and negotiations, 308, 310, 311–4
    consequences of the war, 321, 325
France (navy)
    protection of Patriot commerce, 92, 104–5
    naval preparations and construction, 1, 30, 113–14, 237, 308–9, 310

    naval tactics and doctrine, 115–16, 171, 271–2, 285, 307
    English Channel and Bay of Biscay, 111–12, 147–8, 246–8, 298–9
    West Indies, 169, 172, 275–8
    North America, 111–12, 193–4, 278, 282–9
Franklin, Benjamin, 17
    envoy to France, 104
    peace negotiations, 52, 54, 312–13
Franklin, Governor William, 200, 281
Fraser, General Simon, 81, 85

Gage, General Thomas, 11
    attitude to the conflict, 8, 10, 12, 21
    orders and military operations, 10, 11, 20, 32–3
    treatment of prisoners, 23
Galloway, Joseph, 17, 122, 150
Galpin, George, 214
Galvez, Governor Bernardo de, 239
    support for Patriots, 213
    military operations by, 215–17, 307
    and Yorktown campaign, 278, 290
Gates, General Horatio, 85, 90
    Saratoga campaign, 85–7
    southern command, 181–2
George III, King of Great Britain and Ireland, 24
    attitude to the war, 18, 88, 107, 110, 142–3, 162, 244, 245, 299
    relations with ministers, 110, 143, 299, 300, 316 footnote 12, 324
    comments on commanders, 156–7, 248
Georgia, 96
    British invasion, 69, 108, 110, 128–31
    Patriot and Loyalist militia, 130, 250
    assembly and civil government, 131, 251
Germain, Lord George, 47
    views on the war, 94, 111, 112, 150–1, 243
    orders to commanders in America, 47, 69, 70, 72, 76, 97 footnote 15, 108–9, 150–1, 270, 272
    dispatch of reinforcements, 70, 107, 151, 157, 243

Germain, Lord George (*continued*)
  need for Loyalist support, 108–9, 151, 173
  southern strategy, 108–9, 128, 130–1, 173, 270, 272
  use of Indians, 151, 223, 226
  assessment of, 89, 292, 299
Germantown, Pa, battle of, 80
Gibraltar,
  siege and relief of, 159–62, 244–5, 309–10
  Spanish claims and designs on, 140, 238
  and the Peace, 314
Girty, Simon, 222
Gloucester, Va., 280, 288
Gnadenhutten massacre, 221
Grant, General James, 127–8
Grasse, Admiral Francois Joseph Paul, Comte de
  orders, 239, 298
  West Indian operations, 275–8, 305–8
  Yorktown campaign, 243, 274, 278, 281–2, 284–5, 286, 287, 289, 290
  assessment of, 290–91
Graves, Admiral Thomas, 194, 277, 279–80
  Capes of Virginia battle, 284–5, 289
Great Lakes Indians, 217–18, 219
Greene, Nathanael, 56–7, 119–20, 188
  army strength, 252, 256–7, 261
  attitude to the militia, 188–9, 198, 259
  and partisan leaders, 252, 260, 261
  Congress and the states, 198–9, 261
  southern campaigns, 187–90, 248–62, 302–3
  strategy and tactics, 188–9, 207 footnote 100, 249, 252, 254, 256–7, 302
  view of British, 190, 252
  assessment of, 303
Green Spring, Va., battle of, 279
Grenada, battle of, 157
Grenville, George 2–3
Grey, General Sir Charles, 79, 152
Guadeloupe, 110

Guichen, Admiral, Comte de, 169
  orders to, 169, 170, 247
  naval operations by, 171, 172, 196, 246–8, 309, 310
Guilford Court House, NC, battle of, 254–5
gunpowder (saltpeter), 27, 91

Haldimand, Governor Frederick, 225, 226, 229, 231
Halifax, NS, 34, 50, 94, 107, 156, 158
Hamilton, Colonel Henry, 217–18
Hancock, John, 27, 118
Hanover, 103, 109
  Hanoverian troops, 25, 160
Hardy, Admiral Sir Charles
  Channel Fleet, 146–8, 160
Harlem Heights, NY, 54–5
Henry, Patrick, 5, 218
Herkimer, General Nicholas, 224
Hesse, Captain Emanuel, 219–20
Hesse, principality
  hire of troops, 46
  field operations by, 55, 57, 61, 78, 128, 177
Highlands, NY
  forts, 57, 71, 86, 154–5, 197–8, 282
  see also West Point
Hillsborough, NC, 182, 183, 253
Hobkirk's Hill, battle of, 258, 259–60
Holland, 114
  neutral rights and naval stores, 200–2
  naval operations by, 200, 245–6, 308, 309
  peace treaty, 314, 320 footnote 85
Holston River settlements, 184, 213
Honduras logwood cutters, 141
Hood, Admiral Sir Samuel, 172
  West Indies, 276–8, 306–8
  Yorktown campaign, 283–4, 289
Hopkins, Commodore Esek, 60
Howe, Admiral Lord Rchard
  appointment and orders, 47–8
  peace commission, 48, 51–2, 54, 59
  naval operations in America, 59, 93–4, 95–6, 124–6
  naval operations in Europe, 308–10
  criticisms of 51–2, 95

Howe, General Sir William, 11, 108
  at Boston, 20, 33, 34
  force requirements and reinforcements, 46, 56, 69, 76, 106
  campaign plans and orders, 47, 50–1, 69–70, 74–5
  attitude to Patriot army, 46, 56, 75, 76
  campaigns by, 51–60, 73, 75–80
  co-operation with Carleton and Burgoyne, 51, 56, 70, 72, 75, 76–7
  missed opportunities, 51–2, 53, 55, 56, 57, 58–9, 78–9, 88, 121
  assessment of, 51–2, 89, 101
  footnote 113
Howe, General Robert, 129, 241
Hudson River, 49, 52, 57, 84, 87, 154, 198, 271, 282–3
  see also North River
Hutchinson, Governor Thomas, 5, 6

Iles des Saintes, battle of, 307–8
Illinois, 218–22
  French population, 218–19, 221
India, 243, 314
Indians, see Native America, also individual nations
Intolerable Acts, 8–9
Ireland
  Irish recruitment in America, 26, 129, 241
  Irish patriot party, 29, 192
  French threat to, 109, 246
Iroquois (Six Nations), 222–31
  early neutrality, 23, 222–3
  splitting of the confederacy, 225,
  invasion of homeland, 227–9, 230–1
  and the peace, 231, 315

Jamaica
  Spanish plans against, 140, 238, 278, 305, 307, 308, 310
  British defence measures, 160, 247, 307
James River, 186, 270
Jay, John, 312–13
Jefferson, Thomas, 35
  as governor of Virginia, 261, 270–1, 273
Johnson, Guy, 222, 223

Johnson, Sir John, 223, 224, 228, 229, 230
Jones, John Paul, 117, 143, 148

Kalb, General Johan de, 179, 181
Kempenfelt, Captain Richard (then Admiral), 146
  naval cruises, 247–8, 266
  footnote 68
Kentucky, 218, 219, 220
Keppel, Admiral Augustus
  command of Channel Fleet, 114–17, 146
  First Lord of Admiralty, 308
Kiashuta, warrior chief, 223, 229
Kingsbridge, NY, 49, 54, 62
King's Mountain, battle of, 184–5
  value of irregular warfare, 185
Knox, Colonel Henry, 33–4, 290
Knyphausen, General Wilhelm von, 174
  field operations, 78, 193

La Fayette, Marquis de, 79, 170, 192
  field commands, 122, 123–4, 125
  in Virginia, 271, 272–3, 279, 283, 289
Lake Champlain, 23, 71, 72, 80, 81, 84, 88
Lake George, 82, 84, 86
Langara, Admiral Don Juan de, 161
Laurens, Henry
  president of Congress, 117–18
  peace envoy, 202, 312, 319
  footnote 81
Laurens, Colonel John, 242
Lee, Arthur, 29
Lee, Charles
  operations, 48, 58, 123–4
  relations with Washington, 58, 67, footnote 99, 123–4
Lee, Major Henry, 158
  in the south, 188, 252, 253, 254, 260, 262
Leslie, General Alexander
  southern operations, 186, 187, 248, 249, 250, 303
Lewis, Brigadier Andrew, 213
Lexington, Ma, 11

Lincoln, General Benjamin, 82
    in the south, 129, 131, 159, 174, 289, 290
Long Island, 194
    military operations, 49, 51–2
Louis XVI, King of France, 30, 237, 239, 240, 324
Louisville, 221
Luzerne, Chevalier de, 237
    advice to de Grasse, 274, 281, 295 footnote 72

McCrea, Jane, 83
McIntosh, General Lachlan, 218
Mahan, Colonel Ezekiel, 259,
    Mahan tower, 259, 262
Manhattan, 53–6, 242, 272, 281
Manley, Commodore John, 93, 94
Marion, General Francis, 180
    operations by, 183, 185, 186, 259, 260, 262
Martin, Governor Josiah, 20, 44
Martinique, 110, 127
    (Fort Royal Bay), 276, 277, 306–7
Maryland
    and Articles of Confederation, 36, 242
    Continentals, 181, 188 250, 254, 255, 259
Massachusetts
    opposition to Britain, 7, 8, 9, 14 footnote 14
    military operations by, 156
Mercantilism (Navigation Acts), 1–3, 6
Mid-Atlantic region
    religious and ethnic composition, 42
Middlebrook, NJ, 75, 77, 152
Middleton, Sir Charles
    appointment and reforms, 145, 146, 199
    view of naval affairs, 149–50
militia
    Minutemen, 11, 12
    see individual states and regions, Loyalists and Patriots; also Washington and Greene
Mingo Indians, 217, 229
Minorca (Port Mahon)
    Spanish claims and attacks, 140–1, 238, 246–7

garrison, 160, 161, 244–5, 246–7, 301
    and peace, 314
Mississippi River
    British settlements, 213, 215–6
    and peace negotiations, 313
Mobile, 216
Mohawk Indians, 223, 225, 229
    see also Joseph Brant
Mohawk River and Valley, 225, 230–1
Monck's Corner, 175, 260, 262, 302
Monmouth Court House, battle of, 123–4
Montgomery, General Richard, 25, 28–9
Montreal, 24, 29
Moore's Creek Bridge, battle of, 44
Morgan, Daniel
    northern campaigns, 26, 29, 85–6
    in the south, 188, 249–51
Morristown, NJ, 62, 73, 74, 75
Motte-Piquet, Admiral La, 157, 245
Murray, General James, 18, 247, 301

Natchez, 213
Native America
    military operations by, 211–31
    talks with the Patriots, 23, 211, 315
    as allies of the British, 72, 80–1, 84, 130
    and the Spanish, 216, 217
    methods of warfare, 84, 220, 224, 226–7
    see also individual Nations
Necker, Jacques, 237, 244, 263 footnote 6
Nevis, 314
New Bedford, Ma, 126
Newcastle, Thomas Pelham Holles, Duke of, 324
New England, 2
    religion and ethnicity, 16, 41–2
    militia, 28, 33, 82, 85, 86
    military raids against, 31–2, 73, 94, 126, 154–5, 284
Newfoundland
    fishery, 313, 314
New Hampshire
    militia, 82, 83–4

New Jersey, 42
  Loyalists, 62–3, 59, 74, 261
  militia, 58, 60, 76, 193
  Continental line, 241
New Orleans, 213, 215
Newport, RI
  as a British base, 59, 93, 125, 158
  as a French base, 193–4, 196
  see also Rhode Island
Newtown, battle of, 228
New York City, 49–50
  British control of, 19, 158, 173, 272, 300–1, 304, 314
  Loyalists, 174, 257–8
  as a naval base, 59, 279–80
  see also Clinton and Washington
New York State, 42, 49–50
  devastation of, 230
Niagara, 3, 228, 229
Ninety Six, SC, 176, 186, 260–2
Norfolk, Va., 43
North, Lord Frederick, 300
  earlier economies, 95, 113, 114
  sustainability of the war, 109–10, 142–3, 299
  conciliation initiatives, 6–7, 11, 48
  burdens of office, 109–10, 143, 300
  raising of supplies, 162, 244
  assessment of, 324
North Carolina, 42–3
  military operations in, 178–87, 180–1, 183–90, 248–59
  Loyalist support, 130, 180, 183, 253, 255–6, 258
  Patriot militia, 250, 252, 253–5, 256
  backcountry, 42–4, 184
North River, 51, 54, 55, 274
  see also Hudson River

O'Hara, General Charles, 251, 280, 289
Ohio River, 217–22
  Indian peoples, 217–22
  see also Shawnee, Delaware and Mingo
Oneida Indians, 223–4
  and Patriots, 225, 228, 230, 315
Onondaga
  Iroquois council chamber, 223, 225, 228

Ordnance Board, 91–2
Oriskany, battle of, 224
Orvilliers, Admiral Comte d', 111, 115–16, 147–8, 160
Oswald, Richard, 312
Oswego, 228, 231

Paine, Thomas, 32, 60
Palliser, Admiral Sir Hugh, 95
  court martial and aftermath, 116–17, 146, 161
Paoli Tavern, battle of, 79
Parker, Admiral Hyde, 171, 246
Parker, Admiral Sir Peter, 93
  Carolinas expedition, 44–5, 212
  West Indies, 161, 277, 278
Parliament, Acts of
  Stamp Act, 3, 4–5, 17
  Declaratory Act, 5–6
  Intolerable Acts, 8
  New England Restraining Act, 19
  Prohibitory Act, 34, 59, 90
Parliament
  debates and speeches, 5, 52, 299–300, 315
  sovereignty of, 5, 6, 9, 52, 111
partisans
  in the south, 180, 183–6, 188–90, 253, 258–62
Peace of Paris (1763), 1, 2, 30, 103, 314
peace commission (British), 111, 122–3, 126, 130–1
peace negotiations, 222, 311–15
Pennsylvania, 42
  Continental line, 79, 240–1, 271, 273
Pensacola, 110, 170, 216–17
Petersburg, Va., 186, 270, 272
Philadelphia, 9, 12, 16, 58, 60, 197, 240
  British designs and occupation of, 69–70, 72, 74–80, 88, 106, 108, 110, 122–3, 273, 287
  ladies of Philadelphia, 195
Philips, General William, 257, 271–2, 273
Pickens, Colonel Andrew, 130, 180, 260–1
Pitt, William, Earl of Chatham, 104, 109–10, 163 footnote 16, 324

Pittsburgh (Fort Pitt), 3, 213, 217, 218, 228
Plymouth (England), 145, 147–8
Point of Fork, Va., 273
Pontiac, Ottawa chief, 3
Portsmouth (England), 143, 147
Portsmouth (Virginia)
  as a naval base, 154, 186, 270, 271, 273, 279
Prevost, General Augustine, 129–32, 159, 214
Princeton, battle of, 62, 63
Proclamation of 1763, 3, 4
Putnam, General Israel, 20, 152
Pyle, Colonel John, 253

Quebec
  Quebec Act, 8, 9
  siege of, 28–9, 49

Rankin, Colonel William, 272, 273
Rawdon, Colonel Lord Francis, 129, 251, 302
  southern operations, 181, 258, 259–62, 279
Reed, Colonel Joseph, 60–1
Regulators, 42–3, 44
Richmond, Va., 186, 188, 270, 272–3
Rhode Island
  occupation by British, 59–60, 158
  allied attempts on, 124–5
rifle, 26, 184
  rifle companies, 26, 261
Robertson, General James, 150
Rochambeau, General, Comte de, 170, 190
  orders, 193, 237, 239
  request for reinforcements, 197, 238
  discussions with Washington, 196, 274, 281–2, 304
  at Yorktown, 286, 287, 289, 290
Rockingham, Marquis of, 5, 300
Rockingham Whigs, 244
  and the war, 88, 244, 299–300, 301
  peace negotiations, 312
Rodney, Admiral Sir George, 160, 308
  financial irregularities, 168 footnote 125, 276, 293 footnote 35
  Relief of Gibraltar, 160–1

West Indies, 171–2, 275–8, 305–8, 318 footnote 56
North America, 277–8, 292, 297 footnote 130
naval tactics, 161, 171
relations with other officers, 171–2, 277
Ross, Major John, 230–1
Russia, 103, 46, 239
  Armed Neutrality League, 201, 244–5, 246
Rutledge, John, 16, 131

St Augustine, 110, 216, 217
St Clair, General Arthur, 81, 82, 85
St Eustatius, 202, 276
St Johns (Canada), 25, 28–9, 58, 88
St Kitts (St Christopher's), 304, 314
St Leger, Colonel Barry, 71, 72, 84, 223–4
St Louis, 220, 221
St Lucia, 110, 127–8, 314
St Simon, General, 278, 283
Sandwich, Lord John
  state of the navy, 112–13, 147–9, 165 footnote 58
  ship construction, 94–5, 113–14, 149–50
  strategy and deployment, 94, 107–8, 110–12, 160, 247–8, 305, 323
  and other departments, 91–2, 324
  appointments, 114, 117, 146, 149, 157, 172
  and historians, 112–3
Saratoga, NY, 83, 85, 86–8, 89
  Convention, 87–8,
Sartine, Antoine, 30, 104, 105, 111, 170
Savannah, 129, 262, 300, 305
Schuyler, General Philip
  Indian negotiations, 222, 223, 225
  campaigns, 24, 25, 81–2, 85, 224
  New England distrust of, 82, 85
Scots Highlanders, 43–4, 181
  British regiments, 46, 128, 250
Scots Irish, 227, 241
  support for Patriots, 42
  fighting abilities, 26
Seneca, 224–31
  see also Iroquois
Senegal, 314

Seven Years War, 1, 15, 46–7, 112–13, 162, 324
Sevier, Colonel John, 184, 216
Seyenqueraghta, warrior chief, 225, 226, 228, 230
Shawnee Indians
   and settlers, 212, 217, 218
   campaigns by, 218, 220, 221–2
Shelburne, William Petty, Earl of
   peace negotiations, 311–12, 313–14, 315
Simpson, James, 175, 205 footnote 51
Six Nations, see Iroquois
Solano, Commodore Jose, 170
   West Indies, 172, 278, 307, 308
South Carolina, 16, 42–3
   Patriot governance and planter elite, 30–1, 175, 190
   military operations in, 44–5, 131, 172–90, 248–62, 302–3
   British occupation and administration, 176–7, 190
   Loyalist support, 108–9, 177, 186, 190
   Indian campaigns by, 213, 214
southern provinces and states
   religion and ethnicity, 42–3
Spain (army), 141
   Gibraltar, 159–62, 244–5, 308
   Minorca, 244–5
   Mississippi and West Florida, 215–16, 217, 221
Spain (ministry), 325
   attitude to American conflict, 140, 142, 213
   alliance with France, 105, 141–2, 170
   relations with Britain, 140–1
   war aims, 141–2, 238, 308, 314
   invasion plans, 142, 169, 170
   peace negotiations, 310, 314
   assessment of, 321, 324
Spain (navy), 321
   Strength and condition, 113–14, 141, 144, 147
   Gibraltar and Minorca, 245, 298, 310
   West Indies, 172, 238, 275–8
   English Channel, 147–8, 169, 309
Stamp Act, 3, 4–5, 17
Stark, Brigadier John, 83–4

Steuben, Baron von
   training methods, 120–1
   in Virginia, 188, 252, 253, 271, 290
Stewart, Colonel Alexander, 302–03
Stony Point, NY, 154–5, 157, 158
Stuart, John, 211, 214, 215
Suffren, Admiral Pierre, 239, 243
Sullivan, General John
   campaigns (1776–8), 49, 124–5
   campaign against the Iroquois, 227–9
Sumter, General Thomas, 180
   operations, 182, 185, 187, 260, 262
   partisan indiscipline, 258–9, 260

Tarleton, Colonel Banastre, 176
   British Legion, 176, 249
   southern campaigns, 175, 182, 187, 249–50, 254, 273, 285
   "Tarleton's quarter," 176, 185
Ternay, Admiral Charles d'Arsac, 170, 271, 193
   orders and naval operations, 193–4, 196, 237
Texel, 148, 309
Ticonderoga, 23, 25, 33–4, 58, 81, 88
Toulon, 111–12
Treaty of 1783, 311–14
Trenton, NJ, battle of, 61, 62, 63
Trumbull, Joseph, Commissary, 22, 118
Tryon, Governor, 43, 45, 154–5
Tryon County, NY
   militia, 224, 229, 230

United States of America (after 1783), 325–26
Ushant, 115, 248
   battle of, 116, 142

Valley Forge, 117–20
Vaudreuil, Admiral Louis-Philippe, 247, 248, 304, 306, 308
Vaughan, General John, 87, 276
Vergennes, Charles Gravier, Comte de
   war aims and strategy, 30, 103–4, 169–70, 237–40, 247, 298–9, 308, 325
   relations with Patriots, 30, 237
   peace negotiations, 310–14
   assessment of, 322

Vermont, 244
Vincennes, 219, 221
Virginia, 5
  slavery, 32, 42
  military operations in, 154, 270–5, 278–89
  militia, 182, 250, 254, 290
  state legislature and the army, 126–7, 188, 273
  source of supplies, 154, 189, 257
  and the west, 36, 127, 220, 242
Virginia, Capes of, 283
  battle of 16 March 1781, 271–2
  battle of 5 September 1781, 284–5

War of Independence
  and historians, 41, 313, 321
Washington, General George, 22, 52
  appointment and instructions, 12–13, 28, 79, 315–16
  troop discipline and training, 21, 50, 55–6, 78, 119, 120–1
  recruitment, 27–8, 55, 74, 153, 155–6, 190, 195–6
  army strength, 21–2, 61, 48–9, 73, 74, 272, 274, 281–2
  need for a professional army, 33, 48–9, 55, 73–4, 119, 185
  importance of the army, 49, 75–6, 126
  confidence in the cause, 50, 60, 127, 152, 192, 193, 195–6, 199, 241–2, 305
  mutiny and plundering by troops, 56–7, 77–8, 152, 240–41
  supplies and equipment, 22, 50, 74, 117–20, 199, 230, 240, 281
  strategy and military plans, 22, 33–4, 73, 48–9, 50, 75–6, 153, 157, 193, 271, 272, 304
  importance of New York, 48, 53–4, 194, 242, 272, 274–5, 281–2
  Canada, 25–6, 28, 126–7, 227, 304
  tactics, 52–3, 61–2, 77, 78
  view of British commanders, 22, 26, 33, 75, 155, 158, 199, 287
  conduct of campaigns, 21–3, 268, 48–63, 73–80, 121–7, 154–9, 193–8, 281–91, 303–5
  problem of interstate rivalries, 21, 50
  prisoners and rebel status, 22–3, 52, 185
  treatment of Loyalists, 23, 31, 37 footnote 36, 63
  relations with senior officers, 58, 60, 123, 124, 197–8
  Army council, 26, 33, 53–4, 57, 121–2, 193, 196
  relations with Congress, 61, 79, 118, 119, 190, 199, 315–16
  appeals to the states, 73–4, 274, 281, 304
  importance of French alliance, 152–3, 158, 159, 192, 208 footnote 141, 242, 289–90, 321
  relations with French commanders, 158, 195, 243, 281–2, 290, 304
  handling of French volunteers, 74, 98 footnote 52
  reliance and view of militia, 33, 49–50, 55, 58, 74, 76, 82, 185, 193, 290
  Indians and campaigns against 26, 218, 220, 221, 225, 227–8, 234 footnote 56
  assessment of, 63, 90, 291, 297 footnote 125, 322
Washington, Colonel William, 187, 250, 254, 259–60
Watauga River settlements, 184
  and Indians, 212, 213
Waxhaw, SC, 176
Wayne, General Anthony, 79, 80, 155, 240
  in Virginia, 273, 279
Weymss, Major James, 183, 187
West Indies
  vulnerability of British Islands, 127, 128, 143, 159
  hurricane season and impact on operations, 157, 158, 170, 172, 173, 198, 238, 275, 277–8, 305
West Point, NY, 88, 154, 155–6, 159, 191, 197–8, 240, 241, 271, 272, 274

Wethersfield, Ct, 274
White Cliffs, battle of, 213
White Plains, NY, battle of, 56–7
Williams, Colonel Otho, 252
Williamsburg, Va., 279, 283
Williamson, General Andrew, 130, 213, 215
Willing, James, 213
Wilmington, NC, 249, 251, 256
Wolfe, General James, 71
Women, 119
  ladies of Philadelphia, 195
Wright, Governor James, 131, 174, 177, 251, 258
Wyandot Indians, 217, 221
Wyoming Valley, Pa, 225, 226, 227

Yorktown, Va., 125–6, 273, 275, 279
  battle of, 280–9, 291
  consequences, 298–301, 303–4